Aesthetics and ethics

This major collection of new essays stands at the border of aesthetics and ethics and deals with charged issues of practical import: art and morality, the ethics of taste, censorship, and the objectivity of aesthetic judgments. As such its potential interest is by no means confined to professional philosophers; it should also appeal to art historians and critics, literary theorists, and students of film and the media.

Prominent philosophers in both aesthetics and ethics tackle a wide array of issues. Some of the questions explored include: Can art be morally enlightening and, if so, how? If a work of art is morally better, does that make it better as art? Is morally deficient art to be shunned or even censored? Do subjects of artworks have rights as to how they are represented? Do artists have duties as artists as well as duties as human beings and, if so, to whom? How much tension is there between the demands of art and the demands of life? Is there such a thing as a personal aesthetic and, if so, what justification does it stand in need of? How much agreement can we expect to achieve in ethical and aesthetic matters as compared with scientific ones?

CAMBRIDGE STUDIES IN PHILOSOPHY AND THE ARTS

Series Editors
SALIM KEMAL *and* IVAN GASKELL

Advisory Board

Stanley Cavell, R. K. Elliott, Stanley E. Fish, David Freedberg, Hans-Georg Gadamer, John Gage, Carl Hausman, Ronald Hepburn, Mary Hesse, Hans-Robert Jauss, Martin Kemp, Jean Michel Massing, Michael Podro, Edward S. Said, Michael Tanner

Cambridge Studies in Philosophy and the Arts is a forum for examining issues common to philosophy and critical disciplines that deal with the history of art, literature, film, music, and drama. In order to inform and advance both critical practice and philosophical approaches, the series analyzes the aims, procedures, language, and results of inquiry in the critical fields, and examines philosophical theories by reference to the needs of arts disciplines. This interaction of ideas and findings, and the ensuing discussion, bring into focus new perspectives and expand the terms in which the debate is conducted.

PUBLISHED BY THE PRESS SYNDICATE OF THE UNIVERSITY OF CAMBRIDGE
The Pitt Building, Trumpington Street, Cambridge, United Kingdom

CAMBRIDGE UNIVERSITY PRESS
The Edinburgh Building, Cambridge CB2 2RU, UK
40 West 20th Street, New York, NY 10011-4211, USA
10 Stamford Road, Oakleigh, Melbourne 3166, Australia
Ruiz de Alarcón 13, 28014 Madrid, Spain
Dock House, The Waterfront, Cape Town 8001, South Africa

http://www.cambridge.org

First published 1998
First paperback edition 2001

Printed in the United States of America

Typeset in Melior

A catalog record for this book is available from the British Library

Library of Congress Cataloging in Publication data is available

ISBN 0 521 58513 9 hardback
ISBN 0 521 78805 6 paperback

Aesthetics and ethics
Essays at the intersection

Edited by
JERROLD LEVINSON
University of Maryland, College Park

CAMBRIDGE
UNIVERSITY PRESS

Contents

Contents

Editor's acknowledgments

The core of this collection, historically speaking, is a group of six papers that were delivered at a conference, "Aesthetics and Ethics," organized at College Park in April 1994. They are the essays by Noël Carroll, Ted Cohen, Gregory Currie, Karen Hanson, Richard Miller, and Lynne Tirrell. The essays by Arthur Danto, Mary Devereaux, Berys Gaut, and Peter Railton were solicited after the conference, with an eye to complementing what was already in place.

I thank all of the authors for their excellent contributions, and for their cooperation and understanding during the period in which this project was brought to fruition. I thank also a number of Maryland colleagues who participated in the 1994 conference as commentators and facilitators: John Brown, David Luban, Raymond Martin, Michael Morreau, Karen Neander, Mark Sagoff, Michael Slote, and Allen Stairs.

Support for the conference was provided by the Donald Carey Williams Fund and the College of Arts and Humanities at the University of Maryland, College Park. To both sources I express my sincere gratitude. Without their generous contributions the book you have before you would not have come to be.

Contributors

NOËL CARROLL
University of Wisconsin

TED COHEN
University of Chicago

GREGORY CURRIE
Flinders University

ARTHUR C. DANTO
Columbia University

MARY DEVEREAUX
University of California, San Diego

BERYS GAUT
University of St. Andrews

KAREN HANSON
Indiana University

RICHARD W. MILLER
Cornell University

PETER RAILTON
University of Michigan

LYNNE TIRRELL
University of Massachusetts, Boston

Introduction: aesthetics and ethics

JERROLD LEVINSON

I

This book brings together a number of new essays in an area of growing concern, namely the intersection or overlap of aesthetics and
ethics. Recent developments aside, for the past thirty years or so in
Anglo-American philosophy, aesthetics and ethics have been pursued in relative isolation, with aesthetics being generally regarded as
the poorer, if flashier, cousin. The attention aestheticians have
recently given to moral aspects of art and art criticism, and that ethi-
cists have recently paid to aesthetic aspects of moral life and moral
evaluation, give hope of ending this rather artificial isolation, though
without necessarily forcing us to accede in Wittgenstein's gnomic
dictum that "ethics and aesthetics are one."

The intersection of aesthetics and ethics can be understood to comprise three spheres of inquiry. The first is that of problems or presuppositions common to aesthetics and ethics, the two traditional
branches of value theory. The second is that of ethical issues in aesthetics, or in the practice of art. And the third sphere is that of aesthetic issues in ethics, theoretical and applied.

As it turns out, the concerns of the present collection do not span
the full intersection of aesthetics and ethics as just explained. For
reasons of both unity and manageability, the decision was made to
foreground aesthetics in the present venture. The result is that the
essays fall under the first and second, but not the third ways of
understanding the intersection of the two fields.

Under the first rubric, then, are questions about the logical, psychological, and metaphysical underpinnings of ethics and aesthetics,

1

and whether they are comparable in the two cases. Is there objectivity in ethics and aesthetics? If so, what form does it take, and to what extent does it allow for settling differences by rational methods? Are there aesthetic and moral properties, that is, real features of the world that empirical investigation, broadly understood, can establish the presence of? Are there moral and aesthetic truths, and how are they discovered and defended? What is the place of universality in ethics and aesthetics, as compared with logic or science? How does aesthetic value relate to the notion of value generally? Does aesthetic value rest on some more encompassing sort of concern, to which it contributes, or does aesthetic value, as paradigmatic of what is intrinsically valuable, instead anchor values of other, seemingly more fundamental sorts?

Under the second rubric are questions about the ethical aspects of artistic activity in all its phases – creation, performance, distribution, criticism, and consumption – and of the aesthetic life generally. Can art have moral value, and if so, is such value relevant to its assessment as art? Is it possible for art to be aesthetically excellent and yet morally depraved? Might moral enlightenment come about, perhaps uniquely, via engagement with some forms of art? To what extent are artists accountable for messages implicit in their works or for the effects of their works on audiences? Under what conditions, if any, is artistic censorship justifiable, or even mandatory? Are there no limits on what can, or should, be appreciated aesthetically or dealt with artistically? What, generally, are the moral responsibilities of players in the aesthetic sphere? Is there anything one might call an ethics of response, involving obligations perceivers have toward individual works of art, art as a whole, or themselves as aesthetic agents?

The essays in this collection by Richard Miller and Peter Railton fall clearly under the first rubric, while those by Noël Carroll, Gregory Currie, Karen Hanson, Berys Gaut, Mary Devereaux, Arthur Danto, and Lynne Tirrell fall well enough under the second. The essay by Ted Cohen straddles the divide, serving as a bridge from the most abstract inquiries of the opening two essays to the more concrete investigations of the remaining seven, which tend to focus on particular art forms or particular works of art. Of course, the specific concerns of the essays crisscross in ways that somewhat belie the neat separation under rubrics just proposed. One charge of this introduction will be to outline those concerns as they manifest themselves in each essay and to suggest where the elective affinities among them lie.

II

The rich opening essay by Richard Miller situates aesthetic judgment in the dual context of moral judgment and scientific judgment. Moral and aesthetic judgments are sometimes said to present a strong contrast to scientific judgments in partaking of none of the objectivity of the latter; the former judgments, it is held, are wholly based on and serve only to express merely personal sentiment or feeling. Miller rejects that picture and argues instead for the objectivity of both moral and aesthetic judgments, whose objectivity he finds to be roughly on a par with, if of a lesser sort than, that which scientific judgments can attain.

According to Miller, moral and aesthetic judgments display objective validity insofar as they make rationally defensible claims to *nonperspectival* truth about the moral rightness of actions or the aesthetic value of works of art, a nonperspectival truth claim being one whose pretension goes beyond merely affirming how things are for the judger. Where the objectivity of moral and aesthetic judgments falls short of that characteristic of scientific judgment is in not yielding the *universality* of such judgments. That is, the objectivity that moral and aesthetic judgments enjoy fails to ground a reasonable expectation of *convergence* among qualified seekers after the sort of truth in question. In the aesthetic case, Miller suggests, this owes to the unavoidability of critical blind spots among even optimally qualified judges. Still, aesthetic and moral judgments can be understood as invoking or positing a range of properties or features of the world, often conditional or dispositional ones, that are independent of the state of mind of the judger and that function to make such judgments true or false.

That aesthetic, as opposed to moral, judgment can lay claim to any degree of objectivity, however, seems problematic in light of the following. Such judgment is founded on a response to the direct presence of an object that is, as Miller, following Kant and Sibley, puts it, *unprincipled.* That is to say, the response is one governed by no universal rules connecting perceptual features and aesthetic virtues – or at any rate, none to which the subject has access or can make appeal – and cannot be made, as moral judgment might sometimes be, on the basis of a description of what is to be judged.

The solution to this problem is found, Miller says, in recognizing that aesthetic appreciation, though in this sense unprincipled, has a certain defining *structure* and that one's response, if properly aesthetic, is indicative of a real potential in the object to affect subjects generally. The mark of positive aesthetic response is *enjoyment* – enjoyment that derives from a nonpractical though learninglike engagement with an object. Such response is a rational basis for ascribing to a work the objective capacity to afford enjoyment of at least that degree, and a work is aesthetically valuable in proportion to the highest such learninglike response it can sustain. Yet because of the ever-present possibility of critical insusceptibility or obtuseness, despite optimal training and preparation, there is an asymmetry in judgments of aesthetic value, one related to the failure of valid aesthetic judgments to attain universality; a positive response, if truly aesthetic in form, reliably testifies to the existence of aesthetic value, but a negative response does not reliably testify to its absence, since a responsive blind spot may very well be at work.

For Miller, aesthetic judgments compare with moral and scientific ones, not only in sharing some of the same measure of objectivity, but in yet a deeper way. On Miller's conception of aesthetic appreciation as aimed at a satisfying learninglike response to an object – a conception that echoes Aristotle and Dewey as well as Kant – there is an important connection between aesthetic matters and our cognitive interest in discerning the traits of the natural and human worlds. Aesthetic engagement, on such a conception, is a form of cognitive play in which various features of inquiry – such as discovery, surprise, conjecture, unification, analysis, and synthesis – manifest themselves at turns, but without there being any practical end, scientific or moral, in view.

We also get something like a scale of aesthetic value by asking ourselves, in light of this parallel between aesthetic appreciation and scientific and moral investigation, what processes of aesthetic engagement an intellectually curious and morally serious person would most care about. Miller speculates that aesthetic experience may not only parallel cognitive and ethical inquiry in structure, but also serve as a release valve for the inevitable frustrations and limitations of real-world inquiry in science and morals, and as a surrogate realization of our desires for mastery and closure in those domains. At the end of his essay Miller addresses the related questions of what the role of reasoning in regard to aesthetic response can be, given its lack of governing by principles, and why we are usually determined to get our aesthetic judgments right, avoiding the errors of both under- and overvaluation, despite there being no arguments from which such judgments emerge as conclusions.

The equally rich essay by Peter Railton is also centrally concerned with the objectivity of aesthetic value judgments and their comparability in that respect with judgments of moral value. Railton and Miller also agree, tellingly, in locating the root of aesthetic value in the potential of objects to rewardingly engage, in a perceptual–cognitive way, creatures such as us, constituted as we contingently are.

Like many recent thinkers drawn to make the positive case for truth in matters of aesthetics, Railton takes inspiration from Hume's *Of the Standard of Taste,* with its landmark attempt to reconcile the subjective basis of judgments of artistic worth with their evident claim to being, in many cases, simply right. Obviously, as both Hume and Railton recognize, if judgments of aesthetic value were merely expressions of preference, there would be no debate about them, and no objective import to them when true. Both the authority of aesthetic judgment, that is, its pretension to prescribe preferences validly, and its explanatoriness, that is, its promise to account informatively, if qualifiedly, for preferences actually had, require us to conceive of aesthetic judgments as more than just registerings of personal likes and dislikes.

In seeking the roots of value objectivity, Railton asks whether anything in the "characteristic functions and presuppositions of value attribution" is incompatible with a naturalistic view of the world and our place in it. In his view, the answer is no. Leaving aside the narrowly conceptual question about value attributions – that is, what exactly their semantic or logical differentiae are in contrast to mere ascriptions of preference – Railton focuses instead on our *practices* of attributing value, aesthetic and moral, with an eye to discovering how the objectivity of such attributions could be grounded, given our natures, the nature of the world, and the nature of the interaction between us.

Railton begins with the ineliminable subjectivity of value, understood as a fact about point of view: there is no value without *mattering,* and there is no mattering without a *subject* to whom things matter. The challenge is then set as to how there can be such a thing as *mattering objectively.* The answer would seem to be that some thing matters objectively insofar as the subjectivity or point of view presupposed in a claim of value for the thing possesses an objective character. The task then becomes to say what it is for a subject or viewpoint to be objective. Is it a matter of cognizing a domain of objects and properties independent of the subject, or reasoning in accord with rationally appropriate rules, or perceiving matters in a disinterested and comprehensive manner?

At this point Railton turns for support to Hume, and most specifically to Hume's idea of "true judges," ones whose sentiments of approval and disapproval are more probative, more indicative of real worth, than those of others. Such judges approach objectivity most notably in the third of the senses just sketched, that of *impartiality,* for they judge of an object as it answers to the human capacity for response generally, and not merely in their individual cases. As Railton observes, aesthetic objectivity understood as impartiality has a "horizontal" as well as a "vertical" character: "[I]t is a matter not only of what now pleases the refined judge, but what would please other refined judges at other times, and indeed what would please a very broad range of less refined individuals whose attention has been suitably engaged." In addition, insofar as beautiful objects are such as to produce pleasure in subjects upon being perceived, at least under the right conditions, there is also a place for something like the first sense of objectivity sketched earlier, objectivity as some sort of *match* (correspondence, fit) between the external world and the faculties of the perceiver, and for something like the second sense as well, insofar as the perceiver is called upon to *reason* from experience in regard to the specific beauties the object may present. The "true judge" is thus one whose impartiality of perspective, refinement of discrimination, and rational assimilation of experience optimally suits him or her to discern the degree of match between perceptual objects and human sensibilities, understood in terms of the potential of the former to gratify the latter. "True judges" or ideal critics provide a standard of taste, not through their judgments' constituting what is aesthetically valuable, but through their judgments' reliably indicating the presence of the sort of match between object and subject that is, as Railton suggests, the real basis of aesthetic value.

It is important to note that the refinement, impartiality, and experiential rationality displayed by ideal critics makes them better at *detecting* what objects answer best to the potential for gratification of our cognitive faculties, without making them essentially different from us in what that potential *is.* For were it not so, the judgments of such experts would have little bearing on or authority in our aesthetic lives. It is because we can cultivate that potential in ourselves with no advance limit that we are interested in the identification of what is best fitted to engage our faculties to the fullest. The postulate of a common basic cognitive–sensory–affective response capacity across persons, despite variation in ability to discern objects most apt for engaging with that capacity, explains a good deal about our social practices of aesthetic evaluation. It makes sense, in particular, of our eagerness to learn of the aesthetic judgments of others, especially those we feel are well positioned to inform us about what we may be missing but need not continue to miss.

Of course, the assumption of commonality in our underlying cognitive–sensory–affective makeup – what Railton calls the *infrastructure* of a field of aesthetic value – is open to challenge. Still, were that assumption far from the mark, would our evaluative practices have the shape that they do? Railton suggests not, advancing his case through consideration of how unrecognizable the world of taste would be on contrary assumptions. It is, he concludes, a rather good bet that "there will be some things that excel in their match with our sensibilities, and that can become a source of durable pleasure or interest as familiarity grows, independently of otherwise large variations in personal experience, situation, or culture." The aim of our aesthetic discourse and interaction is, in large part, the identification of those things, together with advice as to how best to appreciate them.

Railton endeavors to show that there is nothing in his naturalistic reconstruction of the standard of taste that is at odds with either the phenomenology or normativity of aesthetic judgment, or the necessary involvement of concepts, such as that of beauty, in experiences of explicitly *aesthetic* character. He also indicates how, on his account, there is truth to both sides of the old conundrum as to whether a thing is aesthetically good because it elicits approval, or elicits approval because it is aesthetically good.

Not all questions of comparative aesthetic value permit decisive settlement, even if the infrastructure of aesthetic value that common human sensibilities provide is in place. There may be no answer to whether vanilla ice cream is superior to chocolate, Dante a better writer than Milton, or Goya a greater artist than Bergman. A Humean account, Railton observes, "is able to suggest why this might be so: neither, really, is a better overall match for widespread human capacities and sentiments." Nor can we expect strictly universal agreement on the artistic virtue of even a Mozart, or uniformity in the aesthetic judgments of even ideal critics across differences in age, humor, gender, and social background – as Hume himself famously noted. Yet, as long as there is sufficient commonality, Railton argues, at least within broad groups, our practices of aesthetic evaluation will not lack rationale. In addition there is evidence, from the not inconsiderable number of works of every variety that have in fact withstood the "test of time," that the ambition of aesthetic judgment to locate objects that widely and durably answer to human capacities for intrinsically worthwhile experience by no means remains unfulfilled.

In the final sections of his essay Railton turns to the nature of moral goodness, construed as what is conducive, generally and impartially, to intrinsically good human life or intrinsic human well-being. In parallel with his understanding of aesthetic goodness, Railton proposes a functional characterization of intrinsic human good as residing in activities or states "that afford a robust and general *match* with human motivational and experiential capacities to produce the kinds of lives people intrinsically prefer."

Though moral assessment appears to differ from aesthetic assessment in a number of ways, such as the nonhypothetical character of the moral and the centrality to morality of balancing and aggregation, Railton manages to show that analogues of these features are present in the aesthetic case as well. Yet despite similarities in grounding and structure, aesthetic and moral value are not, after all, one and the same. Railton concludes his essay by outlining the differences, ones that turn, in his judgment, on matters of scope, scarcity, and obligatoriness. These differences, though, do not threaten the real, if relational – that is, human-sensibility-indexed – objectivity secured for aesthetic and moral evaluations alike.

Whereas the focus in the essays by Miller and Railton is on the intersubjectivity of aesthetic judgments as compared with judgments of other sorts, that is, on the degree of convergence we may rightly expect on the *interpersonal* plane, the essay by Ted Cohen sets that traditional problem to one side in order to address the issue of convergence of aesthetic judgments on the *intrapersonal* plane, that is, within a given individual.

Like Miller, Cohen is convinced that whatever objectivity aesthetic judgments may carry, there are no formulable principles governing the making of them, no exceptionless rules underwriting inferences from descriptive features to aesthetic virtues. Cohen's conviction on this point is anchored directly in an argument of Arnold Isenberg, to the effect that a description of an object can never provide adequate reasons for an aesthetic verdict about it, since descriptions, however detailed, are by nature implicitly general, whereas the qualities that really underlie the verdict are absolutely specific, unique to the object and its clones. This lesson, which Isenberg derived from reflection on the interpersonal case, in which critics strive to bring others to share their aesthetic opinions, is applied by Cohen intra-personally: though the aesthetic judgments of a given individual across a range of objects may exhibit some degree of uniformity or likeness, there is no principle that strictly governs them, or at least none that can be usefully extracted from them. In other words, Cohen claims, the attempt to find logically sufficient but still general reasons for the things one prefers, as opposed to those one does not, is doomed to failure; the descriptive net cast is never fine enough, never adequate to ensure that anything with all the features stipulated will invariably meet with one's aesthetic approval.

Does this mean that one should not seek to discern an order in one's set of aesthetic likes and dislikes? That one should simply reconcile oneself to an unprincipled particularism regarding one's aesthetic being-in-the-world? This is a question, in effect, about the ethical implications of the claimed absence of rule-governedness in matters aesthetic in one's own case, and is answered by Cohen in the negative. The attempt to formulate the objective basis of one's own varied assortment of judgments, even if fated never to succeed, is of value in itself, in that it testifies to one's faith in that set of judgments reflecting an aesthetic *personality* of some sort, rather than being merely a random collection of likes and dislikes. That is to say, the integrity of the self as a locus of aesthetic judgment seems to demand of us that we at least try to discern some order, some rhyme or reason, in our aesthetic responses, that we at least endeavor to work out why, exactly, we admire or relish one thing and not another. If there is a moral imperative to be consistent in one's aesthetic reactions, it seems, it can be no more than that.

Though in the nature of things, Cohen says, we never can work out the why exactly, in the process we learn a great deal about ourselves and the objects that elicit our responses. In addition, others may be helped, through the presumptive reasons we uncover in interrogating our responses, to refine their grasp of their own aesthetic personalities, in harmony with or in opposition to ours. Furthermore, two people may converge in preferring a given thing, yet on divergent grounds; in such cases, articulating presumptive reasons, though it never comes to an end, serves to foreground differences in aesthetic personality that interest us.

What, though, are the minimum conditions for possession of a coherent aesthetic personality, for there being a personal aesthetic *style,* so to speak, evinced in one's collection of aesthetic choices? Although there is perhaps some pressure on one to attempt to rationalize the collection, that is, to locate behind those choices serviceable prima facie reasons for them, the collection may nonetheless reflect a genuine aesthetic persona without that. Cohen suggests, in a tentative vein, that the minimum condition for a personal aesthetic style may lie in the "going together" of one's various choices, such "going together" cashing out, perhaps, in the predictability of some such choices from others, within or across categories. But Cohen resists the implication that such predictions, when successful, rest on underlying principles expressing the full and adequate reasons for those choices in which our aesthetic selves are manifested.

III

The essays by Noël Carroll and Gregory Currie address an issue of long standing, whose roots are in Plato and Aristotle: that of the relevance of morality to imaginative literature and of imaginative literature to morality. The issue, which can be divided into two parts, is this. First, how can fictional narratives, being neither true nor pretending to truth, afford moral insight, instruction, or improvement? How can they give us knowledge of human nature, or of anything else? Second, if imaginative literature has a moral dimension, does this open it to moral assessment, and if so, how does the moral assessment of literature stand to the aesthetic assessment of it? The approaches of Carroll and Currie to this complex issue are singular and innovative, though Currie confines himself mainly to the first part of the issue as just sketched.

In his wide-ranging essay, Carroll argues that fictional narratives can indeed yield moral amelioration and that narrative is thus rightly subject to moral assessment, though there is no moral value to narrative per se. In making his case, Carroll opposes the view he defends, which he labels *clarificationism,* to other, more extreme views on the relation of art to morality, namely *autonomism, Platonism,* and *utopianism.* Autonomism holds that art and morality are entirely disjoint and that the latter is irrelevant to the former, while Platonism and utopianism take art as a whole to be subject to blanket moral assessment, negative in the former case and positive in the latter. Clarificationism, by contrast, maintains only that *some* narrative art, properly engaged with, can deepen moral understanding, through

10

clarifying the content of our moral categories and principles, and that such art is thereby both better morally and better as art. It is the latter, it seems, because ultimately more *absorbing* in virtue of its moral content.

Carroll admits that autonomism, at any rate, has behind it some valid intuitions – in particular, that it appears not to be the function of art in general to promote moral education, and that much art seems to have no moral dimension – but maintains that these are no bar to the qualified assertion of the relevance of morality to art that clarificationism represents. For as Carroll observes, the plain truth is that "certain kinds of artworks are designed to engage us morally, and with those kinds of artworks, it makes sense for us to surround them with ethical discussion and to assess them morally." Serious narratives of human affairs, of course, provide incontrovertible examples of such art.

A central point in Carroll's defense of his position is that artworks of this broad sort, whether novels, plays, films, or songs, are such that proper understanding of them involves more than formally comprehending the patterns they present; it also involves "mobilizing the emotions that are requisite to the text," emotions that are appropriately called forth in relation to this or that character or incident. What this presupposes is a shared background of beliefs and attitudes between artist and audience, some of which will be moral in nature. Furthermore, the very emotions appropriate at one juncture or another are often themselves explicitly moral ones – for example, shame, indignation, or compassion.

This establishes, perhaps, that moral concerns cannot fail to be activated in the course of properly appreciating a wide range of works of art. But how, the autonomist is bound to ask, can this lead to moral enlightenment, and so to a higher estimation of works that offer such, given that one must, by hypothesis, already possess the requisite moral concepts and maxims in order to properly understand the narrative in question? Carroll's response is to question the restrictive notion of moral education implicit in the autonomist's challenge and to portray the moral clarification that some narratives can afford as operating through the reinterpretation and reorganization of moral categories and principles, which results from the confrontation of those categories with the particulars of concrete situations represented in such narratives. To understand a category or principle fully one must know how to apply it concretely, and imaginary situations, if vividly realized, help us to exercise and refine our powers of moral discernment and discrimination. Thus, moral progress may often be a matter not of acquiring new pieces of moral knowledge, but of "reorganizing or refocalizing or regestalting" the moral knowledge we already, if perhaps too abstractly, have in our possession. And moral assessment of a narrative may then rest on the quality of our moral engagement with it, on the degree of reconfiguring or texturizing of our moral conceptual space that it induces, rather than on, say, conjecture as to the probable behavioral consequences of exposure to it. Carroll concludes that even if the primary function of art is to absorb us, whether perceptually, cognitively, or imaginatively, it may certainly do so, and as art, by being *morally* challenging and insightful.

The focus of Currie's essay, as already noted, is not so much the legitimacy of moral evaluation of imaginative literature as the prior issue of how such literature can possibly be a source of real knowledge, of a moral or any other sort, given that imagining things a certain way, in response to a fiction, does not seem like any ground at all for thinking that they are that way.

Currie's response to this challenge, in brief, is as follows. If we conceive of imagination as an activity of role taking, of empathetic enactment of scenarios, it is clear that engaging in imagining may very well issue in practical knowledge, knowledge of how to achieve morally better outcomes than one would otherwise have achieved, in virtue of allowing one to see more clearly what various courses of action, in various complex situations, would really mean for oneself and others. But narrative fictions are often admirably suited to facilitate or enhance this activity of imagining. Hence such fictions, insofar as they serve as aids to practical wisdom, can be of moral worth. The key to their so serving, Currie suggests, is their possessing *realism* of an appropriate sort: being such as to call forth a cognitive and affective response similar to that which would be called forth by real phenomena parallel to those the narrative represents.

In the course of his defense of literary fiction as a potential handmaid to moral development, Currie brings to bear recent work in cognitive psychology on the mechanisms that are most likely involved in imagining how persons will react or behave in various circumstances. Though it is conceivable that we do this by deploying a general *theory* of mind, relating beliefs, desires, and actions, and making inferences on the basis of that, it seems to Currie more plausible that we instead *project* ourselves into specified roles and situations, using ourselves to model the human scenarios in question, and observe the psychological upshot of that. The practice of empathizing with persons in such a manner has, from a moral point of view, two clear benefits: it habituates us to take the interests of others more into account, and it helps us to better grasp what those interests are. Both are relevant to deliberations concerning actions that affect others.

It is, of course, an additional matter to show that fiction provides an arena for imaginative exercise of a distinctive, or even nonsubstitutable, kind, one the lack of which could not be made up by, say, extensive travel or assiduous newspaper reading. But Currie is convinced, in company with Martha Nussbaum and Stanley Cavell, though for reasons not entirely coincident with theirs, that this is indeed so: "Fiction supplements the lessons of experience in a way that *more experience* could not easily do." The reasons, Currie suggests, lie with such features of literary fiction as its disengagement from practicality, the role played by authorial commentary in shaping the imaginative participation of readers, and the sustained and systematic nature of literary delineations of character and circumstance, as well as the extraordinary creativity evidenced in the best of them.

Thus, fiction, in virtue of its especially potent appeal to our imaginations, has a significant capacity to induce moral change, and for better or worse, moral change that is not the result of deliberate decisions to modify one's values. This gives us all the more reason, of course, to be concerned if the fictions most widely consumed in society are more meretricious than meritorious, for they will have ethical effects on consumers of which they are unlikely to be unaware. Among the best sort of fiction, Currie suggests, and on both moral and artistic grounds, is that which displays a high degree of realism of character, thus enabling the sort of imaginative exercise that broadens rather than constricts our understanding of human possibilities of thought, feeling, and action. Currie offers George Eliot's *Middlemarch* as exemplary in this respect.

IV

Berys Gaut, in his incisive essay, mounts a careful argument to the effect that a certain mode of ethical criticism of art is both entirely in place and not such as to exceed the bounds of criticism of art as art. In defending the legitimacy of moral assessment of art, Gaut thus joins ranks with both Carroll and Currie, though the means employed to the common end are rather different. Whereas Carroll's emphasis is on the moral clarification that engagement with narratives can afford, and Currie's is on the moral improvement that imaginative immersion in literature may unconsciously provide, Gaut's emphasis is on the moral quality of the attitudes inherent in or endorsed by narrative works of art, and the interaction of that with the morality of the work's potential readers or viewers.

Gaut dubs his thesis *ethicism.* Ethicism holds that "the ethical assessment of attitudes manifested by works of art is a legitimate aspect of the aesthetic evaluation of those works," and thus that manifestation of ethically commendable or reprehensible attitudes counts toward a work's aesthetic merit or demerit, though of course the manifesting of such attitudes is not by itself either necessary or sufficient for a work's success or failure as art. Gaut is concerned to underscore that ethicism does not entail – though neither does it preclude – the causal thesis that art good in moral respects is morally improving and art bad in moral respects is morally corrupting. Thus, even if ethicism is true, there are no immediate implications as regards, say, the censorship of art.

Gaut helpfully elucidates the role of all-things-considered judgments in assessing works of art aesthetically, the need for a broad notion of the aesthetic in such contexts, and what it is precisely for a nonsentient work of art to manifest attitudes toward states of affairs. But the bulk of his essay is straightforwardly concerned with arguments for, and objections to, the thesis of ethicism.

Among the objections to the thesis, ones Gaut is naturally concerned to defuse, are the following: ethicism errs in blurring the distinction between ethical and aesthetic evaluation; ethicism runs afoul of the fact that certain works of art are better in virtue of their apparent immorality; ethicism is hamstrung from the outset by the fact that the ethical assessment it licenses is simply inapplicable to artistic fictions, which make up the preponderance of works of art, since fictions have no bearing on the real world. In Gaut's opinion, none of these objections withstands examination.

What, then, are arguments *for* ethicism? Gaut considers some that have been offered by others of ethicist persuasion, such as Wayne Booth, David Pole, and David Hume, but, like Beethoven reviewing earlier themes at the opening of the finale of the Ninth Symphony, finds them wanting, if not entirely without virtue. A more promising line of argument, Gaut feels, is the cognitivist one proposed by Martha Nussbaum and Richard Eldridge, which accords to literature

14

a crucial role in the cultivation of moral awareness and sensitivity, and so allows "the moral insights delivered by literary works to enhance their aesthetic worth." (This cognitivist line also receives partial endorsement, of course, in the essays of Currie and Carroll.)

Gaut has reservations, however, as to whether the defense of ethicism that cognitivism affords is not of too large bore, hitting targets one would want to leave undisturbed. He is also skeptical of the radically particularist view of the nature of morality such a defense may presuppose. The central argument in support of ethicism, by his lights, is one turning on the *meritedness of the responses* that a work of art prescribes toward certain events or situations, which is a reflection of the attitudes it manifests toward those events or situations. If such responses are unmerited because unethical, then since there is reason not to respond in such a way, the work is accordingly aesthetically defective. In other words, in seeking to respond to ethically bad art as it invites us to we are necessarily divided against ourselves, and this has got to be laid, negatively, to the account of the artwork that puts us in such a position. In the remainder of his essay Gaut addresses objections to the merited-response argument for ethicism he has put forward.

Karen Hanson's essay also addresses the issue of morality and immorality in art, and reaches conclusions not far removed from Gaut's, though her approach to the landscape is refreshingly different again. Hanson chooses to concentrate on two worries of a moral sort that it is natural to have when considering the realm of art, worries that are in effect mirror images of one another. One worry, of ancient vintage, springs from the conviction that art is deeply *continuous* with life, giving rise to the fear that at least some art is bound, in virtue of its content, to have a morally damaging effect on its consumers. The other worry springs from the conviction that art is inherently *discontinuous* with life, giving rise to the fear that engagement with art, as either consumer or creator, has rather the potential to detach one from reality, with morally harmful results.

Hanson's review of the second of these worries suggests it to have little solid basis. The issue is sometimes raised in relation to photography, such as that of Diane Arbus, which takes as subject matter distressing or unfortunate individuals. That either Arbus or her viewers, in respectively creating or consuming such images, are harming such individuals seems to Hanson difficult to make out. Hanson proposes that it is in the last analysis up to us to connect our responses to representations to our attitudes vis-à-vis the real-world counterparts of those representations, and that we can do this in a morally responsible manner or not. Might it then be the psychical detachment per se putatively demanded by aesthetic appreciation that is ethically objectionable, because implying our moral disengagement from whatever is in evidence? This is implausible; to view with a degree of detachment the observable structure of some phenomenon, in life or in art, does not preclude a more engaged response to its moral import. In Hanson's estimation there is on balance no inherent immorality in engaging with art, for either artist or audience; indeed, creating or consuming art may sometimes be the most appropriate or effective move for a given individual to make in response to some human problem that swims into his or her ken and will not be gone.

Of course, it may often be only a "calculated risk" that devoting oneself to art will pay off in a way that will be humanly justifiable, assessed in retrospect. Invoking Bernard Williams's celebrated notion of *moral luck,* which encapsulates the idea that the moral quality of human actions may not be fully subject to assessment in advance, Hanson affirms its relevance in this context as in any other: ". . . if there is a problem of moral luck, it affects not just art and the artist, but every human enterprise." Thus, a present decision to write a play or paint a picture rather than volunteer for Amnesty International cannot be condemned out of hand.

This brings us to the first, more traditional worry about tension between art and morality, that in trafficking with at least *some* of it we run the danger of being morally corrupted, of becoming more likely to contribute to the evil of the world. (The other worry, by contrast, was that by trafficking with *any* of it we invite and further our own distraction from our moral responsibilities.) Typical of this worry is the question, posed by Justice Warren Burger, of whether exposure to obscene materials in art "adversely affects men and women or their society," or whether art whose thrust is ostensibly sacrilegious, such as certain sculptures of Andres Serrano or novels of Salman Rushdie, causes moral harm. Ascertaining whether that is so is, at a minimum, no easy task. The flip side to this question, naturally, is the question addressed in some of the preceding essays of whether art featuring morally good content brings about moral improvement in its audience. The canonical, though possibly apocryphal, case of the cultivated Nazi officer seems to argue for a negative answer to that question, at least in an unqualified form. (Note that the causal claims involved here are logically independent, though often coupled, that is, affirmed or denied together. But one may be sustainable and the other not, reflecting an asymmetry in the propensity of art to affect the morality of individuals in virtue of its own moral valence.)

Hanson queries the extent to which, in these contexts, aesthetic and moral judgments intertwine or even fuse, and if so, whether the judgments can effectively be teased apart. Certainly, she observes, art making as an activity in the world cannot be exempt from moral criticism. But does the assessment of art *as art* somehow insulate it from moral assessment? Hanson denies this, undermining a purported analogy of artistic content and scientific truth that would forestall that conclusion.

Yet according to Hanson, even if we grant "that the content of art may be subject to moral evaluation, we may still disagree about its import for aesthetic judgment." There are, it seems, two possibilities: either moral assessment of art, though valid, is separate from aesthetic assessment of it, or else moral assessment of art, when present, enters into aesthetic assessment of it. As we have seen, Gaut defends the second of these alternatives, and Hanson is inclined to follow suit, effectively challenging a well-known brief of William Gass's for the absolute disjunction of ethical and aesthetic assessment. Hanson remarks tellingly that our values, albeit of different nominal types, "may be more intimately related than we admit, and that our analytical separation of value areas may simply disclose the partiality of our perspective."

This is not to say that artworks with a moral dimension need be thought of as necessarily carrying *recommendations,* Hanson says, and in this she echoes cautions also voiced by Carroll, Currie, and Gaut against oversimplifying the moral force of artworks, literary or otherwise. Responding to a remark of Lionel Trilling, Hanson observes that insofar as we approve aesthetically of a work whose moral quality we condemn, we are most likely responding to the "power and grace" of the work's presentation of some by hypothesis immoral slant on some human affair. Yet moral defects in art do have a way of revealing themselves, in the end, to be aesthetic defects as well: "[A]rt marked by bigotry and superstition is art deprived, to that extent, of power and grace." Some virtues and vices are aesthetic and moral at the same time, and nowhere is that more evident, Hanson suggests, than in the sphere of art making.

The stage is thus well set for considering perhaps the most notorious example of a work of art admired aesthetically while condemned on moral grounds, namely Leni Riefenstahl's *Triumph of the Will,* a free documentary of the 1934 Nuremberg Nazi Party rally and the subject of Mary Devereaux's thought-provoking essay. As Devereaux succinctly puts it, the problem with *Triumph of the Will* is precisely that it is both evil and beautiful, and that the qualities seem in this case inseparable. Devereaux is thus ultimately drawn, like Gaut and Hanson, to embrace a form of the thesis that aesthetic and moral values do not exist in airtight compartments, but often overlap or interpenetrate.

In the manner of a true case study, Devereaux provides ample detail about the historical background of the film and its process of creation, and offers a trenchant analysis of its power as a work of art, focusing on its structure, narrative strategy, and embodied vision – a vision of the world of National Socialism as "a kind of Valhalla," with Hitler as "both leader and savior, a new Siegfried come to restore a defeated Germany to its ancient splendor," and *das Volk* as one people, united across barriers of age, class, and region in support of *ihre Führer.*

Devereaux considers certain too-easy ways of dealing with the problem *Triumph of the Will* poses for the philosophy of art. One is that the film is merely a documentary that records events distressing in terms of their known historical upshot, and thus that it is only its reminder of those events that makes the film a disturbing one. Another is that the film is not really about its ostensible subject, to wit, the promise and future of Nazism, but is instead a purely aesthetic exercise, devoted to the cult of beauty and not of Hitler. But in light of the inescapable propagandistic intent of *Triumph of the Will* – the intent of the *film,* that is, Riefenstahl's post hoc avowals of personal intent aside – and the centrality of its political message to the impact it makes, such exonerations ring hollow. A valid accommodation with *Triumph of the Will,* Devereaux insists, cannot occur without recognizing that it is successful both as propaganda and as art.

We cannot avoid, then, the fact that *Triumph of the Will's* vision of Hitler and his *Reich* is beautiful, and an implicit commendation of them. Yet that vision is also false and pernicious – a distortion, as subsequent events made all too horribly clear, of the true nature of Nazi Germany. The moral issue for appreciation is thus joined: if I enjoy the film and recognize its artistic worth, am I implicitly condoning its immoral content?

A standard response to this difficulty is to invoke the idea of a distanced or aesthetic attitude toward a work's subject matter, leaving only its form as an object of appreciation. But as Devereaux notes, this simple formalist response is inadequate, since to bracket the substantive content of this film, at any rate, is to neutralize its aesthetic power, its capacity to move us artistically: we can't ignore the message and still perceive the beauty of the work as the work it is. Sophisticated formalism, which takes the *relationship* between a work's manifest content and its embodying form to be the proper object of aesthetic attention, is also found inadequate, if less blatantly so, since although it clearly enjoins a viewer to attend to a work's content, so as to judge the excellence of its expression in the work, it leaves no room, within the confines of aesthetic assessment, for concern with the goodness or truth of that content.

Devereaux proceeds to spell out her preferred resolution of the moral and aesthetic problem posed by *Triumph of the Will*. As she puts it, theory has at this point two ways to go, given the inadequacy of both simple and sophisticated formalism to the task at hand: "We can say that there is more to art than aesthetics, or that there is more to aesthetics than beauty and form." Opting for the latter, Devereaux argues for an expanded notion of the *aesthetic,* one that in effect approximates the notion of the *artistic,* understood as including everything that makes a work of art the very work that it is. On such an expanded notion of the aesthetic, aesthetic engagement with *Triumph of the Will* cannot fail to encompass its message, its glorification of Nazism, for that message is, regrettably, at the very core of the film's achievement as art.

But we are not yet at the end of the problems that the artistic success of *Triumph of the Will* poses. For by rendering something evil beautiful *Triumph of the Will* "tempts us to find attractive what is morally repugnant"; there is thus no denying that it is "potentially corrupting." Devereaux takes up in conclusion the two hardest questions about Riefenstahl's film that we are left with in light of that fact, namely whether we can appreciate the film aesthetically without being morally complicit in it, given the centrality of the film's vision to its power as art, and whether the evil of that vision, central as it is to the work, makes the film any worse as art. Her answer to both questions is a nuanced yes, and is in each case closely informed by the preceding analysis. Devereaux notes, finally, that an important reason to view this film, and to make sure it remains available for viewing, is the singular aesthetic education that it provides: *Triumph of the Will* demonstrates, visibly and vividly, that the conjunction of beauty and evil is very much a possibility for art, one we do well to be keenly aware of.

V

The essay by Arthur Danto, a characteristically stylish and wittily learned one, illuminates yet another corner of the terrain where ethics and aesthetics meet. In earlier essays the spotlight was for the most part on the ethical failings of artworks and the ethical responsibilities of audiences; Danto's essay focuses attention rather on the rights of *subjects* of artworks, and hence on correlative obligations of *artists,* as these arise in the context of representation of real persons. What weight should be given to a subject of representation's desire to appear as she would like to appear or as she envisages herself to be, or at least in ways of which she would not be ashamed?

Danto's main concern is thus, as he puts it, "the ethics of aesthetic degradation." He begins, though, with a broader and prior theme, namely the concern that individuals have for their outward appearances, given all that that betokens. It is exceedingly human not to be indifferent to how we appear to others, and we would seem to have at least a prima facie right to have the looks that, in our view, represent us as we are, even at the expense of the "objective" truth. And yet the significance of an individual's chosen look is often complex, sometimes even opaque, to its bearer. "It is meaning rather than mimesis that must be appealed to in seeing what appearances are in the normal lives of humans," Danto concludes.

What meaning does a person's standard mode of appearing in the world have for that person, and to what extent must that meaning be respected by others, or at least not traduced by them? Just as the physical body has rights against assault and appropriation, so too, Danto suggests, has the "symbolic body," that is, "the body presented symbolically under a system of signals that convey the meaning a person intends to have acknowledged by others." Of course, some are in fact indifferent to appearances, which may reflect an almost exclusive dedication to "higher matters," but the majority of us are not, and so remain open to suffering on this count. If so, then it is surely wrong, disrespectful of personhood, to inflict such suffering wantonly. The

20

"aesthetic degradation" of others, then, seems clearly subject to moral assessment, and may sometimes merit censure. Furthermore, as Thomas Nagel and other moral philosophers have stressed, even what you don't know can hurt you, since not all hurt is *felt* hurt; if others have done damage to your chosen image, you have arguably suffered harm, even if you remain ignorant of the damage.

Danto now connects his inquiry into an individual's right to project the self-image of his or her choosing to two reflections on the particular medium of photography. The first concerns an inherent discrepancy between how people actually look to the unaided eye and how people look in photographs: "[T]here is no immediate assurance that a photographic image coincides with a look, just because there are differences between the speed with which visual images register and the speed with which photographic images do, so that there may be no way we can see something the way the camera shows it." The point is illustrated most clearly later in the essay by reference to Eadweard Muybridge's celebrated still photographs of animal locomotion, which settled questions such as whether galloping horses ever have all four legs off the ground at one time: "We really don't see animals move the way Muybridge shows them moving, or else there would have been no need for the photographs in the first place."

The second reflection concerns the photographer's assertion of authority over his subject, authority "to show the subject as he sees the subject, rather than the way the subject sees himself." This is an authority that, it seems to Danto, can surely be misused, as when photographers ride roughshod over the prima facie rights of individuals to control representations of themselves. At least, Danto suggests, a balance must be struck, varying from case to case.

And consider cases Danto does. Beginning with a scurrilous painted portrait of former Chicago mayor Harold Washington, which Danto takes to be a fairly clear-cut case of pictorial libel, Danto then turns to two contrasting photographic depictions of Warhol-circle transvestite Candy Darling, by Richard Avedon and Peter Hujar. Danto finds Avedon's "an exceedingly cruel image," one in which the photographer "did not simply disregard Candy Darling's values, but forced her to surrender them." On the other hand, Danto finds Hujar's "an extremely moving picture" in which the photographer has portrayed Candy Darling "the way she would have wanted to be shown." The ethical implications, for Danto, are clear: Avedon's picture is, though not libelous, morally blameworthy, while Hujar's is morally praiseworthy.

21

Continuing his contrastive case study, Danto brings his observations on animal motion photography to bear on the photographic depiction of human beings. There are, he says, two kinds of photographs: "stills" and "natural drawings." The latter correspond to looks afforded normal perception, while the former correspond to looks of a sort normal perception is barred from. "The still is a kind of invasion into a world in which our eyes have no natural entry point." In this extended sense, then, Avedon uses his camera to make "stills," whereas Hujar uses his to make "natural drawings." "Cameras do not lie, but photographers do," Danto warns us rather ominously.

In the last part of his essay Danto takes up the topic, to his mind strangely neglected, of the ethics of nakedness. Nakedness, of course, is no longer our natural state – not, at any rate, since the expulsion from the Garden of Eden. Thus, to the extent that there is something wrong about *being* naked – about having one's sexuality on view – is there not something wrong as well about being *represented* naked? On the other hand, we are essentially sexual creatures, and our dignity as human beings must be consistent with both that fact and its acknowledgment, as in, at a minimum, the artistic category of the nude. Danto concludes that it cannot be automatically exploitative to depict human beings in all their sexuality: "As far as showing a subject naked, the morality of that is altogether a matter of how the subject feels about himself as seen that way."

The concluding essay, by Lynne Tirrell, is as much an investigation in social philosophy as one in aesthetics, and its core is a theory of the functioning of language and other forms of communication. Tirrell's dominant concern is the political one of censorship in the arts, cast as the question of whether artistic speech or depiction should be curtailed in any way as regards content. Some of the hardest cases to be confronted on this score, as Tirrell notes, involve the use of materials – words or images – of a derogatory or degrading nature, ones tied historically to modes of oppression, some of them still in force. Tirrell's spirited discussion is aimed at clarifying the extent to which artistic context confers immunity against criticism on grounds of racism or sexism to those who would employ such materials – for example, the word 'nigger' or images of rape – in their works. Most pointedly, the question is what effects various sorts of contextualization have on the usual or primordial force of such words and images. Is that force neutralized or reversed, or does it continue dangerously unabated? And if the latter, can the use of such words and images be condoned after all?

Tirrell frames the issue as a debate between Absolutists and Reclaimers, with Catherine MacKinnon and Andrea Dworkin as prominent representatives of the former position. Absolutists hold that material of a derogatory or degrading nature should, due to its inherently harmful or hurtful nature, be entirely banned, employed in no context whatsoever. Reclaimers deny this, proposing instead that benefits accruing from proper contextualization of such materials can justify whatever negative social valence may still inhere in them. Though her sympathy rests ultimately with the Reclaimers, Tirrell is remarkably evenhanded in her review of this debate, finding considerable justice in both positions. As she observes, Absolutists and Reclaimers are united in their opposition to derogatory terms or degrading images as such. They simply differ in the strategies they advocate for breaking the power of such oppressive signifiers, to wit, outright proscription or creative appropriation.

Tirrell sketches what she calls an *inferential role* theory of meaning and applies this to the matter of derogatory expressions. On such a theory the meaning of an expression is given by its place in a pattern of inferences, governed by commitments, involving speakers issuing licenses to hearers to infer various things, in virtue of the speaker's utterance of the expression in a given context. In speaking, a speaker undertakes linguistic commitments of various kinds as regards his or her utterance, in particular *assertional* (or descriptive) and *expressive* (or attitudinal) ones. Expressive commitments are ones wherein a speaker, by employing a piece of language, commits him- or herself to "the viability and value of a particular way of talking." The issue between Absolutists and Reclaimers partly concerns whether the assertional and expressive commitments of loaded language can ever effectively be canceled and, if so, to what effect. As Tirrell observes, rather delicate operations may be called for: "Reclamation depends upon the possibility of somehow severing the derogation from the term, although not upon the possibility of severing the history of derogation *via* the term." The key question is whether a speaker who employs a term of offense is able, through creative use of context, to control which elements of the term operate within that context. Although as MacKinnon aggressively emphasizes, saying or writing is indeed a kind of doing, "[w]hat deed the words constitute, what the author is responsible for, depends almost entirely on the social and linguistic context in which they appear."

Tirrell turns her attention next to the controversy over pornography, in some ways parallel to that over the use of derogatory language: can images of sexual degradation or subordination, with their undeniable negative valence, be appropriated to socially beneficial ends, or is the hurtfulness they embody necessarily perpetuated, whatever attitude is taken toward them as they are appropriated? Tirrell suggests that Absolutists like MacKinnon overlook aim and point-of-view considerations at their peril, for if no place is made for them it is unclear that even excoriating condemnations of pornography, if complete with evidence, can be allowed. Yet surely there is a difference between a use of degrading images that endorses degradation – to some, the defining feature of pornography – and one that does not, as Helen Longino and others have pointed out. Of course, to have a convincing case for banning everything that truly is pornographic, given the threat to the ideal of freedom of expression such a ban would represent, one would need good reason to think pornography is indeed responsible for significant harm on either an individual or a societal level. But Tirrell does not discount the ability of Absolutists to demonstrate that, nor to show that suppressing pornography on balance furthers free expression, by releasing expression of a sort formerly silenced.

At the end of her essay Tirrell comes back squarely to art, which has been intermittently in view throughout, and plumps for something approaching complete expressive freedom in at least that domain. Drawing on reflections elsewhere of Danto and Devereaux, Tirrell concludes that all material, however derogatory or degrading on its face, and all points of view, however offensive, unpopular, or transgressive, should be fair game for artistic exploration, because of the great good, personal and social, that art promises to afford. Nothing else, suggests Tirrell, can so effectively transfigure the world, make things new, and open up avenues for dramatic change. Yet engaging in art, especially of a radical sort, may require trafficking with all manner of hazardous materials, some of which will, in the nature of things, sometimes be mishandled and some of which may, despite careful handling, still retain a noxious charge. But those are costs we should be prepared to pay. The Absolutist's call for a complete ban on such materials, even where art is concerned, sells short the artist's power of creatively recasting them so as to effect transformation of prevailing attitudes in directions Absolutists and Reclaimers would both applaud.

24

As I hope the foregoing discussion has shown, the ground common to aesthetics and ethics is a fertile one. It is perhaps surprising that it has thus far lain relatively fallow. The ten analytical essays assembled here represent a substantial attempt at cultivating that ground. May they inspire many others.

2

Three versions of objectivity: aesthetic, moral, and scientific

RICHARD W. MILLER

How does the objective validity of aesthetic judgments compare with the objective validity of moral judgments and scientific beliefs? There are two traditional answers. According to one, aesthetic and moral appraisals both utterly lack the cognitive authority of scientific inquiry, since neither kind of appraiser has access to a fact independent of her own judgments and neither is in a position to claim that all who are adequately qualified would share her judgment. For example, emotivists deprive both aesthetic and moral judgments of both kinds of objectivity. According to the other tradition, well-formed aesthetic and moral judgments have the same cognitive authority as well-formed scientific beliefs, because in all three realms the judgment maker is often in a position to assert a truth independent of her judgments, in a claim to which all adequately qualified inquirers would assent. For example, Kant puts the three realms on a par in both ways.

Each of these traditions has distinctive liabilities, which jointly suggest the need to explore a third alternative. The debunking tradition, depriving both aesthetic and moral judgments of all the authority of science, is hard to reconcile with the pervasive aspirations to truth and interests in impersonal argument of apparently rational people engaged in moral and aesthetic judgment. On the other hand, the claims to universality in the elevating tradition often seem wishful thinking.

Elsewhere, I have defended a view of morality and science that rejects the association in both traditions of rational access to appraiser-independent truth with epistemic universality.[1] This alternative approach yields a mixed verdict on the relationship between morality and science: moral inquiry often sustains rational access to

26

appraiser-independent truth (the beginning of the elevating verdict), but (as the debunkers charged) it does not attain the epistemic universality that is within the reach of science. In this essay, I will argue that the mixed verdict extends to aesthetic judgment as well, so that each traditional view was right to put moral and aesthetic judgments on a par, though neither assesses the objective validity of either realm correctly.

I will begin with a brief defense of the mixed verdict on morality and science. Then, I will describe the great barrier to extending the mixed assessment of moral judgment to aesthetic judgment: aesthetic appreciation is based on an unprincipled response to the concrete presence of an object; in the absence of a determinate general principle describing how all contrary responses go wrong, such a response seems a mere autobiographical claim, not a valid ascription of value. Struggling with this barrier to aesthetic objectivity, I will rely on the connection between aesthetic appreciation and the enjoyment of learning, a recurrent theme of the profoundest philosophers of art and literature, from Aristotle to Kant to Dewey. In particular, I will identify aesthetic appreciation with the enjoyment of a learninglike response that does not aim at truth or practical attainments (i.e., useful interventions or virtuous choices). A work has some aesthetic value (roughly) because it is capable of prompting such enjoyment in someone. How much value a work possesses is determined by the highest such response it can sustain, on a scale determined by how much an intelligent, morally serious person would care about various kinds of aesthetic responses. However, what prompts a relevant response in someone might be incapable of prompting it in another competent critic, who may even be rational to deny that the work is ever the object of aesthetic appreciation conferring the value in question.

On this account, aesthetic judgments, like moral judgments, are claims to appraiser-independent truth that are often rational. It is an objective question, independent of the individual judgment maker's response, what are the highest relevant responses a work can prompt in someone; indeed, the aesthetic connection between the work, a learninglike process, and the enjoyment of the process is not guaranteed by anyone's thought that she experiences such enjoyment. Yet one does have rational access to truths about aesthetic value, through standard forms of self-awareness and deference. Nonetheless, blind spots in qualified, informed critics prevent the epistemic universality available in science.

Other enjoyment-based views of aesthetic value could produce a similar mixture, in which one's aesthetic judgment affirms an objective fact – namely, the fact that someone could respond in a certain way – yet the crucial response need not be universal. But (in addition to forcing implausible assessments of particular works) these other, less cognitive theories tend to trivialize aesthetic value, creating implausible exaggerations of the difference between the seriousness of aesthetic judgment and the seriousness of moral judgment. In much of this essay, I will be concerned to show how, in contrast, the connection of aesthetic enjoyment with a learninglike response provides a plausible account of the seriousness of our interest in aesthetic appreciation, accurate aesthetic evaluation, and articulate aesthetic reasoning. This task will begin with the development of the scale of more and less important aesthetic values, a scale that depends on moral and intellectual interests but does not reduce aesthetic importance to importance of other kinds. Then, relying on the connection with learning, I will show why an intelligent, morally serious person would have a profound interest in the most important aesthetic values (construed according to this scale), and why she would be concerned that her aesthetic judgments be reasoned and valid.

In sum, rational aesthetic practice will turn out to attain the same intellectual virtues as moral deliberation, in an unprincipled way. Both activities resemble scientific inquiry in providing rational access to appraiser-independent truth, but both fall short of its epistemic universality.

DIMENSIONS OF OBJECTIVITY

To begin the argument for this conclusion, there is a need to clarify the crucial terms for categorizing and comparing judgments. I use "science" broadly, to include all rational, nonautobiographical inquiry into the nature and instantiation of physical, biological, and psychological properties. I will speak of the technical part of science that posits unobservable mechanisms as "theoretical science." By "aesthetic judgments" I mean judgments of aesthetic value, and I will confine myself largely to positive aesthetic evaluations of works of art.

The most complex preliminary is the description of what is at stake when one asks whether we can claim objective validity for a kind of judgment. This vague question stands for a variety of more specific ones.

One question that might be posed is the question of appraiser independence: do the relevant practices, if well conducted, make it rational for someone to claim that the resulting judgment is true, in a way that she distinguishes from their merely being true from her own point of view? In other words, do the relevant practices put people in a position to claim truth that is nonperspectival?

In all three realms, the answer seems to be yes – though it can be difficult to explain where a skeptical argument has gone wrong on the way to its no. In scientific, aesthetic, and moral deliberation, rational practice results in declarative utterances, which translate into truth claims through the usual Tarskian schema. In each realm, disagreements occur in which people insist, with apparent rationality, that contested predicates really do apply, and not just from their own perspectives. Thus, if one ends up conceding, "It's profoundly moving to me but not to you," one weakens the claim one made in the aesthetic judgment, "The wind instruments' finding and abandoning distinctive voices in Mozart's quintet for piano and winds is profoundly moving." Similarly, if one ends up conceding, "The quintet is a great work given the ideal of musical achievement [or music appreciation] that I embrace, but it isn't given yours," one weakens the claim one made in the standard assertion, "The quintet is a great work."

If the strong claims are rational and routine, there is a further consequence, concerning detection: we often rationally take ourselves to exercise a capacity to detect properties ascribed in aesthetic appreciation, morality, and science. After all, you cannot be rational to refuse, in the face of disagreement, to retreat to the merely perspectival claim (e.g., "This is how it seems to me") unless you take the other to be responding to appearances in an uninsightful way, as opposed to your own, revealing response to the appearances. And we certainly do speak of capacities for insight in each realm, forms of wisdom, expertise, or discrimination, which may also be absent, distracted, or blunted.

The other dimension of the question of objective validity concerns the extent to which reason together with premises uncontroversial enough to be taken as data compel agreement. This is a cluster of questions in which we ask whether people have a right to speak with a universal voice, intending one or another sense of Kant's metaphor. Thus, one might ask when, if ever, a certain practice – say, scientific inquiry or moral deliberation – puts one in a position to suppose that every person rationally responding to one's data would accept one's judgment. Such universality does not follow from the fact that the judgment is a rational, nonperspectival truth claim in the first sense. Perhaps one rationally responded to the data in a distinctive truth-detecting way, from which someone else might depart in an equally *rational* response.

All of the questions along this second dimension are concerned with possibilities of rational dissent. They vary according to the nature of the data that are to rule out rational dissent and according to the nature of the rational dissent that is to be ruled out. For example, one might ask whether the currently available data compel agreement or, alternatively, whether it is a reasonable belief (or a reasonable hope) that the accumulation of data will eventually replace dissent with agreement if all are rational. One might ask whether anyone who actually exists (or has actually existed) could evade the rationally compelling force of the data because of his distinctive way of interpreting data or, alternatively, one could ask whether any *possible* rational person is immunized in this way. Different questions of universality could have different answers concerning the same judgment.

SCIENCE AND MORALITY

Here are the answers to the questions of objective validity in science and in morality that will form the backdrop to my comparison of aesthetic objectivity with moral objectivity. It is helpful to start with science, because (on my broad construal of the term) it is the realm where we are most secure in claims of objective validity.

In rational scientific inquiry, one seeks to confine one's beliefs to those that could ultimately be based on certain minimal assumptions – based on them in the following sense. If one were aware of all the experiences contributing to the rise of the belief in question and if one were, with unimpeded intelligence and attention, to interpret these experiences in accordance with the minimal assumptions, modified as the pursuit of coherence may require, then one would adopt the belief. The minimal assumptions involve prima facie commitments without which no one could learn about the subject matter in question. For example, no one could learn about the properties of material objects if she had no provisional inclination to take sense perception to be reliable.

Of course, one need not work out the derivations employing these minimal assumptions. Still, rational belief is epistemically responsible belief and epistemic responsibility dictates the various precautions by which we try to maintain (and, typically, succeed in maintaining) an adequate connection with the minimal base. For the norms of epistemic responsibility in scientific inquiry are the norms to which any rational epistemic dependent, learning through information exchange, wants all belief conveyors to try to conform. Rational epistemic dependents don't want to subvert themselves by taking on a belief whose formation depended on a premise they would not accept if they were intelligently aware of all the experiences and inferences on which the belief depended. The minimal assumptions are the premises that threaten no such subversion. All learning presupposes them, so all epistemic dependents share them.[2]

This conception of scientific inquiry leads to certain answers to questions of objective validity. We are often in a position to make claims of nonperspectival truth. For the interpretation of one's experiences on the basis of the minimal assumptions licenses such claims (claims that include ascriptions of detection capacity). Often, we are in a position to assert that no one with the same experience could rationally disagree, since tentative commitment to the minimal assumptions is a condition for forming a belief about the subject matter. But theoretical science does sometimes illustrate the possibility that the question of nonperspectival truth might split away from questions of universality. Sometimes, when surprising experiences force some modification of basic principles of causal ascription, in order to preserve coherence, more than one modification is minimal. Ether stress or delayed response, fields or particles, disunified physics or extravagant string theory will reestablish coherence equally well. Then, more than one truth claim may be advanced, and not just as true in a perspective: the claims face each other in a genuine disagreement that reason and evidence cannot now resolve. It is always a rational hope that more evidence and argument will end the disagreement. But surely, there may be some cases in which they will not, when all the evidence is in.

Turning toward the moral part of the backdrop: In morality, too, we are often in a position to make claims of nonperspectival truth. Certainly, in moral judgment, rational people do distinguish what is from how it seems to oneself. A failure to make this distinction would be moral megalomania, a perverse claim that just would be unjust, good bad, right wrong if one's standards were to change in corresponding ways. When true moral judgments are rationally asserted, the judgment maker relies on certain fundamental assump-

31

tions – say, the principle that justice requires equal concern and respect for everyone willing to show equal concern and respect for all. It may be impossible to justify these assumptions through a derivation from non-question-begging premises, but principles that are fundamental in this way are familiar from the minimal assumptions of science. For example, if I had no provisional inclination to take sense perception to be reliable, no non-question-begging premises would be available for a justifying argument in support of the reliability of sense perception. In particular, it would be arbitrary to rely on an inference from the best explanation of the course of my past experience, since it would be arbitrary to have confidence that apparent memories accurately represent past experience in the absence of any trust that current experiences represent the present environment. Finally, in morality as in science, the principles on which we rely include principles of detection, singling out certain processes as truth-enhancing, for example, the emergence of standards of justice on account of the need for a basis for social cohesion that does not depend on unequal coercive power.

So far, morality looks like science. But there are differences when we face questions of universality. For one thing, we never seem to attain the broadest universality that science ever achieves: there is always a possible rational dissenter from our moral judgment who would disagree in response to our evidence, indeed all the evidence that there might be. For there would not have to be any irrationality in the beliefs of a moral nihilist who believed that nothing is just or unjust, good or bad, right or wrong, or morally indifferent. On account of shared nonmoral assumptions, a nihilist could understand our moral discourse well enough to deny that anything corresponds to it. In contrast, someone who is not provisionally committed to the assumptions at the basis of science would not understand enough to dissent. (After all, someone lacking our elementary moral inclinations can deny that what we mean by "justice" exists, while someone lacking even a provisional inclination to respond to experiences with our elementary physical and psychological ascriptions could not even discern that we mean anything.)

In the second place, when disagreement separates actual moral deliberators, we must sometimes give up the minimal hope for reconciliation that is always available in science: it is rational to despair of there ever being evidence that would compel agreement among these judgment makers on pain of irrationality.[3] Thus, though there has been plenty of history since Aristotle, some of his distinctively elitist judgments depend not on ignorance of subsequent data or arguments that might be supplied, but on a view of justice as measured by the highest individual attainment that is promoted by a constitution. This view conflicts with the egalitarian standard I sketched before, according to which deprivations imposed on toilers are not made just by cultural achievements of others (e.g., in late Tsarist St. Petersburg, or even classical Athens) that depend on those exactions. We can say where Aristotle went wrong and how, in a way that attributes his belief to a source of distortion. For example, it reflects the absence of pressure to base social cohesion on consensus, in his world. But his set of fundamental principles is self-immunizing. He could criticize our distinctive way of moral learning as sentimental distortion and weak-willed retreat from the mob.

Why are the limits of rational disagreement broader in morality than in science? I will conclude this comparison with a speculative answer.

The difference in the scope of rational disagreement depends on the different interests and resources guiding the different kinds of discourse. Suppose that two people have arrived at their statements rationally and the question is whether they are both concerned with a single property (which one may be affirming, one negating). The answer depends, in part, on the goals that are essential to communication concerning this kind of property. For the intrinsic function of a type of communication partly determines what counts as successful communication, that is, genuine agreement or disagreement.

An essential goal of communication concerning moral judgments is to resolve conflicts of interest in a noncoercive, nondeceptive way, persuading people to restrain interests they would otherwise pursue – that is, persuading them without relying on force or misinformation to produce conformity. If this goal did not guide participants in a practice of communicating judgments, it would not be a practice of communicating moral judgments – as opposed, say, to commands or nonmoral prohibitions.[4] So a proposed standard of successful moral communication is too strict if its accurate application in regulating moral communication interferes with conflict resolution when this is not necessary to advance other intrinsic goals of moral discourse.

Moral discourse can serve its goal of conflict resolution only if important terms of moral appraisal are readily available as means by which people potentially in conflict can signal their willingness to accept the same resolution. Since different people are willing to suppress self-interest on a variety of different grounds, the conditions in which acceptance of an important term of appraisal signals agreement had better be permissive. For example, there had better be a basic term expressing the choiceworthiness of institutions that utilitarians, perfectionists, and Kantians could all rationally apply when their different standards for non-self-interested preference favor the same institutions. So people with different fundamental standards, engaged in discourse governed by the communicative goal, can mean the same property by the term – "just," if they are English speakers. In general, people applying different basic standards will count (within broad limits) as talking about the same moral subject – a permissiveness that carries over to situations of disagreement as well.

Admittedly, another interest, most centrally expressed in monologue, is essential to moral discourse, an interest in scrutinizing one's own actions and inclinations so that one can respect oneself without hiding from oneself. Because of this interest, a reduction of moral appraisal to the assessment of what will help people to get along would not be adequate. In pursuing the goal of integrity, one employs principles that are one's own resources for choice, a practice of self-scrutiny in which one is prepared to use these principles to criticize other people as well. Taken together, the two interests basic to moral discourse are best served if each individual relies on her own first principles in arriving at moral judgments while a variety of different ultimate principles are taken as means by which different people can investigate a common subject matter.

Turning to science, broadly construed: An essential goal of communication concerning physical and mental properties of nonmoral kinds is the use by each of us of the rest of us as means to extend our senses and reasoning capacity, acquiring beliefs which will overcome limitations in experience, memory capacity, and analytic technique that burden any human being.[5] As part of this cooperative desire, each wants the others to avoid the conveyance of beliefs that she would not accept if she had all relevant experiences and mastered all relevant analytic techniques. (This is not an essential aspect of moral practice, because people engaged in moral communication are not necessarily engaged in using others as moral advisers.) So here genuine communication is an effort to use terms as others would if they responded to the experiences in the background of one's own attributions. We pursue this goal by seeking ultimate justifiability on the basis of our common, minimal principles. Thus, disagreement in the face of common evidence cannot be rational and genuine except in the abnormal circumstance in which two different ways of modifying shared principles in light of common evidence are both as conservative as the evidence allows.

AESTHETIC OBJECTIVITY IN PERIL

Against this backdrop, certain comparisons of moral and aesthetic judgments will not occur – for example, the familiar assessment that we are in no position to claim any objective validity in either realm. But does aesthetic judgment have a title to as much objective validity as I have claimed for moral judgment? Two facts suggest that rational aesthetic practice does not lead to judgments with the same authority. First, aesthetic judgment seems to depend on spontaneous response to the concrete presence of its object in a way that isn't appropriate to a rational claim to nonperspectival truth. Second, our confident aesthetic assertions don't seem to be backed up by a repertoire of aesthetic principles sufficient to rule out contrary responses as misguided.

Suppose that someone has acquired aesthetic expertise. He could rely on someone, lacking such expertise, to report the perceptual features of an object. But no matter how much he interrogates the witness, he will never acquire a basis for rational aesthetic judgment, unless he manages to make the object concretely present to himself, so that he can respond to this presence. In sharp contrast, someone who is morally wise can form a moral judgment by relying on trustworthy nonmoralizing reports of others. Indeed, our moral judgments of laws and policies are almost entirely formed in this way.

Rational nondeferential aesthetic judgment would not depend, in this way, on concrete presence unless it depended on a spontaneous response to the object, the validity of which did not depend, in turn, on following a rule describing what properties of the object make for the aesthetic value in question. If there were such rules, aesthetic expertise could involve grasping them and the unaesthetic but observant witness could supply the rest. But it seems quite mysterious that an unprincipled response to the concrete presence of an object should make it rational to claim nonperspectival truth, to claim that something does not just stir my emotions but is profoundly moving, that it is not just beautiful to me but beautiful.

In the face of this challenge, a friend of aesthetic objectivity might extrapolate a response from Hume's or Kant's writings, a response that seeks a positive answer to all of the questions of objective validity: even though we lack principles describing what features of a work produce aesthetic value, anyone who fully grasps the concept of aesthetic value is implicitly committed to certain principles concerning what makes an aesthetic evaluator competent and relevantly attentive; the value of a work is its capacity to prompt appropriate responses in all appreciators with these qualifications. Thus, Hume thinks (roughly) that a beautiful work would evoke pleasure in all critics with certain qualifications whose relevance is truistic – practice, delicacy, and the like. Kant thinks (very roughly) that a person's judgment of ("free," i.e., purely formal) beauty is validated by the availability to all of her enjoyment of the harmonious interplay of her cognitive faculties in a process in which she is unconcerned with reaching a true conclusion, doing what is morally right, or changing the world to her advantage. Though the occurrence of such harmony is unpredictable, everyone's cognitive equipment is the same, so what can create such enjoyable harmony in one can create it in everyone. In either view, the truth of an aesthetic judgment is a nonperspectival matter of how all well-qualified judges would respond, even though the response itself is unpredictable.

One problem with a universalizing defense of aesthetic objectivity is that it makes our normal view of the validity of our aesthetic judgments suspiciously speculative. We seem rational to take our aesthetic judgments to be valid on many occasions when it would be rash to suppose that every judge with the Humean virtues would respond with the same positive feeling. We don't confine aesthetic assertion to Homer, the Bible, and the like. I am rational to regard my verdict on the film *The Piano* as valid, but it seems a bit daffy for me to claim that everyone at every period who has the virtues of practice, good sense, comparison, and so forth would respond with my kind of appreciation. No doubt, as Kant proposes, the capacity of reason and evidence to compel agreement in science depends on common ways of organizing experience, ways that are enjoyment-driven, motivated by curiosity in the face of disorder, and satisfaction at the achievement of order. But if we ever know that shared basic cognitive processes dictate the enjoyment we feel, it is when we discern prettiness, the satisfaction of universal form-seeking of a lovely flower or a nice piece of wallpaper. If Kant's theory is generalized to encompass all aesthetic judgments, the extrapolation makes my assertion that I have rightly judged *The Piano* a wild speculation in cognitive psychology. (Indeed, Kant presents pretty flowers and neoclassical wallpaper as his prime examples of free beauty when he introduces the phrase in the *Critique of Judgment,* section 16. Music without words is his other example. Kant is said to have had appalling musical taste.)

In addition, there is a particular phenomenon of aesthetic modesty that does not fit equations of aesthetic objectivity and well-qualified universality. Wise appreciators sometimes admit to blind spots, confessing that their general competence does not give them access to values that others detect. Pauline Kael says that Fassbinder is one of her blind spots. And someone who treasures the grace and richness and warmth of Jean Renoir's movies might well have problems with an art that depends on constant stylistic posturing in the distanced portrayal of those who do not overflow the stereotypes that contain them. I think that Kael may well be admitting that Fassbinder has merit that she cannot see for herself – in spite of appropriate attention and Humean virtues. This would be an incoherent admission according to the aesthetics of universality. But the phenomenon is routine.[6]

Note that the Humean virtue of unprejudiced acceptance of the goals of a work does not help here. If you say that what Fassbinder is trying to do is to make films that unsentimentally accept and even pity dominance by stereotypes and surface, Kael will, no doubt, accept this and say that his project fails, in her experience of it. The claim that she would succeed in feeling pleasure at the project if she tried hard enough seems either wishful thinking or the irrelevant thought that you can brainwash yourself into liking anything.

The available uncontroversial aesthetic principles have turned out to be too sparse to support a claim to respond as every sufficiently qualified appreciator would. Can we, then, fall back on the narrower claim of ideal consensus that I conceded to morality, each claiming that her aesthetic response would, in any case, be shared by those who are guided by certain fundamental, rational, but rationally rejectable principles to which she is committed? No. One seems to have no defensible determinative principles, value-constituting or competence-constituting, uncontroversial or not, commitment to which would make one's aesthetic evaluation compelling for all who share the same nonevaluative perceptions.[7]

AESTHETIC OBJECTIVITY REGAINED

Against the backdrop that I painted at the start, the failure of the universalizing accounts is not the end of the project of giving aesthetic judgment the same title to objective validity as moral judgment. After all, rational, nonperspectival *moral* truths did not require a response to the nonmoral facts that every rational person would share. Detaching Kant's account of judgments of free beauty from his quest for universality, we can use it as a clue to the way to put aesthetic and moral judgment on a par.

The grain of truth in Kant's theory of taste is that an aesthetic judgment must be valid when it corresponds to an enjoyed process of response whose enjoyability is based on achievements like those of learning even though its goal is not truth, right action, or useful intervention. I will develop this idea as follows. Aesthetic appreciation is the enjoyment of a process of responding to an object that is not directed at learning but that is sufficiently like learning; this learninglike process might have elements of passive reception, surprise, exploration, imaginative construction, discovery, the achievement of coherence, or the perception of underlying normality. (I will address the question of what is "sufficiently like learning" toward the end of this essay. But even this bare list of common elements should suggest abundant links between valuable aesthetic engagement and the experience of inquiry.) Such a learninglike process, if enjoyable, will involve the achievement of order in the face of threatened disorder – for reasons that are not cognitively fancy. What is enjoyable is interesting and what is interesting is not boring. So there must be aspects of disruption. But unresolved disruption is not enjoyable. So there must be aspects of order. Something that is created to provide such enjoyment that can, in fact, provide it to someone is a work of art with some aesthetic value. More precisely, it must be capable of prompting such a response in a person with the basic cognitive equipment and the unavoidable neediness and lack of control characteristic of human beings. This gives aesthetic value the same scope as the norms of rational scientific inquiry and the most fundamental moral norms. (Something that is *not* a work of art has aesthetic value if someone who is intellectually and morally mature could respond to it with aesthetic appreciation.)

Any general description of aesthetic value makes a large claim. I can hardly discharge all the burdens of my general description by the end of this essay, and it would be crass Kant worship to suppose that the echo of his theory reduces the ultimate obligation to do so. However, there is space for a few gestures, which do, I hope, establish the initial plausibility of the link between aesthetic value and enjoyment of a learninglike process.

Three versions of objectivity

The aesthetic value of a work is what gives a point to looking at it, hearing it, or reading it – that is, a point that does not consist of acquiring truths or means of coping or living morally. Apart from enjoyability, whatever else gives point to the process of taking in the work gives it one of the nonaesthetic varieties of value, instead. So we seem on safe (and utterly familiar) ground in supposing that aesthetic value is, by its nature, based on some form of enjoyment.[8] What kind of enjoyment? In general, what is enjoyable includes sensations, feelings, and moods, the pleasures that pills can, these days, provide. But what gives a work of art its value is not provided equally well by one of these pills. For the objects of aesthetically relevant enjoyment, we should look to processes, extending over time, in which the person taking in the work also plays an active role (which can be, and usually is, spontaneous and unselfconscious).

When one reflects on an enjoyed process of taking in a work that has a bearing on aesthetic value and tries to make explicit its scenario, its play-by-play, terms for processes of learning always seem apt: mystery and solution, the discovery of surprising implications, the deepening appreciation of potential, the ultimate encompassing of tense ambiguities, the discovery of order in apparent chaos, and so forth. In any case, this is my play-by-play. I hope it is that of my readers as well. Note, too, that teaching someone how to appreciate a type of work (poetry, say, or Post-Impressionist painting) is naturally carried out in this mode. Of course, teaching and learning about art also produce knowledge of historical circumstances and artistic conventions and techniques. But this learning leads to scholarship that is value-blind unless it facilitates an otherwise unavailable appreciation of "what the author [composer, painter, or whoever] did in the work," an appreciation that involves enjoyment of a process due to the work which has a learninglike scenario even though its goal is not learning, not even learning truths about art.

In addition to these gestures at aesthetic life, a certain gesture toward philosophical authority is not entirely callow. The connection of aesthetic value with the enjoyment of a learninglike process is hardly a distinctively Kantian move. I have already alluded to parallels in Aristotle and Dewey. Indeed, there seems to be no major statement about aesthetic value that does not connect it with enjoyment of some kind of learninglike process, at least when the statement is charitably construed. For example, the familiar association of aesthetic value with the appreciation of complex order had better not allude to the sort of ordered complexity that is instantly and eas-

39

ily grasped, like an arrangement of thirty-six matchsticks prescribed in a matchstick puzzle. But in canceling this implication, one will connect aesthetic interest with processes of taking in the work in which order is won in the face of resistance, that is, processes like explanatory discovery. Similarly, to the extent to which Tolstoy does not confuse aesthetic value with something else, he describes a process like gaining access to another's mind that art distinctively affords. And so on, throughout the canon.

Unless, implausibly, philosophical discussions of aesthetic value have been all, utterly misguided, aesthetic value must be based on something like enjoyment of a learninglike process. Assuming, from now on, that this initial proposal *is* plausible, I will develop it in ways that answer some central questions about aesthetic judgment, including those that determine the relation of the objectivity of aesthetic judgments to the objectivity of moral ones.

So far, my explicit proposal has sketched conditions for having some aesthetic value, the minimum attained by nice wallpaper and pretty flowers. To see what greater value might involve, let us first see how the notion of aesthetic appreciation might accommodate more diverse and specific aesthetic values. In aesthetic appreciation, the learninglike process one enjoys can be more or less sustained, complex, or surprising. One's enjoyment can be more or less intense or prolonged. Finally, one can enjoy the learninglike response in an emotional way, enjoying it sadly, perhaps, or with pity and terror. In more or less obvious ways, these varieties of aesthetic appreciation correspond to the terms of serious critical appraisal. One can rank these responses in value (leaving much appropriate indeterminacy in the ranking), by asking what specific kinds of aesthetic appreciation an intelligent, morally serious person with relevant background knowledge – that is, someone meeting Hume's prescriptions for critical competence – would care about more if special limits to leisure and energy were no problem and if she did care about aesthetic value. If someone enjoys the richer, more sustained, yet more unpredictable structure of Beethoven's op. 131 quartet as compared with his op. 18, no. 1, but doesn't care *more* about the former response, then either he is too tired for the more strenuous delights or he lacks interest in the solution of large problems, which marks him as intellectually sluggish. Here the cognitive helps to rationalize our aesthetic assessments. Similarly, if an appreciator isn't especially interested in the combination of terror and pity that Aristotle describes, he is not a morally serious person. So the moral also helps to rationalize our aesthetic assessments. The interests that move someone who functions well intellectually and morally organize the specific, autonomous kinds of aesthetic appreciation into a kind of normal scale. The highest point on the scale at which a response that someone could have to a work is located determines its aesthetic value.[9]

The connection of the normal scale with important aspects of intellectual and moral competence helps to explain the risk of insulting someone by challenging his ascriptions of major aesthetic value. It is different when one merely expresses a strong distaste for something someone likes – brandy alexanders or sushi, for example – even if he likes it a whole lot.

In making these connections with intelligence and morality, I do not mean to suggest that aesthetic responses are valuable (much less aesthetically valuable) only to the extent to which they facilitate moral or intellectual interests. The relevant perspective is that of intelligent, morally serious people who care about aesthetic appreciation for its own sake. An intelligent, morally serious person will have nonmoral, nonintellectual interests (e.g., an interest in amusement) just in virtue of being human. In virtue of being intelligent and morally serious, she will enjoy certain processes in ways that draw her to purely formal achievements of art as well, enjoying those aspects of intellectual and moral life independently of their payoff in truth or moral virtue. (For example, someone intelligently engaged in inquiry will enjoy finding solutions that require much effort but that, once found, simplify thinking about vast congeries of propositions – the sort of intellectual findings that attract such aesthetic labels as "elegant.") For these and other reasons, rankings on the normal scale need not correspond to relative moral or intellectual value. Still, the role of intelligence and morality in the normal scale is bound to seem artificial unless there is some intrinsic, if indirect, relation between the interests served by aesthetic appreciation and the interests guiding scientific inquiry and the pursuit of moral virtue. Later, I will try to establish such a connection, arguing that what makes enjoyment aesthetic is, in part, its satisfaction of certain needs that are created and thwarted by intellectual and moral learning.

If this account of the content of aesthetic judgments is right, then in making an aesthetic judgment one can rationally assert a truth when one's judgment essentially depends on a non-rule-governed response to the concrete presence of the work. If one's own response constitutes aesthetic appreciation, then the specific ways in which one responds are an adequate basis for ascribing specific aesthetic virtues ("The woodwinds are engaged throughout in a poignant struggle to find a musical genre in which they are at home"), and the specific virtues are a basis for claiming that the work attains at least a certain rank on the normal scale ("Anyone who appreciates this work as it can be appreciated should at least acknowledge that it is a major work worthy of a great composer"). There are no laws or valid rules that say which properties of an object (i.e., properties that an aesthetically insensitive person might recognize) prompt aesthetic appreciation. So if one does not defer to others' aesthetic judgments in making such evaluative claims, one's basis must be one's own response to the concrete presence of the object.

But is this a basis for a claim of nonperspectival truth? Granted, on the present account of the content of aesthetic judgments, the subject of the aesthetic claim itself is, nonegocentrically, someone's possible appreciation. But one's own aesthetic appreciation is supposed to be sufficient for locating a work at least that high on the normal scale. So there might seem to be no way to explain why the confession "It's moving [beautiful or whatever] to me, but not to you" is normally a retreat from the claim, "It's moving [beautiful or whatever]." By the same token, this account of aesthetic value seems incompatible with obvious facts about the detection of aesthetic value (a capacity that must exist if we have access to nonperspectival aesthetic truths). Contrary to our obvious fallibility, it seems to leave no room for anyone's falsely ascribing aesthetic value on the basis of his own response.

To see that all the standard elements of rational nonperspectival truth claims are in place, one must first see the room there is for wrongly thinking that one has appreciated something aesthetically. That will involve wrongly thinking that one has enjoyed the learninglike response I described, rather than enjoying something else. Even when the question is whether something possesses mere aesthetic value, as nice wallpaper does, such missteps in self-awareness are conceivable. One might be enjoying the thought that others would approve one's approval, or one's enjoyment might consist of satisfaction at having recognized that the object fits some conventional rule. When values farther up the normal scale are in question, mistakes are much more likely. Perhaps I think that my viewing of Fassbinder's *The Bitter Tears of Petra von Kant* is intensely yet unsentimentally pitying, when really my pity is inspired by thoughts of empty wretched people prompted by the viewing.

Getting it right aesthetically, when one ascribes specific virtues and abstract values on the basis of one's own response, is a matter of authenticity, the accurate identification of the object of one's response. It is like getting it right about whether one loves a person or lusts after a person or is in love with a mood or fantasy that the person serves. Indeed, the question of whether a person is lovable is a good analogue for the question of whether a work has a certain aesthetic value. As in all questions of the identity of the object of a response, one is rational to rely primarily, in one's own case, on attention to one's own feelings and to answers and imaginings that spontaneously occur in the course of self-interrogation – access that, nonetheless, one does not, rationally, treat as infallible. (In relying on someone else's aesthetic expertise, one relies on her authenticity and her self-insight.)

Despite the fact that accurate autobiography is sufficient for valid aesthetic judgment, the shift to "It is for me, though not for you" is normally a retreat. Normally, in saying this, one moves back from a claim to have enjoyed a learninglike response in a certain emotional way to the much weaker claim that one felt pleasure or an emotion *occasioned* by the work, while the other did not. Perhaps hearing the woodwinds stirred my emotions, but only by producing a reverie about loneliness and friendship that moved me on its own. A different usage of ". . . for me, though not for you" is certainly imaginable: "It is moving for me, though not for you" *could* be a way of attributing a blind spot to the other. Then there is no retreat from the unqualified assertion. But usually, this step beyond unqualified assertion would be pointlessly insulting.[10]

The other dimension of objectivity involves the issues of epistemic universality that distinguish scientific belief from moral judgment. As part of this distinction, we are supposing that when a true moral judgment is rationally affirmed, there is sometimes no rational hope that all the evidence there will ever be would provide everyone engaged in moral judgment with compelling reasons to affirm it. Aristotle's blind spot about hierarchy would keep him from some of our judgments about justice even if he responded rationally to the accumulation of evidence.

Aesthetic judgment shares this lack of universality, along with the achievement of rational access to truth. For here, too, appraisers often regard their blind spots as sources of genuine insight. The hope that every critic with traits whose relevance must be acknowledged by all who grasp the concept of aesthetic value would, if he or she took part in enough discussion and scrutiny, arrive at the same

43

assessment of Fassbinder, Brecht, or Ronald Firbank is wishful think-ing. Suppose that in viewing *The Bitter Tears of Petra von Kant* I really do enjoy a process like wondering whether a person overcome by a passion for another is ridiculous or serious, in love or in love with her emotions, abject or in touch with life's value; suppose I really am stirred and deeply amused by this process, a process like moving from each hypothesis to its opposite and finally finding that the oppositions are not so significant after all; and suppose that in the enjoyed process I am not actually engaged in finding truths or gain-ing practical or moral insight. Despite all this, some others who have all the general traits relevant to critical competence will still fail to be moved by *their* viewing. Some of them will both not get it and, rationally, doubt that there is anything there to get. They will take me and others like me to be kidding ourselves, misidentifying enjoyment that is really due to our cultivating a sentimental wish that narcis-sism should be grander, deeper, and subtler than it is, cultivating this wish under a self-deceptive mantle of tough-mindedness. There is every reason to suppose that such disagreements will continue, even among Humean critics, as long as the work is accessible to anyone. Still, I would be in a position to claim the work has substantial aes-thetic value, and my claim would be true. Again, since the question is whether the film provides enjoyment with a suitable object, there is an analogy with the epistemology of love: John could be in a posi-tion to say that his relation to Mary sustains genuine love, even though Bill thinks it does not, Bill has whatever traits contribute to competence in such judgments, and there is not even a rational hope that Bill's eyes will be opened to the flourishing of this love.[11]

It might seem, nonetheless, that aesthetic judgments, unlike moral judgments, share the following feature of typical scientific beliefs. *If* someone were to possess all of one's evidence and if it were his total evidence as well, he could not, rationally, disagree with one's con-clusion. This appearance of conditional universality is made tempt-ing by the following fact. In offering a description of the basis for one's aesthetic judgment, one can provide what might be counted as a description of the experience that made one's judgment appropri-ate *and* a description that forces anyone to share one's judgment if she acknowledges the validity of the description and has no inde-pendent reason to reject the judgment. For example, asked why I regard the Mozart quintet for piano and woodwinds as a work of genius, I might mention my delight and surprise at the work's daring combination of scrambling exploration and ultimate unity as the

woodwinds restlessly yet coherently create the characteristic problems and solutions of one genre after another – now working as a collective piano, now as the orchestra in a piano concerto, now as if they
were a string quartet, now ever so tenuously combining as though a
suitable special genre for woodwind voices in all their individuality
had finally been found. Any rational person engaged in making aesthetic judgments would respond to this same "evidence," namely to
the same delight and surprise at the same process, by ranking the
work high on the normal scale. For all its philosophical frills, my
characterization of my response to the Fassbinder film was, similarly,
a description of an evaluatively compelling experience. Indeed,
there is always an articulate and cogent answer to the question
"What is it about your experience that makes you regard this aesthetic judgment as right?" which would describe a basis for only one
conclusion.

In fact, universality on this basis is not a form of universality that
distinguishes science from morality. In moral discussion, too, I can
describe the experience on which I based my conclusion in a way
that compels the conclusion if the validity of the description is
accepted and no contrary experiences are brought to bear. For example, asked for the basis for my judgment that Newt Gingrich's pro-
posals are unjust, I might cite my outrage at their cruel effects on the
poor, a response that would lead even Speaker Gingrich to my judgment if he thought the description was accurate and had no further,
contrary moral experience to offer. Of course, this connection would
not impress the Speaker. The judgment is implicit in my tendentious
way of describing what led me to it, when I describe the condemnation as based on outrage at cruelty. And the same can be said of
the aesthetic descriptions that create the appearance of universality.
The tendentiousness can be part of the description of how one
responded, as in my claim to have been stirred and deeply amused,
not just titillated, by the shifting perspectives of *Petra von Kant*. The
tendentiousness can also be part of a description (perhaps, a superfi-
cially neutral description) of what one responded to. If, listening to
the quintet, I responded to the achievement of coherence in the face
of constant shifts, the work has value. But coherence, in this context,
is the good sort of unity, distinct, say, from superficial unity through
dogged loyalty to conventional harmonic patterns. (The former is
what provides enjoyment, for its own sake, of a process like the
achievement of understanding, while the latter properly prompts
nothing more than recognition of the creator's craftsmanship and

learning.) Brahms lovers describe their pleasure on hearing Brahms's First Symphony as a response to the first sort of unity, while a Brahms hater would claim that their pleasure depends on misidentifying what is really unity of the second kind. (Cf. Shaw on the *German Requiem:* "an attempt to pass off the forms of music for music itself, especially those forms which have received a sort of consecration from their use by great composers in the past.")[12]

Of course, if possession of all one's evidence is construed as requiring endorsement of a description of one's response that entails the judgment at issue or if it is construed as requiring sharing an attitude including affirmation of the judgment, then in all three realms of judgment one can expect possession of one's evidence to lead to agreement in one's judgment on the part of everyone who is rational. But such construals trivialize the status of typical scientific beliefs. What is distinctive about their authority is that the rational scientific believer is often in a position to take the evidence with a bearing on his belief to be rationally compelling to those who share it as their total evidence, when evidence is construed as consisting of non-tendentious findings, namely falling on the observational side of an appropriately contextual observational–theoretical distinction.

"But," someone might object, "something quite analogous is true of aesthetic observations. When Humean critics disagree about value judgments, they must experience the work in different ways, ways that are not intrinsically value-laden. If the Brahms lover is right and the Brahms hater is wrong about the unity a work achieves, then the Brahms lover genuinely hears the music as unified, while the Brahms hater does not. The underlying difference is no more evaluative than the difference between one who does and one who does not see the duck in the duck–rabbit figure. If all Humean critics took in works in the same perceptually structured ways, then all would agree. That they do not so take works in is the source of rational despair about achieving the universality of science. Here, as opposed to the moral case, the crucial difference from science involves the tendency for the scientific community to acquire sufficiently similar perceptual resources."

I think this is a misdiagnosis of aesthetic disagreement, due to another tempting misunderstanding of the epistemic implications of critical discourse. A Brahms hater, if trained in ways that she regards as generally relevant, will be able to hear a long passage as unified by the prolonged pedal points Shaw liked to mock. But this won't be unity she enjoys, or enjoys in a moving way – and she does not think this unity is the real object of the Brahms lover's emotion. Majestic, as opposed to pompous, unity is what she will not concede, but this puts us in the sphere of my disagreement with Speaker Gingrich, not in the realm of the duck–rabbit.

Here the role of authenticity in aesthetic arguments tends to confuse us. A debunker is committed to explaining the stirring emotions that others feel as due to something other than the features of their experiences that make these experiences sufficiently like learning. So a debunker will often charge that the enamored are not responding to what is really there. (Shaw's worst insult is that Brahms turns out "the description of music positively by tons," rather than music itself.)[13] However, rather than discerning a purely perceptual comment, we should understand the debunker to be charging that the enjoyment the enamored do undergo, which would otherwise put the work high on the normal scale, is not enjoyment of a learninglike experience. This will not support so much as a hope (much less a requirement) that common, evaluatively neutral experiences lead to common evaluations by Humean critics. For the link between experience and enjoyment may be present for some, missing in others, and each side may enduringly lack resources to overcome this difference.

But what of special cases, such as Mozart's or Shakespeare's greatest works? Mightn't an appreciation of their greatness (after sufficient scrutiny and training) be a condition for a full grasp of the concept of aesthetic value by anyone who makes aesthetic judgments, so that at least in these cases aesthetic judgment approaches the universality of science at its most secure? Perhaps so (though one thinks worried thoughts about Tolstoy's disdain for Shakespeare and Hume's blithe assumption that everyone of taste would rate Bunyan as a tiny molehill beside Addison's great Tenerife). Still, similarly paradigmatic moral judgments have a similar standing. Anyone who actually makes moral judgments must regard torturing babies for the fun of it as wrong, on pain of lacking a full grasp of the concept of moral wrongness.

Where aesthetic judgment may attain a higher universality is in its capacity to exclude rational nihilism. A moral nihilist could rationally deny that wrongness exists, denying that others' moral revulsion is a means of discerning any distinctive property. In a way, an aesthetic nihilist must go further, since he must deny that the crucial way of responding – here enjoyment of a learninglike process that does not aim at truth or practical attainment – occurs at all. It is not clear that such a stark denial could be part of the best explanation of all psychological data in any rational framework for explaining them. For rational inquiry itself seems to be enjoyment-driven, even though it is directed at finding out the truth. By its nature, inquiry leads from frustration to a search for satisfaction in which the inquirer enjoys successful inference, clarification, discovery, and heightened perspicuity. Just as a rational agent would think himself deprived by a life of pleasurable feeling delivered to his supine body through electrodes, a rational believer would think himself deprived by a life in which true beliefs were reliably delivered through electrodes, without any achievement of justification on his part. So it is not clear that any rational inquirer could deny the existence of aesthetic value, since this is tantamount to denying the enjoyability of learninglike processes for their own sake. Perhaps, then, one should say that the cognitive authority of aesthetic judgment is pretty much on a par with that of moral judgment, but a little bit higher.

THE SERIOUSNESS OF AESTHETIC LIFE

The means by which I have given aesthetic judgment a similar degree of objective validity to moral judgment might seem to separate these kinds of judgment in implausible ways elsewhere. It might seem that a theory basing valid aesthetic judgment on an unprincipled response must underrate the importance of reasoned arguments for and against aesthetic judgments. It might seem that a theory identifying aesthetic values with kinds of enjoyment must make it irrational of us to be as concerned as we often are to arrive at a *valid* aesthetic judgment when we experience a work of art. Finally, it might seem that talk of enjoyment that is directed at a learninglike response to an object, not just occasioned by perceiving it or thinking about it, is at best a loose metaphor, making the objective validity of aesthetic judgment loose and metaphorical as well. I will conclude by showing how an account basing aesthetic value on the enjoyment of a learninglike process can respond to these fears.

An intelligent person engaged in forming *moral* judgments must engage in moral deliberation. For his morality will involve commitment to general principles that are hard to apply to particular cases. People engaged in aesthetic judgment do often engage in reasoning. Why should there be this parallel with moral judgment if the validity of aesthetic judgments consists of the availability of a kind of unprincipled response?

Part of the answer involves the public and facilitating role of aesthetic reasoning. Often, such discourse is a means of enabling others to enjoy a learninglike experience by appropriately directing their attention and expectations. The reasons given are, in effect, directions for achieving an aesthetically appreciative response. Still, to sustain the full parallel between moral and aesthetic reasoning, one must explain how aesthetic reasoning can play a potentially private role of putting aesthetic judgments to the test, and justifying or debunking them. This can happen because what puts a work at the interesting, higher levels of the normal scale is enjoyment produced in a certain way, a way that must be capable of further articulation if it exists. I wasn't moved by the drama of the woodwinds' struggle to find room for their distinctive voices if there is no way in which they struggled and no way in which the phases of their struggle were moving: so I had better be able to articulate this drama. Quite generally, since aesthetic value is based on enjoyment of a learninglike process, the enjoyment that gives a work its value must be articulable in the language of learning, in terms of surprise and discovery, apparent randomness and the dawning recognition of order, and so forth.

The second problem – which is much more troubling – concerns the seriousness with which people take the goal of objective validity in the two realms of judgment. Someone engaged in moral judgment is rationally concerned to arrive at an objectively valid judgment. *Of course,* this concern is rational: if her judgment is false, she may wrong someone in relying on it; taking truth and falsehood to be merely perspectival would involve moral megalomania and the abandonment of the pursuit of moral insight on which her self-respect depends. Similarly, people engaged in enjoying art in the ways that lead to aesthetic judgment are concerned that their judgments be right. They question their own judgments, and are frustrated and humbled when they decide that their judgments were misguided. This seems a rational concern for rightness, too. But why is it, if the goal is the aesthetic one of enjoyment rather than the moral goal of avoiding wrongdoing? Before, the question "Is it really moving?" turned out to be like the question "Am I really in love?" But relying on a false answer to the second question can lead to disaster. In the first case, why care if the work is really moving, as long as one's emotions are enjoyably stirred up?

I find this question so difficult that I will approach it after facing a related question that must be confronted in any case. Do all intelligent, morally serious people have reason to especially care about the kinds of aesthetic appreciation that confer especially high value on a work of art? After all, the intensity and length of the pleasurable feelings experienced are nothing special. I have to confront this question because I assumed that such people do especially care about those kinds of response when I associated high value with a high position on the normal scale.

Ironically, my suspiciously subjective account of aesthetic validity provides two objective reasons, reasons compelling for all intelligent, morally serious people, to have a special interest in art with serious aesthetic value. First of all, human intelligence seeks the enjoyment of learning. It involves the interest in problems and satisfaction in their solution that are inherent in curiosity. Yet an intelligent human investigating the world can never achieve full satisfaction in her solutions. There is always the chance that reality will prove her wrong and the likelihood that her solutions will prove misleading when she applies them to further problems. What seem productive clues and meaningful mysteries often lead nowhere, which is not much fun. Such a person will seek relief from the anxiety and disappointment of actual inquiry in learninglike processes that are especially demanding yet ultimately secure from the world's confusions. She will have a special need for the works of art that have special value. (Yeats writes, "The poet . . . is part of his own phantasmagoria and we adore him because nature has grown intelligible, and by so doing a part of our creative power.")[14]

Second, an intelligent person will be aware that she does not experience the world as others do, that her living is colored by characteristic thoughts, expectations, and emotions in a way that is not quite the same as anyone else's. And she will face the enormous frustration, to any curious person, of not knowing what it is like to live in the distinctive way of anyone else. We need to resist submersion in others in our actual encounters with them. We would lose our boundaries and go crazy otherwise. Still, this limitation is an enormous frustration to anyone's curiosity, a barrier to her coping with others, whether for the sake of advantage or love, and an impoverishment of the sensitivity on which moral competence often depends. Indeed, the lure and the danger of transcending personal boundaries produce a painful tension in the background of every person's life. The utter separateness of one's self from the persons and things around one is a source of profound loneliness, yet psychic absorption into the world would be self-annihilation. The distinctive individual tone of a person's life is a matter of the distinctive expectations, emotions, and experiences of coherence and normality with which the person responds to the world. So, seeking escape from these dilemmas of isolation and immersion, one will be grateful for processes that do *not* threaten the integrity of the self, in which one's responses are shaped in different ways by expectations and emotions and norms, and in a coherent way, another way of making sense of the world. One will have another serious need for art of serious value.

The reasons for caring about major aesthetic values ought to be present in some form in all aesthetic values, in a resemblance between minor and major virtues that does not trivialize the latter. We can now see how the general identification of aesthetic appreciation with enjoyment of a learninglike process not directed at truth or practical attainment makes this so. Any enjoyment of a process that is learninglike yet not concerned with actually learning about reality comforts us with characteristic joys of learning that are freed from the anxieties that actual inquiry requires; in minor art, the comfort is small, but it is there. Less obviously, but more profoundly, any such enjoyment helps us to evade the metaphysical pain of being repelled both by the loneliness of independence from one's world and by terror at losing oneself in it. In actual learning, one struggles with the independence of the world from one's mind; in aesthetic appreciation, attitudes and skills normally deployed in that struggle are activated without risking defeat by recalcitrant reality. Granted, the evasion of the metaphysical pain is especially well sustained by the long processes combining self-forgetfulness with the experience of active engagement characteristic of serious aesthetic value. But the same relief is afforded by all art for at least a while and to some extent. As Winnicott speculated, a work of art comforts us as a teddy bear comforts an infant, by creating a zone that is neither wholly 'me' nor wholly 'not-me.'[15]

Any plausible rationale for taking aesthetic value to be a deeply important aspect of life must somehow connect it with our strivings for knowledge or virtue. Yet such a rationale for the importance of art threatens to trivialize art in another way, by making the importance of art depend on its usefulness as an aid to nonaesthetic values. If serious aesthetic value is a substantial response to needs that intellectual and moral inquiry must create *and* must thwart, then it is appropriately connected to truth and virtue yet *not* subordinated to them.

Now, let us return to the original question of why intelligent, morally serious people care about getting it right in evaluating works of art. Of course, this is a question about nondeferential aesthetic judgment: commercial considerations to one side, one cares about the aesthetic judgments of experts to the extent to which they will facilitate one's self-sufficient achievement of the same insight. The question is why it is rational to be so anxious to avoid either undervaluing or overvaluing in the judgments that flow out of one's current experience of a work.

As far as the question concerns the avoidance of undervaluing, the rationality of our concern is clear. Undervaluing normally reflects an experience that is lower on the normal scale than the work might provide, hence a missed opportunity for satisfactions that an inquisitive, morally sensitive person will especially value. Even in the abnormal, Huck Finn–like case in which one's aesthetic appreciation really is as valuable as the work can provide, yet some hidebound tradition leads one to locate one's enjoyment lower than it actually deserves to be, there is a loss in the undervaluing itself. One is not as apt as one would otherwise be to return to the work, to deepen one's appreciation of it, or to seek out similar works with the eagerness appropriate to the interests they serve.

But why is the fear of overvaluing rational? (After all, we *fins esprits* do sometimes regard our aesthetic nicety as a burden.) If one has the interests underlying the normal scale, then overvaluing will occur in one of two ways. The first is the way of superficiality: in one's enjoyment of an experience of problems and solutions, the problems are less demanding or the solutions less effective than one thinks. The second is the way of sentimentality: one takes oneself to have gained access to an alternative rich and comprehensive way of responding to the world when in fact the work has simply triggered responses that are part of one's standard emotional equipment. In itself, overvaluing leads to spending time on certain works that would better be spent on deeper, emotionally richer works, to achieve satisfactions that are of greater interest. In addition, the attraction to the superficial or sentimental that is revealed in the discovery that one has valued a work too highly is cause for concern on another ground. There is a danger of experiencing deep, emotionally rich works in a shallow, sentimental way. So one needs to struggle against one's own superficiality and sentimentality, to drive oneself to achieve the best that works can provide. For all these reasons, it is rational to have a stance of fear of overvaluing – at least at those times that one will rationally set aside for pursuit of the two interests in serious value. (For most of us it would be neurotic not to relax the sense of taste when viewing late-night TV.)

Once we appreciate that the seriousness of art has distinctive roots, different from what makes morality such a serious matter, we may gain vital material for clarifying the most troubling distinction in my account of aesthetic judgment, the distinction I have often made between the enjoyment of a learninglike response to the work itself and the enjoyment of a thought or reverie occasioned by the work. (Without this clarification, the whole account can seem a loose metaphor, to be applied according to the aesthetic appraiser's whim.) Traditionally, such distinctions have been explained formalistically, by detaching the genuinely aesthetic response from beliefs and emotions outside the experience of art. But formalist strictures are either excessive or useless here.

It would be an excess of formalist puritanism to require that aesthetic enjoyment never depend on thoughts of what one has encountered in the world outside art or on feelings prompted by appreciation of parallels between perceived qualities of the work and emotion-laden experiences in nonaesthetic life. Often, one could not fully appreciate wit without recognizing the elegance with which it captures truth, or fully appreciate tragic power without recognizing that real horrors and dilemmas of being human have been honestly confronted.[16]

A milder formalism might seem helpful now: responses based on associations with the real world or nonaesthetic life that the work occasions must be no more than the raw material for the total process to which aesthetic enjoyment itself responds. But mild formalist metaphors of raw material worked up and elements combined are not much help in distinguishing aesthetic appreciation from enjoyment of thoughts or emotions that are merely occasioned by a work. Manipulative melodramas use emotions as raw materials, prompting responses in ways that do depend on the serial order of the emotions evoked – but they work the materials up in a nonaesthetic way. On the other hand, isolated details, such as the first, soaring measures of Beethoven's Eighth Symphony, can add to the genuine aesthetic power of a work in ways that do not depend on their structural role.

What is the difference, then, between aesthetic appreciation and the mere enjoyment of a series of thoughts and emotions prompted by the work? How can the difference be described without reducing aesthetic judgment, in the end, to the application of aesthetic principles? The lame answer entailed by my account of aesthetic value is that the object of aesthetic enjoyment must be a process of hearing, seeing, reading, or otherwise scrutinizing the work that is sufficiently like those in which we learn about the world, but enjoyed apart from an interest in acquiring truths, avoiding wrongdoing, or deciding on useful interventions. The answer is lame until more is said about what makes enjoyment have such a process as its object. I think the further answer is, roughly, this. The process enjoyed is learninglike enough for genuine aesthetic appreciation if the enjoyment of aspects of the process that make it resemble learning depends on its serving those distinctive needs for art that are inevitably created and thwarted by learning, the need to overcome the frustration and disappointment of actual striving for truth, and the need for merging into different ways of responding without threatening the integrity of one's self.

Any pretty wallpaper and any absorbing tale serve those interests to some degree, relieving cognitive anxiety or loosening the constraints of self-containment. But a strong response to a mere melodrama does not derive its intensity or richness from demanding problems and their solutions or from a diverse yet distinctive way of experiencing the world. That is why the power of the work is not aesthetic power. One can say, in the language of my initial formulation, with its echo of Kant, "The object of powerful enjoyment was not enough like a process of learning." One can say, as we usually do, "The emotion wasn't earned; it wasn't honestly there; it didn't come out of the drama itself." Or one can say, "The strength of the enjoyment wasn't due to the depth of the satisfaction of those longings that are inevitably created and thwarted in scientific and practical inquiry." The three kinds of condemnation come to the same thing.

In the other counterexample to mild formalism, the opening of Beethoven's Eighth Symphony, needs of those who long for large yet effortless solutions and intimacies are satisfied by an immediate achievement of free movement that respects constraining harmonic rules and by sudden access to a way of feeling that is at once extremely volatile and extremely well ordered. The learning that such a process is like is the sudden dawning of a revelation – but freed from the responsibility to make sure that apparent revelation is real and purified of the detachment that is part of even the most direct glimpse of what life is like for another.

It might seem that the need to appeal to our distinctive interests in art when explaining the content of aesthetic judgments debunks talk of objective validity in connection with aesthetic judgments. For

54

interests, after all, are a subjective matter. But objects can fall under a predicate as a matter of fact when interests determine how far the predicate extends. Objects are tables or chairs as a matter of fact. Their fitting their artifact category depends on meeting certain requirements of structure and serving certain interests. Similarly, what fits the category of aesthetic appreciation must involve the enjoyment of a process of contemplation or scrutiny with elements of learning and must involve that enjoyment because the process serves certain interests. Aesthetic judgments, unlike most moral and scientific judgments, are evaluations of things in terms of their capacity to serve distinctive functions. Nonetheless, they are perfectly factual.

Notes

I am indebted to Jerrold Levinson and Raymond Martin for their helpful comments on earlier versions of this essay.

1. See Richard W. Miller, "Ways of Moral Learning," *Philosophical Review* 94 (1985): 507–56; *Fact and Method* (Princeton, N.J.: Princeton University Press, 1987), esp. chaps. 2, 4, 8, 9, and 10; and *Moral Differences* (Princeton, N.J.: Princeton University Press, 1992), chaps. 1–5.
2. I describe this connection between responsible cooperation and the norms of scientific inquiry in more detail in "The Norms of Reason," *Philosophical Review* 104 (1995): 205–45.
3. I take it that no actual person who has not been misled by bad arguments is a moral nihilist. In any case, I have in mind disagreements among those who make moral judgments, i.e., the moral ascriptions from which moral nihilists forbear.
4. I have in mind the practice of communicating moral judgments in which a moral nihilist does not participate. The moral nihilist is a semantic parasite on this activity. If no one made judgments as to what is good, bad, right, wrong, just, unjust, or morally indifferent, the moral nihilist could not single out the target of his stance, by asserting the nonexistence of any property that could make true a certain kind of statement.
5. Could people engage in scientific assertion independently, with no such cooperative goal? If so, this practice would not be governed by the communicative goals that properly regulate the scope of genuine communication with our actual terms of scientific assertion. And in any case, each monadic inquirer would be constantly engaged in cooperation with her past and future selves, trusting herself to have been concerned in the past to extend her future resources and attempting now to be worthy of such future trust (a trust that will be essential, since current experiential bases for belief formation are largely, inevitably, soon forgotten).
6. Most of us would be willing to fill in the following schema in a variety

of ways: "I cannot get very far into the hallowed works of X. If I had all generic critical virtues, I expect I still would not get it. But X lovers include people such as Y, so obviously perceptive on other subjects that I accept their insight here." For example, I have discovered that I am one of many who would instantiate "X" with "Dickens" and "Y" with "Leavis."

7. Competence-constituting principles will be especially important in grounding moral judgments if, as some insist (e.g., W. D. Ross and John McDowell), accurate moral judgment sometimes requires weighing competing prima facie considerations in the absence of any rule assigning weights in virtue of general properties of the case at hand. Still, the weighing will be insightful only if there is a general rule, perhaps rationally rejectable, describing attitudes, commitments, or experiences that would lead anyone to the same judgment, if rational and informed. Otherwise, one would have to claim superior moral insight while accepting that there is nothing in virtue of which one's insight is superior. Such epistemic arrogance is incompatible with moral insight (a claim that is a substantive moral principle as well as a metaethical constraint). Aesthetic judgment is unprincipled even in comparison with moral judgment as seen in a plausible morality of sentiment.

8. Of course, this is enjoyment in a broad sense, which need not consist of fun. Those who profoundly enjoy a performance of *Lear* do not have great fun. Jerrold Levinson, "Pleasure and the Value of Works of Art," *British Journal of Aesthetics* 32 (1992): 295–306, offers a number of warnings about aesthetic pleasure that also apply to the broader category of aesthetic enjoyment.

9. Admittedly, it can remain appropriate to ascribe an abstract ranking to a work when the work has become so inaccessible that ascription of a corresponding specific form of enjoyability is no longer appropriate. But the inappropriateness of the specific ascription is pragmatic and reveals nothing important about the sources of aesthetic value. Among the Elizabethan dramas one notch lower than *The Spanish Tragedy*, there must be some melodramas that were once subjects of intense, sad, suspenseful appreciation of a sort that ranks a work as good but that no one, no matter how scholarly and imaginative, could so enjoy today. We still, tenselessly, ascribe the abstract ranking "good." *The Stranger from Ipswich* is a good drama. But it *was* a moving drama. It isn't any more. I think our diffidence concerning the specific attributions reflects nothing deeper than the desire not to mislead. The standard point of making a specific aesthetic appraisal is to help and invite the audience to respond to the work in that way. The invitation so to enjoy *The Stranger from Ipswich* is pointless now. But it wasn't once, so the play is good.

10. The claim that accurate autobiography is enough to validate any aesthetic judgment is not as lax as it seems, since a great deal of specialized knowledge and training may be needed to make possible a particular aesthetic enjoyment, especially one ranking high on the normal scale.

Still, if one ignores the ranking of aesthetic enjoyments and their general connection with learning, then my proposal to identify the aesthetic value of a work with a capacity to provide enjoyment for someone *will* seem wildly permissive, even if Humean prescriptions for critical competence are imposed. As Alan Goldman notes, in "Aesthetic Versus Moral Evaluations," *Philosophy and Phenomenological Research* 50 (1990): 721, if beauty were the capacity to cause pleasure in some knowledgeable critic, virtually anything would be beautiful. By the same token, Goldman's neglect of those resources for an aesthetics that makes the highest relevant enjoyment decisive affects his stimulating discussions of aesthetic objectivity. In particular, I believe that this neglect is largely responsible for the "anti-realist" conclusion he has drawn from our shared denial of universality in aesthetic response, his inference that there is "no fact of the matter" concerning aesthetic value when Humean critics disagree ("Realism about Aesthetic Properties," *Journal of Aesthetics and Art Criticism* 51 [1993]: 31).

11. Why isn't someone's attribution of a critic's dissent to a blind spot grounds for the charge I previously directed at overly aestheticizing moralities, "too arrogant to be insightful"? In the case of aesthetic judgment, the affirmer of a controversial ascription of value can rely on first-person access in the identification of the object of enjoyment. This grounding in mere psychological access need not involve any foolish arrogance, since the ultimate aesthetic issue is whether someone can have enjoyment of a certain kind. In contrast, moral issues are not questions of whether someone can be in a certain psychological state. This is part of the reason why it is arrogant and wrong to persist in a moral assessment that is not shared when one does not think that contrary assessments depart from any appropriate principle.

12. George Bernard Shaw, *Music in London* (New York: Vienna House, 1973), 1: 228. In this review, as in all his Brahms debunking, Shaw clearly does not question Brahms's sincerity, but contrasts the real process of listening to works by Brahms with what Brahms and his admirers think the works provide.

My diagnosis of this false appearance that aesthetic judgment has the universality of scientific belief only entails that a tendentious description is always *one* natural way of justifying an aesthetic evaluation. This would require the availability of a large number of important terms of aesthetic description that have an evaluative component in their normal use – the moderate position on description and evaluation that Alan Goldman proposes as common ground in the illuminating exchange between Jerrold Levinson and Goldman in "Being Realistic About Aesthetic Properties," *Journal of Aesthetics and Art Criticism* 52 (1994): 351–6. On the other hand, my endorsement of the Kantian thought about the unprincipled nature of aesthetic judgment probably requires Frank Sibley's much more radical claim, in "Aesthetic Concepts," *Philosophical Review* 68 (1959): 351–73, that a fully explicit, adequate set of reasons for an aesthetic evaluation must itself describe the work in terms that have an evaluative component. In addition to considerations I previously sketched, my sympathy with Sibley rests on my acquaintance with what critics have written. I have never encountered a cogent critical argument in support of an evaluation that did not rely, almost always quite explicitly, on tendentious characterizations of the work.

13. Shaw, *Music in London,* 228. I hope it is clear that music is the art form most receptive to the analysis I am criticizing.

14. W. B. Yeats, "A General Introduction for My Work," *Essays and Introductions* (New York: Macmillan, 1961), 509.

15. See Donald Winnicott, "Transitional Objects and Transitional Phenomena," *Collected Papers: Through Paediatrics to Psychoanalysis* (London: Tavistock, 1958), 229–42.

16. Not that formalist puritanism has lacked distinguished adherents, including Arnold Isenberg, Cleanth Brooks, and W. K. Wimsatt. It is none too easy to say how their arguments have gone wrong, without making the discovery of truth into a goal of aesthetic appreciation, contrary to my account of aesthetic value. In "Truth in Beauty," *American Philosophical Quarterly* 16 (1979): 317–25, I present a detailed case against this formalism, in terms compatible with the perspective of the present essay.

3

Aesthetic value, moral value, and the ambitions of naturalism

PETER RAILTON

INTRODUCTION

Here's a story that Hume, I believe, would have liked.[1]

Someone I know once led a group of U.S. journalists on a tour of Germany. The tour was part of a public relations effort by a German company, so naturally the journalists were prone to be skeptical of what they saw and heard. One of the stops was a sort of clearing-house where professional tasters made judgments about the quality, readiness, price, and so on of wines from various vineyards and regions. To display their skill to the journalists, the tasters performed blind tests – the journalists would pour wine from numbered bottles into unlabeled cups and then bring them to the tasters, who would attempt to identify the number of the wine. The tasters did so well that one of the journalists thought there must be a trick. He therefore surreptitiously contrived to pour wine from two different bottles into a single cup before submitting it to the tasters. He stood back to watch the reaction. The first taster washed the wine over his tongue, spat it out, and pronounced: "Hmmm . . . Something's the matter here . . . maybe you accidentally poured some wine into a cup that wasn't empty? I think I can taste some of number ten, but there's also a bit of something more like number seventeen or . . ." After leaving the clearinghouse, the journalist later confessed the trick to his host. "You know," he said, "those guys are really onto something."

What they are onto, of course, is a set of complex perceptual qualities that make up the taste of wine. Does this show anything about whether they might also be onto the qualities that make up taste *in* wine? Evaluation, we all believe, is a profoundly subjective phe-

59

nomenon. And yet we may ask, Mightn't it also be objective? Indeed, might value lie precisely at the intersection of the subjective and objective? So I will claim. Such a claim, if it could be made out, might help us to get beyond a certain initial skepticism about evaluation, a dark unease over what sort of thing value is and how it might find a place in the world.[2]

Other, perhaps decisive, grounds for skepticism could still lie ahead. To be sure, evaluative talk is an important part of our daily lives – it seems impossible to imagine life without it. But that isn't much of an endorsement of any particular evaluative discourse. We can see that, over time, many forms of evaluative discourse have come and gone. (Think, for example, of evaluations in terms of nobility, or male and female honor.) Evaluative discourse is by its nature bound up with a great deal else in thought and culture, even as it aspires to something more. Thus, evaluative forms can have the rug pulled out from under them when our overall view of the world changes. (Think, for example, of evaluations in terms of piety.)

At present, moral and aesthetic evaluation – our chief concerns here – are, by and large, still standing. Indeed, one might say that they have come wholly into their own only within the modern period (a point to which we will return). But there unquestionably are insistent forces tugging at *their* rugs. The contemporary intellectual world is one in which cosmology is done by physicists rather than theologians, in which no guiding intelligence seems to have written value into the world. Perhaps a conception of value thoroughly acclimated to the contemporary world must view all evaluative talk – morality and aesthetics included – as a *projection,* much as Feuerbach held the secret of the Holy Family to be the human family. This thought naturally finds expression in the claim that value is subjective. The objective purport of evaluation rings out, but finds no echo.[3]

Evaluative talk is at risk in part because of its objective purport.[4] If evaluation were no more than the expression of preference, then its place in the world would be fairly secure. There is some, but not much, controversy over the reality of human desires and preferences. Evaluation is of course closely tied to preference – preference is surely the main point of entry into evaluation – but evaluation has further ambitions. A companion who says to us as we descend the steps on our way out of the Annual Young Artists show, "I don't know much about art, but I do know what I like – and I don't like *that,*" is signaling that he does not pretend to be pronouncing an aesthetic judgment. One seemingly needs more than strong preferences if one is to claim authority on value. Indeed, we even speak of value as *explaining* preferences, as for example when we contrast a case in which we believe that the acclaim received by a work of art is attributable to mere fashion – and no doubt soon will pass – with a case in which we believe that a work's acceptance has been won over time by a growing recognition of its merit. The critical pretensions and explanatory ambitions of value discourse would come to nothing if talk of value were no more than the shadow of our preferences.

Coming to terms with these ambitions presents us with various philosophical challenges. We might seek to characterize the *concept* of value – to give an analysis that would capture the difference in meaning between unadorned claims of preference and attributions of value. But we might in a more explanatory spirit ask whether anything in the *characteristic functions and presuppositions* of value attribution – and, especially, of attributions of objective value – renders talk of objective value incompatible with a sober, naturalistic view of ourselves and our world. Answering this second question certainly presupposes some competence on our part in the language of value – else how would we know what to look for? Yet we might have sufficient competence to raise and answer questions about functions and presuppositions without being able to produce a satisfactory conceptual analysis. To show that the wherewithal exists within the natural world to sustain talk of objective value would not be tantamount to giving a naturalistic reduction of value. As G. E. Moore recognized, even if goodness is an unanalyzable, non-natural concept, the goodness of anything still supervenes upon its natural features.[5] In consequence, even a non-naturalist's claims about value cannot be vindicated unless the world contains natural properties capable of playing whatever roles our evaluative practices call for.[6]

In this essay I propose largely to set aside the first, conceptual question about value. I will assume that we have sufficient working understanding of the meaning of 'value' in general – and of 'moral value' and 'aesthetic value' in particular – to ask some central questions about how objectivity in value and valuation could be possible for creatures like us in a world like ours. This project is therefore largely independent of partisan debates within the metatheory of value.

I will pair moral and aesthetic value in part because I believe each can help us to understand the potential objectivity of the other. From moral value we will borrow a vertical-and-horizontal model of objectivity that arguably (surprisingly?) fits the aesthetic case. From aesthetic value we will borrow the idea that value can be objective and nonhypothetical without standing in a necessary relation with claims of obligation, an idea that arguably (surprisingly?) fits moral value. To begin, however, we will look somewhat generically at notions of subjectivity and objectivity in value.

THE SUBJECTIVITY OF VALUE

In what sense is value subjective? A proper answer would be fairly complex and would force us to examine a number of central tendencies in "modern culture." It says a great deal about us that the man in the street (or the undergraduate in our classroom) is so ready to agree that value is "subjective" and so quick to elide this to "arbitrary." The task of the present essay is not, however, intellectual history. Instead, we need to ask whether we can locate a compelling case for saying that subjectivity is essential to value.

I believe the best case to be a highly abstract one. According to this case, value enters the picture when *mattering* does. (Nihilists thus have hit on an apt phrase when they say, "Nothing matters.") If we imagine a world without any locus of mattering or concern – say, a world composed entirely of oxygen molecules in random motion – no issues of value would arise internal to that world. Within that stark world it couldn't matter less what happens, because it doesn't matter at all. If to this world we add some beings to whom something matters, then questions of value might have a foothold. It matters quite a lot to us how we fare – for example, whether there is any oxygen in *our* vicinity. Some philosophers are drawn to the thought that ours is really, at bottom, a stark world: when viewed as the physicist sees it – viewed "objectively," according to some – it is no more than molecules in motion. But the "no more than" seems gratuitous. There is a striking difference between our world and the original oxygen world, for ours is one in which some of the molecular goings-on constitute mattering.

Of course, this mattering might just be desire – likes and dislikes, and their associated psychology. And this has seemed an inadequate ground for value in general or objective value in particular. As Bertrand Russell wrote:

I cannot see how to refute the arguments for the subjectivity of ethical values, but I find myself incapable of believing that all that is wrong with wanton cruelty is that I don't like it.[7]

It was natural for Russell to phrase the question of whether the objectivity of morality could be upheld in terms of whether good and evil also matter in some larger, more objective sense. He put it like this: "Are good and evil of importance to the universe, or only to man?"[8]

This formulation of the problem of "mattering in some objective sense" or "mattering objectively," however, makes a positive solution seem out of the question. For what could it possibly mean to say that good and evil matter *to the universe* – or anything remotely like that? If "mattering objectively" means something like "mattering from an objective standpoint" and if a standpoint is objective only if it is free of subjectivity, then we seem to have reached a dead end. For a standpoint without any subjectivity is a standpoint with no point of view – which is to say, no standpoint at all.

A genuine, nonmetaphorical standpoint or point of view is always a locus of experience, centered on a subject ("Archibald's standpoint" or "my cat's standpoint") or somehow composed of subjects ("the standpoint of Local 1099" or "the standpoint of future generations"). Fortunately, Russell's formulation is idiosyncratic: our forebears were far more likely to ask whether *God* cared than what the universe might think. This suggests an approach. If an ideal, divine subject were thought by its nature to occupy a standpoint that could underwrite "mattering objectively" and provide an appropriately nonsubjective standard of value, mightn't we mortal subjects accomplish something along the same lines by *achieving* a suitably similar standpoint? So, naturally, we are led to ask in what ways subjects can be objective.

THE OBJECTIVITY OF SUBJECTS

Subjects can, we think, be more or less objective. Three notions of objectivity in particular seem important.

1. We often speak of objectivity in belief or perception as a matter of whether one reliably cognizes an independently existing domain of objects and their properties.[9] Because of its worldly focus, let us call this the *objectual* sense of objectivity. A subject who, owing to preconceptions or other limitations, systematically distorts or misrepresents the world around him lacks this sort of objectivity. "Try to be objective," we admonish, "try to see things as they are rather than as you think they are, or wish they were." The representational efforts of subjects, such as reports, testimony, or even paintings, can also be more or less objective in this sense. Of course, perfect objec-

tivity of this sort seems unattainable by beings like us, since our perceptual and cognitive processes involve mechanisms that could not function without some preconception or bias. But when all goes reasonably well, our preconceptions and biases can promote very considerable objectual objectivity.

Although thinking of objectivity in this way orients us toward "the external world," it could hardly demand the banishment of subjectivity. On the contrary, objectivity in representation, belief, or assertion requires the real presence of a representer, believer, or asserter. An undetected stratum of ice in Antarctica may more accurately reflect the local magnetic field 55,000 years ago than any current believer's thinking, but the ice layer is in itself a mere object, not a locus of representations. Subjects, on the other hand, are such loci and can be more or less objective to the extent that they possess epistemic and semantic capacities which nonaccidentally result in representations that approximate features of the world around them.

2. A second familiar way of conceiving the objectivity of subjects shifts the focus away from relations to the external world. A subject can be objective in virtue of reasoning in accord with rules or conditions that are either demonstrably valid or (in some other sense) deliberatively appropriate for subjects regardless of their individual variability. Let us call this *deliberative* objectivity.

In this case, too, subjectivity is not eliminated as a precondition for objectivity. Only subjects are capable of self-regulation through the self-imposition of rules or conditions on reasoning. Unconstrained subjectivity can of course undermine this sort of objectivity, because subjects are prone to mistaking their particular, contingent thoughts for something universally rational or valid. That is a kind of reifying illusion. But if subjects were *genuinely* to recognize a rule or condition as valid and to commit themselves to following it, this would implicate them in no reifying illusion at all. Since this second conception locates objectivity in rules or conditions for subjects rather than a relation to external metaphysics, it is (for want of a better term) a 'subjectual' rather than objectual conception.[10]

3. The third familiar way in which subjects can be objective is often described as disinterestedness, though seldom without an also-familiar caveat: 'disinterested' means not "unengaged" but something more like "displaying a general, impartial regard combined with a serious – and not merely instrumental – engagement." What this comes to is not easy to say, but we can often (even in the face of substantive disagreements) reach consensus about what we are look-

ing for in a suitably disinterested mediator, judge, referee, or adviser, or about how to go about identifying one. To avoid the unwanted associations of 'disinterested', let us call this third conception the *impartialist* conception of objectivity.

This third notion has both objectual and subjectual affinities. On the one hand, impartiality in perspective is a way of overcoming incomplete or biased representation of the matters at stake; on the other hand, there certainly is no presumption in the idea of impartiality that the matters at stake are wholly objectual – wholly independent of us or our activities.

HUME'S ACCOUNT

If value has its origin in subjects, and if subjects can in these three ways be more or less objective, do we therefore have in hand the requisites for capturing the notion of objective value? Hume begins his own account of aesthetic judgment by despairing of both objectualist and deliberative approaches. First, the objectualist:

> There is a species of philosophy, which cuts off all hopes of success in such an attempt, and represents the impossibility of ever attaining any standard of taste. (6)

This view, he goes on, treats judgments of taste on the model of judgments of independently existing properties of the object appreciated. Yet matters of taste are essentially tied to "the common sentiments of human nature," according to Hume (7).

Hume then argues that the linkage of value to sentiment equally implies that the standard of taste cannot be objective in the second sense:

> It is evident that none of the rules of composition are fixed by reasonings *a priori,* or can be esteemed abstract conclusions of the understanding, from comparing those habitudes and relations of ideas, which are eternal or immutable. (7)

Does the involvement of sentiment preclude altogether the possibility of a genuine objectivity in aesthetic judgment? Hume notes a certain tendency of common sense to embrace this thought, and he reflects upon the familiar proverb *de gustibus non disputandum est:*

> ... the proverb has ... determined it to be fruitless to dispute concerning tastes. ... [C]ommon sense, which is so often at variance with philosophy, especially with the sceptical kind, is found, in one instance at least, to agree in pronouncing the same decision. (6)

And yet now it is Hume who wishes to play the antiskeptic. He notes that

... there is certainly [also] a species of common sense, which opposes [this proverb], or at least serves to modify and restrain it. Whoever would assert an equality of genius and elegance between Ogilby and Milton or Bunyan and Addison, would be thought to defend no less an extravagance, than if he had maintained a mole-hill to be as high as Tenerife, or a pond as extensive as the ocean. Though there may be such persons, who give the preference to the former authors; no one pays attention to such a taste; and we pronounce, without scruple, the sentiment of these pretended critics to be absurd and ridiculous. (7)

If sentiment – rather than independent reality or pure reason – is at the core of taste, how are sentiments themselves to be thus evaluated?

[The real] foundation [of rules of composition] is the same with that of all the practical sciences, experience; nor are they any thing but general observations, concerning what has been universally found to please in all countries and ages. (7)

This foundation can exist even if sentiment "only marks *a certain conformity or relation between the object and the organs or faculties of the mind*" (6, emphasis added). Here, then, is the sort of antiskeptical position on value that Hume will seek to make a place for: many questions of taste *are* justly disputable, for they are not proprietary matters to be referred only to one's own sentiments; rather, they are questions, at least in part, of *general* sentiment. We begin to see here a role for the third conception of objectivity, impartiality. Humean objectivity in aesthetic judgment has, one might say, a *horizontal* as well as *vertical* character: it is a matter not only of what now pleases us, but what would please us and others across time and space. I must "conside[r] myself as a man in general" (15). Of course, any actual aesthetic *experience* is individual and particular, and for that reason no single experience (or content thereof) affords the touchstone in aesthetic evaluation.

We shall be able to ascertain [beauty's] influence not so much from the operation of each particular beauty, as from the durable admiration which attends those works that have survived all the caprices of mode and fashion, all the mistakes of ignorance and envy. (8–9)

As this way of framing things indicates, Hume's account of beauty gives it sufficient independence from particular reactions that it can be cited in the *explanation* of experience:

The same Homer who pleased at Athens or Rome two thousand years ago, is still admired at Paris and at London. All the changes of climate, religion, and language, have not been able to obscure his glory. (9)

Because it is a general matter of whether "a certain conformity . . . really exist[s]" rather than a direct content of experience, beauty – or "glory" – can explain not only individual experiences, but also patterns of similarity in experience.

It emerges that, for Hume, although no questions of taste are resolvable a priori, many aesthetic judgments are as definite and determinable as "matters of fact" in the a posteriori objectualist sense. Let us call the relation of conformity between objects and general "organs or faculties of the mind," such that the objects are "by the structure of the mind . . . naturally calculated to give pleasure" (10), a *match*. Although this match may not itself be a content of direct experience, it is a frequent cause of experience, so that the "conformity or relation between the object and . . . the mind" is not for us simply an esoteric, speculative matter. Rather, our familiar experiences – especially as developed and shared across individuals and over time – suffice to give us reasonably secure knowledge of it.

Though in speculation we may readily avow a certain criterion in science, and deny it in sentiment, the matter is found in practice to be much more hard to ascertain in the former case than in the latter. . . . [N]othing has been more liable to the revolutions of chance and fashion than these pretended decisions of science. The case is not the same with the beauties of eloquence and poetry. Just expressions of passion and nature are sure, after a little time, to gain public applause, which they maintain for ever. (18)

VALUE'S INFRASTRUCTURE

This notion of a match needs considerable refinement. We must, for example, sharpen its characterization so that emphasis is placed upon attention to the object itself and to perceptually based experience of it (rather than some other means by which it might cause pleasure in us). Hume writes: "[A] critic . . . must . . . allow nothing to enter into his consideration, but the very object which is submitted to his examination" (14–15). But this is too strong. The meaning of a work, for example, will depend upon the context in which it was created. And Hume indeed immediately amends his exclusion:

. . . every work of art, in order to procure its due effect on the mind, must be surveyed from a certain point of view, and cannot be fully relished by persons whose situation, real or imaginary, is not conformable to that which is required by the performance. (15)

We must, further, make sure our understanding of *pleasure* is broad enough to include a range of intrinsically sought-after experiences. And we must ask *which* humans Hume has in mind.

Hume speaks of what is "universally found to please," but that is for him a term of art. Human variability is surely enough, he admits, that nothing will meet universal approbation (17). Moreover, great delicacy is needed to form a just opinion of an object (13). Neither of these considerations will eliminate the prospect of a standard of taste, however, as long as there is sufficient underlying similarity among humans to permit the existence of (what I will call) the *infrastructure* for a suitable *field of value.*

The picture of Hume's approach I have been sketching here should be distinguished from another, perhaps more familiar way of characterizing his view. According to the present account, Hume is *not* offering a *definition* of 'beauty' (or necessary truth conditions for statements of the form "*x* is beautiful") in terms of the consensual responses of a particularly sensitive subgroup of humanity, the experts. Rather, he is giving an account of the features of human sensibility and the world we inhabit in virtue of which aesthetic value can exist and afford a domain of objective judgment, a domain in which expert opinion is possible. The "joint verdict" of expert opinion is offered by Hume as a solution to the problem of finding a *standard* of taste, not as a way of saying what constitutes aesthetic value. Delicacy of sentiment, freedom from prejudice, extensive practice, comparative knowledge, and so on are important so that the expert critic can discern matches, that is, can "discer[n] that very degree and kind of approbation or displeasure which each part is naturally fitted to produce" (13). To be a reliable detector of matches is no cinch:

... it must be allowed, that there are certain qualities in objects which are fitted by nature to produce those particular feelings [of beauty and deformity]. Now, as these qualities may be found in a small degree, or may be mixed and confounded with each other, it often happens that the taste is not affected by such minute qualities, or is not able to distinguish all the particular flavors, amidst the disorder in which they are presented. (11)

Those of us with ordinary tastes will often miss these differences, even though the differences could be expected to manifest themselves in ordinary experience in the long run as experience extends across an increasingly large and diverse population of individuals in an increasing variety of contexts. The generalized "test of time" thus has great discriminatory power even with regard to subtle differences. Hume explains how individual experts can also possess this sort of discriminatory power:

Where the organs are so fine as to allow nothing to escape them, and at the same time so exact as to perceive every ingredient in the composition, this we call delicacy of taste. (11)

An analogy may be useful. We might think of a much more literal sort of match, the fitting together of parts in a complex machine. Superficial inspection of a machine may show the parts to fit nicely, turn easily, work smoothly. But the long-run reliability of the machine depends upon much finer tolerances than superficial inspection can reveal, tolerances in the thousandths of inches detectable only by delicate measuring devices. These differences will tend to reveal themselves over time, as a machine (or type of machine) is subject to repeated use in various settings. Engineering and manufacturing standards for tolerances, materials, and so on are developed along these lines.

Hume himself is drawn to a mechanical analogue, borrowing Fontenelle's image of "a clock or watch":

[T]he most ordinary machine is sufficient to tell the hours; but the most elaborate alone can point out the minutes and seconds, and distinguish the smallest differences in time.[11]

A clock or watch can afford a more or less reliable standard of time. A perfectly precise timepiece could afford a true standard. In Hume's day, the most pressing need for high accuracy and reliability in timepieces was the famous "longitude problem" of navigation at sea. For a timepiece to be a true standard, its reading would have to remain – no matter where or how transported – in perfectly regular correspondence with solar time at a fixed location on the globe, say, Greenwich, England. Being a true standard of time in this sense is clearly not the same as constituting time. The connection between the reading of any particular clock and fixed-location solar time (an alignment between a point on the earth's surface and the position of the sun) is nomological, not definitional.[12]

Of course, unawareness of tiny differences is not the only way we misjudge matches. We can also be misled by "caprices of mode and fashion," by "ignorance and envy" (9), or by lack of experience and narrowness of understanding:

[A] true judge in the finer arts [possesses] strong sense, united to delicate sentiment, improved by practice, perfected by comparison, and cleared of all prejudice. . . . (17)

THE THIRST FOR TASTE

True judges can exist because there is a *subject matter* with respect to which they can develop expertise, authority, and objectivity. This subject matter is afforded by the underlying sensory and cognitive structures that we share with other humans and, in particular, with such judges. If refinement on their part led to a fundamental alteration in their underlying sensory and cognitive structures, they might be subtle judges, but their "joint verdict" would no longer represent expertise about *our* taste, or *human* taste. We differ from the experts not so much in what matches best and most durably the potentials of our underlying structures as in how well we can detect these matches. As a result, we accord greater authority to those with genuinely acute and experienced palates, and greater authority to ourselves as our palates become more acute and experienced.

This deference to more acute and experienced palates is not mere snobbery or acquiescence in a cultural hierarchy. Rather:

Many men, when left to themselves, have but a faint and dubious perception of beauty, who yet are capable of relishing any fine stroke which is pointed out to them. (19)

The enjoyments identifiable and accessible through heightened sensibility, we learn from experience, are very great, widely available, and little dependent upon "the good or ill accidents of life."[13] Thus,

a delicate taste of wit or beauty must always be a desirable quality, because it is the source of all the finest and most innocent enjoyments of which human nature is susceptible. (12)

Partly for this reason, and perhaps also partly for other, less instrumental reasons, Hume believes that we are moved to be concerned about whether we are good judges, and that a man cannot be satisfied with himself if he suspects that he is mistaking trendiness for beauty, or "suspects any excellence or blemish . . . has passed him unobserved" (12).

This doctrine – of the fundamental similarity of underlying sensory and cognitive structures and resultant widespread availability of the special enjoyments attending real difference in excellence or beauty – helps us to explain various readily observable phenomena.

First, to return to the story with which we began, it helps us to see why, in purchasing wine wholesale (or in selecting tea or coffee for import, or blending whiskey, or preparing tobacco, or choosing the raw materials for perfume) businesses devoted to commercial success rather than to higher aesthetics nonetheless purchase the services of expert tasters, whose palates (or noses) are vastly more discerning than our own. Of course, such companies do seek the opinion of tasters of only typical sensitivity – they carry out "field trials" of products before release and in order to make continuing changes. But if I (and many others like me) can't tell the difference between two wines, why should the company that seeks to sell wine to me (and many others like me) employ people with expensive taste buds to select and blend wine? The answer is that the broad population *can* taste these differences or, perhaps more accurately, can *respond* to these differences in forming its preferences. Of course, we don't as individuals fully realize these potentials – any one of us might fail to respond to particular differences on particular occasions, and almost all of us would fail to identify them clearly or reliably. But even so seemingly straightforward a matter as maintaining the constancy of taste of a product to a broad population of consumers requires a taste-testing procedure of considerable refinement – available ingredients are seldom perfectly constant in character (or cost), and within broad populations over time there will be a nearly full representation of the various components of our sensory potentials. "You can fool all of us some of the time, and some of us all of the time, but you can't fool all of us all of the time," Lincoln once said in a different context.

Second, this doctrine of fundamental similarities helps us to understand our social practices of evaluation. We seek not only to have good taste, but to be taken as having good taste and to identify other possessors of good taste. We are relentless producers and consumers of opinions, advice, and guides. Our conversation often turns to the exchange of judgments, and we are eager to share our enthusiasms and to find confirmation of our judgments in the opinions or experiences of others. We hardly obey the maxim of not disputing matters of taste. And though such disputes may lead to an impasse, we have both familiar ways of mitigating difference – we can retreat to the language of expressed preference – and an inveterate tendency to continue to seek agreement. Shared judgment yields a gratifying confirmation and bond, as well as useful evidence that our taste and enjoyment are no fluke. If we were grossly unrealistic in continuing to seek out judgments shared among friends and companions, or

71

shared with various critics, authorities, or wider circles, one would not expect the practice to have gone on so long and so vigorously.

The bustling commerce in aesthetic evaluations is, after all, almost entirely voluntary. No threat of an Aesthetic Judgment Day is needed to bring us to scrutinize our aesthetic evaluations, or to pay heed to them in choice. Bookstores bulge with guides, and newspapers and journals do a steady business in reviews. We readily pay for reliable restaurant ratings, travel great distances to view recognized natural wonders, and freely swap judgments on music or movies. Some people, of course, pay little attention to all this – they can't be bothered. Where, if anywhere, are they going wrong? We see them, I think, as *missing something,* as partly blind. It would not be uncommon for us to say that such people have a good reason to pay more attention to aesthetic matters – what they fail to appreciate is something very much worth having. It would be uncommon, I think, to speak of such people as exhibiting a necessary irrationality or incoherence. There are substantive goods out there of which they are unaware, but that is more like a deficit in knowledge than a kind of inconsistency. Its price is an impoverishment or truncation of their lives.

THE COMMONALITY ASSUMPTION

All this is very breezy. Just how plausible is Hume's assumption of commonality in our underlying sensory and cognitive structures, sentiments, and so on? Rather than attempt to answer this directly, let us begin with the opposite hypothesis and see how things would look. Assume that variability in underlying human sensory and cognitive capacities and sentiments is very great and thoroughly unsystematic. Consider two scenarios.

Scenario 1. Greater knowledge and experience do not tend to produce any general similarity or stability in judgment. Objects that please some of us could not be expected to please others, even with increasing familiarity, and there would be little predictability from one person's likes and dislikes to another's or from one person's likes in one area to her likes in another. What would someone who does not know me intimately learn about what she might expect from a performance or a meal upon hearing that I thought it wonderful? What pleasure or reward could arise from sharing such judgments, or from "trying out" particular judgments of mine against the judgments of others and finding agreement? Discovering commonalities and differences would be rather more like discovering that others have the same or different birthdays, a curiosity perhaps, but not evidence of much else. As a society, we would lack not (the equivalent of) the chance coincidence of shared birthdays, but rather (the equivalent of) the institution of common holidays, special days publicly observed, capable of playing a collective role across a broad population. One of the more important sources of social solidarity would be missing, and it would be fairly bootless to ask whether someone was good-looking, to consult gastronomic guidebooks, to offer the opinion that a given morning is beautiful, to debate the excellence of films, or to discuss the charm of cities. There would be, in effect, no regular commerce in taste. Chefs, designers of public buildings, and film directors could not rely upon their own reactions, or the reactions of those around them, to gauge "effect." If words such as 'beautiful' and 'delicious' were in use, they would have a social role and force much closer to expressions of mere preference, and the language of preference itself would lose much of its familiar predictive value.

Scenario 2. As before, except that powerful cultural institutions are in place to attempt to regiment opinion on what is or is not excellent, or beautiful, or delicious. Natively, our sensations and sentiments are not much alike, but we are under strong social pressure to conform to established norms concerning which colors are harmonious, which natural phenomena are awe-inspiring, which writers are moving, which mornings are beautiful. How successful might such cultural hegemony be expected to be in the absence of an infrastructure of shared faculties – how much like existing social practices and institutional pressures would this be? While it would be impossibly naive to deny that the authority of institutions or the desire to belong make important contributions to shaping our tastes, it would seem equally naive to imagine that all of the current spontaneous commerce in taste could be sustained by pressures or urges to conform. Indeed, in this scenario one would have to imagine, I think, that the exercise of taste would have a social character much more like etiquette or morality than it currently does: here is what is expected of you; from youth upward you are told that this is for your own good; you will lose your standing in the community if you depart from standards of taste; and so on. There is, indeed, an element of taste in society that has just this character – the cultivation of "good taste." And it does have its characteristic effects, among which are also a certain cynicism and resistance as well as deference. What is more difficult to imagine, however, is that the whole bustling, ungrudging world of taste – a world ranging from Best of Boston readership polls to oral sagas and folk melodies carefully passed along for generations in remote hills and islands – could be explained in this way.

How far we in the actual world are from the arbitrary variation from subject to subject in sensation and sentiment in these scenarios is measured by how different our world seems from either Scenario 1 or Scenario 2. This, along with the manifest similarity among *Homo sapiens* in respect to the physiology of sensation, seems ground for believing there to exist sufficient similarity to provide the infrastructure among us for a very large *field of aesthetic value:* there will be some things that excel in their match with our sensibilities, and that can become a source of durable pleasure or interest as familiarity grows, independently of otherwise large variations in personal experience, situation, or culture. If the cultivation of expert palates led to the outright replacement of common capacities and sensibilities by others, it would be difficult to explain why we heed the opinion of expert critics or why commercial enterprises rely so much upon expert tasters. Hard-to-detect failures of match can, of course, easily be masked by temporary enthusiasms, lack of familiarity, small variations in personal experience and sensitivity, or the distraction of other factors. The masking by such features of a failure of match cannot, however, be expected to last forever. Hume, at least, was sure it could not.

To reconnect with our notion of the objectivity of subjects, we can say that the judgments of Humean experts *combine* the three sorts of objectivity discussed earlier: objectual (their strong sense allows them to detect minute but real differences in the things themselves), deliberative (they reason properly from experience and possess clear ideas),[14] and impartialist (they compare and are free of prejudice). What they must possess as well is a set of structures and capacities for sensation, cognition, and sentiment that are largely shared with the rest of us.

A DIVISION OF LABOR

But surely, one can argue, when I judge a work of art to be excellent I am not making a complex descriptive claim about its capacity to match widespread human sensibilities. Such a claim would merely be a species of general causal judgment and would account for neither the *normative* character of aesthetic claims nor the *phenomenology* of aesthetic judgment. Moreover, is not Hume himself famous for insisting that value judgment be linked to the will, a view that has become the foundation of modern antidescriptivism? Would not G. E. Moore rush to point out that one can intelligibly say, "Yes, we can agree that this object matches widespread human sensory capacities and sentiments in such a way as to produce robust and lasting enjoyment, but can we not still intelligibly ask whether it is beautiful?" Have I so bungled the interpretation of Hume as to make him guilty of a "naturalistic fallacy" in aesthetics?

There is nothing in the present reading of Hume to set such worries in motion. We have not supposed that Hume's ambition was to give an account of the concept of Beauty, the meaning of 'beauty', or the peculiar phenomenology of experience under aesthetic concepts. His main interest, we have suggested, lay elsewhere, in examining the worldly infrastructure of aesthetic evaluation and asking whether it would support a species of objective judgment or a standard of good judgment.

Is it anachronistic to imagine that Hume himself might have divided the questions in anything like that way? Is there evidence that he distinguished the task of giving a definition or conceptual analysis from giving an account of the function or infrastructure of a discourse? In fact, he seems to have just such a distinction in mind in the *Treatise,* when introducing his discussion of pride and humility:

The passions of PRIDE and HUMILITY being simple and uniform impressions, 'tis impossible we can ever, by a multitude of words, give a just definition of them, or indeed of any of the passions. The utmost we can pretend to is a description of them, by an enumeration of such circumstances, as attend them.[15]

The "attending circumstances" he goes on to illuminate are the characteristic *objects, causes,* and *effects* of these passions (the section is subtitled "Of pride and humility; their objects and causes"). This gives, if you will, a partly functional characterization of the role played by pride and humility in our mental economy and collective lives. How is Hume able to discuss these features in detail without defining the relevant concepts?

[A]s these words, *pride* and *humility,* are of general use, and the impressions they represent the most common of any, every one, of himself, will be able to form a just idea of them, without any danger of mistake.[16]

Let us, then, have a philosophical division of labor, and distinguish five elements in a Humean (or at least Hume-inspired) account of beauty.

1. *The beautiful things* are those things (if any) genuinely possessing beauty. We know something of Hume's opinion on this matter – for example, he believed that Homer and Milton wrote beautiful things, vastly more beautiful than Ogilby did. Hume claims, not implausibly, that many judgments of what is beautiful are sufficiently uncontroversial that denying them outright would only earn one the name of a crank.

2. *The beauty-making characteristics,* or "beauties," are those features of an object or performance in virtue of which it is beautiful. The works of Homer and Milton, for example, are made beautiful by their language, form, narrative structure, evocative power, insight, originality, and so on. These features engage our sensory and cognitive capacities and our sentiments in ways we find intrinsically enjoyable, and the more deeply and intensely so upon greater familiarity and broader experience. Some examples:

In all the nobler productions of genius, there is a mutual relation and correspondence of the parts. . . . (16)

[This poet] charms by the force and clearness of his expression, by the readiness and variety of his inventions, and by his natural pictures of the passions. . . . (8)

These are general features, which works may possess in various degrees and combinations. Moreover, they may be found alongside other features – for example, lack of coherence and extreme improbabilities – that produce intrinsically "disagreeable" experiences, even disgust (7–8). The aesthetic value of a work depends upon the balance of its beauty-making characteristics and its ugly-making or indifferent features. In Ariosto's work, for example, ". . . the force of these beauties has been able to . . . give the mind a satisfaction superior to the disgust arising from the blemishes" (7–8). Given the *general* character of the beauty-making features, Hume believes, there are *principles* concerning such relationships. Moreover, these principles may be somewhat genre-specific. Poetry, Hume notes, cannot be held to the normal principle of discourse that we should aim to say what is true, since "[m]any of the beauties of poetry, and even eloquence, are founded on falsehood and fiction . . ." (7). However, other principles are at work: "[Poetry] must be confined by rules of art, discovered to the author either by genius or observation" (7).

3. *The functional characterization of beauty,* as suggested in Hume's account, has been our principal focus here. It is a characterization of the typical objects, causes, and consequences of the experience of beauty and of judgments of taste, including the roles played by such experiences and judgments in artistic creation and our thoughts and practices more generally. I have attributed to Hume a functional characterization of beauty as a particular sort of robust and general match between objects or performances and widespread human sensory capacities and sentiments – "[t]he relation, which nature has placed between the form and the sentiment" (9) – that permits these objects and events to bring about intrinsically sought, perceptually based experiences in those who become acquainted with them. Features that can play this role are beauty-making features; things that can play this role are the beautiful things. As Hume writes:

Did our pleasure really arise from those parts of [Ariosto's] poem, which we denominate faults, this would be no objection to criticism in general: it would only be an objection to those particular rules of criticism, which would establish such circumstances to be faults. . . . If they are found to please, they cannot be faults, let the pleasure which they produce be ever so unexpected and unaccountable. (8)

Because this characterization of what makes for beauty is largely functional, it follows that were we humans significantly different in our sensory and cognitive capacities or our sentiments, different things would be beautiful and different features would be beauty-making characteristics (of which more later). Moreover, if we humans showed arbitrary individual or temporal variability in the relevant capacities and sentiments, there might be no identifiable group of objects and features that could fulfill the functional characterization robustly, stably, or generally enough to warrant uncontroversially (or perhaps at all) the name 'beautiful' or 'beauty-making'. Indeed, in such circumstances, we would not see the familiar social commerce in taste, patterns of deference to expertise, and so on: ". . . all the general rules of art are founded only on experience, and on the observation of the common sentiments of human nature" (8).

4. *A standard of taste or beauty* is a means for reliably detecting or measuring how well the functional characterization is met in particular cases. Though the standard does not itself constitute beauty, coming to see how such a standard could exist may nonetheless reveal a good deal about the nature of beauty. Hume's standard of taste – the "joint verdict" of those of greatest force and delicacy of sentiment, freedom from prejudice, and breadth of experience –

points us both to the subjectuality of aesthetic value, the impossibility of removing sentiment from the equation to leave a purely objectual form of judgment, and to its sources of objectivity.

It is, of course, not always easy for us to make the sorts of discriminations that would enable us to discern whether certain objects please chiefly because they are in vogue or have certain salient but superficial characteristics, or because they genuinely possess beauty-making characteristics. The latter, were we to attend closely to them, would be a source of lasting pleasure even after fashions have changed or acquaintance grew. We wish to create and surround ourselves with objects that can be sources of rich, perceptually based pleasure, objects moreover that will provide the occasion for shared pleasures among family and friends, that will call forth the admiration of others, and that will afford deeper satisfaction the better we know them. A standard of taste, if it could be established, would help us make these choices. It would help us, too, to resist a too-ready dismissal of objectivity in taste in view of the diversity of actual opinion.

5. *The concept of beauty* is something (in principle) different from either standard or functional characterization. Though we are all familiar with the word 'beauty', it is no simple matter to say what this concept might be. Even if we suppose there to be a definite concept lying behind our use, philosophical opinion differs as to what in general a concept is or does. One fairly common view is that a concept is (inter alia) what we must internalize if we are to become competent speakers in a given area of discourse. On this view, the concept of beauty is what we must grasp in order to understand judgments of beauty and to make novel and appropriate judgments of beauty on our own. Grasp of this concept, further, may be seen as making it possible for us to have what we might call *distinctively aesthetic experience*. Distinctively aesthetic experience is different from the experience of perceptually based pleasure merely as a causal consequence of characteristics that would qualify as beauty-making. A pleasurable awe at sunsets is something we seem to share with many beasts. Distinctively aesthetic experience is also different from the experience of those with an entirely intuitive grasp of various beauty-making characteristics – those who possess the practiced eye or hand of a skilled artisan, say, but who do not represent things to themselves in terms of (a general-purpose notion of) beauty. Wittgenstein offers as a model of "appreciation" a tailor or clothes cutter studying the length of a customer's suit with his practiced eye and saying "Too long" or "All right."[17] On a Humean account, this can be understood

as a kind of sensitivity on the cutter's part to the beauty-making characteristics. A clothes designer, by contrast, might observe the same suit when the cutter's work is finished and pronounce, "A beautiful suit – just right in proportion and fit." Both make perceptually based judgments that are responsive to beauty, but perhaps only the designer is appropriately said to deploy the concept of beauty and to have a distinctively aesthetic experience. Full grasp of distinctively aesthetic concepts involves the higher-order idea that an object may *merit* certain responses on our part, thanks to its beauty. Mastering the concept beauty, as opposed to merely being able to appreciate or be responsive to beauty, involves a (perhaps tacit) understanding that beauty is *normative* for attitudes such as appreciation and for practices such as artistic and artisanal creation.[18] This, of course, is a commentary rather than a reductive analysis.

As far as I know, Hume does not attempt to give an analysis, reductive or otherwise, of the concept of beauty. Instead, he seems to assume (along the lines of his discussion of pride and humility) that we are familiar enough with this notion that he can without any such definition proceed to develop an account of what such judgments are founded upon and how there might be a standard for assessing them, even if actual opinion on matters of beauty seems remarkably diverse.

Hume proceeds by considering the objects of aesthetic assessment, the causes of perceptually based pleasure, the sources of stability and convergence in aesthetic judgment, and also familiar patterns of deference in judgment. From these he develops an idea both of what makes for beauty and of what, correspondingly, would make for a difference between true judges of beauty and those who can only pretend to possess genuine expertise. He believes we can, like the U.S. journalist at the German wine tasting, be led to see that some critics are "really onto something," such that their judgments can carry authority that extends beyond merely personal or arbitrary preferences. This acknowledgment that there *is* something there to be onto – rather than a "free-fire zone" of preference and undeserved prestige – is one expression of the idea that there is the requisite human infrastructure for a field of aesthetic value.

We began by thinking of value as essentially subjective, arising from *mattering*. In any nonmetaphorical case of mattering, we should be able to fill in the formula "*x* matters to *y* for *G*." Hume, in effect, fills in this formula in the case of taste by replacing *y* with humankind and *G* with reliable conduciveness to perceptually based, intrinsically desirable experience. Things of aesthetic value matter to us in virtue of the possibility of robust matches with our capacities and sentiments.

The match between Homer and our capacities is not altogether unlike the match of the chemical structure of sucrose with the physiology of the sweetness receptors on the human tongue, which enables us to explain why sugar tastes sweet. This is not an account of the phenomenology – it does not explain "why sugar tastes like *that*." Instead, it explains why sugar (and various similar substances) might reliably cause sensations of a kind that, when they occur, we want them to continue (at least up to some point of satiation). This match might, in the case of sugar as in the case of Homer, be independent of fashion, indoctrination, or particularities of "climate, religion, and language."[19] When a work of art or natural phenomenon is in this way a quite general match for our capacities and sentiments and, further, when the intrinsically desirable experiences it helps produce are such that they become more intense and ramified with further and more discriminating experience of the object (again, at least up to some point of satiation), we have arrived at "the catholic and universal beauty" (8). It will be complained that this is too broad and does not distinguish aesthetic experience from other forms of pleasurable, perceptually based experience. But for Hume's purposes, this is a virtue of the account. In particular, it helps us to see how beauty might have a noncircular explanatory use.

VALUE-BASED EXPLANATIONS

This sort of account, with its division of labor between the beautiful things, the beauty-making characteristics, the functional characterization of beauty, a standard of taste, and the concept of beauty, allows Hume to vindicate the explanatory ambition he exhibits when he seeks to attribute Homer's long-standing success to the "glory" of his work (9).

Consider the perennial question: "Do we like it because it is beautiful, or is it beautiful because we like it?" Both claims seem to have plausibility. Hume can explain why this is so – without circularity, and even for expert opinion.

We like it because it is beautiful. Beauty can substantively explain preference. There is, on Hume's account, a difference between preferences that arise in virtue of an object's possession of the right sort of match with our sensory and cognitive capacities and sentiments, on the one hand, and preferences that arise because an object is in fashion, or is recommended by prestigious individuals, or possesses superficial pleasingness, on the other. In the first sort of case, but not the second, the beauty of the object explains our liking it. For its beauty is *constituted by* its possession of the properties that make for the right sort of match – its "beauties," as Hume calls them, "which are naturally fitted to excite agreeable sentiments" (9). This sort of explanation is possible even for the "joint verdict" of expert judges – what makes them different, and what makes them tend to converge in judgment more than the rest of us, is their greater and more reliable sensitivity to the characteristics that make for a robust match. Consider a parallel: solubility is a match of sorts between the chemistry of the solute and the activity of the solvent. Is this just a matter of the former dissociating in the latter? Then solubility could not *explain* the dissociation. But now note the following contrast: a molecule of calcium carbonate (which is very sparingly soluble in water) that dissociates into ions the moment it is placed in water because it happens to be struck by a cosmic ray at that time versus a molecule of calcium chloride (which is readily water soluble) that breaks into parts at such a moment because of the normal electrochemical properties of interaction with water to produce dissociation of the molecule. Both the calcium carbonate and calcium chloride molecules could in the circumstances be said to "dissociate when placed in water," but only one case is explicable in terms of solubility. The same distinction can be applied to preferences: I might come to prefer an object I experience – be I expert or layman – as the result of the operation of a match with common underlying perceptual and cognitive capacities on my part, or as the result of suggestibility, or faddishness, or (even) a chance cosmic ray's effects on my neurons.

It is beautiful because we like it. Beauty has been functionally characterized in terms of a capacity to produce (in a certain way) intrinsically desirable experiences in us. In this sense, if we did not possess certain perceptually based capacities for liking and disliking, nothing could be beautiful – the infrastructure for the field of aesthetic value would be absent.

The explanation Hume offers for why Homer still pleases, despite "changes of climate, religion, and language," is that such changes "have not been able to obscure his glory" (9). For Homer's glory to do its job of shining through, it has not been necessary that his readers possess the concept of "aesthetic value" or that they judge his work to be beautiful – it is enough that the work win their admiration as a result of those features in which its beauty consists. Suppose, for example, that scholars are correct in saying that the idea of the fine arts and associated distinctively aesthetic concepts – including the contemporary notion of aesthetic taste – did not emerge until the eighteenth century.[20] Equipped with these concepts, our appreciation of Homer might grow and ramify in various ways, but there will also remain a great deal that is common to the admiration won by Homer in ancient Athens and contemporary London. In particular, at least some of this admiration will be attributable to his work's possession of those features in virtue of which it is a robust match for our sensibilities. The "ground-level" experiences that underwrite aesthetic value thus need not possess a peculiar, aesthetically tinged phenomenology. The beauty of an object can therefore explain why it inspires singular interest or has achieved an enduring popularity, even if we imagine that many of those who have been drawn to it or moved by it do not deploy distinctively aesthetic concepts or enjoy distinctively aesthetic experiences. Moreover, the beauty of objects can help explain why humans have chosen to shape or decorate them just so, or to give these objects a conspicuous place in their lives, even before the emergence of a going practice of actively judging their aesthetic value as such. Indeed, one might go so far as to suggest that it is the existence and enjoyment of beautiful things that explain why aesthetic concepts emerged, seemed to make sense, and could form the basis of a coherent, enduring practice that yields judgments we find worth making and following.

Once aesthetic concepts have been introduced, we can readily be led into distinctively aesthetic appreciation and evaluation. The pleasure we feel on attending intrinsically to a given beautiful work can be accompanied or even enhanced by a judgment of its beauty; this sort of appreciative experience may have a special place in understanding the nature and value of art.[21] But whether a given object is such as to achieve a match that "by the structure of the mind be naturally calculated to give pleasure" (10) is a matter of its causal powers and their fit with our sensory and cognitive apparatus, and not a content of immediate appearance. We can become as accustomed to making this sort of causal inference in the case of value as any other, and so may find ourselves making almost immediate perceptual judgments. Works can strike us as beautiful, much as situations can strike us as dangerous or words can strike us as misspelled.

It is an empirical question whether there are beautiful objects –

objects capable of playing the role of being beautiful – and so an empirical question whether there are any credible "aesthetic explanations." Perhaps Homer's long-lasting admiration is best explained by the prestige of cultural icons from ancient Greece. Hume might be able to convince us that he has identified a standard of taste, and yet we might find that no actual objects or performances meet it. This would be a very great surprise, perhaps, but if humans are much more diverse than Hume takes them to be, it would be comprehensible. I take it to be a strength of the Humean approach sketched here that it enables us to understand in a principled way why the observed diversity of human opinion is evidence for skepticism about beauty. This remains a strength of the approach even if we are inclined to agree with Hume that, in the actual world, the human diversity that would remain once variability in knowledge, experience, sensitivity, perspective, and partiality were taken into account, would not be sufficient to shake our confidence in aesthetic value.

This is not to say that all questions of aesthetic value permit determinate answers. Hume compares aesthetic judgment to the distinguishing of mountains from molehills, and there we find determinacy enough: Mozart really is superior to Lully. But it is well known that determinacy breaks down once we deal with smaller mountains and larger hills. We need to find an infrastructure of judgments of taste that affords as much, but no more, determinacy in these judgments than we believe there actually to be. It is important to be able to account for the perennial popularity of a Beethoven or an Ellington, and the entirely predictable charm of fall foliage and Alpine meadows. But a theory of the infrastructure of aesthetic value need not yield a determinate ranking, or even much by way of comparability, in all cases. There is, for example, surprisingly little call for genre-unspecific aesthetic evaluations. Does anyone think that we cannot judge Beethoven and Shakespeare great until we can rank them? Indeed, an account of value's infrastructure should help us to understand why we do not think there is an answer to questions like "Who writes better, Dante or Milton?" or, for that matter, "Which tastes better, vanilla or chocolate ice cream?" A Humean account is able to suggest why this might be so: neither, really, is a better overall match for widespread human capacities and sentiments; whatever decisive preferences we do find across individuals on these choices seem attributable to differences in the individuals themselves, differences that greater experience, sensitivity, and so on reveal to be equally basic.

MAD (NO – ECCENTRIC) AESTHETICS AND
MARTIAN AESTHETICS

The Humean account of the functional characterization of beauty enables us to understand a number of familiar features of our value discourse, but also something a bit less familiar, yet nonetheless (I think) intuitively comprehensible.

Suppose we reflect upon the possibilities of genuinely alternative aesthetic communities – not alternative cultures of *Homo sapiens,* whom we might imagine we could bring (thanks to the underlying similarity in their perceptual and cognitive apparatus) to see things as we do, but communities possessing radically different physiologies and, therefore, a different aesthetic infrastructure.

Imagine Martians. Might there be something deserving the name 'Martian beauty' even if it were quite different from what we recognize to be beauty?[22] How would we understand this? How would we interpret "This image leaves us cold, but it possesses true Martian beauty"? Such a remark certainly need not mean that Martians find it to have the distinctive qualities *we* identify as beauty-making – for example, particular structures, symmetries, harmonies, and palettes. For we can understand well enough that Martians might be sufficiently dissimilar from us that they would not find excitement or delight in the forms or palettes that please us. Martians might even have quite different senses. Yet don't we understand well enough what it would be for them to have a distinctively aesthetic practice of *evaluating beauty?* It would be (inter alia) for them to have a practice using distinctive terms, which they take to be normative, for those objects that have a general, robust match with *their* sensory and cognitive capacities for experiences *they* intrinsically desire.

Looked at from this perspective, we might say that it is very unsurprising that we humans find sensory delight in symmetry, given the world in which we evolved. In our world, the animals that have interested us and our ancestors (as prey, menace, or mate) are overwhelmingly symmetric along at least one axis. Indeed, the vast majority possess bilateral symmetry when confronted in the most salient way, head-on.[23] We should therefore expect that not all symmetries interest us equally. This expectation appears to be borne out in (for example) architecture, where bilateral symmetry in the front elevation of a building clearly has been a powerful organizing feature of admired buildings and monuments over time and across cultures, while symmetry along other axes and radial symmetry (viewed, say, from overhead) have played a much smaller role. Martians themselves might, along with their fellow Mars-bound creatures, possess radial symmetry, or perhaps no simple form of symmetry at all. They might find the front elevations of our great pyramids, cathedrals, totems, stately houses, tombs, and burial mounds to be disturbingly unbalanced ("bottom heavy," say) or unrelievedly dull.

Turning this thought back on ourselves, should we be unsettled in our aesthetic practices to learn that the matches we detect are distinctively human matches and might properly be said to constitute *human beauty* rather than a "catholic and universal beauty"? We are Earthlings, and we should not be embarrassed by the contingency and worldliness our tastes display. We seem to share with bees a high regard for showy flowers, with bears a taste for honey and berries, and with crows and gulls an attraction to sunsets. An austere Martian world of radially symmetric, intelligent subterranean life that drew its nutrition from minerals in the soil and absorbed solar energy from the soil's warmth might find none of these aspects of Earth the least aesthetically interesting, yet they could be rhapsodic about our hot mud springs and undersea manganese nodules. Does our aesthetic discourse depend for its interest and authority on a claim that Martian beauty is at best only Martian beauty, while human beauty is beauty itself?

Of course, there might be a substantive *universal aesthetic*. Perhaps every form of intelligent life capable of sensory experience would thrill to Bach's *Magnificat*, at least once the work and its conventions were familiar enough.[24] But this is vastly speculative, and in any event one wonders whether such a condition could possibly be necessary for our practices of attributing greater or lesser aesthetic value to be in good order. It would seem sufficient to meet the criticism that "mere" human beauty is "not sufficiently objective" to point out that the functional description of beauty *is* universal, and that it is an objective (though subjectual) matter what, if anything, meets that description for us.

There is, however, what might be seen as a much greater threat nearer home. We deceive ourselves, I suspect, if we think Mozart would please every human, even every human freed of prejudice and capable of fine discrimination. But if Mozart's music isn't "objectively beautiful," what is? How essential to our aesthetic practice is strictly universal *human* agreement? Hume himself concedes that

human tastes are variable even when there is no prejudice, ignorance, or want of discrimination, for there seems to exist some degree
of basic variation in the human physiology and condition.

> ... where there is such a diversity in the internal frame or external situation
> as is entirely [free of "prejudice, ... want of practice, or want of delicacy"],
> and leaves no room to give one the preference above the other; in that case a
> certain diversity in judgment is unavoidable, and we seek in vain for a stan-
> dard, by which we can reconcile the contrary sentiments. (19)

The process of aging, for example, is for Hume a ground for "blame-
less" diversity in taste. "A young man, whose passions are warm,
will be more sensibly touched with amorous and tender images, than
a man more advanced in years ..." (20). Yet for a field of value to
exist and to function as the ground of an aesthetic practice, we might
think, there must be a *sufficiently extended* population showing *sufficient degrees* of similarity in the relevant respects. Something like
this is not out of the question. Not only are young and old quite broad
groups, but long-standing experience suggests that the young and old
are enough alike to support a notion such as 'a beautiful sunset' or 'a
beautiful person' or 'a magnificent building' without elaborate qualification.

The social role of the aesthetic vocabulary clearly depends upon
some degrees of commonality, at least within broad groups. Beauty
has vertical (intrapersonal) and horizontal (interpersonal) objectivity. But consider now the following sort of case. I have met a learned
man who insists that, try as he might, he can find no beauty in music
written after 1800 comparable to that of earlier music. Let us suppose
that he is *not* disputing whether any music written after 1800 is such
as to robustly match widespread human capacities and sentiments.
And let us also suppose that his unusual preference is not attributable to lack of experience, errors in thought, or lack of acuity on his
part. He and we can, I think, understand each other quite well. We
can imagine how it could be that his capacities and sentiments are
functioning well and sensitively, and yet the work of Beethoven,
Stravinsky, and Monk will not speak to him. We have learned that he
is different: an eccentric or unusual (perhaps in the way a colorblind
person is unusual), but not irrational or foolish. He is even an authority of sorts, but mostly for those more like him than we seem to be.
We don't feel much pressure to share all his tastes (just as we don't
feel much pressure to share a colorblind person's relative lack of
interest in the Venetian school of painting). The existence of blame-
less eccentrics (as Hume might call them) serves to remind us of the

contingency of our tastes – they really do depend upon what we are like, and the principles of taste are "nearly, if not entirely, the same in all men" (17). But all this leaves the infrastructure of aesthetic judgment essentially unchanged. The unthreatening understanding we possess of just what sort of authority our eccentric possesses reveals our tacit recognition of the functional character of beauty.

AN EXAMPLE?

In his political writings, Hume emphasized that in matters of morality one should not expect the sorts of radical new discoveries that have characterized natural science.[25] Social practices and norms have been hammered into shape by generations of conflict, compromise, and experience, he thought, and thus embody a kind of accumulated wisdom about the conditions under which men and women can live together with moderate calm and mutual advantage. To think that these could be radically challenged on speculative moral grounds he considered to be a mark of poor judgment.

We might balk at the extent of Hume's conservatism. After all, some of the very innovations that seemed terribly at odds with traditional practice in Hume's day have become part of current conventional wisdom about how best to live. But he has a point: there is a certain riskiness about claims of value unattached to long-evolved practices. And one might expect this point to apply equally to aesthetic judgment.

Consider a rather careless parallel. Historically, composers we regard as "serious" or "highbrow" have drawn deeply from rhythms, harmonies, melodies, and voices that evolved over centuries of folk musical practice: playing together, singing together, dancing together – sharing music and also shaping music and the instruments on which it was performed. The great composers before the emergence of distinctively modern music obviously did not simply reproduce these forms, and often pushed them in new directions. Yet they remained in many ways strongly attached to these forms, and their popular audience was surprisingly broad by contemporary standards.[26]

In this century, by contrast, we have seen in certain conspicuous strands of "serious" music the emergence of styles of composition and forms of instrumentation and performance that have deliberately separated themselves from this folk musical past and that do not lend themselves to informal, shared, rhythmic, and melodic appropriation – these were in effect left to the domain of more "popular" composers and performers. The widespread perception that, however

excellent and interesting such "serious" composition as total serial-
ization and concrete music might be in various respects, it is unlikely
to achieve the widespread acceptance or the lasting greatness of (say)
nineteenth-century "serious" music could be given a Humean diagnosis in terms of a loss of connection to musical traditions that had
finely developed matches with widespread human sensibilities.
Contemporary "serious" music certainly draws on various beauty-
making features in ways that make it possible to form relative judgments of merit. No doubt, too, it has expanded our understanding
of the possible sources of beauty. But we should not be surprised
if much less of it survives the "test of time" or enters into the repertoire of works widely deemed great music and spontaneously
demanded by audiences and informally performed by individuals
and groups across broad populations. At the same time, the idea of a
match with general human capacities is not hostage to any particular
tradition. This idea helps us to understand why the music, visual
arts, or cuisine of another culture might come to us as a real revelation, despite a lack of connection to our particular cultural history.
And it holds out the prospect not only of pluralism and syncretism,
but of genuine cultural innovation, the discovery of powerful
matches previously unknown or undeveloped. Twentieth-century
"serious" visual art has surely demonstrated this – and so has twentieth-century popular music, there being no reason to expect that
successful aesthetic innovation must come from "high-" rather than
"lowbrow" origins.

SOME FEATURES OF AESTHETIC VALUE, ACCORDING TO
THE PRESENT ACCOUNT

Thus we arrive at a view about the nature of aesthetic value with the
following characteristics.

First, it is (in principle) *naturalistically grounded;* that is, nothing
lying outside the domain of the natural seems required in order for
the functional characterization to be met. Aesthetic judgment can be
seen to call upon actual human sensation and its capacities, as qualified by familiar forms of knowledge and causal inference. However,
a naturalistic ground is not, we have stressed, the same thing as a naturalistic reduction of the concept of aesthetic value.

Indeed, nonreductionists can recognize the importance of providing a naturalistic ground of some sort, for most nonreductionists hold
that aesthetic value *supervenes* on nonaesthetic, natural features of

the world. This Humean account could therefore answer to their purposes as well – if it is even roughly right about how aesthetic value is constituted, it would enable us to see how the natural world might provide the wherewithal to underwrite aesthetic judgment.

Second, because it involves a *functional characterization* of beauty, it enables us to understand how aesthetic value might be multiply realized in diverse populations. We can see the sort of role aesthetic evaluation would play for such populations, what kind of information about the world (and their relation to it) such talk would carry, and the conditions under which it might guide a useful, stable practice and discourse.

Third, it is *phenomenologically thin*. The experience of aesthetic value, on such a view, need not be an experience presenting itself under an aesthetic concept. Both in our own individual developmental histories and in human history in general, genuine experiences of beauty can exist and can shape our behavior before the emergence of distinctively aesthetic concepts. A young child's experience of pleasure in examining an autumn leaf or hearing a lullaby may be appropriately explained by the beauty of the leaf or song, even if she does not yet grasp the concept of beauty. Beauty, indeed, can explain why certain things come to be liked. The Humean account is entirely compatible with recognizing as well a special kind of experience that does involve perceiving an object "under an aesthetic concept"; it simply does not treat such experience as the fundamental response to examine if one is to see how the field of aesthetic value is underwritten.

Fourth, this account is (in principle) *critical*. That is, it can help us to understand how some judgments or tastes could be better based or more authoritative than others, and it points us to specific ways in which such authority or grounding can be gained. In matters of taste, we show some deference – in ourselves and in seeking the opinion of others – to preferences based upon greater knowledge, wider experience, and finer discrimination. This pattern of deference reflects the generalizing ambition of aesthetic value discourse, its claim to speak not for a momentary personal experience, but on behalf of beauty and excellence. At the same time, the existence of a practice with this ambition hardly ensures that the world is such as to vindicate the practice. This, too, shows critical potential: the account preserves the skeptical possibility that there is no such thing as genuine aesthetic value. However, the fact that some works of artistry or artisanship, folk tunes, scenic vistas, and foods do seem to have withstood the "test of time" is evidence that outright skepticism about aesthetic greatness is implausible.

Fifth, as we have seen, this account can help us to understand some of the *motivation* to take aesthetic judgment seriously. If, as Hume supposes, our underlying sentiments and sensory capacities are much more similar than they are different, then we learn what can robustly, durably please us when we learn what is genuinely beautiful or what meets the "joint verdict" of experts' standards. These pleasures are, Hume stresses, both powerful and widely available.

The good or ill accidents of life are very little at our disposal; but we are pretty much masters [of] what books we shall read, what diversions we shall partake of, and what company we shall keep.[27]

This observation stresses the contribution of a developed taste to individual enjoyment. The Humean account also possesses a sixth feature of note: it is *social,* drawing our attention to the extent to which our aesthetic practices depend upon a community of relevantly similar individuals and unite us with that community. An account of aesthetic value should help us to understand the importance in human society of the sharing of taste and of aesthetic experiences. Our enduring proclivity toward public spectacle, public monuments, the celebration of icons of beauty, the vigorous commerce in taste, the development of shared styles in dress and building – these are among the most impressive features of human existence. Archaeological evidence suggests that they emerged early across the globe, even in societies of modest surplus. It therefore makes sense that our aesthetic vocabulary, once it emerged, had terms of appraisal subject to a double objectification: not only what appeals as one grows more knowledgeable, broad-minded, and discriminating (vertical objectivity), but also what appeals widely across society and time (horizontal objectivity).

Is there any reason to expect extensive similarities across individuals in their perceptual and cognitive faculties? Speculative evolutionary thinking suggests that the similarities are bound to be very great indeed. The problem of trying to predict others' behavior, or to coordinate our behavior and expectations with theirs, would seem impossibly complex unless our own sensations, thoughts, and sentiments were reasonably good models for the sensations, thoughts, and sentiments of others. Moreover, in a species such as ours, which has gained its livelihood for nine-tenths of its time on this planet as communities of foragers who shared food among themselves and found mates exogamously, the benefits of having our tastes be close models of one another's – despite other differences – would be very significant.

All this is compatible with a good deal of slack or unspecificity in the infrastructure of aesthetic judgment. Cultural variations may fix ideas of aesthetic worth in cases where (what Hume might call) native faculties do not. A shared culture of judgment and exchanged opinion is part of how societies self-identify and distinguish themselves. This connects with some of the most powerful sources of human motivation – the need to belong, to have an identity, to know one's community. One knows one is at home by the look of things – the idea of a proper house, a proper way of dressing, a proper way of talking.

Seventh, this account is *incomplete.* Perceptually based pleasure might in itself be enough to secure the beginnings of a theory of aesthetic value, but it cannot be the whole story. Beauty – our principal focus here – is not the only dimension of aesthetic evaluation, which concerns itself also with other ways that works might intrigue us, challenge us, or instruct us. How, for example, are we to explain in terms of sensory pleasure the following remark, concerning the words of a plaintive traditional work song of Koreans mining in Japan?

This is not the sort of thing one calls a favorite poem. Not, that is, unless a favorite poem is one that has made its home in your mind, one that has permeated your very depths and refuses to be moved.[28]

We had better make room in a theory of aesthetic value for a favorite poem in this latter sense – poems that give us experiences that are almost too much to bear (and yet that we also cannot bear letting go of), not just poems that fill us with delight. Completing a Humean account requires at the least that we move from something like "pleasure" to something more like "intrinsically sought experience." Not all intrinsically sought experiences are pleasant. But this formulation is still too vague to be satisfactory.

Eighth, and last, this account makes aesthetic value remarkably similar in certain respects to *moral value.* Looking at the two together might help us see a bit more clearly how objectivity in evaluation is possible in either case. So let us turn briefly to morality.

MORAL VALUE

Intrinsic moral value has not been the central category of philosophical attention in ethics in this century; that has been *moral obligation*

91

or *the moral 'ought'*. In the words of P. H. Nowell-Smith's classic introduction, *Ethics:*

Practical discourse . . . consists of answers to practical questions, of which the most important are 'What shall I do?' and 'What ought I to do?'[29]

More recently, however, judgments of moral value – of what makes a life, a person, an act, a practice, a trait of character, and so on *morally good* – have begun to receive greater attention.

A number of conceptions of moral value, and of its place within moral assessment generally, exist side by side. An important distinction among them traces the line between accounts of "that which constitutes the intrinsic value (or source of intrinsic value) in distinctively moral actions or attitudes" – for example, conscientiousness, a good will – and accounts of "those features of acts, motives, outcomes, etc. which count favorably from a moral point of view."[30] The former conception is especially concerned to identify "distinctively moral actions or attitudes"; the latter is prepared to find moral value in actions and attitudes done for nonmoral reasons, for example, out of friendship, loyalty, or generosity. Because we have been concerned here with aesthetic value chiefly in the sense of "those features of objects or performances which count favorably from an aesthetic point of view" rather than "that which constitutes the intrinsic value (or source of intrinsic value) in distinctively aesthetic acts or attitudes," it is appropriate in the present context for us to consider a conception of moral value of the second sort in making our parallel.

The most influential conception of moral value of this second kind treats it as based upon two elements. First, there are the *intrinsic goods* humans are capable of realizing, the stuff of a good life. Classical hedonists recognize only one such good, happiness. Pluralists imagine that there might be many – happiness, aesthetic experience, accomplishment, autonomy, integrity, and so on. Perhaps the goods are all experiential, perhaps some are not. What is common to these views is that intrinsic good is in some sense *nonmoral*. That is, intrinsic goods do not depend for their desirability upon their moral character or contribution. Nor do they depend for their recognition upon distinctively moral concepts. Thus, there is something desirable about experiencing happiness or avoiding pain, even prescinding from the question whether the experience is morally deserved or undeserved. The archetype of such an intrinsic nonmoral good is individual well-being, so let us use it as our example.

Perhaps the most widely held account of individual well-being understands it in terms of what is intrinsically desirable with regard to the course of one's life. What is this desirability? Mill famously remarked that the sole evidence it is possible to produce that something is desirable is that we actually desire it.[31] *Actual* desires concerning the course of one's life may, however, be based upon mistaken information, lack of experience, irrationality, inattention, and so on. Mill, acknowledging this, held that the true standard on the question is afforded by the settled views of those of wide experience.[32] Like Hume, Mill seems to have assumed considerable similarity across individuals, such that he could speak of "the permanent interests of a man as a progressive being."[33]

We can, I think, describe this notion of desirability in much the same terms as those used earlier for the grounding of aesthetic value. Using the division of labor already suggested, we can distinguish a *functional characterization* of intrinsic human well-being in terms of those activities or states – if any – that afford a robust and general *match* with human capacities to produce the kinds of lives or experiences they intrinsically prefer. The hedonist, for example, argues that only happiness affords a robust and general intrinsic motivator, so that nothing matches – at least for humans – except owing to the happiness it affords. We test such hypotheses by examining how we might best explain the seemingly intrinsic preferences we possess. Thus, the hedonist defends his substantive account by appealing to a functional characterization. Desires arising from peer pressure, erroneous assumptions, imperfect acquaintance, or lack of sensitivity are explained away as not accurately reflecting such matches. Mill's discussion of desire as *evidence* of desirability thus makes sense, and his account of the settled preferences of experienced judges falls into place as a *standard* of desirability much like Hume's standard of taste. At least since Moore, there has been a tendency to construe Mill's view as a proposed analysis of the concept of desirability. But we need not see it in this light. Mill might more plausibly be seen as giving an account of what the sort of desirability relevant to well-being consists in, and suggesting, Hume-like, how there could be an infrastructure for a domain of objective judgment about well-being with respect to which experienced judges afford an appropriate standard.

This gives us a rough idea of individual well-being. But what of moral value? For this we need to introduce a form of generalization, such as the notion of a *moral point of view*. This point of view has been variously characterized. It is, however, largely agreed that it is at least in part an impartial point of view concerned with well-being – it is disinterested with respect to particular individuals or groups but positively engaged on behalf of the well-being of any and all individuals. From this point of view, we can ask to what extent various courses of action, or institutions, or states of character, and so on are conducive to the realization of human well-being.

Moral value, as understood by this approach, is parallel in a number of ways to aesthetic value as interpreted earlier. Both possess intrapersonal and interpersonal components, and thus vertical and horizontal dimensions: the contribution made to an individual life as well as the extent to which this contribution extends to the lives of all potentially affected. Moreover, neither aesthetic nor moral value would itself possess a distinctive phenomenology. In both cases, general causal tendencies are in question, and in both cases this permits a kind of noncircular explanation: the reception of a work or a practice, and the convergence of expert opinion on a judgment of it, can be explained in terms of its beauty or its goodness. Finally, in both cases objectivity is obtained without banishing the subjectual.

Notoriously, the notion of a moral point of view presents problems of aggregation and balancing: if an act or institution would not be in all respects optimal for everyone alike, how are we to weigh the various gains or losses within and across individual lives in arriving at an overall assessment? Similar issues should, if the present Humean account is right, attend aesthetic evaluation as well. That we tend not to think of aesthetic judgment as involving aggregation and balancing might be in part the result of the way that paradigms – Beethoven, Milton, Homer – have tended to occupy the focus of attention in aesthetic discussion. Hume himself considers some cases of more middling value. Concerning the vertical (intrapersonal) dimension, Hume writes (as already noted) that Ariosto's poetry is able to "give the mind a satisfaction superior to the disgust arising from its blemishes" (7–8). Concerning the horizontal (interpersonal and intertemporal) dimension, Hume writes (also noted earlier) that works of great aesthetic value will identify themselves by winning more sincere admiration "the longer [they] endure, and the more wide they are spread" (9), that is, the more nearly their match is universal in the human population, even though none can be expected to be fully universal (17). In both moral and aesthetic evaluation, then, assessment is disciplined by objectifying considerations in the vertical and the horizontal. Experienced judges are sensitive to the features that will manifest themselves in moral or aesthetic differences, and therefore often are able, like experienced physicians or mechanics, to grasp a situation and make a judgment that concerns complex causal tendencies "at a glance." But it is not the character of this refined experience that makes the judgments of moral or aesthetic value true.

NONHYPOTHETICALNESS

The parallel structure of aesthetic and moral value may help us to see a familiar feature of moral evaluation in a somewhat different light.

Moral judgment is often said to be nonhypothetical in character. Wittgenstein gives a helpful example:

Supposing that I could play tennis and one of you saw me playing and said "Well, you play pretty badly" and suppose I answered "I know, I'm playing badly but I don't want to play any better," all the other man could say would be "Ah, then that's all right." But suppose I had told one of you a preposterous lie and he came up to me and said "You're behaving like a beast" and then I were to say "I know I behave badly, but then I don't want to behave any better," could he then say, "Ah, then that's all right"? Certainly not; he would say "Well, you *ought* to want to behave better."[34]

Note that in both cases an *evaluative judgment* is made ("you play pretty badly" and "you're behaving like a beast") and is followed by a *practical judgment* ("that's all right" and "you *ought* to want to behave better"). The practical judgments differ in kind: a judgment of permissibility versus a judgment of obligatoriness. A traditional way of explaining this difference is in terms of *reasons for action*. We have a hypothetical reason to play tennis well – if we care about tennis. But we have a categorical reason to eschew beastliness – whether we care or not. If Wittgenstein doesn't care about his tennis game, then he may have no reason to strive to play better; if he doesn't care about his honesty, then he is acting contrary to reason, showing a kind of practical irrationality or incoherence.

But Wittgenstein himself diagnoses this difference in other terms. He says of the second case: "Here you have an absolute judgment of value, whereas the first instance was one of a relative judgment."[35] Picking up on this use of the language of value – though not on his terms 'relative' and 'absolute'[36] – we might say that we are reading these cases in a particular way. We tacitly assume that the only value really at stake in Wittgenstein's playing of poor tennis is his own enjoyment, and so he should suit himself. Suppose, instead, that Wittgenstein is playing against a friend, whom he knows to be facing an important upcoming match and to be secretly hoping that Wittgenstein will serve as a good training partner. Then Wittgenstein's cavalier attitude begins to seem beastly – insensitive to the values at stake. Note that it could still be true that Wittgenstein does not himself want to play any better; it simply no longer is true that the values at issue turn entirely on that fact. Now when we return to the second case, we can see that we are reading it in just this way. We are assuming that the values at stake in Wittgenstein's dishonesty do not turn entirely on his own interest. This manifests itself as a kind of nonhypotheticalness: because the agent's particular purposes in acting are not the complete infrastructure of the evaluative field within which he acts, there are grounds for assessing his act or character that are independent of his purposes. If those elements in the evaluative field to which the agent is insensitive are themselves within the purview of a moral point of view, then his insensitivity is morally evaluable.

Aesthetic evaluation exhibits a similar nonhypotheticalness. Suppose that I am building a house, and you observe that it is uninteresting in design, graceless, or incongruous. "You've designed it pretty badly," you observe. Would my reply, "I know, but I'm not concerned with how it looks" serve to render your evaluation irrelevant or inapplicable? On the contrary, the building will lack or possess beauty-making features whether I or anyone happens to notice or care, and I cannot make this "absolute" judgment inapplicable to me by my own indifference.

Now the question emerges: How natural would it be to describe my failing here as a kind of deliberative or practical incoherence? Do I collide with a categorical reason to care about aesthetics? Is it not more plausible to say that I exhibit a kind of obliviousness to a value (or disvalue) whose presence does not depend upon my particular concerns? One might seize on this difference to argue that moral value is fundamentally disanalogous with aesthetic value, but another reaction is possible: perhaps we moved too quickly from the "absolute" character of the value judgment in the moral case to a particular *explanation* of this absoluteness – perhaps nonhypothetical evaluation can have a grounding other than nonhypothetical imperatives.

As a builder I can, of course, ignore aesthetics. What I cannot do is either exempt my creation from aesthetic assessment or place it into the category of "aesthetic success" by limiting my aesthetic ambitions. As we noted at the outset, aesthetic evaluation has an ambition that extends beyond gratifying personal preference.

I have tried in the earlier sections of this essay to suggest how that ambition might be understood and underwritten by a suitable infra-

structure. If there truly are beauty-making features – such that I am
in principle able to make a building not only that pleases *me* or that
I *think* beautiful, but also that is genuinely beautiful – then this is
owing to an infrastructure that extends well beyond my current concerns. Indeed, we may not need to know anything about authorial
intention in order to make aesthetic assessments, as when we judge
the beauty of phenomena that have no author at all (rock formations,
the morning light over an offshore island, a prairie storm) or objects
not made for any distinctively aesthetic purpose (tools, artifacts, hap-
hazardly evolved urban landscapes). As an ordinary individual, my
sensory capacities and sentiments are part of the infrastructure for
beauty, but only a part.

Return now to Wittgenstein's "outrageous lie." One might have supposed that the possibility of supporting a nonhypothetical negative
judgment of this lie in the face of the liar's evident lack of concern
would depend upon showing that the liar is mistaken – he somehow
rationally *must* be concerned to avoid this particular dishonesty,
whether or not he cares on other grounds. He is *rationally obliged* to
do so. But we cannot assume that moral value – including judgments
of "beastliness" – is always tied so closely to obligation. In the first
place, much of what we assess in terms of moral value – emotions,
traits of character, institutions, social practices – is not under an individual's voluntary control.[37] We cannot even infer from the judgment
that a given practice or trait of character realizes greater moral value
to a practical conclusion that we ought to do whatever is in our power
to bring it about – sometimes striving to bring about an end will have
quite the opposite effect. Nor can we infer from obligation to value. In
a moral dilemma, any particular act one might take could be morally
bad, even though one must (as a matter of practical necessity) act.

Attribution of moral value thus does not appear to be hypothetical
on the reasons for action of the agent or the judge. We may account
for this by noting that the ambition of an assessment of moral value
need not be to tell us what is or is not rationally required. Judgments
of moral value express a quite recognizable kind of moral concern, a
humane concern with human weal and woe, with how institutions,
practices, actions, and so on affect them. We can, I think, understand
the role and infrastructure of such judgments without settling
whether reason requires each of us always to follow them. Indeed,
that is what enables us to ask intelligibly the question of how moral
value and moral obligation, or reasons for action, are related. The
infrastructure of moral value certainly will include the well-being of

the agent or the judge. But, as in the case of aesthetic value, this represents only a part of a broader foundation.

What, then, is the ground of negative moral evaluation, if it is not that there is something incoherent about embodying, or pursuing, that which is morally bad? Well, what is the ground of negative aesthetic evaluation? We are more likely to say that someone is *missing something* by aesthetic indifference, or *impoverishing* himself and others by aesthetically bad creations. Impoverishment is not merely metaphorical here: it is a case of lost value. Perhaps other values compensate, but this one will be gone.

We need to convince ourselves that value can be objective without being tied to something like obligation. Why is it, after all, that the dedicated egoist or contented philistine has so little power to induce skepticism in us by announcing "I could care less" when we raise broader questions of value? Because he seems to us incoherent? Or because we can see so clearly just how there could exist real differences between weal and woe, or between beauty and ugliness, without their commanding *his* interest? Whatever we think of his reasoning, we can see that he is missing something.

Our response is quite different when a Nietzsche or a Marx comes along and provides powerful arguments meant to explode comfortable assumptions about where our values come from and what sustains them. We then are forced to ask whether what we took to be a solidly underwritten field of value is not instead a historically specific combination of prejudice, privilege, *ressentiment,* ignorance, and illusion. Our practices are portrayed by such critics as narrow-minded and in the service of particular interests, in just that area of life where we took them to be broad-minded and universal, sensitive to a wide and comprehensive field of value. This sort of critique mobilizes our own evaluative ambitions against ourselves in a way that the moral or aesthetic philistine professing personal indifference cannot. Our soaring objective purport is brought crashing down to earth, and we are forced to ask anew whether there could be anything that genuinely plays the role of moral or aesthetic value.[38]

CONCLUSION

If aesthetic and moral value are in these ways similar, how are they different? How, in particular, to avoid Bentham's error in assimilating all value to moral value?

The brief answer is that, although both aesthetic and moral value are grounded in intrinsically desired states, and both possess vertical and horizontal dimensions, the states need not be the same in character or cause, and the dimensions can evidently differ.

Even if we consider Benthamite theories of well-being that equate it with an experiential state, still such theories do not characteristically restrict attention to perceptually based experiential states or to the vehicles of sensation the way aesthetic evaluation does. Thus, two performances might possess the same moral value owing to their overall contribution to well-being, while one has much greater aesthetic value than the other. In the case of the former, a considerable component of the good it does may arise from its beauty-making characteristics; in the case of the latter, a lesser aesthetic value might be offset morally by other positive effects on well-being. Aesthetic evaluation thus may concern some features of the world that contribute to moral value, but not all such. Similarly, an act or institution may possess moral value in virtue of protecting people from various sorts of harm, without making any identifiable contribution to the aesthetic quality of their lives.

This is a difference in the *vertical* character of aesthetic versus moral value – the sorts of effects on individual lives that lie at the bottom of these two species of value. The two differ as well in the *horizontal* dimension, even if both moral and aesthetic points of view are held to be informed, unbiased, and so on. The existence of a field of aesthetic value that could underwrite an actual practice of aesthetic evaluation depends upon the existence of sufficient *similarity* in sensory capacities and sentiments in the relevant population. The existence of a field of moral value, by contrast, need not assume this sort of similarity. There will be moral questions about the decent treatment of others, for example, that do not depend upon shared sensibilities (though our ease and confidence in answering them might). Indeed, it is sometimes said that moral value has as its peculiar vocation helping us to fairly assess situations in which underlying sensibilities, interests, and so on are in conflict. Notice, however, that interests may conflict in part *because* sensibilities are shared: because the Mona Lisa is so widely admired, a moral question arises about how best to reconcile conflicting interests in having the work on public display and in protecting its security. Part of this question is aesthetic – for example, do security arrangements substantially obstruct the beauty-making features? But part concerns actual or likely *access* to the work – the possibility of a broad population experiencing the work's value. Here the horizontal dimension concerns actual or likely extent of effect on well-being, not simply the existence of a concentration of beauty-making characteristics that *could* be widely recognized.

These differences in moral and aesthetic evaluation help to explain what otherwise might be thought a puzzling feature of aesthetic evaluation, in contrast to moral or even prudential evaluation: the seeming absence in aesthetic evaluation of a category comparable to that of duty or obligation.[39] On a Humean scheme, property and its associated obligations have their origin in "the conditions of justice," where scarcity and conflicting interests are defining characteristics. If the world were one of perfect abundance, he speculates, we would not have a role for property and related notions of justice.[40] Aesthetic evaluation takes place in pleasant abstraction from questions of scarcity. In part, this is a feature of the nonexclusive character of aesthetic enjoyment. It has a loaves-and-fishes character that permits a single musical composition to yield aesthetic enjoyment, in principle, to the entire globe without diminishing its potential. Moreover, as we have noted, Hume sees us as much better able to control what we read or observe than other elements of our fate or fortune.[41]

Some aspects of moral evaluation have a similar abstraction from the nasty business of supply and demand: when we characterize our moral ideals we are free to ask (for example), "What would be the highest degree of excellence in moral character?" or "What are the best motives?" or "What would a perfect society be like?" These judgments, like aesthetic judgments, concern in-principle concentration, intensity, and extent. In principle, the whole world can derive moral satisfaction from the contemplation of morally singular persons or institutions. Here we reach that area of moral value closest to aesthetics (and furthest from obligation?). It concerns what we deem most admirable and is normative not in the first instance for action – we may think there is no reasonable prospect of achieving the most admirable character, say, and that aiming at this would not be wise – but rather for attitude.[42] Does that mean this species of moral evaluation is not the "business end" of ethics, that it is "mere aesthetics"?

Mere aesthetics! – as if discussing and deciding about what we truly admire or detest were not a central, shaping force in human life. Our views about what is excellent and what is poor, admirable or despicable, exert a dominion over our daily thought and conduct no less extensive than our views about what is right and what is wrong.

How plausible is this quasi-Humean picture of aesthetic and moral evaluation – of their infrastructure, their field of value, their subjectual origin, and their dimensions of objectivity? It has not been my ambition to answer that question here, and in any event, significantly more development of both views would be required before that question could be in good shape for answering. The present picture indicates how the groundwork might exist to support to a reasonable degree the objective and explanatory purport of value discourse, though arguably there are further aspirations in such discourse that it cannot accommodate. It can, for example, yield a quite general characterization of the functional role of beauty, but it cannot ensure that this role will be played by the same characteristics in all populations. In a grand scheme, then, the account of beauty is relational rather than absolute.

Relational is not, however, relativistic or arbitrary. The relational infrastructure might be as broad as a species, perhaps broader.[43] And it can be objective. There might, however, be a further aspiration of our concepts of beauty and well-being, an aspiration that resolutely transcends relationality. If so, then the quasi-Humean approach considered here threatens to unsettle rather than undergird our evaluative practices. For on such an approach, it is distinctly difficult to see how anything could play the role of beauty or well-being independently of any contingent features of our capacities or sentiments. If beauty or well-being must have a universal match – match not only for all actual sentient beings, but for any being that could count as sentient – then the spirit informing the quasi-Humean account would seem to lead us in a skeptical direction. Without sensation or sensibility, what would there be to match?

For my part, I think the aspirations of our talk of beauty and well-being are not so grandiose and empty. As far as I can see, we are well within our rights to say – to those who are listening – that the world is full of many beauties, that life can be good, and that aesthetic and moral value therefore matter.

Notes

I would like to thank Kendall Walton, David Hills, and Michael Smith for helpful conversation. Over the years, Allan Gibbard has much influenced my thinking about matters of value. Jerrold Levinson, David Hills, and Kendall Walton kindly provided comments on an earlier version of this essay, which I hope I have put to good use. I owe a special debt to Jerrold Levinson for his patience.

1. Cf. the famous anecdote Sancho Panza tells about his kinsmen, as recounted by Hume in "Of the Standard of Taste," reprinted in *Of the Standard of Taste and Other Essays, by David Hume,* ed. John W. Lenz (Indianapolis: Bobbs-Merrill, 1965), 10–11. Hereinafter, unattributed page references in the text are to Hume's essay in this reprinting.

2. Belief, too, one might say, lies at this intersection. (For some discussion, see P. Railton, "Truth, Reason, and the Regulation of Belief," *Philosophical Issues* 5 [1994]: 71–93.) The two claims characterize a shared aspect of the two key ingredients in a broadly Humean picture of agency: degrees of belief and degrees of value. This feature of straddling objective and subjective emerges as especially important in trying to develop a Humean account of *free, rational agency.* But all that is a long story.

3. Cf. John Mackie's thesis of "the subjectivity of value" in his *Ethics: Inventing Right and Wrong* (Harmondsworth: Penguin, 1977). Mackie holds that were God *not* dead, objective value could have a place in the world (48, 203–8).

4. Do noncognitivist accounts of value avoid this risk? After all, they deny that evaluative talk attributes a distinctive class of properties to the world, and so need not be guilty of *that* sort of projection. However, since the aspiration to objectivity seems endemic to evaluative discourse (at least in the case of moral and aesthetic value), even the noncognitivist must give some account of whether and in what sense this aspiration can be made good. For an example of a norm-expressivist working toward a naturalistic understanding of how the objective purport of evaluative discourse might be vindicated, see Allan Gibbard, *Wise Choices, Apt Feelings* (Cambridge, Mass.: Harvard University Press, 1990).

5. Moore wrote: "It is true, indeed, that I should never have thought of suggesting that goodness was 'non-natural', unless I had supposed that it was 'derivative' in the sense that, if a thing is good (in my sense), then that it is *follows* from the fact that it possesses certain natural intrinsic properties. . . ." From G. E. Moore, "Reply to My Critics," in *The Philosophy of G. E. Moore,* ed. Paul Schilpp (La Salle, Ill.: Open Court, 1968), 588.

6. Moore was, famously, a cognitivist about moral judgments and a Platonist about properties. Giving up these positions – embracing noncognitivism about moral language or minimalism about properties – would not, however, remove the challenge of exhibiting compatibility between the functions of value discourse and the nature of the nonevaluative world. For noncognitivists and minimalists do not abandon supervenience (indeed, they often take it to be a conceptual feature of moral value), and so do not avoid the challenge of asking whether the world contains the requisites for our evaluative practices to be sustained.

7. Bertrand Russell, "Notes on PHILOSOPHY, January 1960," *Philosophy* 35 (1960): 146–7. I owe this reference to David Wiggins's essay "A Sensible

Subjectivism?" in his *Needs, Values, Truth* (Oxford: Basil Blackwell, 1987), 185.

8. B. Russell, *The Problems of Philosophy* (New York: Oxford University Press, 1969), 155.

9. Cf. Crispin Wright's idea of "correspondence to the facts": ". . . in our practice of the discourse, we interact in a cognitive-representational manner with matters that are independent of us." From his *Truth and Objectivity* (Cambridge, Mass.: Harvard University Press, 1992), 175. Here he is speaking of objectivity in a realist's sense.

10. I once thought I had a better term in 'subject-ive'. I didn't. 'Subjectual' at least cures the chronic hiccough of that locution. See "Subject-ive and Objective," *Ratio* 8 (1995): 259–76.

11. David Hume, "Of the Delicacy of Taste and Passion," as reprinted in *Of the Standard of Taste,* ed. Lenz, 28.

12. The public visibility in his day of the longitude problem perhaps makes it unlikely that Hume was thinking of a timepiece as itself the *determinant* of true time, rather than as a more or less reliable standard. In the context of marine navigation, one could not even stipulate that the "convergence" reading of timepieces of a particular kind would by definition give the "true time" at a given location – the revolution of the earth would not be constrained to obey these timepieces, and so actual worldly location could not be guaranteed to correspond to differences between the "convergence" reading of such watches and local solar time. See Dava Sobel, *Longitude* (New York: Walker, 1995).

13. Hume, "Of the Delicacy of Taste and Passion," 26.

14. Hume writes, ". . . reason, if not an essential part of taste, is at least requisite to the operations of this latter faculty" (16). Of course care is needed here. Hume meant reason to include not only sound reasoning, but also a "sound understanding" of the empirical features and factual context of an object of judgment (16–17), which many nowadays would not ordinarily deem to be part of reason proper.

15. David Hume, *A Treatise of Human Nature,* ed. A. Selby-Bigge (Oxford: Clarendon, 1888), 277. I am grateful to an unpublished paper by David Aman on Hume's account of pride, which cited this passage.

16. Ibid., 277.

17. He also notes, "That [someone] is an appreciator is not shown by the interjections he uses, but by the way he chooses, selects, etc." See Ludwig Wittgenstein, *Lectures and Conversations,* ed. Cyril Barrett (Berkeley: University of California Press, 1966), 7.

18. For an example of an account of aesthetic value that, unlike the Humean account discussed here, makes essential use of higher-order aspects of aesthetic experience, see Kendall Walton, "How Marvelous! Toward a Theory of Aesthetic Value," *Journal of Aesthetics and Art Criticism* 51 (1993): 499–510.

19. Apparently, if a sugar-based mixture is injected into the amniotic sac, a human fetus will begin drinking the amniotic fluid. This has been used

as a way of administering medicine directly to the fetus. Hume uses the analogy between "bodily taste" and sugar, on the one hand, and "mental taste" and beauty, on the other (11).

20. See Paul Oscar Kristeller, "The Modern System of the Arts," in his collection of essays, *Renaissance Thought and the Arts* (Princeton, N.J.: Princeton University Press, 1964).

21. There certainly is room here for the idea of distinctively *aesthetic* pleasures, pleasures that are possible only thanks to the taking of an evaluative attitude toward a work – finding beauty in it, say – and perhaps also thanks to the special enjoyment or excitement one can have precisely from finding it so fine. On this point, see again Walton, "How Marvelous!"

22. I am plainly indebted here to David Lewis's discussion of pain in "Mad Pain and Martian Pain," reprinted in his *Philosophical Papers* (New York: Oxford University Press, 1983), 1: 122–32.

23. Some fish apparently manifest a fear response or mating behavior if presented with schematic wire constructions that display bilateral symmetry but otherwise do not much resemble a fish.

24. Lewis Thomas once considered the proposal that the radio-frequency signals beamed into space in our search for intelligent extraterrestrial life take the form of Bach's compositions, though he worried it might be "bragging." See his *Lives of a Cell* (New York: Viking, 1974), 45.

25. David Hume, "Of the Original Contract," reprinted in his *Political Essays,* ed. Charles W. Hendel (Indianapolis: Bobbs-Merrill, 1953), 60–1.

26. See Lawrence Levine, *High Brow and Low Brow: The Emergence of Cultural Hierarchy in America* (Cambridge, Mass.: Harvard University Press, 1988). The importance of shared rhythmic and melodic performance is, like our taste for fruit, something we seem to have in common with a very wide swath of other species. No doubt it is connected to some very deep sources of social solidarity and identification.

27. Hume, "Of the Delicacy of Taste and Passion," 26.

28. Morisaki Kazue, from a passage in *My Imaginary Marriage to My Motherland,* trans. Kazuko Fujimoto, in "Singing Voices from the Bottom, of the World: One of My Favorite Poems," *Concerned Theater Japan* 2 (1973): 165. I am indebted to an unpublished essay by Brett de Bary, "'Two Languages, Two Souls': Morisaki Kazue and the Politics of the Speech Act," for bringing this passage to my attention.

29. P. H. Nowell-Smith, *Ethics* (Harmondsworth: Penguin, 1954), 11. More recently, Bernard Williams has diagnosed the preoccupation of contemporary moral philosophy with an obligation-based "moral system" as a chief defect. See B. Williams, *Ethics and the Limits of Philosophy* (Cambridge, Mass.: Harvard University Press, 1985).

30. Sigrun Svavarsdottir emphasized a similar distinction in her Ph.D. dissertation, "Thinking in Moral Terms" (Ann Arbor: University Microfilms, 1993). I am grateful to her for enlightening discussion.

31. John Stuart Mill, *Utilitarianism,* ed. George Sher (Indianapolis: Hackett, 1979), 34.

32. Ibid., 10–11.
33. "On Liberty," reprinted in *Utilitarianism and Other Essays by John Stuart Mill,* ed. Mary Warnock (New York: New American Library, 1962), 136.
34. Ludwig Wittgenstein, "Lecture on Ethics," *Philosophical Review* 74 (1965): 5.
35. Ibid.
36. And setting aside his use of the term 'ought' for now. See note 37, below.
37. See, e.g., Robert Adams, "Motive Utilitarianism," *Journal of Philosophy* 73 (1976): 467–81. What of Wittgenstein's remark tying 'beastliness' (seemingly) directly to a corresponding '*ought*'? The transition will seem immediate and unproblematic as long as the 'ought' is taken in a moral sense; if we take it in a rational sense, we can see room for question. Beastliness may be conceptually linked to moral error, but is it so linked to rational defect?
38. A functional understanding of value can, it seems to me, enable us to see both why a Nietzschean or Marxist critique can be genuinely unsettling, and why it might also appropriately be viewed as itself an alternative aesthetic or moral position – to the extent, that is, that it seems to offer an alternative to play the functional role of value. How fully this claim could be sustained in either case is a matter requiring discussion in its own right.
39. In prudential evaluation, the principal source of conflict of interest occurs over *time* when, for example, one would gain from deferring the realization of an attractive benefit or be harmed in the long run by yielding to current temptation.
40. Hume, "Of the Origin of Justice and Property," in his *Political Essays,* ed. Hendel. Hume's thought here needs supplementation, presumably, by an account of scarcities that are not affected by material abundance, e.g., human relationships that cannot simply be "replicated" owing to the abundance of alternative partners or the capacity to produce new offspring.
41. Hume, "Of the Delicacy of Taste and Sentiment," 26. We see here, too, the influence of the modern idea of Art or Fine Arts, and the carving out of a special evaluative space for taste as apart from other species of judgment of the usefulness or suitability of an object.
42. I am indebted to Elizabeth Anderson for framing questions about the nature of value in terms of its purporting to be normative for attitude.
43. As always, with allowances made for unusual individuals.

On consistency in one's personal aesthetics

TED COHEN

INVITATION TO THE TOPIC

This essay is a work in progress and therefore tentative for the usual reasons, and it is tentative also because my hope is to reveal a topic where, to the best of my knowledge, none has so far been noticed. I think it may be harder to persuade you that this is a good, rich topic than it is to answer the questions it yields. In fact, I might settle for attracting you to the topic even if I fail to persuade you of my answers to its questions.

Perhaps because of the influence of Cartesian epistemology, and also because of a temptation to model aesthetics on ethics, considerable attention has been given in modern aesthetics to what are called "interpersonal" matters. How are we to understand the fact that one person *A* has likes and dislikes that coordinate (or conflict) with the likes and dislikes of some other person *B?* Can we say that *A* is right or somehow superior to *B,* or is there no way of comparing the affective conditions of *A* and *B* so as to vindicate one and denigrate the other?

This concern is at least as old as Hume and his marvelous essay "Of the Standard of Taste," wherein he takes up precisely the question of whether it is possible for something – a standard – to "confirm" *A* and "condemn" *B.*[1]

I wish to introduce a different question, although one of the interests in this question may well be how it is related to the interpersonal questions. It is this intrapersonal concern: How are we to understand the convergence in *A* alone of his particular likes and dislikes? How are these related to one another, if at all?

106

On consistency in one's personal aesthetics

I would like to set this topic, at least initially, as an extremely general question. If I might speak very roughly of one's "aesthetic personality," then how is this personality constituted? How is it integrated, so that it amounts to something more – or other than – a concatenation of atomistic aesthetic expressions?

I would like to avoid begging questions about "taste," about what it is and whether it has an objective component, and whether it can be evaluated. And I would like to avoid becoming entangled in questions about the relation of feelings to judgments, as well as any number of other good questions that occupy philosophers of art. My aim is to introduce this topic in such a general and neutral way that its salience will remain whatever one's favorite way of describing aesthetic responses might be.

I will suppose it typical of any person that he has certain preferences, certain likes and dislikes, and that he makes certain judgments. These preferences, likes, and judgments may be expressed in various ways, and their relations to one another are not obvious. I make no distinction between art and any other kind of object toward which one may have preferences and likes, and about which one may make judgments. I mean to attempt to talk about an aesthetic personality conceived very broadly and certainly not limited to its attachment to works of art.

I will get under way by rehearsing some old matters having to do with the epistemology of aesthetic judgments, matters from our youth and before. Let us suppose an aesthetic judgment is some judgment of evaluation made about a work of art, or perhaps about some other kind of thing, and that the judgment looks baldly something like 'x is good' or 'x is better than y' or, possibly, in an eighteenth-century sense of the word 'beautiful', 'x is beautiful' or 'x is more beautiful than y'. The eighteenth century was absolutely certain, so sure that it gave very few arguments, that these judgments were intimately connected with feelings in those who make the judgments. In the crudest versions of this view, 'x is good' is "analyzed" as 'I like x', where 'I' is taken to refer to whoever asserted 'x is good'. Some versions of what has been called "emotivism" may actually have given this analysis. More sophisticated versions have been available since the eighteenth century. From Hume we have something more or less on the order of 'I like x, and I am the right kind of judge', and from Kant we have 'I like x and every one ought to like x'. I will not discuss these formulations, because I believe I can either bypass them or go right through them in order to set the issue I wish to introduce.

Thinking something is good or beautiful, or whatever, must have something to do with liking the thing, but it is difficult to say just what the connection is. This sentence is odd, perhaps, but not inconsistent:

'It's good but I don't like it.'

This sentence is not even so odd:

'It's not good or beautiful, but I like it.'

I distrust analogies and other connections between aesthetics and ethics, but we might try this: if we think of an ethical saint as someone who invariably does the right thing, we might think of an aesthetical saint as someone who always likes the right things. This reference to the "right things," however, suggests a commitment to an objective or at least interpersonal conception, and I wish to avoid that. As a hedge, then, we might think of a thoroughgoing man of taste as someone who at least always likes what he thinks good, thinks good whatever he likes, and so on. Now I dare say no one is quite like that. There are always gaps between what one likes and what one thinks good, and conversely. To find someone whose personal likings coincide perfectly with what he thinks good, one might turn to someone sufficiently indoctrinated in some philosophical theory that he thought all it *means* for him to find something good is that he likes it (and conversely). There may be such people, fresh out of beginning philosophy courses, perhaps, but I regard such people as disingenuous or else corrupted by theory, and I will not consider them.

'It's good but I don't like it' seems to require some explanation. That an explanation is called for indicates that 'It's good' implies or intimates or at least suggests that everyone should like it; or it suggests at least for the speaker – the person who asserts that it's good – that *he* should like it.[2] Notice that it doesn't matter whether x really is good, or even whether in general it makes sense to assume that 'x is good' has a truth-value. All that matters is that the speaker has chosen to say 'x is good', and that seems to require of the speaker either that he like x or that he have some story about why he does not despite being willing to say that x is good.

One may think of the need for such a story to arise during interpersonal discussions or arguments, but I wish to locate it entirely within one person. An advantage of this location is that it preserves an interesting phenomenon, a phenomenon that seems to disappear when interpersonal cases are analyzed in terms of crude emotivism. If A and B are faced with x, then perhaps A asserts 'x is good' and B denies this, asserting 'x isn't good'. (I find it useful to go over this old-time stuff in order to get rid of it by getting through it.) If 'x is good' is taken to have as its content only 'I like x', then the apparent disagreement between A and B disappears. Instead of A asserting 'p' and B asserting 'not-p', we actually have 'I like x' asserted by A, and 'I don't like x' asserted by B, and that amounts not to 'p' and 'not-p' but to 'A likes x' and 'B doesn't like x', and these two propositions have no logical connection besides being consistent with, and independent of, each other.

A THESIS OF ARNOLD ISENBERG'S

Let us turn to A alone and his responses to two objects, x and y. A likes x. If he asks himself why he likes x, suppose his answer is he likes x because 'R' is true of x, that is, R is the reason he likes x, that is, he likes x because Rx. In "Critical Communication," an essay half a century old that is finally, I hope, becoming a classic, Arnold Isenberg observed that Rx can never be a successful reason for claiming x to be good if, as Isenberg thought, that claim has to do with liking x.[3] It won't do as a reason with which one might persuade an opponent, according to Isenberg, because the opponent will always refuse the general proposition that R's are good, and he will refuse because he rejects the proposition that he will invariably like anything of which R is true.[4] Unlike Isenberg, I am considering a single person not involved in an interpersonal wrangle, but I wish to preserve his point. The point is that this person A will always know of some other object y, either one he is acquainted with or one he can imagine, of which R is true but which he does not or would not like.

The first question I wish to raise is this: If A is looking for the reason why he likes x, and the best he can come up with is R, what is his logical situation when he realizes that he does not like y and that R is as true of y as it is of x? How do these three propositions strike you?

(1) A likes x because Rx.
(2) A does not like y.
(3) Ry.

Do they seem to you to make an inconsistent conjunction? Not as they stand, I suppose, because A might not realize Ry. Let us put that in, and also suppose that (1) implies that A is aware of Rx and believes that it is on account of Rx that he likes x. Then we have something like this:

(1) A likes x.
(2) A believes he likes x because Rx.
(3) A does not like y.
(4) A believes Ry.

Do you think there is an inconsistency in this foursome? Surely there is a kind of incongruity. A will most likely take the awkwardness to be pressing enough that he will attempt to escape it, and his likeliest maneuver, seemingly the easiest one, will be to give up the second proposition. He will try to refine his conception of what it is in x that elicits his liking. He will refine 'R', looking for a way to make it more specific or detailed. The result will be some other statement of the reason he likes x. Call this R^*x. If this maneuver works, A will be able to concede that indeed Ry, but he doesn't like y anyway, and his liking of x is on account of R^*x. It is indeed true that Rx, but it is only because of R^*x that A likes x.

Now if some other object, z, is presented, which is R^* but which A does not like, then A will resume his efforts to make R more specific, hoping to find something, R^{**}, which is true of x but not of z.

I hope this procedure is familiar, even though I have described it clumsily, in terms of exceeding abstraction. You can render it concrete by supplying examples of your own, but I will begin a few examples here just to make sure I am clear in describing the phenomenon.

A friend of mine, someone with exceptionally refined taste and an ability to explain why she likes what she likes, once pronounced against the typical products of an organization called the Bombay Company. Perhaps you know this company. It makes things like campaign chests and tables, constructions of wood and brass, mostly looking like the furniture used by the British in India and elsewhere in the Empire. I thought she was inveighing against attempts to make things that look like what they are not, and so I was surprised some weeks later when we were together in the furniture department of a store and she expressed admiration for some tables in what was called a "Shaker design." The tables had the simple top and tapered legs characteristic of the furniture made by the Shakers a century ago (I think). In my customary agreeable manner, conciliatory, inquiring, congenial, I asked how she could like this furniture when she did not care for the productions of the Bombay Company.

The question is whether my friend needed to make any answer at all.

The same friend some time later objected to my suggestion that she have a rubber doormat inside the door of her summer home, and she explained her objection in terms of an aversion to having rubber – which she thought of as a naturally outdoors substance – inside the house, although she might admire it outdoors. A short time later she bought a mat that was, in fact, a carpet remnant. When I discovered that the carpet material was entirely acrylic, I asked why acrylic was acceptable when rubber was not.

The question is the same: Does my friend need any answer? Could it not simply be that she finds acrylic but not rubber acceptable indoors – period?

I have had many such conversations with this friend, and they have not been confined to items like furniture and floor coverings. More often than not they have had to do with official high art, but their structure is the same. She does not particularly care for much of the music of Aaron Copland. She does not like the treatment of the Shaker hymn tune in *Appalachian Spring,* for instance, and when I have inquired into this, she has said that she finds it disagreeable that a folk tune should be so duded up. I mention the use of folk tunes by Liszt, Bartok, and others, some of which uses she does like, and she feels the need to explain more specifically what she finds wrong with Copland's efforts. It is, perhaps, that in the case of this tune, the melody has an appealing simplicity and purity all its own, and this character is damaged by the symphonic attention Copland forces on it. I attempt to counter by citing telling examples of the use of Romanian and Hungarian melodies and others in the works of various twentieth-century composers, some of these melodies being equally simple and uncluttered.

She does not like *Rodeo* much, and in this case she does not like the attempt at a formal exposition of some allegedly "national" music. I cite Verdi's *Aida,* Mozart's *Abduction from the Seraglio,* and Puccini's *Madama Butterfly* as equally disturbing efforts at the appropriation of national or ethnic music, and, furthermore, I insist, Verdi's and Mozart's attempts at Egyptian and Turkish music, if heard in this way, are far more ludicrous than Copland's essay at what he imagines to be the music of the U.S. Southwest. And, of course, my friend has a reply to this, pointing out the enormous imaginative distance between Verdi and Mozart and their subjects, by comparison with Copland's presumed appropriation of some national music of his own.

And so these conversations go. As a matter of fact, my friend and I have found these exchanges so invigorating that we have gotten married, thereby increasing the time available for them. And each of them does require time, for, as I shall be saying presently, each exchange might go on forever, at least as far as its internal logical possibilities are concerned.

As it happens, my friend and wife has a passion for orderly thinking. She extends it to at least some aesthetic matters, and she undertakes to explain all these preferences. Her explanations are clear and often compelling and illuminating, and I would be glad to pass them along; but I want to raise the question whether such explanations – or the hope for them – are essential in the integration and coherence of one's aesthetic personality.

Does one feel that if one's reason for liking a thing does not also make one like some other thing possessing the same characteristic, then one has not yet identified the real reason for one's liking? And is this feeling a sense that one is inconsistent or at least incomplete in one's self-understanding? I think something like this obtains when one reflects on one's affective life. I want to ask how sensible it is to pursue this ever-greater refinement.

I begin by endorsing and amplifying an extremely bold claim of Arnold Isenberg's. You may persuade me to retract my endorsement, but I will go with it for now. Isenberg says:

There is not in all the world's criticism a single purely descriptive statement concerning which one is prepared to say beforehand, 'If it is true, I shall like that work so much the better'. . . .[5]

And shortly after this, he reiterates,

The truth of R [the reason] *never adds the slightest weight to V* [the verdict], because R does not designate any quality the perception of which might induce us to assent to V.[6]

Isenberg is speaking principally of reasons given in texts of art history and art criticism, but his point applies to any description whatever, any description one might cite as the reason why one likes something. He is making the point with reference to arguments between *A* and *B*, with *A* trying to prove to *B* that *A*'s judgment of *x* is correct. I will adapt the point to *A*'s self-understanding, but it is the same point.

If Isenberg is right, then

A will never find an R adequate to explain his liking of x which does not also include some other thing, also R, which A does not like. Then A's progressive refinement in his reason, first to R* and then to R**, and so on, is ultimately hopeless.

I would like to think of this hopeless pursuit in this way: Of course, it is not just *R* in general that explains one's liking for *x:* it is *R* in the context of any number of other features of *x* that does the trick, and that is why it is natural to refine *R,* searching for the particularity of *R's* efficacy in the case of *x.* But it is the absolute specificity of *x* that must be attended to, and what this requires, ultimately, is that one arrive at an *R* so particularized, so specific, so parochial that *R* will be true of *nothing but x.*[7] But then it is awkward to think of *R* as a reason. It seems the essence of a reason, after all, to be *general,* to have at least an in-principle application to cases besides the one at hand. If *R* is only a reason why one likes *x* and has no presumptive application in any case not identical to *x,* then in what sense is *R* a *reason?* It is this point, I believe, or something like it, that induced Stuart Hampshire to say, three years after the Isenberg essay,

I conclude that everyone needs a morality to make exclusions in conduct; but neither an artist nor a critical spectator unavoidably needs an aesthetic, and when in Æsthetics one moves from the particular to the general, one is travelling in the wrong direction.[8]

"Moving in the wrong direction," I suppose Hampshire thinks, because one cannot get to the end of the line. And, Hampshire says, there is no unavoidable need to go in that direction at all.

I offer this contrary hypothesis:

It is indeed necessary to move toward the general if one is to understand something very important about oneself, although it is indeed not logically required; and the movement is an expression of one's faith in one's own coherence, even though one might know that the sought generality is forever out of reach.

There are two motives behind the search for these reasons – I mean the reasons one likes what one does, despite the conviction that the reasons may not be found, and perhaps cannot be found. The first is the virtually transcendental need to understand why one likes those things. The second is the desire to find coherence and congruence within one's own aesthetic personality. I will begin to try explaining both motives, but first I should say something about affections for which one may have no reason at all.

113

KANTIAN FORMULATIONS

It has been suggested to me that it is important to distinguish judgments of affection or approval for which we have no reasons from those we are prepared to support. Michelle Mason, in particular, suggested that it is only those judgments Kant calls "judgments of taste" for which we feel a need (or an ability) to give reasons, while other "aesthetic judgments" are made without reasons.

This distinction does not translate easily into Kant's idiom, for the very reason that, if Kant is right, then we *cannot* give reasons in support of our judgments of taste exactly because such judgments are without predicate concepts, and it is only through such concepts that any other judgment could lend support to a judgment of taste. But Mason has an important idea. As Kant sees it, it is only those aesthetic judgments which are judgments of taste that connect us to other possible judges. Such judgments, that is, have a kind of "public" character not shared by other judgments of feeling. Because of this publicity, one's judgment of taste can conflict with someone else's judgment. Thus, Kant supposes the clash between two such judgments to be a genuine logical opposition, while there could be no such opposition in a pair of any other kind of aesthetic judgment. This logical opposition, however, can have no resolution, according to Kant, because no logically relevant *argument* can be adduced on either side. No 'R' can stand in as a reason for either judgment, not because no 'R' could be true, but because no 'R' could *imply* any genuine judgment of taste.[9]

Despite Kant's radical denial of even the possibility of supporting one's judgment of taste, Mason is right to identify these judgments as the ones Kant thinks relevant. They are "reflective" judgments, judgments one puts forward and holds in opposition to the judgments of others. Are they, then, the only kinds of judgment I should be concerned with in my worries about consistency? I am not sure about this. In the first place, I am concerned not with how one's judgment may coordinate with another's judgment, but with how one's judgment may coordinate with one's other judgments. How does one's own array of likings, preferences, and so on make a coherent unity? Which of one's judgments (or likings) should I be thinking of?

I will settle for this: Sometimes when one likes x, or judges x to be good, one finds sense in the question 'Why do you like x?' (or 'Why do you think x good?'), and finds it sensible to reply, 'Because of R'. I think there may be variation in our estimates of when this will be a sensible exchange. For instance, some will think of answering 'Why do you like the taste of artichoke, or the color red, or the smell of bay rum?' and others will regard these questions as pointless. I take no stand on the matter. I wish to speak very generally about those preferences and likings for which one *does* care to give a reason, and I see no need (at least not here) to say just which preferences and likings those will be or to insist that they will be the same for everyone. Nor do I see a need to worry about whether the R one might cite is a "reason" or a "cause," because what is at stake is how the possessor of these affections puts them together.

I take the liberty of neglecting to refine the conception of one's "defensible" aesthetic judgments precisely because I mean to speak only of how one relates these judgments to one's other judgments, and so all that matters, for the moment, is how the judge himself sees these things, and not whether he does or should see them as everyone else does.

SOME LESSONS FROM FRIENDSHIP

For some time now I have been insisting that a way to understand our relation to works of art is to reflect on our relation to other people.[10] Some object to this analogy, but I will persist in it here, or at least in a version of it. I ask you to contemplate replacing someone who means something to you, someone you care for, say, a friend. Suppose you are explaining to someone, perhaps to yourself, why this person is a friend, why you care for him. You enumerate his characteristics, those features of his personality and behavior in virtue of which you are his friend. Refer to any characteristics you like, put as generally or specifically as you like. Jonathan is trustworthy, you say, and he is witty, and he is sympathetic, and he plays a nice game of straight pool, and he chews with his mouth closed, and he never interrupts when you are speaking, and he is always on time, and he sings your praises, and he pays his own way. Go on with this list as long as you can or as long as you like. When you have finished, we will produce someone who fits your bill exactly, who has every characteristic you mentioned. Of course, this person will not be a perfect substitute for Jonathan, not a replica, not a clone. My point is not only that this new person is not going to be mistaken for Jonathan, but that you cannot even be sure you and he will be friends. Your relation with Jonathan is specific, peculiar to the two of you. As much as you may try to identify the components of your fraternity you will have to admit that you cannot get them reflected in the inherently general language of description, and that is why you will not be able to say (in a refraction of Isenberg's claim) that if this new person has characteristics 1, 2, 3, and so on, you will befriend him just as you have befriended Jonathan.

I do not aim to be giving a sappy encomium to the impenetrable essence of friendship, although I am not afraid to be doing that. I mean to call attention to the special click of affection, and the fact that the affection eludes formulaic representation. Having done that, I invite your interest in why one might persist in developing the formula even in clear awareness of the impossibility of getting it right. Of course, there is no logical compulsion, nor any moral imperative, in thus attempting to explicate these ties that bind, and yet there is a wonderful mystery to wander around in. Just what is it, after all, that draws you to Jonathan? Why do you want to know? *Because it tells you more about Jonathan, and it tells you more about yourself.*

There is an encyclopedia more to be discovered when you reflect on your relationship with Jonathan in light of the relations you have to others. Suppose there is someone, Saul, who shares almost all Jonathan's characteristics and yet is not also a friend of yours, nor is ever going to become one. And there is a third person, David, whom you are also a friend of, although he shares none of the characteristics that seem to underpin your affection for Jonathan. What do you make of all that? And what do you make of the fact that David and Jonathan have deep affection for one another, and that each has ambivalent relations with Saul?

I put it to you that one of the surest paths to self-awareness is the investigation of your linkages to others. What kind of person are you? Well, you are the kind of person who is a friend of Jonathan, and also of David, but not of Saul. Do you need to know that about yourself? Yes, I say, although there is no logical requirement, nor any moral one; and that is a good point: the human need for this kind of self-understanding is not brought by logic or analytic morality, and for that very reason, it is an intrinsic, self-generated need. In a word, it is *human*.

As I have noted, the situation customarily under examination is this: *A* likes *x*, *B* doesn't like *x*, and the question is, what can be done to resolve this incongruity (if, indeed, it is an incongruity and if, indeed, anything can be done to resolve it)? I have hoped to interest you in the intrapersonal situation in which *A* likes *x* but does not like *y* when, seemingly, *A*'s "reason" for liking *x* ought to bring him to like *y.* Now I would like to mention another situation, although only in passing, in the hope of interesting you in yet another unexamined failure of aesthetic congruity.

It may happen that both *A* and *B* like *x*, but do not seem to do so for the same reason. In such a case, just as in the one in which *A* and *B* do not share a liking for *x*, there is some failure to *share*. *B* likes *x*, but when *A* attempts to articulate the basis for *A*'s affirmative response to *x*, *B* finds that this is not his ground for liking *x*. This case can be much more frustrating than the one of disagreement in liking, because now both *A* and *B* seem to be missing something, although they both are getting *something*. And in some cases of this kind, either of the judges may feel that the other is just "not getting it," not finding or focusing on what is most significantly there in *x* to respond to.

Those of us who love movies find ourselves in this situation from time to time. Many of my friends, for instance, are fond of Billy Wilder's *Some Like It Hot*. But many of these fans seem to me to find only superficial attractions in the movie, while I remain convinced that my own high opinion of and affection for it are grounded in something my friends either do not see or do not credit.

Such examples lead immediately to worries about whether the idea of "liking" something is not too broad, too crude, too undifferentiated; and I'm sure it is. There can be more than one reason for liking something, there can be reasons for liking it and also for detesting it, and the idea of *liking* itself is in need of refinement. But I will attempt no refinement in this essay. I want to induce an interest in the question of the consistency of one's aesthetics, and I will settle for that, along with this passing reminder that the search for aesthetic coherence leads through more than one kind of tangle.

The search for self-consistency, or self-coherence, does not lead in only one direction. The central case I have been worrying about is this: *A* likes *x*, *A* doesn't like *y*, *y* and *x* are similar, so that *Rx* and *Ry*; and when all this obtains, *A* gives up the idea that *x* and *y* are significantly similar, deciding that although *Rx* and *Ry*, it is not, after all, because of *Rx* that *A* likes *x*. And this leads to some discovery, *R*x*, as the real reason why *A* likes *x*.

That is not always what happens. Sometimes *A* remains persuaded that he likes *x* because of *Rx*, and his dislike of *y*, which is also *R*, is simply a stubborn puzzle. This state of affairs is the one Hume describes in this way:

But when we show him an avowed principle of art; when we illustrate this principle by examples, whose operation, from his own particular taste, he acknowledges to be conformable to the principle; when we prove, that the same principle may be applied to the present case, where he did not perceive or feel its influence: He must conclude, upon the whole, that the fault lies in himself, and that he wants the delicacy, which is requisite to make him sensible of every beauty and every blemish, in any composition or discourse.[11]

Hume is talking about how to silence "the bad critic," but I wish to stay with the case of *A* alone, trying to sort out his likes and dislikes. *A* knows he likes *x*, and he believes strongly that it is on account of its being *R* that he likes *x*. Now he encounters *y*, doesn't like *y*, but is faced with the fact that *y* is as truly *R* as *x* is. He may decide, as Hume says, that his own taste is not strong and consistent enough to deal with *y*, or, of course, he may reappraise his sense of the reason why he likes *x*, hoping for something *y* does not have in common. If he does the former, then he is stuck with something like the proposition that he *should* like *y*, at least as far as he can tell, because *y* has what he thought he liked in *x*.

A may be able to get no farther than this. This seems to me a difference from comparable situations in ethics and epistemology. This is not a case of action, or of belief, at least not in the last instance. In aesthetic matters, if Isenberg and perhaps Hampshire are right, in the end it is a matter of feeling, and no principles can dislodge them. I think it is a common opinion that this is how things stand. Here is a personal statement of the opinion from a recent book:

I accept responsibility for my actions and words, and my processes of rational thought can fairly be judged competent or incompetent. For my feelings, desires, fears and hopes, I accept no responsibility at all; they simply happened to me, like health and sickness, good weather and bad.[12]

In one's moral life perhaps one feels like doing *x* and not doing *y*, but if one becomes convinced that one *should* do *x*, and is convinced by some reason which also obtains in the case of *y*, one will be forced to conclude that one should also do *y*, and may then do *y* despite not feeling like it. There is in ethics, at least in this simple way of considering things, a difference between feeling and action, whereas in aesthetics there seems to be just feeling. This is not to deny that persistent attention to some object *y*, which shares the relevant characteristics with an already-liked *x*, might lead one eventually to come to like *y* as well. It is, however, to insist that one's liking for *x* and dislike of *y* are rock-bottom facts, the facts making up one's aesthetic personality. And if one's feelings about *x* and *y* seem not to go together comfortably, seem perhaps, so to speak, inconsistent with one another, there is nothing one can do to mend things, nor is there anything one might subscribe to that would fix the situation. If one believes in the objectivity or verifiability or salience of propositions like 'x is good' held independently of any feelings, then one might move, as Hume suggests, to a view that both x and y are good although I like x and dislike y. The acceptance of 'x is good' as if forced by one's other beliefs will be a kind of amelioration, but the feelings remain, and it is these feelings and their mutual consistency in which I hope to interest you. I hope to have done that, but whether or not I have succeeded, I will leave off this topic now and turn briefly to another one. This other one may be thought of as concerning consistency, but it is more aptly thought of in terms of coherence or congruence. I am not sure what the best term is.

PERSONAL STYLE

How do a person's aesthetic choices and preferences go together to make a whole? It may be too strong a term, too pompous or presumptuous, but I think I am asking how a person's aesthetic personality is manifest in a *style.* The question of style in a work of art is certainly not a new topic with me, and in fact it is not a topic of this essay at all. Some of the most useful work on it has been done by Richard Wollheim and, following Wollheim, by Jenefer Robinson in her "Style and Personality in the Literary Work."[13] Commenting on the "verbal elements" present in the writing of Henry James, Robinson says:

Moreover, negatives, abstract nouns, non-transitive verbs, elegant variation and so on are verbal elements which at first sight seem to have nothing in common. What links them all together, however, as elements of "James' style" is their use in the artistic acts James performs: they are all elements of his style because they all contribute to the expression of his personality and attitudes.[14]

I think this is an exceptionally useful way to think of the verbal components in a literary style, but what I wish to ask about is not the expression of personality and attitudes, but the personality and attitudes themselves. What links *them* together? A bit before this remark about the verbal elements of style, Robinson summarizes her general conception of literary style:

I have argued that a literary style is a way of performing "artistic acts," describing a setting, portraying character, manipulating plot and so on, and it is the writer's way of performing these acts which is expressive of all those standing traits, attitudes, qualities of mind and so on that together form her personality.[15]

This, too, seems to me a very promising way of thinking of literary style, but, again, I wish to ask not about the literary or artistic style that expresses a personality, but about the personality itself. What is *its* form? How is it consistent, coherent, unified? It is good to say that *x, y,* and *z* are related because they all come from *A,* but I want to ask what relates them *in A.*

Before moving to that too-grand-sounding topic, I will pause to mention the collective manifestations of what might be thought of as someone's aesthetic sensibility.[16] I am thinking of fairly simple and common examples, most easily thought of in terms of predictions. If someone likes certain pieces by Mozart and the early Beethoven, we are not surprised to find him liking pieces by Haydn. If someone likes cannelloni and tagliatelle, it is not surprising to find he also likes fettuccine and manicotti. So far this seems not so different from the earlier discussion of the presumptive liking of similar things; but we can expand the range of relata, noting that it becomes ever less clear how to explain the relations. The person who likes pasta may well drink pinot grigio with his meal and have an espresso after. What does liking Mozart and early Beethoven go with? Liking certain styles of painting and literature? Perhaps, but of course there are people with strong preferences for musical works and very little interest in either painting or literature. There are musical people, visual people, literary people. A person with strong, deep interests in literature who cares little for painting is a recognizable kind of person. I would dare to call his a kind of sensibility. What do you think?

I think I can begin better with a seemingly more mundane example of the expression of aesthetic personality, one which moves completely away from these preferences for various official objects of art. Let me urge you to think about how people dress. A man is wearing trousers, a jacket, a shirt, a belt, shoes, socks, and a tie. How do these items go together?

Certainly I do not claim that these components do always "go together." I want to ask about how they do, when they do, and whether something seems missing when they do not. We are inclined to think that things go together when, given some of them, we are able to predict others. It is not a surprise when a man who wears standard, conservative Brooks Brothers clothing to work and to evening affairs turns up wearing boat shoes when he is on an outdoor outing. You are surely able to supply many examples of this kind, having to do with dress, with food, and, of course, with art. I am happy to leave to you the pleasant and instructive task of formulating examples.

GOING ON

There is a nearly irresistible temptation to think, whenever given *a*, *b*, and *c* we succeed in going on to predict *d*, we must be "going on" with reference to some principle or rule, some schematic precept that displays the links holding *a*, *b*, and *c* together and extending to *d*. Let me call this presumed general rule 'ϕ'. There is a strong, abiding conviction that there is a ϕ, that there must be a ϕ.

This is not quite the same as, but is reminiscent of, the conviction, for instance, that because we are able to go on speaking and understanding English, there must be some grammatical rules describing what we are doing. Faced with a universal inability to articulate ϕ, one may attribute the knowledge of ϕ to all who are engaged in the activity anyway, insisting that the knowledge is implicit or unconscious or whatever. However one attempts to account for this presumed knowledge in the face of practitioners' inability to evidence it in any way besides carrying on the activity, one believes that ϕ *can be formulated* and one pursues its formulation.

But now I have referred to three principles, or rules, underlying human expressions, and they may not be so much like one another. First was the matter of simple likes, dislikes, and the rest. Call its principle '*P*' (for preferences). Next was the topic of dress – and whatever else is like that. Call its principle '*S*' (for style). And now I have thrown in the question of one's use of language. Call its principle '*G*' (for grammar).

The phenomena overlying *P* and *G* seem different. One's preferences just *are* whatever they are, however much they may be predicted or explained by this hypothetical *P*. One's use of language seems different. It involves doing something and, perhaps, in some sense choosing what to do, while one's likes and dislikes just are what they are and, in some sense, are immune to choice. Dressing oneself, on the principle *S*, may seem like either of the others. If we think of dressing as a matter of choosing what to wear, perhaps as the result of some deliberation, then it is something like speaking, and *S* is like *G*. But we might think of dressing as just a matter of buying and putting on what one likes, and then *S* is more like *P*.

CONSOLATION

These matters need considerable untangling, but with this slight clarification and at least a nod to indicate that I see a mess in the making, I will leave them as they are for now and go on to suppose that the search for any of them may be urged on one as a project of self-understanding.

Is it like this with one's preferences and one's style? Do we believe that if there is a coherent aesthetic personality being exhibited, then there must be some *P* or *S* which explains its coherence? And what if we cannot find it? What if one cannot locate it in one's own case? There are, at first, two possibilities: either I have not looked deeply enough, not been analytically and imaginatively acute enough to find the principle, although it is indeed there to be found, or I doubt that my aesthetic choices, preferences, and likings do after all exhibit a style – I doubt, that is, that they do go together. If I settle for the latter, then am I admitting some failure on my part? Is it a failure to achieve an integration in my aesthetic character? Should I think that I am a man who has not succeeded in getting himself together? Should I worry about that?

And what if the deep truth is a third possibility: I do continue to believe in a coherence in my aesthetical self, but not only can I not locate its principles, I am convinced that it is impossible to do so. What then? There is, perhaps, consolation and instruction in these remarks, which were made by a very fine, very deep artist and critic in the course of his attempt to explain the success of some lines of Walt Whitman:

Of course we critics do our best to probe into poetry to try to ferret out the inner core of poetry. We know that we shall never get at the heart of poetry. We can never "pluck out the heart of its mystery," as Hamlet said. But still we try to go a little deeper down, though we know the task is endless, and perhaps one of the beauties, one of the joys of criticism, is in knowing that you are attempting something impossible, because there is something noble, I think, in the fact of attempting impossible things. Even Satan felt that it was his dignity to fight almighty Omnipotence.[17]

I would not presume to improve on Borges, although I note that Danny Herwitz has guessed that when Borges speaks of the nobility of hopeless struggle, he may well mention Satan, but surely he is thinking of Don Quixote. What I take from Borges's observation, combined with my own efforts in this essay, is this summary inference:

Explaining the coherence – the total sense – in a work of art is like explaining the coherent style of another person, and both are like explaining one's own aesthetical self. None of these explanations, in the end, is possible, and all must be attempted.

Is that a good thing or a sad thing?

On consistency in one's personal aesthetics

I cannot answer a single one of the questions raised in this last part. I hope to interest you in them. I have come to realize that it is my style to attempt to raise questions without answering them. I do not know that this is a matter of my personal aesthetics, but I might not mind if it were.

Notes

This essay began as an invited lecture for the University of Maryland Department of Philosophy's D. C. Williams Memorial Conference in the spring of 1994. It was improved – considerably, I hope – as a result of discussions there, and of later discussions of later versions in the University of Michigan Humanities Institute and Department of Philosophy and in the University of Chicago informal aesthetics workshop. Of particular help in the workshop were Stephen Burton, Michelle Mason, Gaby Sakamoto, Joel Snyder, and Lauren Tillinghast.

1. David Hume, "Of the Standard of Taste," reprinted in *Essays Moral, Political, and Literary,* rev. ed. (Indianapolis: Liberty Classics, 1987), 229.
2. Analyzing 'It's good but I don't like it' is reminiscent of working on Moore's paradox, trying to analyze 'P and I don't believe P', although there are striking differences.
3. Arnold Isenberg, "Critical Communication," *Philosophical Review* 58 (July 1949): 330–44. I will give citations to a reprinting of this essay in William Elton (ed.), *Aesthetics and Language* (Oxford: Basil Blackwell, 1959), 131–46.
4. There is a gap in Isenberg's argument, a missing, unargued premise. Isenberg assumes some close, rather simple relation between a willingness to say that something is good and having a liking for that thing. This is irrelevant to my purposes because I am concerned only with the likings and not with judgments about goodness.
5. Isenberg, "Critical Communication," 139.
6. Ibid.
7. This is probably not quite true, at least not of every *x*. For instance, if one likes roses in general, it may be possible to find an *R* which is the reason one likes this particular rose and which would also be a reason one would like any rose whatever, or at least many roses.

   Cases like this seem sufficiently infrequent, tame, and unthreatening not to require any attention in this essay. They may be important in other contexts, however, and I might note, in passing, that Kant makes a mess of just this example when he discusses the relation between 'This rose is beautiful' and 'Roses in general are beautiful'.

   In §8 of the *Critique of Judgment,* trans. Werner S. Pluhar (Indianapolis: Hackett, 1987), on page 59, Kant insists that the judgment of taste is singular, and he says, "For example, I may look at a rose and make a judgment of taste declaring it to be beautiful. But if I compare many singular roses and so arrive at the judgment, Roses in general are beautiful, then my judgment is no longer merely aesthetic, but is a logical judgment based on an aesthetic one."

I find it impossible to make sense of this remark. The difficulty is pointed up inadvertently by Werner Pluhar when he appends this explanatory note: "In the *Logic,* Kant spells out the (familiar) distinctions between universal, particular, and singular judgments in terms of inclusion and exclusion, total or partial, of the spheres of subject and predicate concepts, and also distinguishes universal from general propositions. . . ."

But there is no predicate concept employed in a judgment of taste; the word 'beautiful' does not signify the presence of such a concept, but rather indicates what Kant calls "a predicate of feeling." If 'Roses in general are beautiful' is, as Kant says, a logical judgment, then in this judgment 'beautiful' does indicate the use of a predicate concept. Where does this predicate concept come from? How could a judgment using the concept be "based on" judgments that do not use the concept? If, on the other hand, it is the predicate of feeling indicated by 'beautiful' in the singular judgments that is again employed in the general judgment, then there is no reason to declare 'Roses in general are beautiful' a logical judgment, for it has no genuine predicate concept. Suppose the use of 'beautiful' in an aesthetic judgment has this import – I am pleased and everyone ought to be pleased. If this import carries over to the general judgment based on singular ones, then the general judgment itself is also an aesthetic judgment. Putting it loosely, and in an un-Kantian idiom, the problem is this: Either 'beautiful' means the same in both judgments or it doesn't. If it does, then both judgments are of the same kind. If it doesn't, then there is no way to base one judgment on the other. Of course, the two occurrences of 'beautiful' might have different but connected meanings, but I can find no way to articulate this connection that is both plausible and congruent with the rest of Kant's text, and if there is no way to do this, there is no way to credit Kant's comparison of the two judgments.

8. Stuart Hampshire, "Logic and Appreciation," *World Review* (1952). I cite a reprinting of this essay in William Elton (ed.), *Aesthetics and Language* (Oxford: Basil Blackwell, 1959), 161–9. This is the concluding remark, on page 169.

9. I think Kant is committed to this extreme position, effectively denying the possibility of any kind of defense of one's judgments, despite the attempts of many sympathetic commentators to identify some kind of "formalist" Kantian aesthetic criticism. This is not a place to defend my opinion of the logic of Kant's position, but I note that I have attempted some softening and amplification of that position in "An Emendation in Kant's Theory of Taste," *Nous* 24, no. 4. (1990): 137–45, and "The Relation of Pleasure to Judgment in Kant's Aesthetics," in *Kant and Critique:*

New Essays in Honor of W. H. Werkmeister, Synthese Library, vol. 227, ed. R. M. Dancy (Dordrecht: Kluwer, 1993), 117–24.

10. E.g., in "The Very Idea of Art," *NCECA Journal* 9, no. 1 (1988): 7–14.
11. Hume, "Of the Standard of Taste," 236.
12. Kenneth Dover, *Marginal Comment* (London: Duckworth, 1994).
13. Jenefer M. Robinson, "Style and Personality in the Literary Work," *Philosophical Review* 94, no. 2 (1985): 227–47. I will cite a reprinting of this essay in George Dickie, Richard Sclafani, and Ronald Roblin (eds.), *Aesthetics: A Critical Anthology,* 2d ed. (New York: St. Martin's Press, 1989). References to Wollheim's work can be found in Robinson's essay.
14. Robinson, "Style and Personality," in *Aesthetics,* ed. Dickie, Sclafani, and Roblin, 459.
15. Ibid., 458.
16. Perhaps 'aesthetic' is a needless qualifier.
17. Jorge Luis Borges, "Walt Whitman: Man and Myth," transcription of a talk given at the University of Chicago, January 30, 1968, *Critical Inquiry* 1, no. 4 (1975): 714–15. To save space I have abbreviated Borges's remarks to the point of mutilation. My apologies.

5

Art, narrative, and moral understanding

NOËL CARROLL

With much art, we are naturally inclined to speak of it in moral terms. Especially when considering things like novels, short stories, epic poems, plays, and movies, we seem to fall effortlessly into talking about them in terms of ethical significance – in terms of whether or which characters are virtuous or vicious, and about whether the work itself is moral or immoral, and perhaps whether it is sexist or racist. Undoubtedly, poststructuralists will choke on my use of the phrase "naturally inclined," just because they do not believe that humans are naturally inclined toward anything. But that general premise is as needlessly strong a presupposition as it is patently false. And, furthermore, I hope to show that my talk of natural inclinations is hardly misplaced here, for we are prone to respond to the types of works in question in the language of moral assessment exactly because of the kinds of things they are.

Moreover, we do not merely make moral assessments of artworks as a whole and characters in particular; it is *also* the case that these moral assessments are *variable.* That is, we find some artworks to be morally good, while some others are not; some are exemplary, while some others are vicious and perhaps even pernicious; and finally other works may not appear to call for either moral approbation or opprobrium. So, though we very frequently do advance moral assessments of artworks, it is important to stress that we have a gamut of possible evaluative judgments at our disposal: from the morally good to the bad to the ugly, to the morally indifferent and the irrelevant. And it is this availability of different judgments that I am referring to as the variability of our moral assessments of artworks.

Very frequently, then, we make variable moral assessments of artworks. I take this comment to be no more than a pedestrian observation about our common practices of talking about art or, at least, certain kinds of art. But even if the observation is pedestrian, it is, oddly enough, hard to square with some of our major traditions in the philosophy of art. For the ideas (1) that we make moral assessments of art and (2) that these moral assessments are variable each offend certain well-known and deeply entrenched viewpoints in the philosophy of art, albeit in different ways.

First, there is the position in the philosophy of art – which may be called *autonomism* – that has exerted a great deal of influence on thinking about art since the eighteenth century and that continues to muddy our intuitions about art even today. Speaking very broadly, according to the autonomist, the artistic and the moral realms are separate. Art has nothing to do with moral goodness, or with badness, for that matter, and moral value neither contributes anything to nor subtracts anything from the overall value of the artwork. From the perspective of the autonomist, the fact, if it is a fact, that we spend so much time talking about morality with regard to so many artworks appears to be virtually unintelligible – perhaps it can be explained only by attributing deep and vast confusions to those who indulge in such talk.

For the autonomist, an essential differentiating feature of art is that it is separate from morality; this is the autonomist's underlying philosophical conviction. Thus, from the autonomist's point of view, that we make moral assessments of certain artworks is a mystery that must signal either our lack of taste or lack of understanding. For the autonomist, the problem is that we make moral assessments of artworks at all, since, philosophically, the autonomist is committed to the view that all artworks are separate from or exempted from considerations of morality.

On the other hand – to make matters more complex – we are also the beneficiaries of other philosophical traditions that, although they, contra autonomism, find no special problem in our making moral assessments of art, nevertheless consider it mysterious that our moral assessments should be variable. For one of these strands in the philosophy of art – call it *utopianism* – leads us to presume that, in virtue of its very nature, art, properly so called, is always morally uplifting, while yet another strand – call it *Platonism*–regards all art as morally suspect, once again due to its essential features. Both tendencies are clearly philosophical in the strong sense, inasmuch as their overall assessments of the morality of art are entailed by or rest

127

upon conjectures about the essential nature of art. And, though the utopian and Platonic traditions espouse opposite conclusions in this matter, they do at least appear to agree in precluding the possibility of *variable* moral assessments of artworks, since for the utopian all art is morally good, while for the Platonist all art is morally bad.

Undoubtedly, the Platonic tradition is the oldest and best known of the two.[1] This tradition situates art in ever-expanding circles of guilt. First, Plato himself chides art for proposing characters who are bad moral role models. But then – perhaps due to the recognition that there may be good moral role models in art – Plato argues that the problem is with the way in which art – mimetic art – is engaged and consumed. For that involves *identification,* and, for Plato, identifying with others is immediately morally suspicious. Here, of course, Plato was not simply thinking of designated actors taking on roles; he also believed that ordinary readers of dramas would become involved in a species of identification with others as well, inasmuch as they spoke the lines of characters. That is, in Athenian households, people would read plays aloud; thus, as they read the dialogue, Plato worried that they would somehow "become" someone else (namely, the character whose lines they recited).

This was putatively grounds for moral alarm, not only because the characters in question might be ethically vicious and because it would threaten Plato's ideal of the social division of labor, but also because it would destabilize the personality. Moreover, were one to challenge the generality of Plato's condemnation of art on the grounds that not all art is what Plato calls mimetic and, therefore, not mired in identification, Plato would respond with another argument, claiming that all art is by its nature aimed, in one way or another, at the emotions and, thereby, undermines the righteous reign of reason in the soul.

Nor is the Platonic spirit dead today. It thrives in our humanities departments, where all artworks have become the subject of systematic interrogation either for sins of commission – often in terms of their embodiment of bad role models or stereotypes – or for sins of omission – often in terms of people and viewpoints that have been left out. Furthermore, if none of these strategies succeeds in nailing the artwork, then it is always possible to excoriate it for – as followers of Lacan and Althusser like to say – positioning subjects, that is, for encouraging audiences to take themselves to be free, coherently unified subjects, a self-conception that is always thought to be a piece of ideologically engineered misrecognition and that is instilled by the formal structures of address of the mass communication media.[2] (Ironically enough, whereas Plato thought that the problem with art was that it destabilizes personalities, the contemporary Platonists of the Althusserian–Lacanian dispensation complain that art in fact stabilizes subjects, though for nefarious ideological purposes.)

Perhaps utopianism emerged as a response to Platonism. Once the Platonic prejudice was in the air, it called forth a rival that was its exact opposite number (a kind of situation that frequently occurs in philosophy). To the charge that all art is morally suspect, the utopian responds that in certain very deep respects art is by nature ultimately emancipatory. For Herbert Marcuse, for example, art is always on the side of the angels, because due to the ontology of fiction and representation, core art-making practices, artworks have the capacity to show that the world can be otherwise, thus entailing the conviction that it is at least possible to change it – an obvious precondition for radical praxis.[3]

In all probability, Marcuse's idea owes something to Schiller's thought that insofar as the aesthetic imagination is free from nature – in fact, on Schiller's account, it gives form to nature through its free play – the aesthetic imagination is said to be a precondition for moral and political autonomy.[4] But, be that as it may, Marxists like Marcuse and Ernest Bloch nevertheless tend to think that art is essentially liberatory by virtue of the ways in which artworks, ontologically, are distinct from mere real things. In virtue of this constrast, art, so to say, is always on the side of freedom, as far as they are concerned. Indeed, Sartre thought that prose fiction writing was so indissolubly linked to freedom that he claimed it would be impossible to imagine a good novel in favor of any form of enslavement.[5]

The autonomist position is also often taken to be a response to Platonism, and there are perhaps even historical grounds for this conjecture. Inasmuch as the autonomist argues that art is essentially independent of morality and politics, the autonomist goes on to contend that aesthetic value is independent of the sort of consequentialist considerations that Plato and his followers raise. Art on the autonomist view is intrinsically valuable; it should not be subservient to ulterior or external or extrinsic purposes, such as producing moral consequences or inducing moral education. For the autonomist, anything devoted to such ulterior purposes could not be art, properly so called.

Autonomists are also able to bolster their case with supporting arguments. For example, they argue that moral assessment cannot be an appropriate measure of artistic value, since not all artworks possess a moral dimension. We can call this the *common-denominator argument,* because it presupposes that if any evaluative scale can be brought to bear on art, then it must be applicable to all art. That is, any measure of artistic merit must be perfectly general across the arts.

Moreover, the autonomist may challenge the specific notion that art is an instrument of moral education. For if moral education delivers knowledge and that knowledge can be distilled into propositional form, then art cannot be a moral educator, on two counts: first, because much art has few propositions to preach, thereby raising the common-denominator question again, while, second, that art which has something to say that can be put in the form of maxims – like the punch lines to Aesopian fables or the entries in Captain Kirk's log at the end of *Star Trek* episodes – usually delivers little more than threadbare truisms. That is, where artworks either blatantly and outrightly express general moral precepts, or are underwritten by them, those principles or precepts are typically so obvious and thin that it strains credulity to think that we learn them from artworks. Instead, very often, it seems more likely that a thoughtful preteenager will have mastered them already.

Yes, there is an argument against murder in *Crime and Punishment,* but surely it is implausible to think that it requires a novel as elaborate as Dostoyevsky's to teach it, and even if Dostoyevsky designed the novel as a teaching aid, did anyone really learn that murder is wrong from it? Who, by the time he is able to read such a novel with comprehension, needs to be taught such a truism? In fact, it is probably a precondition of actually comprehending *Crime and Punishment* that the readers already grasp the moral precepts that motivate the narrative.

So it seems that art neither teaches nor, for that matter, does it discover any moral truths on a par with scientific propositions. And if an artwork pretends to such a role, such truths as it disseminates – understood as propositions – could unquestionably be acquired just as readily by other means, such as sermons, philosophical tracts, catechisms, parental advice, peer gossip, and so on. Art, in other words, is an unlikely means of moral education, and even where art professes to have some interesting moral maxims to impart, it is hardly a uniquely indispensable vehicle for conveying such messages.

Of course, the autonomist, utopian, and Platonic tendencies each face many problems. For example, there are scarcely any grounds for

Plato's anxieties about identification – neither for the case of the actor, nor for the case of the reader or the spectator. For as Diderot pointed out long ago with respect to the actor, no one could become Oedipus and continue the performance.[6] If I became as jealous as Othello, I would surely forget my lines and my blocking, as well as my rehearsed gestures and grimaces.

Nor do audiences standardly identify cognitively or affectively with characters; not only do we know more than Oedipus does through much of the play, but when Oedipus is crushed by feelings of guilt, we do not share these feelings. Instead, we are overtaken by rather distinctively different feelings of pity for Oedipus. We do not share Oedipus's internal experience of self-recrimination, but have concern for him from an external, observer's point of view.

Moreover, Plato's worries that art heightens the rivalry between reason and the emotions are misplaced because there is no cause to conceive of the emotions and reason as locked in ineliminable opposition. Reason – that is to say, cognition – is a constituent of the emotions rather than an alien competitor. Thus, it is possible to join Aristotle in regarding arts as such and theater in particular as ways of educating emotions such as pity and fear by means of clarifying them – to put a Collingwoodian spin on the notion of *catharsis* – by providing spectators with, or, more accurately, by presenting cognition with, exemplary or maximally fitting objects for certain emotions such that our capacity to recognize the appropriate objects of said emotions and our disposition to undergo these affective states in the right circumstances are enhanced.

And, of course, the problem with the Lacanian Marxists, our contemporary Platonists, is even easier to pinpoint. For insofar as they identify structural features of mass communication – such as film projection[7] – as the source of all evil, they are in the embarrassing position of lumping every attempt at moral and political progressiveness along with *Triumph of the Will*.

Utopianism confronts rather the same problem, but from the other direction. Given certain conceptions of the nature of art, the utopian is driven to put *Triumph of the Will* in the same boat as genuinely progressive art, because of the utopian conviction that, simply in virtue of being art, *Triumph of the Will* has something morally positive about it. Or, to put the matter in more fashionable jargon, all art must have its emancipatory moment. Thus, the utopian approaches the artwork with a research program – namely, find the emancipatory moment. This can lead to some fairly long stretches of interpretive fancy. I once heard a critic of this persuasion locate the emancipatory moment in *The Godfather* as its yearning for community – after all, everyone wants a family.

Utopianism seems highly improbable. It appears entirely too facile and convenient that the ontology of art should be able to guarantee that all art is morally ennobling. Indeed, I find the conclusion that art is necessarily complicit in moral progress, since by its nature it acknowledges that things can be otherwise, to be a deduction that appears to go through simply because its central premise is so vague and amorphous. The notion that art shows that things can be other than the way they are is too indefinite and unspecified a hook, to my mind, upon which to hang art's moral pedigree. Nor, even if we accept this rather obscure, if not equivocating, derivation of art's moral status, can we be satisfied that its conclusion coincides neatly with reality, since pre-theoretically it is rather apparent that there are irredeemably evil artworks.

Finally, I would protest that the utopian position strikes me as unduly sentimental. Basically, the utopian is committed to the view that art is always morally valuable. But the conceit that art should always turn out to be among the forces of light is nothing but a pious, deeply sanctimonious wish-fulfillment fantasy. (Perhaps a less tendentious way of framing this objection is to complain that utopians make art a category of commendation rather than of classification.)

If it were only the Platonic and utopian traditions that stand in the way of the commonsensical observation that the moral assessment of art can be variable, we could easily affirm common sense. However, as already noted, there is the even more comprehensive objection to moral discourse about art, namely the view of the autonomist who claims that there should be no moral assessment of art whatsoever – indeed, that moral discussion of art is of the nature of a category error. This, of course, flies in the face of ordinary critical and discursive practice with respect to most literature, film and theater, and a great deal of fine art. But the autonomist remains unconcerned by this anomaly, convinced that art is categorically separate from morality and politics.

Nevertheless, the acceptability of this conviction is hardly self-evident; and the fact that art, or at least much art – including, for example, art in the service of religion, politics, and social movements – does not appear disjoined from the realm of moral value, *in conjunction with* the fact that autonomists are not very good at coming up with a satisfying, clear-cut principle with which to demarcate the boundary between art and everything else, makes autonomism a far from overwhelmingly persuasive doctrine.[8] For in a great many cases of art, the putative impermeability of art to other sorts of practices, including morality, seems counterintuitive. What credibility can the autonomist position have when one realizes that simply in order to comprehend literary artworks, one must bring to bear one's knowledge of ordinary language and verbal associations, as well as one's knowledge of "real-world" human nature and everyday moral reasoning?[9]

And yet autonomism has some strong intuitions on its side, too – intuitions with which any philosophical attempt to develop an account of a general relation between art and morality must come to terms. Those intuitions include the following:

1. Not all artworks have a moral dimension, and it is therefore unintelligible to attempt to assess *all* art from a moral point of view.

2. Art is not an instrument of morality and so should not be assessed in terms of its moral (a.k.a. behavioral) *consequences.* It is not the function of art to produce certain moral consequences, so it is a mistake to evaluate art in light of the behavior to which it gives rise, either actually or probably. Art is not subservient to ulterior purposes, such as morality or politics.

Furthermore, in addition to this putatively conceptual point, it can be added that we still understand virtually *nothing* about the behavioral consequences of consuming art. For example, we have no precise, reliable account of why the incidence of violence is high in Detroit but low in Toronto, where the respective populations are exposed to the same violent entertainment media, nor do we have anything but exceedingly general ideas about why there is less violent crime in Japan than in the United States, despite the fact that Japanese programming is far more violent than ours. At this point, the notion of a *difference in cultures* may be solemnly intoned, but that is not an explanation. It is what needs to be explained if we are to determine the differential behavioral responses to popular art. Thus, given this, it may be argued that since we don't know how to calculate the behavioral consequences of art for morality, we should refrain from evaluating art in light of moral considerations.

3. It is not the function of art to provide moral education. This is not merely a subsidiary of the preceding point. It can also be bolstered by the observation that if art is supposed to afford moral knowledge of a propositional variety, then the maxims that are generally derivable from artworks are rather trivial. They are so com-

monly endorsed that it makes no sense to suppose that artists discover them, or that readers, listeners, and viewers come to learn them, in any robust sense, from artworks.

I would like to develop a philosophical account – by which I mean a general account – of one of the most important and comprehensive relations of art to morality. This account, moreover, is meant to accord with our practice of making variable moral assessments of artworks. I should also like to explain why, with certain types of artworks, it strikes us as natural, rational, and appropriate that we tend to talk about them in terms of morality. But, at the same time, I will try to develop this account in such a way that it confronts or accommodates the objections of the autonomist.

Autonomism is an attractive doctrine for anyone who approaches the question of the nature of art with essentialist biases, that is, with the expectation that everything we call art will share a *uniquely* common characteristic, one that pertains distinctively to all and only art. This is the card that Clive Bell plays when he announces that unless we can identify such a common, uniquely defining feature for art, then when we use the concept, we gibber.

Of course, by declaring art to be utterly separate from every other realm of human praxis, the autonomist secures the quest for essentialism at a stroke, if only by negation, by boldly asserting that art has nothing to do with anything else. It is a unique form of activity with its own purposes and standards of evaluation, generally calibrated in terms of formal achievement. That those standards do not involve moral considerations, moreover, can be supported, the autonomist argues, by noting that moral assessment cannot be an appropriate measure of artistic value, since not all artworks possess a moral dimension. We have already called this the common-denominator argument. It presupposes that any evaluative measure that applies to art should be applicable to all art. But since certain kinds of works – including some string quartets and/or some abstract paintings – may be bereft of moral significance, it makes no sense, so the argument goes, to raise issues of morality when assessing artworks. Moral evaluation is never appropriate to artworks, in short, because it is not universally applicable.

Moreover, that we are willing to call some artworks good despite their moral limitations – despite the fact that their moral insights may be paltry or even flawed – fits as nicely with the autonomist posit that art has nothing to do with morality as does the fact that with certain works of art, questions of morality make no sense what-soever. The autonomist accounts for these facts by saying that art is valuable for its own sake, not for the sake of morality, and that art has unique grounds for assessment. Art has its own purposes and, there-fore, its own criteria of evaluation.

But however well autonomism suits some of our intuitions about art, it also runs afoul of others. Historically, art seems hardly divorced from other social activities. Much art was religious and much art has served explicitly political goals. Are illustrations of the exemplary lives of saints, or biblical episodes, or pictorial biogra-phies of Confucius, or celebrations of the victories of empires and republics to be thought of as utterly disjunct from other realms of social value? Such works are obviously designed in such a way that viewing them from the perspective of "splendid" aesthetic isolation-ism renders them virtually unintelligible. Such works are made in the thick of social life and demand to be considered in light of what autonomists are wont to call nonaesthetic interests as a condition of their comprehensibility. Thus, though a taste for essentialism may create a predisposition for autonomism, the history of art and its reception makes the thesis that art is categorically separate from other realms of human praxis somewhat suspect.

To understand a literary work, for instance, generally requires not only that one use one's knowledge of ordinary language and verbal associations, drawn from every realm of social activity and valua-tion, but also, most frequently, that audiences deploy many kinds of everyday reasoning, including moral reasoning, simply to under-stand the text. How can the negative claims of autonomism – that art is divorced from every other realm of social praxis – be sustained in such a way as to render literary communication intelligible?

Or, to put the matter differently, much art, including literary art in particular and narrative art in general, has propositional content that pertains not only to the worlds of works of art, but to the world as well. In the face of such an indisputable fact, it is hard, save by an excess of ad hocery, to swallow the autonomist conviction that art is always divorced from other dimensions of human practice and their subtending forms of valuation.

If the negative claim of autonomism – that all art is in pertinent respects separate from other social practices – seems problematic, its positive project is desperately embattled. For no one, as yet, has been able to come up with a characterization of what is uniquely artistic that resists scrutiny for very long. Here the notion of disinterestedness plays a large role, one too complicated for me to rehearse here. Suffice it to say that talk of the aesthetic dimension is perennially popular, but after two centuries of discussion still inconclusive. That is, no one can give a persuasive account of what it might be in a sufficiently comprehensive way that would provide a model for art as we know it. Thus, since no autonomist seems to be able to say successfully, in a positive way, what art – its nature, purpose, and schedule of evaluation – is, the hypothesis seems like so much posturing. What persuasiveness it commands appears to rely upon a promissory note, drawn on the conviction that a certain preconception of essentialism is an unavoidable desideratum, though, as I hope to show, the preconception in question may misconstrue the nature of at least certain kinds of art.

Autonomism rides on the unexceptionable observation that art appears to aim, first and foremost, at being absorbing. The so-called aesthetic experience is centripetal. Thus, if the artwork essentially aims at our absorption in it, then it is valuable for its own sake. The thought that art is valuable for its own sake, in turn, is believed to entail that it is not valuable for other reasons, especially cognitive, moral, and political ones. However, this conclusion is a non sequitur. For, in ways to be pursued at length in what follows, some art may be absorbing exactly because of the way in which it engages, among other things, the moral life of its audience. That is, just because we value art for the way it commands our undivided attention does not preclude that some art commands our attention in this way just because it is interesting and engaging cognitively and/or, for our purposes, morally.

The autonomist is certainly correct to point out that it is inappropriate to invoke moral considerations in evaluating *all* art. This premise of the common-denominator argument is right. Some art, at least, is altogether remote from moral considerations. And, in such cases, moral discourse with reference to the artworks in question – say, a painting by Albers – may be not only strained and out of place, but conceptually confused. Nevertheless, the fact that it may be a mistake to engage moral discourse with reference to some pure orchestral music or some abstract paintings has no implications about whether it is appropriate to do so with respect to *The Grapes of Wrath, Peer Gynt, The Scarlet Letter, Anna Karenina, 1984, Potemkin, The Ox-Bow Incident, Antigone, The Bonfire of the Vanities,* and *Beowulf,* since artworks such as these are expressly designed to elicit moral reactions, and it is part of the form of life to which they belong that audiences respond morally to them on the basis of their recognition that that is what they are intended to do, given the relevant social practices. These works have moral agendas as part of their address to the reader to such an extent that one would have to be willfully blinkered to miss them.

The common-denominator argument presupposes that there must be a single scale of evaluation that applies to all artworks. Whether or not there is such a scale – a controversial hypothesis if there ever was one – can be put aside, however, because even if there is, that would fail to imply that its underlying property was the *only* evaluative consideration that could be brought to bear on every artwork. For in addition to, for example, formal considerations, some artworks may be such that given the nature of the works in question, it is also appropriate to discuss them in terms of other dimensions of value.

We may evaluate eighteen-wheelers and sports cars in terms of their capacities to locomote, but that does not preclude further assessments of the former in terms of their capacity to draw heavy loads or of the latter to execute high-speed, hairpin turns. These additional criteria of evaluation, of course, are related to the kinds of things that eighteen-wheelers and sports cars respectively are. Similarly, the conviction that there may be some common standard of evaluation for all artworks, even if plausible, would not entail that for certain kinds of artworks, given what they are, considerations of dimensions of value, beyond the formal, such as moral considerations, are out of bounds.

It is my contention that there are many kinds of art, genres if you will, that naturally elicit moral responses, that prompt us to talk about them in terms of moral considerations, and that even warrant moral evaluation. The common-denominator argument cannot preclude this possibility logically, for even if there is some global standard of artistic value, there may be different local standards for different art genres. Moreover, with some of these art genres, moral considerations are pertinent, even though there may be other genres where bringing them to bear would be tantamount to a category error.

Certain kinds of artworks are designed to engage us morally, and, with those kinds of artworks, it makes sense for us to surround them with ethical discussion and to assess them morally. Thus, in order to deflect the autonomist's common-denominator argument, we need simply adjust the domain of prospective theories about the relation of art to morality to the kinds of artworks where ethical discourse and moral assessment are intelligible. Consequently, I will restrict the scope of the theoretical framework that I am about to advance to narratives, specifically human narratives (including anthropomorphized ones like *The Wind in the Willows, Charlotte's Web, Animal Farm,* and *Maus*). This is not to suggest that narrative is the only art genre or category where moral assessment is pertinent – portraiture may be another – but only that it is a clear-cut case. That is, narratives like *Lord of the Flies, To Kill a Mockingbird, Vanity Fair, Pilgrim's Progress, Beloved, L'Assomoir, Germinal,* and *Catch-22* are such obvious, virtually incontestable examples of morally significant art that they provide a useful starting point for getting out from under autonomism.

The common-denominator argument cannot be taken to have shown that it is never appropriate to assess artworks morally, but only, at best, that it is not always appropriate to do so. This allows that sometimes it may be intelligible to assess artworks morally and, I submit, that artworks that are narratives of human affairs are generally the kind of thing it makes sense both to talk about in ethical terms and to assess morally. Moreover, there are deep reasons for this.

As is well known, narratives make all sorts of presuppositions, and it is the task of the reader, viewer, or listener to fill these in. It is of the nature of narrative to be essentially incomplete. Every narrative makes an indeterminate number of presuppositions that the audience must bring, so to speak, to the text. All authors must rely upon the audience's knowledge of certain things that are not explicitly stated. Authors always write in the expectation that the audience will correctly fill in what has been left unsaid. Shakespeare presumes that the audience will not suppose that Juliet's innards are sawdust and, with respect to *Oleanna,* David Mamet assumes that the audience will suppose that his characters possess the same structure of beliefs, desires, and emotions that they do and that the characters are not alien changelings possessed of unheard-of psychologies. When the author of a novel about the eighteenth century notes that the characters traveled from one country to another, she expects that, unless she wrote otherwise, we will not imagine that the characters were teleported. No artist can say or depict everything there is to say or to depict about the fictional events she is narrating. She depends upon the audience to fill in a great deal and that filling-in is an indispensable part of what it is to follow and to comprehend a narrative.[10]

Moreover, the kinds of details that authors rely on audiences to supply come in all different shapes and sizes, ranging from facts about human biology to facts about geography, history, politics, religion, and so on. In many cases, the author relies upon what we know or believe about human psychology in order for her narratives to be intelligible. For example, in *Eugénie Grandet,* Balzac presumes that the audience has enough understanding of the ways of the human heart to see how it is that Eugenie's betrayal at the hands of her cousin can precipitate an irreparable bitterness that turns her into the very image of her father. Likewise, in the *Symposium,* Plato supposes that the reader knows enough about flirtation to understand the erotic triangle with Agathon at its apex in order to appreciate the sly maneuverings of Socractes and Alcibiades. And in *The Bluest Eye,* Toni Morrison relies on the reader's understanding of human psychology to see how Pecola's plight derives from her aunt's displacement of her maternal concerns from her own family to that of her white employers inasmuch as the white family can provide her with the material conditions that will enable her to take pride in running a functioning household.

But the audience's activity of filling in the narrative does not simply have to do with recognizing what the text suggests or implies of presupposes about the contours of its fictional world and about the nature and psychology of the human characters that inhabit that world. To understand a text properly also involves mobilizing the emotions that are requisite to the text. Properly understanding Trollope's *Dr. Wortle's School* involves feeling distrust toward Robert Lefroy, while anyone who does not find Uriah Heep in *David Copperfield* repugnant would have missed Dickens's point. One does not understand Hemingway's *For Whom the Bell Tolls* unless one admires Robert Jordan's restraint, just as the reader must ultimately find Casaubon despicable in order to "get" *Middlemarch.* Similarly, "getting" *Medea,* it seems to me, requires finding her actions finally appalling, whereas anyone left unmoved by the experiences of the members of the Joy Luck Club would find the point of that novel incomprehensible.

A narrative by its very nature is selective and, therefore, incomplete in certain specifiable senses. It is for this reason that the successful author requires an audience that can bring to the text, among other things, what is not explicit in it. This further dictates that, to a large extent, the author and the audience need to share a common background of beliefs about the world and about human nature, as well as a relatively common emotional life. That is, authors generally not only possess a shared cognitive stock with audiences, but a shared emotional stock as well. The author designs her work with an implicit working hypothesis about the knowledge that her anticipated reader will bring to the text, along with knowledge of how the reader will feel toward the characters. For unless the readers feel toward the characters in certain ways, they will be unlikely to comprehend the narrative.

Of course, the cognitive stock that the audience needs to possess in order to properly understand a narrative fiction includes not only knowledge of geography and human nature, but moral knowledge as well. And the emotions that the audience brings to bear on a narrative are not only shot through with moral concepts, in the way that, say, anger is – insofar as "being wronged" is conceptually criterial for feeling it – but the relevant emotions are themselves very often moral emotions, such as contempt for wanton brutality and the indignation at injustice that pervades almost every page of *Uncle Tom's Cabin.*

One cannot, for example, admire Schindler in the way the film *Schindler's List* encourages if one does not feel that the Nazis are morally loathsome. And even melodramas, like *Back Street,* typically evoke an emotional response that is a mixture of moral admiration for the protagonists – often as a result of recognizing the nobility involved in their self-sacrificing behavior – and sorrow over their adversity.[11] There is no "melodramatic" response, just as according to Aristotle there is no tragic response, when the audience misconstrues the moral standing of the relevant characters. Nor is it likely that there can be a successful narrative of any substance that would not rely on activating the moral powers of the readership.[12] And finally, of course, in the general case, the author can rely on the audience sharing the relevant cognitive and emotive stock because the audience and the author already share a roughly common culture.

In his *Letter to M. D'Alembert on the Theater,* Jean-Jacques Rousseau argues that theater cannot transform a community morally or reform it.[13] Rousseau believes this because he points out that in order to succeed an author has to write within the moral framework of his times. As Rousseau notes, "An author who would brave the general taste would soon write for himself alone."[14] That is, there are "market pressures," so to speak, that incline authors to design their works in such a way that they rely on a fit between their narratives and a roughly common cognitive, emotive, and moral stock that is shared by the readers, viewers, and listeners who make up the expected audience of the work. If there were no such common background, there would be no communication, since there could be no uptake.

A narrative is built so that its anticipated audience can understand it, and in order to understand a narrative properly, an audience will have to mobilize its knowledge and its emotions, moral and otherwise, in the process of filling in a story. This means that in order to understand a narrative properly, we must use many of the same beliefs and emotions, generally rooted in our common culture, that we use to negotiate everyday human events for the purpose of filling in and getting the point of stories. In this sense, it is not the case that the narrative teaches us something brand new, but rather that it activates the knowledge and emotions, moral and otherwise, that we already possess.

That is, the successful narrative becomes the occasion for exercising knowledge, concepts, and emotions that we have already, in one sense, learned. Filling in the narrative is a matter of mobilizing or accessing the cognitive, emotive, and moral repertoire that, for the most part, we already have at our disposal. Narratives, in other words, provide us with opportunities to, among other things, exercise our moral powers, because the very process of understanding a narrative is itself, to a significant degree, generally an exercise of our moral powers.

Because successful narratives are so inextricably bound up with the opportunity they afford for the exercise of our moral powers, it is quite natural for ethical concerns to recur frequently when we discuss stories. Insofar as narratives necessarily depend upon activating our moral beliefs, concepts, and feelings, it comes as no surprise that we should want to discuss, to share, and to compare with other readers our reactions to the characters, situations, and overall texts that authors present to us with the clear intention of eliciting, among other things, moral responses. That is, it is natural for us to think about and to discuss narratives in terms of ethics, because narratives, due to the kinds of things they are, awaken, stir up, and engage our moral powers of recognition and judgment.

If this account is correct, and if we suppose, in addition, that learning is a matter of the acquisition of interesting propositions heretofore unknown or of freshly minted moral emotions, then, as the autonomist argues, in the standard case there is no learning when it comes to the vast majority of narrative artworks, since those artworks antecedently depend, as a condition of their very intelligibility, upon our possession of the relevant knowledge of various moral precepts, and of concepts of vice and virtue, and so on. Nor do narratives invest us with and thereby teach us new emotions; rather they typically exercise the emotions we already possess. So the autonomist's case against the hypothesis that the relation of art to the emotions cannot be one of moral education looks persuasive.

And yet it does seem that the operative sense of learning in the autonomist's argument is too restrictive. For there is another sense of learning – both moral and otherwise – that the autonomist has ignored and that applies to the kinds of activities that narrative artworks abet. It is this: that in mobilizing what we already know and what we can already feel, the narrative artwork can become an occasion for us to deepen our understanding of what we know and what we feel. Notably, for our purposes, a narrative can become an opportunity for us to deepen our grasp of the moral knowledge and emotions we already command.

This conception of the relation of art, especially narrative art, to morality might be called the *transactional view* (because of its emphasis on the transaction between the narrative artwork and the moral understanding), or it might be called, as I prefer to call it, the *clarificationist view,* in honor of the most prized transaction that can transpire between the narrative artwork and the moral understanding. Clarificationism does not claim that, in the standard case, we acquire interesting, new propositional knowledge from artworks, but rather that the artworks in question can deepen our moral understanding by, among other things, encouraging us to apply our moral knowledge and emotions to specific cases. For in being prompted to apply and engage our antecedent moral powers, we may come to augment them.

In the course of engaging a given narrative we may need to reorganize the hierarchical orderings of our moral categories and premises, or to reinterpret those categories and premises in the light of new paradigm instances and hard cases, or to reclassify barely acknowledged phenomena afresh – something we might be provoked to do by a feminist author who is able to show us injustice where before all we saw was culture as usual. Thus, in *Up the Sandbox,* Anne Richardson Roiphe juxtaposes adventure fantasies with the daily chores of a housewife in order to highlight the inequality of the latter's life when compared to her husband's.

A play like *A Raisin in the Sun* addresses white audiences in such a way as to incite vividly their recognition that African-Americans are persons like any other and therefore should be accorded the kind of equal treatment for persons that such audiences already endorse as a matter of moral principle. The play does this by showing that the dreams and the family bonds of the major characters are no different from those of other persons, thereby prompting the subsumption of African-Americans under a moral precept concerning equal treatment that the audience already believes. This, in turn, encourages the white audience to form the moral judgment that the way in which the prospective white neighbors of the black family respond to their purchasing a house in their neighborhood is wrong.

In this case, as in many others, it seems accurate to describe what goes on in the white audience as a discovery about something it already knows; that is, audience members put together previously disconnected belief fragments in a new gestalt in a way that changes their moral perception. Here it is not primarily that white audience members acquire a new piece of moral knowledge; rather they are prompted to make connections between the beliefs they already possess.

The characters and the situations presented by the play afford an occasion to reorganize or reshuffle the moral beliefs that the white audience already has at its disposal. Its system of beliefs undergoes clarification. Its grasp and understanding of what it already knows is deepened in a way that counts, I contend, as learning, though it may not primarily be a matter of learning an interesting new proposition, since in some sense, the white audience already knows that African-Americans are persons and that persons deserve treatment as equals. They might even be able to recite the relevant syllogism, but it would not strike home. What the play succeeds in doing is to create a situation that encourages the audience to forge a salient connection between heretofore perhaps isolated beliefs. We are given an opportunity to deepen our grasp and our understanding of what we already know in a way that also counts as learning, though not necessarily as a matter of learning interesting, nontrivial, new propositions.[15] Rather, it is more a matter of grasping the significance of the connections between antecedently possessed knowledge.[16]

I intend here to draw a contrast between knowledge and *understanding* such that understanding is meant to mark our capacity to manipulate what we know and to apply it with a sense of intelligibility – not simply to have access to abstract propositions and concepts, but to employ them intelligibly and appropriately. Understanding is a capacity to see and to be responsive to connections between our beliefs. A person with understanding has the ability to find her way around in the mental geography of her own cognitive stock.[17] Understanding is the ability to make connections between what we already know. With understanding, we acquire increasing familiarity with concepts and principles that are at first bewildering. Understanding is the activity of refining what we already know, of recognizing connections between parts of our knowledge stock, of bringing what we already know to clarity through a process of practice and judgment.[18]

We may possess abstract principles, like "All persons should be given their due," and abstract concepts, such as "Virtue is what promotes human flourishing," without being able to connect these abstractions to concrete situations. For that requires not only knowing these abstractions, but understanding them. Moreover, it is this kind of understanding – particularly with respect to moral understanding – to which engaging with narrative artworks may contribute.[19] For narrative, as we have seen, involves the exercise of moral judgment and it is through the exercise of judgment that we come to understand moral abstractions.

Inasmuch as understanding is often a function of correctly classifying things, fictional narratives frequently present us with opportunities to deliberate about how to categorize behaviors and character traits, and thereby they can enhance our capacity for classifying the human environment – by linking abstract concepts to percepts in ways that can make us more sensitive to applying them to real-world cases. As I have already suggested, it seems to me that the work of many feminist novelists has been to get people to reclassify a great many everyday practices under the category of injustice.[20]

Moreover, insofar as the emotions involve a conceptual component – in terms of formal criteria for what can serve as the object of an emotional state – it is coherent to talk about deepening our emotional understanding. This involves treating the narrative as an occasion for clarifying our emotions or, as Aristotle might put it, of learning to apply the right emotion to the appropriate object with suitable intensity.

As is probably apparent, for the clarificationist, engaging with or coming to understand a narrative artwork can itself simultaneously be a process of deepening one's own moral understanding. Recognizing that there is something deeply wrong with Emma's "guidance" of Harriet in Jane Austen's classic is not only a requisite recognition for properly understanding the novel; it also deepens our moral understanding by providing us with a penetrating portrait of interpersonal manipulation, which, though well intentioned, is ultimately self-deceptive as well as wicked. Moreover, the fact that we must resist the allure of Emma's otherwise attractive moral character before we reach this insight about the wrongness of her interference with Harriet's life makes reading the novel *Emma* all the more serviceable as an occasion where we have the opportunity to expand our moral understanding, though not our knowledge (insofar as we already knew the abstract maxim that treating people merely as a means is immoral).[21]

On the clarificationist view, learning from a narrative artwork through the enlargement or expansion of one's moral understanding is not well described as a *consequence* of engaging with the story. Understanding the work, enlarging one's moral understanding, and learning from the narrative are all part and parcel of the same process, which might be called comprehending or following the narrative. When reading a novel or viewing a drama, our moral understanding is engaged already. Reading a novel, for example, is itself generally a moral activity insofar as reading narrative literature typically involves us in a continuous process of moral judgment, which continuous exercise of moral judgment itself can contribute to the expansion of our moral understanding. When reading a novel, we are engaged in a moral activity already insofar as our powers of moral judgment and understanding have been drawn into play, and, as we shall later see, our moral assessment of a narrative artwork may rest upon the quality of that moral activity or experience, rather than upon speculations about the probable behavioral consequences of reading, hearing, or viewing that fiction.

Moreover, by talking of the expansion or enlargement of our moral powers, I am not speaking metaphorically, since the process of understanding that I have in mind concerns making *more* connections between what we already know or believe, while by the notion of exercising our moral understanding I mean to signal that successful narrative artworks, as a condition of intelligibility, compel us to make moral judgments.

In order to avoid obscurity, it will be useful for me to provide some examples of the way in which narrative artworks can enhance the understanding. As Sir Philip Sidney and Immanuel Kant point out, we are often possessed of general propositions that are very abstract and that we may not be able to connect with particular situations.[22] That is, they are so abstract that they leave us at a loss about how to apply them. But narrative artworks can supply us with vivid examples that enable us to see how to apply abstractions to particulars. For example, *King Lear* gives us an arresting example with which to understand the general proposition that "a house divided shall not stand"; Brecht's *Three Penny Opera* exemplifies the principle that the quality of moral life is coarsened by poverty; *Measure for Measure* shows how power corrupts; the early-twentieth-century film serial *Judex* dramatizes the adage "Judge not, lest ye be judged"; while *Oedipus Rex* supplied the ancient Greeks with a percept to match the admonitory precept "Call no one happy until he is dead."

This recognition of the importance of examples for moral understanding, of course, was also acknowledged by medieval theologians in their recommendation of the use of the *exemplum,* a recommendation that can be traced back to Aristotle's discussion of illustrations in his *Rhetoric.* Much modern moral theory has placed great emphasis on rules in its conception of moral deliberation. However, this overlooks the problem that often our moral rules and concepts are too thin to determine the particular situations that fall under them. That requires moral judgment, and the capacity for moral judgment is exactly what is ideally exercised and refined through our encounters with narrative artworks. Narrative artworks, that is, supply us with content with which to interpret abstract moral propositions. Here, it is not my intention to disparage the role of rules in moral deliberation, but merely to point out that rules must be negotiated by the capacity for judgment, which capacity can be enhanced by trafficking with narrative artworks just because narrative artworks typically require moral judgments in order to be intelligible.

For example, Mary Shelley's *Frankenstein* exemplifies the point that evil proceeds from nurture, not nature – from the environment and social conditioning, or the lack thereof – and, hence, that blame must be apportioned with respect to this principle. Moreover, as this example should indicate, the way in which moral understanding is enhanced by narrative artworks need not be thought of as a matter of the fiction supplying readers with templates that they then go on to match to real cases. For, obviously, there can be no real case anywhere like the one portrayed in *Frankenstein.* Instead, the moral understanding can be refined and deepened in the process of coming to terms with this story and its characters, especially the monster and his claims to justice. We are not in a position to measure real-life cases on a one-to-one basis against the story of *Frankenstein,* but after reading the novel our moral understanding may be more sophisticated in such a way that we can identify cases of injustice quite unlike that portrayed in *Frankenstein.* Thus, we see why authors need not, and frequently do not, trade in typical cases, but favor extraordinary ones (consider *The Brothers Karamazov*) in order to provoke an expansion of our moral powers.

In addition, just as narrative artworks enable us to clarify our moral comprehension of abstract principles, so too do they enlarge our powers of recognition with respect to abstract virtues and vices. In *Pride and Prejudice,* Jane Austen presents the reader with an array of kinds and degrees of pride in order to coax the reader into recognizing which type of pride, as Gilbert Ryle puts it, goes best with right thinking and right acting,[23] while in *Sense and Sensibility,* she contrasts these traits through the characters of Elinor and Marianne Dashwood in a way that the reader should come to see redounds morally to the former's virtue. Similarly, so many western novels and movies, like *Shane,* are about restraint, about its proper scope and limits, as exemplified in a case study.

Molière's comedy *The Miser* and Erich von Stroheim's film *Greed* are obvious examples of the way in which narratives limn the nature of the very vices their titles name, while in Chekhov's *The Cherry Orchard,* we are offered a striking contrast between worldly prudence and imprudence in the persons of Lopukhin and Madame Ranevskaya – a contrast staged over the cherry orchard whose loss, due to Madame Raneskaya's obliviousness to real life, deals a shattering blow to her family.

In *Barchester Towers* by Trollope, Mr. Slope exemplifies a paradigm of manipulativeness, whereas in Dickens's *Bleak House,* the reader gradually comes to see Mr. Skimpole's charm and frivolity as a form of callous egoism, thereby receiving a lesson in what, *avant la lettre,* we might call the passive–aggressive personality. That *Bleak House* and *Barchester Towers* were originally released in serial form, of course, encouraged readers to compare their moral judgments of evolving characters and situations with one another between installments, much in the way that contemporary soap operas provide communities of viewers with a common source of gossip, where gossip itself has the salutary function of enabling discussants to clarify their understanding of abstract moral principles and concepts, as well as their application through feelings, by means of conversation and comparison with others.[24]

Narratives involve audiences in processes of moral reasoning and deliberation. As the father in *Meet Me in St. Louis* considers moving to New York, the viewer also weighs the claims of the emotional cost such a move will exact on his family against the abstract claims of the future and progress. And, of course, some narratives present readers with moral problems that appear not to be satisfactorily resolvable, such as Maggie Tulliver's romance in *The Mill on the Floss.* This too seems to enrich moral understanding by stretching its reflective resources as one struggles to imagine a livable course of action.

As Martha Nussbaum argues, not only may narratives serve as models of moral reflection and deliberation, they may offer occasions for moral understanding. Nussbaum, of course, believes there is little legitimate room for moral principles and abstract moral concepts in literary-cum-moral understanding, emphasizing, as she does, perception as the model for moral reflection.[25] However, though I do not want to preclude that there may be cases of the kind of moral perception that Nussbaum valorizes, I do not feel any pressure to deny that there are also cases where the moral understanding comes to appreciate abstractions via concrete narratives. Why not have it both ways – so long as we acknowledge that the process of reflection involved in understanding narrative artworks is at the same time a process of moral understanding, often, at least in the most felicitous cases, involving the reorganization and clarification of our moral beliefs and emotions.

Rousseau, it will be recalled, claimed that theater could not reform its audience, since a public art form, like theater, had, in order to persist, to root itself in the beliefs and moral predispositions that its audiences already embraced, lest the work appear unintelligible to them, only, in consequence, to be rejected out of hand. Now surely Rousseau is right that, in the standard case, living artworks must share a background of belief and feeling with their audience. But Rousseau oversteps himself when he infers from this that art cannot reform its audiences, at least incrementally. For often moral reform is a matter of reorganizing or refocalizing or "re-gestalting" what people already believe and feel.

For example, by calling attention to and emphasizing the fact that gays and lesbians are fully human persons one can often convince heterosexuals that gays and lesbians are thereby fully deserving of the rights that those heterosexuals in question already believe should be accorded to all persons. And, of course, this type of gestalt switch, which often contributes to the refinement of moral understanding, is easily within the grasp of narrative, as topical novels and films, such as *Gentleman's Agreement, To Kill a Mockingbird,* and *Philadelphia,* attest.

Undoubtedly, these particular examples are sometimes criticized for trafficking in victims who are too pure, too saintly, or too unrealistic and, so, in that sense, are somewhat misleading in the long run. But I think that, in the short run, these choices are certainly tactically justifiable in order to get the job done, where the job in question is to prompt the reconfiguration of thinking about Jews, Blacks, and gays. And to the extent that people can be incrementally enlightened by narratives that operate on the audience's antecedent framework of ethical beliefs and emotions, Rousseau is wrong. For moral reform can be achieved by deepening our moral understanding of that which we already believe and feel.

By focusing on the nature of narrative and by taking note of the way in which narratives require audiences to fill in stories by means of their own beliefs and emotions – including, unavoidably, moral ones – I think that I have shown why it is natural for us to discuss narrative artworks in terms of ethical considerations. For, simply put, much of our readerly activity with respect to narratives engages our moral understanding. It is a failure of neither intelligence nor taste to discuss narrative artworks in virtue of their moral significance, given the kind of artifacts that stories are. For given the nature of narrative, the activity of reading, in large measure, is a matter of exercising our moral understanding. It is appropriate to think and to talk about narrative artworks in light of morality because of the nature of narrative artworks and the responses – such as moral judgment – that they are meant to elicit as a condition of their being intelligible, *given the kinds of things they are.* It would, rather, be a failure of intelligence and taste if one did *not* respond to narratives morally.

Moreover, if what I have argued so far is compelling, then perhaps the clarificationist picture of the relation of morality to (narrative) art can also suggest certain grounds for the moral assessments that we make of characters and of complete narratives as well. Obviously, the moral judgments and understandings achieved in response to a narrative artwork differ in at least one way from those essayed in everyday life, since the moral experience that we have in respect to a narrative artwork is guided by the author of the story. There is a level of moral experience available from the narrative that depends on the guidance with which the author intends to provide us. I contend that our moral assessments of the narrative, then, can be grounded in the quality of the moral experiences that the author's guidance is designed to invite and abet.

Some narratives may stretch and deepen our moral understanding a great deal. And these, all things being equal, will raise our moral estimate of the work, which may, in turn, also contribute to our artistic evaluation of the work, insofar as a narrative artwork that engages our moral understanding will be all the more absorbing for that very reason. *Emma,* as I have already suggested, is an example of this sort. On the other hand, narratives that mislead or confuse moral understanding deserve criticism – as does Michael Crichton's recent, morally frivolous novel, *Disclosure,* which pretends to explore the issue of sexual harassment through a case that really has more to do with thriller-type cover-ups than it has to do with sexual politics. Here the problem is that the novel is essentially digressive, and, in that respect, it misfocuses or deflects our moral understanding from the issue of sexual harassment. Likewise, narratives that pervert and confuse moral understanding by connecting moral principles, concepts, and emotions to dubious particulars – as often happens with cases of political propaganda – also fare badly on the clarificationist model, since they obfuscate rather than clarify.

The recent film *Natural Born Killers,* for example, advertises itself as a meditation on violence, but it neither affords a consistent emotional stance on serial killing, nor delivers its promised insight on the relation of serial killing to the media, if only because it neglects to show how the media might have affected the psychological development of the relevant characters. Indeed, its very title – *Natural Born Killers* – would seem at odds with the hypothesis of media-made murder. The media references in the film seem to divert our attention from the moral issues at hand, and in confusing, or even perverting, our moral grasp of the issues, they are, along with the film as a whole, candidates for moral rebuke.

Throughout this essay, I have emphasized the importance in narratives of enlisting the audience's emotional response to the situations they present. Because of this, narratives can be morally assessed in terms of whether they contribute to emotional understanding, where that pertains to morality, or whether they obfuscate it. For example, in many fictions about psychotic killers, like *Silence of the Lambs,* the murderers are presented as gay. Gayness is part of their monstrosity, and the audience is encouraged to regard these killers with horror. Gayness is thus represented as unnatural. Gayness and monstrosity are superimposed on each other in such a way that gayness is turned into a suitable object of the emotion of horror.

This is to mismatch gayness with a morally inappropriate emotion. It is to confuse homosexuals with the kinds of creatures, like alien

150

beings, that warrant emotional responses of fear and disgust. But to engender this kind of loathing for homosexuals by enlisting a response to them that is emotionally suitable for monsters is morally obnoxious as a result of the way in which it misdirects our feelings. It confuses matters morally by encouraging us to forge an emotive link between gayness and the horrific.

The ways in which the quality of our moral experience of a narrative artwork can vary, either positively or negatively, are quite diverse. Many different things can go right or wrong in terms of how our moral understanding is engaged or frustrated by a narrative artwork. Thus, it is unlikely that there is a single scale along which the qualities of all our moral experiences of narratives can be plotted or ranked. And since we possess no algorithm, we will have to make our moral assessments on a case-by-case basis, aided, at most, by some very crude rules of thumb, like those operative in the preceding examples.

For example, in the movie version of *Schindler's List,* in the scene where Schindler leaves the factory, director Steven Spielberg manhandles our emotions by trying to force us to accord Schindler a level of moral admiration that the character has already won from us. As Schindler whines about his Nazi lapel pin, we are coerced into virtually subvocalizing, "It's okay Oskar, you're a hero and the pin probably helped you fool the German officers anyway." Here, our moral emotions are engaged, I think, excessively. But, of course, this flaw is rather different and nowhere as problematic as the case of the gay serial killers. In that case, the emotions get attached to morally unsuitable objects for the wrong reasons. At least Schindler appears to be the right kind of object for the emotion in question.

On the clarificationist model, moral assessments of narrative artworks can be grounded in the quality of our moral engagement with and experience of the narrative object. This engagement can be positive, where our moral understanding and/or emotions are deepened and clarified, or it can be negative, where the moral understanding is misled, confused, perverted, and so on. Moreover, there are many ways in which moral understanding and feeling can be facilitated. For example, a novel may subvert complacent views, prompting a reorganization that expands our moral understanding, where such an expansion may count as a good-making feature of the work.[26] And, of course, many narrative artworks, perhaps most, engage our moral understanding and emotions without challenging, stretching, or degrading them. Such narrative artworks probably deserve to be assessed positively from the moral point of view, since they do exercise our moral understanding and emotions, but maybe it is best to think of them as morally *good, but without distinction.*

One advantage of grounding our moral assessments of narrative artworks in the quality of our moral engagement with said artworks in comparison with attempts to base our moral assessments on the probable behavioral consequences of reading, hearing, and viewing such narratives is that we have little or no idea about how to determine with any reliability the consequences of such activities for real-world contexts. And if we can't predict the consequences with precision, there seems to be no acceptable method here. But, on the other hand, using ourselves as detectors, we can make reasonable conjectures about how those who share the same cultural backgrounds as we do are apt to understand and be moved by given characters and situations. That is, it is difficult to imagine participants in Western culture who could mistake Iago for noble or Darth Vader for generous.

The clarificationist, then, can deal with those who are suspicious of moral assessments of art on the grounds that such assessments appear to rest on unwarranted presumptions about the behavioral consequences of consuming artworks. For the clarificationist contends that the moral assessment here is keyed to the very process itself of consuming the narrative artwork and not to the supposed behavioral consequences of that process. This is not to deny that the way in which narrative artworks might interact with our moral understanding may have repercussions for behavior. Nor would I reject the possibility that certain narrative artworks might be censored, if (but that is a big *if*) it could be proved that they cause harmful behavior on the part of normal readers, listeners, and viewers systematically. Rather, the clarificationist merely maintains that the moral assessment of narrative artworks continues to be possible, as it always has been, in the absence of any well-confirmed theory about the impact of consuming narratives on behavior.

Moreover, the version of the relation of narrative to moral understanding that I am advancing must be distinguished from the closely related view recently propounded by Frank Palmer.[27] Palmer, following Roger Scruton, maintains that literature, in mobilizing the kind of moral understanding I have been discussing, feeds and strengthens the moral imagination's capacity for knowing what it would be like to be, for example, a Macbeth, and that this exercise of the imagination is thereby linked to practical knowledge. That is, for

Palmer, moral understanding, enriched in this way, has a role in determining what to do. Knowing what it would be like – what it would feel like – to be a Macbeth should figure in our deliberations about doing the kind of things Macbeth does. Indeed, in general, knowing what it would feel like to do *x* is something one should consider before doing *x*. For instance, if as a result of such an exercise of the imagination one thinks that doing *x* would bring about insufferable discomfiture, that should count as a reason for not doing *x*.

But I am skeptical about this link to the behavioral consequences of consuming narrative fictions, because I think that with respect to most narratives, the audience's role is more of the nature of an observer and that the contribution that narratives make to moral understanding has primarily to do with the assessment of third parties rather than with deliberation about action. Palmer's theory seems to me to suggest a reversion to the notion of identification. This is not to say that moral understandings garnered from literature can have no impact on action, but only that the link, where there is one, is less reliable than Palmer seems to believe.[28]

Furthermore, I think that imagining what it would feel like to be a character is not the norm in experiencing fictions. We are more often in the position of onlookers or observers of how the characters feel. Thus, Palmer's theory does not offer a comprehensive picture of the relation of the moral understanding to narrative artworks. At best, it tracks a special case.

Not only can the clarificationist meet the objection that we cannot assess art morally because we lack the wherewithal to gauge the behavioral consequences of art. The clarificationist can also explain how art might have something to *teach,* even though the maxims and concepts it deals in are so often routinely known. For narrative art can educate moral understanding and the emotions by, in general, using what we already believe and feel, mobilizing it, exercising it, sometimes reorienting it, and sometimes enlarging it, rather than primarily by introducing us to interesting, nontrivial, new moral propositions and concepts.[29]

Since I have attempted to ground moral assessments of narrative artworks in what might be broadly construed as a learning model, it may appear that I have walked into the cross hairs of the autonomist's contention that artworks cannot be instruments of moral education, nor have it as their function to promote moral education. However, though I think I have shown how moral learning can issue from commerce with narrative artworks, I have not proposed the reduction of narrative art to an instrumentality of moral education. For the learning that may take place here, though it emerges because of the kind of work a narrative artwork is, need not be the aim of the narrative artwork, but rather a concomitant, one of which the author may take no self-conscious notice. If it is the purpose of the narrative artwork to absorb the audience in it, to draw us into the story, to capture our interest, and to stimulate our imagination, then it is also apparent that by engaging moral judgment and moral emotions, the story may thereby discharge its primary aim or purpose by secondarily stimulating and sometimes deepening the moral understanding of the audience.

It is not the function of a narrative artwork to provide moral education. Typically, the purpose of a narrative artwork is to absorb the reader, viewer, or listener. However, frequently the narrative may bequeath moral learning to the audience while in pursuit of its goal of riveting audience attention and making the audience care about what happens next, by means of enlisting our moral understanding and emotions. That is, what the author explicitly seeks is to engage the audience. And engaging the audience's moral understanding may be a means to this end.

The autonomist is correct in denying that narrative art necessarily serves such ulterior purposes as moral education. Nevertheless, that does not preclude there being moral learning with respect to narrative artworks. For in those cases, which I believe are quite common, moral learning issues, in a nonaccidental way, but rather like fallout or a regularly recurring side reaction, as the author seeks to absorb readers in the narrative by addressing, exercising, and sometimes deepening our moral understanding and emotions. This need not be the author's primary intention, but it happens very often in narratives of human affairs where it is our moral interest in the work and our moral activity in response to the work that keep us interested in the object for its own sake.

In conclusion, I have tried to show why we are naturally inclined to advert to morality when we discuss narrative artworks, and I have also attempted, in the teeth of autonomist objections, to ground the variable moral assessments we make concerning narrative artworks in our experience of the work.[30] Throughout, I have focused on one very important relation between morality and the narrative artwork, specifically on the way in which the narrative artwork unavoidably engages, exercises, and sometimes clarifies and deepens moral understanding and the moral emotions. Indeed, it is my contention that this is the most comprehensive or general relation we can find between art, or at least narrative art, and morality.

Undoubtedly, there may be other relations between art and morality. Some narratives, like the story of the Roman general Regulus, are designed to make virtues, such as honesty, more and more attractive (in a way that might suit Plato's suggestions about the moral education of the young), while other narratives, like "The Pied Piper of Hamelin," are meant to make vices, like dishonesty, seem profoundly ill-advised. However, such overt moral didacticism is not the mark of most narratives, but only of a limited segment, often dedicated to children.

Likewise, some narratives are devoted to extending moral sympathies by inducing some of us to see things from foreign or alien points of view. For example, in *Beloved,* Toni Morrison invites us to understand why a slave mother might prefer to kill her child rather than to have the child grow up in bondage. But though this is an undeniable way in which a narrative might address its audience, it is not a phenomenon operative in all or even most narratives of human affairs, since not all narratives typically possess viewpoints that differ in any appreciable degree from those of their audiences.

Thus, I have stressed the way in which narrative artworks generally, given their nature, unavoidably bring moral understanding into contact with narrative artworks as virtually a condition for comprehending them. I have pursued this line of attack because it seems to me to rest on the most pervasive stratum of the relation of morality to narrative art – though, of course, I would be the first to agree that other strata also welcome further excavation.

Throughout this essay, I have tried to indicate why we are so naturally inclined to considerations of morality when we think about, discuss, and evaluate narrative artworks. I have argued that this disposition is connected to the nature of narrative artworks that concern human affairs. In this respect, I wish to urge that it is not a category error to talk about morality with reference to narrative artworks, given the kinds of things they are. Moreover, contra autonomism, since narrative artworks are designed to enlist moral judgment and understanding, morally assessing such works in light of the quality of the moral experience they afford is appropriate. It is not a matter of going outside the work, but rather of focusing right on it.

Notes

I would like to thank Jerrold Levinson, Alex Neill, Berys Gaut, Sally Banes, Kendall Walton, Stephen Davies, Denis Dutton, Ismay Barwell, William Tolhurst, David Novitz, Ivan Soll, John Brown, John Deigh, David Michael Levin, Peter Lamarque, Gregory Currie, Jim Anderson, Jeff Dean, Richard Kraut, Michael Williams, Meredith Williams, Robert Stecker, and David Bordwell for their comments on earlier versions of this essay. They, of course, are not responsible for the flaws in my argument; I am.

1. See Plato's *Republic,* Books 2, 3, and 10.
2. The founding essay in this line of thought is "Ideology and Ideological State Apparatuses (Notes Towards an Investigation)," by Louis Althusser in his book *Lenin and Philosophy* (London: New Left Books, 1971). This approach has been extremely influential in the humanities and notably still is in film studies. For a critical overview, see Noël Carroll, *Mystifying Movies* (New York: Columbia University Press, 1988).
3. See Herbert Marcuse, *The Aesthetic Dimension: Toward a Critique of Marxist Aesthetics* (Boston: Beacon Press, 1977).
4. See Friedrich Schiller, *On the Aesthetic Education of Man (in a Series of Letters)* (Oxford: Oxford University Press, 1967).
5. See Jean-Paul Sartre, *What Is Literature?* (London: Methuen, 1983).

    Sometimes Martha Nussbaum sounds as though she may be a member of the utopian school, at least with respect to novels. For example, she contends that "the genre itself [the genre of the novel], on account of some general features of its structure, generally constructs empathy and compassion in ways highly relevant to citizenship." At points, Nussbaum qualifies this in various ways – by claiming that she is speaking only of the *realist* novel or by acknowledging that not all novels are *equally* valuable for citizenship. But, at the same time, she is prone to speak of the novel in general, or at least the realist novel, as a form generically conducive to positive moral perception. But clearly to speak this way would require gerrymandering the extension of the class of things to which the concept of the novel (or even realist novel) applies. The novel, at least in the classificatory sense, is not always morally beneficent. There are evil novels. When Nussbaum refers to the genre of the novel, she must be using that notion honorifically, even if she writes as though she is using it descriptively. See Martha Nussbaum, *Poetic Justice: The Literary Imagination and Public Life* (Boston: Beacon Press, 1995), 10.
6. Denis Diderot, in *The Paradox of Acting, and Masks or Faces?* (New York: Hill & Wang, 1957).
7. For a sympathetic account of this approach, see James Spellerberg, "Technology and Ideology in the Cinema," reprinted in *Film Theory and Criticism,* ed. Gerald Mast and Marshall Cohen (New York: Oxford University Press, 1985), 761–75.
8. For an account of why autonomism maintains its grip on the philosoph-

ical imagination, see Noël Carroll, "Beauty and the Genealogy of Art Theory," *Philosophical Forum,* 22, no. 4 (1991): 307–34.

9. This sort of criticism is developed by R. W. Beardsmore in *Art and Morality* (London: Macmillan Press, 1971).

10. Much of the filling-in that audiences do with respect to narratives involves mobilizing the schemas they use in order to navigate everyday life. For example, when encountering a fictional character, we use what some theorists call the *person schema* in order to fill out our under-standing of a character. Thus, Arthur Conan Doyle need not inform us that Sherlock Holmes has only one liver rather than three because, unless informed otherwise, we will use our standing person schema to form our conception of Sherlock Holmes. Our person schema is a default assump-tion, and authors presume that we will use it to fill in their characters, unless notified otherwise by the text. Moreover, insofar as we constantly deploy everyday schemas, like the person schema, to understand narra-tives and fictional characters, the doctrine of autonomists – like the Rus-sian Formalist Boris Tomashevsky – that art, including literature, and life are separate must be false. Most narratives are unintelligible unless the audience accesses everyday person schemas, as well as other sorts of schemas, in order to follow and comprehend narratives of human affairs. The penetration of life into art is, therefore, a necessary condition of nar-rative literature. It is not a category error.

   On person schemas, see Murray Smith, *Engaging Characters: Fiction, Emotion and Cinema* (Oxford: Clarendon Press, 1995), esp. chap. 1.

11. This characterization of melodrama is defended by Flo Leibowitz in "Apt Feelings, or Why 'Women's Films' Aren't Trivial," in *Post-Theory: Reconstructing Film Studies,* ed. David Bordwell and Noël Carroll (Madison: University of Wisconsin Press, 1996), 219–29.

12. One can imagine an avant-garde novel designed to stifle or to derail the reader's propensity to respond to human events morally. However, experiments of this sort are likely to have as part of their purpose reflex-ively calling attention to our typical expectations and, in that respect, would involve drawing attention to our standard, moral response by forcefully deactivating our moral powers and intuitions. But even this subversion of expectations would have our typical moral response as a background, and, in fact, such experiments might be undertaken, as they frequently are, for moral reasons – such as disparaging and/or dislodg-ing the reader's "sentimental bourgeois" tendency to read moralistically.

13. Jean-Jacques Rousseau, *Letter to M. D'Alembert on the Theater,* in *Poli-tics and the Arts,* ed. Allan Bloom (Ithaca, N.Y.: Cornell University Press, 1973).

14. Ibid. 19.

15. This view is defended at greater length in Noël Carroll, *A Philosophy of Mass Art* (New York: Oxford University Press, forthcoming), chap. 5.

16. I would not wish to deny that there is a sense in which one might describe what the audience has learned by means of a general proposi-

tion. Perhaps, one might describe the reaction to *A Raisin in the Sun* in terms of the audience's possession of a new proposition – that African-Americans deserve equal treatment. But I don't think that the audience has simply deduced this from other general propositions that it holds antecedently. That is something it could have done by rote. Rather, audience members come to see that this perhaps already known moral fact is deeply embedded in their structure of moral beliefs. That is, they come to appreciate it in the sense that one appreciates a chess move. They not only acknowledge that it follows from their beliefs in a formal sense, but apprehend its interrelation to other beliefs in a way that also makes those other beliefs more vivid and compelling inasmuch as their relevance is brought home powerfully with reference to a particular case. What goes on might be better described as "re-gestalting."

Phenomenologically, it is not like simply acquiring a new proposition such as "The sum of 47,832 + 91,247 = 139,079." Rather, it is a matter of an abstract proposition falling into place resonating in a larger system of beliefs. Merely describing what happens as the acquisition of a new proposition, even if in some sense this is formally accurate, misses this dimension of the transaction.

Of course, I would not want to deny that *some* narrative artworks convey general moral propositions to audiences of which they were hitherto unaware. Perhaps from *Native Son* readers learned that racism literally brings its own worst nightmares into existence. However, it is my contention that this is not the standard case. In the standard case, the narrative artwork functions more as a vehicle for promoting (or, as we shall see, degrading) moral understanding by activating moral propositions already in our ken.

17. See Neil Cooper, "Understanding," *Aristotelian Society,* suppl. vol. 68 (1984): 1–26.

18. On one view of the morally educative powers of narrative, it is supposed that audiences derive interesting, novel moral propositions from texts and then apply these propositions to the world. I agree that this is not an accurate, comprehensive account, because most of the propositions derivable from narratives are truisms. But this is not the picture of the educative powers of narrative that I advance. I agree that narratives generally play off the moral beliefs and emotions that we already possess and that we already employ in our intercourse with the world. However, in *exercising* these preexisting moral powers in response to texts, the texts may provide opportunities for enhancing our existing moral understanding. Thus, the direction of moral education with respect to narratives is not from the text to the world by way of newly acquired moral propositions. Rather, antecedent moral beliefs about the world may be expanded by commerce with texts that engage our moral understanding. In stressing the world-to-text relation between moral understanding and narratives rather than the text-to-world relation, my position converges on one defended by Peter Lamarque and Stein Haugom Olsen in their *Truth, Fiction and Literature* (Oxford: Clarendon Press, 1994).

19. Charles Larmore, *Patterns of Moral Complexity* (Cambridge University Press, 1987), 21.
20. This view is close to one expounded by Alex Neill. However, in emphasizing fictional narratives as paradigm cases of the grammatical investigation of concepts, I think that Neill makes the consumption of - narratives too philosophical. Readers and viewers may recognize the appropriateness of certain concepts to fictional behaviors and character traits, but that sort of recognition can occur without insight into the formal criteria or grammar of the concepts. Neill's immensely stimulating paper, "Fiction and the Education of Emotion," was read at the 1987 meetings of the American Society of Aesthetics in Kansas City.
21. See Gilbert Ryle, "Jane Austen and the Moralists," *Oxford Review,* no. 1 (1966): 8.
22. Sir Philip Sidney, "An Apology for Poetry," in *Criticism: The Major Texts,* ed. Walter Jackson Bate (New York: Harcourt, Brace, Jovanovich, 1970), 82–106. Immanuel Kant, "Methodology of Pure Practical Reason," in *Critique of Practical Reason* (Indianapolis: Bobbs-Merrill, 1956), 82–106. See also what Kant says about judgment in "On the Common Saying: 'This May Be True in Theory, but It Does Not Apply in Practice,'" in Immanuel Kant, *Political Writings,* ed. Hans Reiss (Cambridge University Press, 1995), 61.
23. Ryle, "Jane Austen and the Moralists," 8.
24. On this view of soap operas, see Noël Carroll, "As the Dial Turns," in *Theorizing the Moving Image* (Cambridge University Press, 1996), 118–24.
25. See, e.g., Martha Nussbaum, "Perceptive Equilibrium: Literary Theory and Ethical Theory," in *Love's Knowledge: Essays on Philosophy and Literature* (New York: Oxford University Press, 1990), 168–94.
26. This sort of value is stressed by numerous authors. It is a view that is important to acknowledge. However, it can be overdone when theorists isolate the subversive power of narrative as *the* morally significant power of art in general or of literature in particular. It is one moral contribution that novels, plays, films, and so on can make to moral understanding. But it is not the only one, since non-morally-subversive narratives can also make a contribution to moral understanding. Overemphasizing the subversive power of certain narratives can suggest a distinction between "literature" and other sorts of narratives, which distinction poses as classificatory but which is ultimately honorific. In this light, such a view may be a subspecies of utopianism. Some theorists who emphasize the morally subversive value of literature include Bernard Harrison, *Inconvenient Fictions: Literature and the Limits of Theory* (New Haven, Conn.: Yale University Press, 1991); R. W. Beardsmore, "Literary Examples and Philosophical Confusion," in *Philosophy and Literature,* ed. A. Phillips Griffiths (Cambridge University Press, 1984), 59–74; John Passmore, *Serious Art* (LaSalle, Ill.: Open Court, 1991); Richard Eldridge, "How Is the Kantian Moral Criticism of Literature Possible?" in *Literature and Ethics,*

ed. Bjorn Tysdahl et al. (Oslo: Norweign Academy of Science and Letters, 1992), 85–98.

27. Frank Palmer, *Literature and Moral Understanding: A Philosophical Essay on Ethics, Aesthetics, Education and Culture* (Oxford: Oxford University Press, 1992).

28. The reservations I have raised concerning Palmer's view may also be relevant to Gregory Currie's account of the moral psychology of fiction, given the emphasis that Currie places on our putative simulation of the situations of characters. I worry about whether simulation isn't identification all over again. Rather than simulating or identifying with characters, I think that our relation to characters is typically that of onlookers or outside observers. Undoubtedly, how the character feels from the inside is relevant to our responses to her, but when she feels sorrow over her misfortune, we typically pity her for the sorrows she palpably feels, and this is not something that *she* does. The object of our emotion is different from the object of her emotion. Moreover, I am also not convinced that simulations à la Currie play much of a role in our moral deliberations, since we are aware that the pertinent scenarios are made up. For exposition of the simulation theory, see Gregory Currie, "The Moral Psychology of Fiction," *Australasian Journal of Philosophy*, 73, no. 2 (1995): 250–9. A simulation theory is also advanced by Susan Feagin in *Reading with Feeling: The Aesthetics of Appreciation* (Ithaca, N.Y.: Cornell University Press, 1996). For further criticism of the simulation view, see Carroll, *A Philosophy of Mass Art*, chap. 5.

29. The caveat "primarily" is meant to allow for the possibility that, in exceptional cases, the kind of reorienting, reorganizing, and re-gestalting that I have been talking about may yield some new nontrivial proposition or concept. This is not, I contend, the general course of events, but I would not wish to argue that it could never happen. However, it is rare enough that it cannot provide the basis for a general theory of fictional narratives and moral understanding. Moreover, it should be stressed that even where there is the acquisition of a new proposition or concept, the fictional narrative itself provides no probative force for the acquired "knowledge," since the fiction is made up. If the proposition is to be justified, it must find warrant in the real world. (The concession that new propositions may be acquired in the process of deepening our moral understanding of fictional narratives is a response to a comment by Jerrold Levinson. But I remain skeptical about his suggestion that the fictional narrative can serve as part of the data base for newly acquired principles and concepts.)

30. In response to my suggestions about the moral assessment of artworks, some autonomists might say that though I have shown how some artworks might be evaluated *morally*, nevertheless this sort of moral assessment is never relevant to the *aesthetic* assessment of artworks. I have tried to deal with this objection in "Moderate Moralism," *British Journal of Aesthetics* 36, no. 3 (1996): 223–37. See also Berys Gaut, Chapter 7, this volume.

6

Realism of character and the value of fiction

GREGORY CURRIE

Imagination is usually contrasted with knowledge, as imaginative literature is contrasted with fact or purported fact. Legitimate distinctions underlie these contrasts: imagination is not knowledge, nor is fiction factual assertion. But don't separate these ideas completely. Imagination might be a source of knowledge; in imagining things, we might thereby come to know (possibly other) things. And if fictions are aids to imagination, they may lead indirectly to knowledge.

Such a claim is likely to get a skeptical response. True, imagination is often cited as a source of recollection; if you want to recall the number of windows in your house, imagine walking around in it, counting them. But that is not an example of imagination resulting in knowledge you didn't previously have.

Some will argue that imagination can never lead to new knowledge: if imagination is to have reliably factual content, it must be content you already know, though you might not know you know it, as you don't know, before the imaginative exercise, that you know how many windows your house has. If we think of imagination as something like an inferential process, it does look as if imagination could at most be knowledge-preserving, rather than knowledge-increasing; if I merely imagine something happening without knowing that it did, and draw conclusions from that, then surely none of the conclusions can count as knowledge, though they might be true.[1]

But imagination is not an inferential process; at least, there is a legitimate and familiar use of "imagination" which refers to something that is not an inferential process. Imagination in this sense is a process of role taking, or empathetic enactment. I will argue that imagination in this sense can lead to knowledge, that it can lead in particular to knowledge of how to act so as to achieve outcomes that are morally better than those you would have achieved without the imaginative exercise. I will argue that this kind of imaginative process is capable of being enhanced by works of fiction.

I start with some remarks on realism in fiction and then give a theory about the nature of imagination. I next claim that imagination has a number of functions, which are connected in complex ways. I describe an important and illuminating bit of psychological evidence for the connection. I then outline what I see as the role of fiction in all this, return briefly to realism, and conclude with responses to some objections.

A REALIST'S PROJECT

No view according to which we can learn from fiction could be true unless some form of realism about fiction were true. To learn is to come to stand in some sort of relation to the real world, and fiction could not be an aid to learning anything unless the worlds of fiction were systematically related to the real world.[2] The idea that there is such a systematic relation is rejected by a great many literary theorists, often on the basis of extremely feeble arguments.[3] But while it is perfectly reasonable to hold that some version or other of realism is true, it is not an easy matter to say which. The details of my own version will emerge later as a natural accompaniment to the picture I shall present of how we learn from fiction; for now I shall merely indicate the form of that realism.

Elsewhere I have argued, against conventionalist accounts, that pictures are characterized partly by relations of likeness that they bear to their subjects.[4] We don't normally mistake pictures of things for the things they represent, but still, the most plausible account of our capacity to recognize what pictures represent involves postulating similarities of visual appearance between the pictures and the things. So I am a realist about pictorial representation, and my realism is a version of the view that pictures and the things they represent are alike. But the ways they are alike are not describable in absolute, observer-independent terms; rather, their likeness consists in the sharing of certain qualities of shape and color sufficient to provoke the same responses within the visual systems of normal human observers in normal conditions. The respect in which pictures and their subjects are alike is to be explained in something like the way we explain the similarity between things that are, say, red.[5] So my realism is what others have called a "response-dependent realism."[6]

The question then arises as to whether there is some comparable version of realism worth defending in relation to other media. Let us take the literary case. Clearly, if literature is like the real world it is not like it in respect of visual appearance. Literary works themselves don't look like anything, and my copy of *Middlemarch,* if we ignore the incidental cover illustration, does not look like its characters and events, nor does it look like any real people and events. But there are ways in which we respond to things that do not depend on their visual appearances. In particular, it might be that works of literary fiction, with their descriptions of fictional characters and their activities, are capable of calling forth from us imaginative responses that are similar to those called forth by our encounters with real people. That is what I will argue for here, and so I shall give support to the view that there is a generic version of realism that, through its appeal to the idea of *calling forth a like response,* enables us to count pictures and mimetic fiction as realistic, without engaging in any equivocation on the meaning of the term "realism."

If works of literature – and of narrative fiction generally – have the capacity to affect us in ways significantly like the ways the world can affect us, then the idea that we can learn from fiction becomes at least very plausible. What my programmatic realism does not say is how this learning comes about. To that I now turn.

PLANS AND VALUES

It is commonly said that fiction engages the imagination. But how, in doing so, can fiction affect our moral (and other value-oriented) perceptions, preferences, and principles? Elsewhere I have argued that we can get moral knowledge from fiction through acts of imagining. Briefly stated, my argument was this. Assume that we are capable of choosing, and changing, our values and that an important part of that process is one of imagining situations in which we pursue the values that are rivals for our attention. If that act of imagining goes well, then it may illuminate those values for us, giving us an indication of the consequences for ourselves and for others of holding those values and pursuing the things to which those values attach. Of course, imaginative projects of this and other kinds do not always go very well. In particular, it is often hard for us to sustain an imaginative exploration of a complex situation. That is where fiction comes in. Fictions can act as aids to the imagination – holding our attention, making a situation vivid for us, and generally drawing us along in the wake of the narrative. If they help us to enter empathically into the lives of the characters, we can come to feel what it is like to be those characters, make their choices, pursue their goals, and reap the rewards and costs of their actions. And by doing all this in imagination rather than by simply trying out values in the real world we avoid the costs of bad choices.

We need not think of this as a process by which we learn *facts* about what is right or good, though a moral realist might see it partly in that way. We might instead see it as a process by which we learn to *behave* in various desirable ways; moral knowledge may be, in part, practical rather than theoretical knowledge. And if it is that kind of knowledge that we get from fiction, then we have an explanation for the seemingly rather embarrassing fact that it is nearly always impossible to state, without descending into triteness, what you learned from a fictional narrative. Just as my inability to offer you a theory of bicycle riding is no objection to the claim that I know how to ride a bicycle, so my inarticulateness in the face of the question "What did you learn from *Middlemarch*?" is no refutation of the claim that I did, indeed, learn something from it.

While I emphasized in my earlier essay that moral choices might involve practical rather than propositional knowledge, the focus on moral choice still encouraged a perhaps too intellectual picture of the moral life. It is easy to think of the moral life as one defined by moral choices, and so in part it is. But seriously considered moral choices are probably quite unusual events in most lives, yet those lives can be good, bad, or morally indifferent. Many, perhaps most, of our moral failures come about not because we choose the bad over the good, but because our choices, whatever they are, are not well planned. The capacity to plan will not guarantee moral responsibility: grossly immoral people can plan their actions with terrifying precision and forethought. But such people are rather exceptional; at least a good deal of regrettable conduct is the upshot of failure to anticipate circumstances, the consequences of actions, the reactions of others. Most of us would be better moral agents if we changed only one thing about ourselves, that is, if we changed from being not very good planners to being better ones.[7]

But the imperative to plan goes beyond the requirement that we plan the route from the present state to a particular desired outcome;

we need to plan for our own cognitive and moral development so as to be better able to plan for desired outcomes. So there is first-, second-, and possibly higher-order planning to be done. Some of that, particularly at levels above the first, involves the formulation of long-term plans. We need, to some degree, to plan our lives. I will argue that imagination is an important aid to planning and that fictions can enhance the planning function of imagination.

Being a good planner does not mean systematically planning everything you do. Some acts owe all or some of their value to their being unplanned: a spontaneous show of affection is probably more valuable than a calculated one.[8] But experience suggests that lives that are to some considerable degree planned and based on a realistic understanding of the likely outcomes of various courses of action, especially in connection with long-term goals like career choice and child raising, go better than lives that are not: better for the agent, and better for those who depend on her. But what is this planning process and what, in particular, has it to do with imagination?

TWO WAYS TO PLAN

Planning might be done in two ways. It might first be done by deploying something like a theory: in planning action, we have some beliefs about what happens under what circumstances, and in particular about how people are likely to react in those circumstances. We then explore a particular course of action by drawing conclusions about its effects, and especially its effects on people's states of mind, including our own, and the effects of these on behavior. We would then compare what are judged to be the likely outcomes according to some preferability rating, itself based on further beliefs we have about what kinds of outcomes we are most likely to find rewarding.

Planning of this kind certainly occurs; think of economic planning. And, as I shall argue further on, much planning of a more personal nature probably does consist partly of such theory-driven activity. But it is hard to believe that all the planning we do, including that of which we are scarcely conscious, is of this kind. Think of the planning we do when we construct our next chess move, settle on the most winning way to ask someone for a date, or decide how to move into the side street against heavy oncoming traffic. For one thing, the inferences involved in these sorts of cases would seem to be extraordinarily complicated, with a vast number of premises and intermediate steps required in order to get to the goal: a decision about what is best to do. That would certainly be the case where, as in my examples, what you decide to do depends on what you reckon someone else will decide to do; and a great deal of morally relevant action is of that kind.[9] For another, the experience of planning – unless one does it in an unnaturally cerebral fashion – does not seem to fit very well with the model. The experience of planning suggests a rather different process: a process involving the imaginative projection of the self into the situation that characterizes one or another candidate strategy. We imagine ourselves undertaking the contemplated action, and we see, in imagination, what the consequences are. Planning by imaginative projection would not be a wholly reliable method of planning. It might be a great deal less reliable than a really scrupulous and comprehensive inferential probing of the various alternatives. But it would probably be quicker, and it might, given limitations of knowledge and inferential power, be the only realistic possibility. But imaginative projection probably works best when undertaken in conjunction with at least a scaffold of theory. You imagine how these events might turn out and then review the imagined outcome, redoing the projection when you realize you need to take into account more or other circumstances.

Imagination might help us to decide what strategy to adopt in solving a problem or attaining a goal, while not helping us at all in carrying out the strategy. It is one thing to know what strategy to adopt; it is another to have the ability to adopt it. If imagination helped us only in deciding what strategies to adopt, the knowledge it gave us could all be counted as propositional knowledge; it would be a matter of knowing that the best strategy in the circumstances is S. Might it also give us the knowing-how of skills and abilities? There is evidence, admittedly somewhat limited, that imagination can improve our abilities. Experimental results suggest that people can improve their performance on various tasks not only by repeatedly carrying out the tasks, but by *imagining* carrying them out.[10] Work in this area has naturally concentrated on the acquisition of skills of which some objective measure can be made, and thus on the acquisition of manual and other bodily performance skills. It is not as easy to establish that imagination helps us to negotiate, say, complex social interactions. My hypothesis, however, is that it does and that the phenomenology of imaginative experience supports this.

If we are planning our actions, and we imagine ourselves acting first this way and then that, there must be some criterion by which to judge the success or failure of the imagined outcomes; otherwise, the imagining could not lead to a decision about what actually to do. In some cases, such as when we are choosing among imagined distinct physical actions on the way to a well-determined and concrete goal, each imagined action will display its own success or failure. For example, the "Tower of Hanoi" problem is a standard task used to assess people's executive functions – something about which I will say more later. You are given a number of vertical rods, some with colored rings stacked on them; the problem is to find the most economical way to move the rings so that they come to be on a given rod in a specified order. A good way to solve the problem is to shift the positions of the rings *in imagination,* seeing thereby whether a given act of shifting contributes effectively to the goal or gets you stuck. If you attend properly to the imagined process, it will be evident what the effect of a given move is. Piecing together a successful solution will then be just a matter of concentration. But what about negotiating a difficult interview, partitioning your time between the demands of philosophy and your stamp collection, or deciding between a life with X and one with Y? How do we tell whether the imagined outcome of some planned strategy is a good one with respect to such problems and goals as these? Here there is not an antecedently identifiable goal; rather, one wants to do *whatever will be for the best,* whatever that turns out to be. There might be a number of ways to solve problems of this kind, but an important one would surely be this: in imagining the outcome, we imagine experiencing that outcome, and in imagining experiencing it, we experience – actually experience, that is – an emotion.[11] We can get some idea about the quality of the outcome from the nature of the emotion. Imagined outcomes that are desirable are responded to, in imagination as in real life, with contentment, happiness, or joy, undesirable ones with frustration, sorrow, anger, jealousy, and the rest. In experiencing these states, we come to learn something about what it would be like really to experience the outcome in question, and thus something about its desirability as a goal.[12]

THREE ROLES FOR IMAGINATIVE PROJECTION

I hope the line I am taking is recognizably an application of Collingwood's model of historical understanding through imaginative reenactment – an idea that has recently been pressed into service to explain how we come routinely to understand the mental processes of those around us.[13] Elsewhere I have argued that there is a further role for such projection.[14] Fiction reading consists of imaginatively projecting yourself into the position of one who is reading a text and gaining from it knowledge of the events it describes. The reader of Conan Doyle "plays the part" of someone who is reading and learning from a factual account of the activities of a detective and his medical companion. On this view, then, apparently quite disparate activities – comprehending other people's motives, planning actions, and reading fiction – tap the same mental capacity.

Whether this view is correct is, of course, a matter for empirical psychology and not for a priori philosophy. Is it correct? The current evidential situation is somewhat confused, but there are some data that seem to me extremely suggestive. They concern people with autism, and the probably closely related condition called Asperger syndrome.[15] Autistic subjects have difficulty understanding, communicating, and socially interacting with other people; even those with high levels of language use find it difficult or impossible to negotiate conversations and other social interchanges in an effective way. Also, one of the earliest signs of childhood autism is a lack of pretend play.[16] This absence of interest in make-believe usually continues in later life, since older people with autism tend to be interested in the rote learning of facts rather than in fictional stories.

These aspects of autism are well known, and for some time researchers have been trying to connect the capacity to understand other minds with a capacity for spontaneous pretend play, on the grounds that people with autism tend to lack both.[17] Much more recently, however, it has been shown that there is another incapacity connected with both autism and Asperger syndrome: executive function deficits.[18] Roughly speaking, this means that people with autism tend to have difficulty in planning effective strategies for action, and in particular in being flexible in problem solving so as to respond effectively to changed circumstances – something probably connected with the well-known and very marked preference of such people for rigid routines and ordered, predictable environments.

Autism is an extremely complex and bewildering condition, and sufferers exhibit a considerable range of incapacities, most of which vary considerably in degree. Yet the three incapacities I have just described, concerning mentalistic understanding, pretend play, and planning, are probably the most consistent symptoms. This conjunction is rather remarkable. It suggests that the capacity to understand the minds of others, to engage in make-believe, and to plan one's actions are closely connected, and that all three rely on something

168

other than general knowledge and intellectual capacity, since we know that autism can be found within the normal range of intelligence and occasionally in the higher range. That is exactly what the theory I have outlined suggests – that these three capacities depend on the operation of a faculty of imaginative projection that is not itself reducible to general reasoning or theoretical knowledge. It is tempting to hazard the guess that autism is, or at least that a primary component of it is, an inability to project oneself imaginatively into the situations of others and into purely hypothetical situations.[19]

FICTION AND LIFE

I have linked three activities as functions of imaginative projection: understanding other minds, planning, and engagement with fiction. I want to note now how closely linked the first two are, for the same act of imaginative projection could serve both functions. I see that Smith is miserable, and I speculate on the cause of his misery. I imagine doing the things I know or guess Smith to have done, and the act of so imagining causes in me feelings akin to those of misery. I now suppose that I understand Smith's misery as the outcome of states produced in him by the things he has done and the events he has experienced as a result. I know, or believe I know, something about his mental life. But I also know or guess something about how I would feel in that situation, for it is by placing myself, in imagination, in that situation that I came to understand his response to it. And if I know, or have a belief about, how I would respond, I am starting to plan, since to plan is to have a view about which actions would have good or desirable outcomes and which would not. So projecting myself into the life of another has, potentially, the double function of telling me about his mental life and about my own possible future course of action; whatever I do, I had better make sure that things don't turn out *that* way for me.

These are two potential functions of imaginative projection. Both of them have a moral significance. In empathizing with others I come to share their mental states, which powerfully reinforces my tendency to take their interests into account. (It may also be that empathy is the *source* of our moral sense, but that is a more controversial proposition.) And the same process makes the actions and outcomes of others guides to my own planning. So two of the three functions of imaginative projection are united not merely by their common etiology, but by their mutually reinforcing contribution to the moral

169

life. What of the third function: imaginative engagement with fiction? Does that also have a role in our moral lives? That it does is an occasionally explicit assumption behind the project of realistic fiction. George Eliot put it very forcefully: "Art is the nearest thing to life, it is a mode of amplifying experience and extending our contact with our fellow-men beyond the bounds of our personal lot."[20]

But the objection to this is well known: what is the value of art, in this case, mimetic literature, if it is merely a substitute for life? Eliot's remark about art extending our experience "beyond the bounds of our personal lot" seems open to the objection that the greater opportunities for travel available to us now, together with global news media, render fiction redundant. What I want to do is offer a defense of Eliot's remark that shows how fiction supplements the moral lessons of experience in a way that *more experience* could not easily do.

I said that imaginative projection into the lives of others can help us to plan our own lives as well as to understand theirs. Unfortunately, such acts of projection are much more likely to be helpful for short-term than for long-term planning. The occasions on which we most naturally have recourse to imaginative projection are those where we are confronted by some current word or deed of another that we need to understand in terms of its mental causes, or where we need to predict what someone will do next. We then project ourselves into the situation of the other as it seems relevant to that explanatory or predictive project. If it is successful, the projection gives us a glimpse of the inner life of another, but it will probably not give us the big picture: the background of personality, habit, and formative experience that helps to constitute the person as he currently is. Having got what we immediately want from the projection we move on to other things. One of the values of realist fiction is the opportunity it gives us to engage in a systematic sampling of the character's life, conveniently revealed to us at crucial junctures by the narration. By living that life, or important moments in it, in imagination, we may learn something about how to see our own lives as connected wholes capable of being structured in a planned way.

We may learn more from imaginative projections if we give conscious, critical attention to their results. Two other features of the fictional scaffolding assist this reflection. One is the fact that the projection takes place, exactly, as part of the relatively disengaged activity of reading fiction. This allows us to dedicate scarce mental resources to the task of reflecting on the result of the projection,

whereas in real life we cannot easily take time off from our obligations as social agents. The other is that a well-made narrative, with
illuminating commentary, may be just the thing to encourage and
guide that reflection. The commentary might not take the form of
explicit statement; it could be a showing rather than a telling. So we
need not think of commentary as the province of a particular kind of
literature. In my sense, it is just whatever there is in the mode of presentation of the fiction that enhances projection.

There is nothing in this account of what fiction provides that could
not, in principle, be provided by something else. Instead of reading
Middlemarch I could imagine the lives of people of my own invention, shaping their characters and fates as closely to my own circumstances as possible. But that would require more creativity than I or
most people happen to possess; good fictions give us, through the talents of their makers, access to imaginings more complex, inventive,
and instructive than we could often hope to make for ourselves. Con-
structing my own imaginings would also require of me a prodigious
capacity to stand aside from my own immediate desires, since a natural tendency is to rig the narrative so as to get from it the lesson we
want to hear. Better on the whole to listen to the narrative of another,
more competent teller of tales. In this way we can think of fictions as
just further examples of endogenously supplied survival mechanisms. Drugs aid the body's natural defenses against disease, clothes
keep us warmer than skin alone could, and fictions aid our natural
capacity to plan our lives.

This might sound like an absurdly didactic theory of fiction; it
would be if it were offered as an account of why we have fiction, or
why we like fiction, or as a complete theory of how fictions are to be
judged. It is none of those things. I don't say that fiction flourishes
because it is an aid to planning. For all I know (or care, for present
purposes), fiction's role as a planning aid has nothing to do with fiction's success. In particular, the reasons that readers are willing to
project themselves imaginatively into the lives of fictional characters
may have nothing to do with desiring to be better planners. The reason we project ourselves into the lives of the characters is most likely
the same reason we project ourselves into the lives of real people:
because we want to learn more about them. Learning to plan is probably no more than a by-product of that. Nor is fiction to be judged
wholly in terms of the degree to which it succeeds as a planning aid;
some of what we focus on by way of aesthetic analysis of the work is
quite unrelated to that function. Still, the capacity of a work to

encourage us to undertake informative projections is probably a strong indicator of aesthetic value in this sense: a work that is valuable as measured by this criterion is likely to be valuable as measured by other important criteria as well. If a work encourages successful projections, that will be because it has various features, and those features are likely to be of the kind we think of as positive indicators of literary value. To encourage a systematic and reflective sequence of projections the work is almost certain to have (i) an arresting and well-constructed narrative, (ii) characters whose inner lives seem worth probing, and (iii) narration that is helpful without being alienating through its intrusion. Such a work will have significant aesthetic value, not because it encourages projection, but because it has features that subserve its capacity to encourage projection.

So far, this characterization of imaginative projection suggests that it must take our preferences and emotional tendencies as fixed, and use fiction simply to guide us in the ways we can satisfy those preferences and tendencies. If that were so, fiction would have no implications for moral change. But fiction can assist moral change. Imaginative projection can help us to value responses that are not naturally our own, by enabling us to experience them in a new and revealing way. Here is an illustration. Throughout most of the narrative of *Persuasion,* Anne Elliot is oppressed by her thoughts of Captain Wentworth and of their previous acquaintance; the thought of him is painful to her, and more painful is any mention of him and certainly any meeting with him. But exactly what is the quality of that feeling or those feelings of oppression? Austen is unspecific, and it is hard to imagine an author whose writing could adequately convey it. But readers may have a quite vivid sense of that feeling of oppression, because they come to feel something like it themselves; projecting themselves into Anne's situation, they come to know something about what (it is fictional that) she feels – something that, if my experience is anything to go by, is remarkably easy, despite the barriers of biology, time, and culture that stand in the way. And in so projecting themselves, readers may come to know something else. They will not only feel Anne's oppression, but feel the lifting of that oppression on those occasions, of which there are many, when her thoughts turn sympathetically, or with ironic humor, to the troubles, real and imagined, of other characters. The reader who, through imaginative projection, feels that oppression lifting comes to know something about the value of good humor, concern for others, and forgetfulness of self.[21]

Earlier I emphasized the extent to which the moral life need not be defined in terms of moral choice. How does that square with my little illustration of the encounter with fiction as a cause of value-change? Surely change of values is *choice* of values, though it need not always be a very conscious and reflective choice. Not so. If we think of fiction as providing us with vicarious experience of values (or, properly speaking, of experience of situations that embody values), we are free to think of the value-change induced by fiction as more closely akin to the changing tastes of the wine connoisseur. You don't choose a preference for certain tastes; you acquire it as a result of exposure to those tastes. Fiction, by exposing us, in imagination, to morally charged experiences, may change our values in the same way.[22]

FICTIONAL REALISM

I said that this discussion of imaginative projection would be keyed to a certain kind of fiction that I called "realistic" and that is often thought of as best exemplified in works like *Middlemarch* (surely a work about the consequences of inadequate imaginative projection). We are now in a position to give a partial characterization of this sort of realism. I shall call it "realism of character." Given what was said earlier about empathy, it follows that one very important way of understanding the minds of others is by imaginatively projecting ourselves into their situations, seeing how we respond to their situations in imagination. To the extent that our own minds are models of theirs,[23] we are then able to understand their thoughts and actions on the basis of our own imagined response. I say that a work possesses realism of character when it enables us to engage in that same kind of empathic understanding with its characters. When we can respond *that way* to its characters, we are responding to fiction as to life.

Is such realism a useful instrument for thinking about literary works? If the test of realism in literature is the work's capacity to call forth from us responses we find in our repertoire of responses to our fellow humans, then few if any works of literature would wholly fail the test of realism; one of the disconcerting things about narrative fiction is the capacity of the most formulaic, unlifelike works to present us with characters we can at least make sense of and in whom we may even invest a certain amount of concern. Does such realism distinguish between anything and anything else?

Yes, but mostly by degrees. Certainly, in the sense of realism I am trying to get at, very little literature could count as *wholly* unrealistic. But in some works, through incompetence or through design, the characters of the fiction do, at least partly, resist our imaginative projections: their responses to situations, their words, and even their thoughts – insofar as the author lets us know what they are – seem not to be those we would have in their situations. In these cases, when we engage with the fiction, trying to guess what will happen, trying to fill in its background of unstated presuppositions and undescribed events, we need to rely more than usually on inferences about such things as the author's intentions or the constraints of form and genre the work conforms to.[24] Such works are unrealistic; at least, they are notably less realistic than some others.

Perhaps my label "realism" is misleading. It applies only to some works in some kinds of arts, so it is not realism about art or literature in general. And it is not an ontological thesis, as realisms commonly are. It says only that there are significant commonalities between experiencing art and experiencing the world of people and other (non-art-world) objects, whatever "experiencing the world of people and objects" turns out to be. If any of a whole range of antirealisms about persons, stars, and physical objects generally turned out to be true, and experiencing these things turned out not to be a confrontation with wholly external, mind-independent entities, my realism about art would not be affected.

But a more realistic realism than mine would not be appropriate, though it is sometimes tempting. We say, unreflectively, that stories are realistic when we think their events and characters have things significantly in common with real events and characters. The trouble is that fictional things, considered in themselves, are as unlike real things as they could possibly be. Taken all in all, Elizabeth Bennet, being the creation of someone's imagination, confined to the pages of a book, is less like any human being than any one human is like any other. The realism of her story can consist in nothing more than its calling from us a response similar in important ways to our responses to real people.[25] That, at any rate, is the only realism I can allow.

THREE OBJECTIONS

There are a number of reasons for being skeptical about this account of the value of fiction and of the nature of realism in fiction. I shall end by very briefly considering three of them. The first we might call the "psychological diversity objection." It says that, as a matter of fact, people are too psychologically diverse for there to be any good reason to think that a character of fiction can be a useful peg on which to hang our own imaginative explorations of value, goals, and strategies. Real people don't resemble each other much, so what reason is there to think that a significant number of them will resemble any fictional character sufficiently to gain much from putting themselves in the character's shoes? (This thought would also constitute an objection to the characterization of realism of character given in the preceding section.) The second objection we might call the "simplification objection." According to this objection, the moral and more generally evaluative issues raised by fiction are usually, and perhaps inevitably, presented in a way that radically simplifies – and thereby ultimately falsifies – our real moral experience of the world. On this view, our responses to literature would count as a very poor guide to our responses to life. The third objection is related to the second and will be called the "unreliability objection." It claims that while fiction may on occasion give rise to true belief about morally responsible action, it is too unreliable to give rise to knowledge. Let us take these objections in turn.

What reason is there to think that we are all significantly alike mentally? Recall my adoption here of the projectivist's view of imagination. On this view, I am able to attribute to others beliefs and desires so as to explain and to predict their behavior, not, or at least not primarily, by employing a folk theory of the mind, but by imaginatively projecting myself into their situations. Roy Sorensen has argued that if projection theory is correct, we may expect agents within a given population to be mentally similar, because being mentally average will confer a selective advantage.[26] The more like others I am, the more reliable will be the process of mental projection I engage in, the more I will be able to work out what others believe and desire, what they believe I believe and desire, and what they desire I believe and desire. That way, I will be better able to cooperate with them when cooperation suits me, and to compete with them when it does not. That way I have a better chance of surviving and breeding. And as people's minds bunch more closely around the average, the pressure to be average increases, because by being average there are more and more people I can successfully simulate. It is certain that we are not wholly alike. But we may be more alike than we are apt to acknowledge.

As for the simplification objection,[27] that literature simplifies, that it abstracts from the complex flow of events that any real life situation would present, that it foregrounds some events and makes others recede – this cannot be denied. This would not be an objection if we adopted the theoretical conception of the imagination outlined in the section of this essay titled "Two Ways to Plan." If to imagine situations is to theorize about them, it would be unambiguously a virtue of literature that it simplified and selected, because that is what effective theorizing requires. But if we think of imagination in projective terms, we cannot so easily accept the essentially simplifying role of literature, because the projective conception asks us, apparently, to think of literature as a kind of substitute for life. The simplification objection says, exactly, that literature is not very much like life at all.

But the advocate of the projective conception should not say that literature is straightforwardly a substitute for life, and therefore something capable of instructing us just to the extent that our experience of it reproduces our experience of life. The projectivist ought to say that literature functions not merely to reproduce the experiences we would have in a real-life situation which mirrored that of the text, but rather to refine that experience. One of the troubles with experience of the world is that it is hard to discriminate finely between things that are objects of a given experience and things that are not. Exactly what was my reaction in that situation a reaction to? It is often difficult to say that it was a reaction to this aspect rather than to that one, or to calculate the degrees to which it was a response to either. Literature, exactly by *not* reproducing the rich confusion of life, offers us idealized scenarios within which we can focus our attention on distinguishable traits and outcomes, seeing how we respond in imagination to them alone, or at least in manageably small combinations. On this view, fictions are moral thought experiments, which, like the idealizing thought experiments of physics and economics, abstract from confusing factors like friction and consumer ignorance. And like those thought experiments, they are instructive to the extent that, in so abstracting, they give results that do not differ dramatically from the results we would get if we took the confusing factors into account. Certainly, not all fictions are instructive in this sense; it is common enough to observe that many fictions, by concentrating exclusively on the value of romantic attachment unconnected with other real-world concerns, distort the satisfactions that romance is likely to provide in any world remotely like our own. The point is that literature may be instructive, not that it must be.

This last point leads naturally to the third objection, that while imaginative engagement with fiction can, on occasion, lead to true belief about how it would be best to act, and to the making of more effective plans for future action, it cannot lead to knowledge. It is notoriously a matter of dispute as to what the difference between mere true belief and knowledge is – or even whether there is a difference.[28] But I will assume that there is one and that the difference has to do with the reliability of the belief-forming process: a widely though certainly not universally held view among epistemologists.[29] Framed in terms of this assumption, the objection would then be that engagement with fiction is too unreliable a process of belief formation to count as knowledge; it may on occasion lead to a true belief about how to achieve a good or valuable outcome, but it is sufficiently likely to lead to a false one to defeat the claim of the true beliefs to be formed by a reliable process. Notice that the interest of this question would to some extent survive the discovery that reliable true belief isn't knowledge. For reliable true belief would still be a significant category, and the question whether projection gave reliable true belief would remain a significant one.

I have said that I am here interested in moral "skills" and "know-how" as much as in propositional knowledge of moral rightness, and it might be thought that this objection has no force as an objection to the claim that fiction can give us moral know-how. But the objection can be restated: if the value of fiction lies in its capacity to enable us to do things, what reason is there to think that the effect of the average fiction on the average reading citizen is an improved capacity for moral action? After all, a change of capacity is desirable only if the exercise of the changed capacity is sufficiently likely to bring about a desirable result. The thought is that fictions simply do not make that sufficiently likely.

How likely "sufficiently likely" would have to be for this pair of arguments to go through is unclear. But let us grant that, taking all the occasions on which engagement with fiction leads to belief about value, the proportion of true beliefs so formed is small enough for the argument about theoretical knowledge to go through. And let us grant, correspondingly, that, taking all the occasions on which engagement with fiction leads to change in morally relevant capacities, the proportion of changes that constitute improvements is small enough for the argument about practical knowledge to go through. But then the projectivist's response should be that she is not claiming that the process of imaginative engagement with fiction is, *on all occasions of use,* a reliable belief-forming process or a reliable improver of moral capacities. Are electron microscopes aids to knowledge? Surely they are. Would you or I, scientifically ignorant, unskilled in the use of the device and unable to interpret its data, get knowledge by using it? Surely not. As a matter of fact, electron microscopes are used almost always by those well able to benefit from them, but the knowledge-enhancing capacity of these instruments would not be diminished if the rest of us suddenly got in on the act. The claim that engagement with fiction can lead to knowledge of value should be treated similarly. It is certainly not the claim that any process of imaginative projection, provoked in any way by any kind of engagement with any work of fiction, will lead to knowledge of whatever kind. A proper specification of the claim would involve appeal to things like the necessity for critical reflection on the nature of the imaginative experience, a familiarity with the genre of the work and its rhetorical resources, as complete and as vivid an understanding of the content of the story presented in the work as could reasonably be expected – together, of course, with the specification that the work itself be of a certain kind, since many works of fiction have little capacity for moral instruction, even in the hands of the most discriminating and sensitive reader. This may sound the most unpromising of promissory notes, but I will not attempt to make it good here. I have sought merely to indicate the direction in which the projectivist would seek an answer to this third objection. Note that, by gesturing in this direction, the projectivist suggests an important role for the critic in deriving morally relevant knowledge from fiction. The successful critic can help us rise to the imaginative occasion of the work, or else alert us to its spurious message.

So along with the moral value of *fiction,* I assert the possibility – and the value – of moral *criticism.* Despite the excellent example of writers like Wayne Booth and John Gardner, moral criticism is not currently fashionable. But the present condition of the critical community will not, I hope, last forever.

Notes

This essay, a companion to my "The Moral Psychology of Fiction," *Australasian Journal of Philosophy* 73 (1995): 250–9, is the product of reflection on two works by psychologists: Nicholas Humphrey, *Consciousness Regained* (Oxford: Oxford University Press, 1983), and Keith Oatley,

Best Laid Schemes (Cambridge University Press, 1992). Thanks to Jerry Levinson for comments on various drafts.

1. See Paul Taylor, "Imagination and Information," *Philosophy and Phenomenological Research* 42 (1981): 205–23.
2. That there literally are worlds of fiction is something I dispute, but for present purposes it will have to do as a shorthand; see my *The Nature of Fiction* (Cambridge University Press, 1990), chap. 2.
3. For a healthy response to such arguments see, e.g., Robert Alter, "Character and the Connection with Reality," in his *The Pleasure of Reading* (New York: Simon & Schuster, 1989), 49–76.
4. See my *Image and Mind* (Cambridge University Press, 1995), chap. 3.
5. See, e.g., John McDowell, "Values and Secondary Qualities," in *Morality and Objectivity,* ed. Ted Honderich (London: Routledge, 1985), 110–29.
6. See, e.g., Philip Pettit, "Realism and Response Dependence," *Mind* 100 (1991): 587–623.
7. This is not to deny that there are other ways we could improve morally.
8. As Mark Johnston emphasizes in his "Dispositional Theories of Value," *Proceedings of the Aristotelian Society,* suppl. vol. 62 (1989): 139–74.
9. A telling example of this is given by Adam Morton, who examines the difficulties of explaining, by appeal to knowledge of theory, how it is that we make the decisions we do make in playing a simple game where our next move depends on an assessment of the other player's likely subsequent moves ("Game Theory and Knowledge by Simulation," in *Mental Simulation,* ed. M. Davies and T. Stone [Oxford: Basil Blackwell, 1995], 235–46).
10. For elaboration of a theory about how this occurs and for references to the experimental literature, see Gregory Currie and Ian Ravenscroft, "Mental Simulation and Motor Imagery," *Philosophy of Science* (forthcoming).
11. Here I am particularly indebted to Keith Oatley's *Best Laid Schemes.* But I do not go all the way with Oatley in his attempt to define emotions by linking them with plans.
12. Are the emotions experienced in imagination themselves real emotions? I think this is a purely verbal question. See my "The Paradox of Caring: Fiction and the Philosophy of Mind," in *Emotion and the Arts,* ed. Mette Hjort and Sue Lavers (Oxford: Oxford University Press, 1997).
13. See R. G. Collingwood, *The Idea of History* (Oxford: Oxford University Press, 1946). For more recent developments see the essays in two volumes edited by Martin Davies and Tony Stone, *Folk Psychology and Mental Simulation* (Oxford: Basil Blackwell, 1995). My "Imagination and Simulation" in the second of these two volumes explores other connections between imaginative projection and the aesthetic.
14. See my "Paradox of Caring."
15. A useful introduction to autism is Uta Frith, *Autism: Explaining the Enigma* (Oxford: Basil Blackwell, 1989), though I strongly dispute her theoretical conclusions. Frith has also edited a collection of essays, *Autism and Asperger Syndrome* (Cambridge University Press, 1991).

16. See S. Baron-Cohen, J. Allen, and C. Gillberg, "Can Autism Be Detected at 18 Months? The Needle, the Haystack and the CHAT," *British Journal of Psychiatry* (forthcoming).

17. The work of Alan Leslie has been particularly influential in this area. See, e.g., his "Pretence and Representation: The Origins of 'Theory of Mind,'" *Psychological Review* 94 (1991): 412–26. For criticism, see my "Imagination and Simulation."

18. S. Ozonoff, B. Pennington, and S. Rogers, "Executive Function Deficits in High-Functioning Autistic Children: Relationship to Theory of Mind," *Journal of Child Psychology and Psychotherapy* 32 (1991): 1081–1106, and idem, "Asperger's Syndrome: Evidence for an Empirical Distinction from High Functioning Autism," *Journal of Child Psychology and Psychotherapy* 23 (1991): 704–7. See also Paul Harris, "Pretending and Planning," in *Understanding Other Minds,* ed. S. Baron-Cohen, H. Tager-Flusberg, and D. J. Cohen (Oxford: Oxford University Press, 1993), 228–46.

19. See my "Simulation Theory, Theory Theory and the Evidence from Autism," in *Theories of Theories of Mind,* ed. Peter Carruthers and Peter K. Smith (Cambridge University Press, 1996), 242–56.

20. From an essay of 1856. Quoted in Oatley, *Best Laid Schemes,* 257.

21. Kendall Walton emphasizes the role that fiction can play in teaching us about how others feel and about how we would feel in other circumstances. See his "Make-Believe and Its Role in Pictorial Representation and the Acquisition of Knowledge," *Philosophical Exchange* 23 (1992): 81–95.

22. The analogy is in some ways not very apt, since we need not think of a connoisseur of morals as indulging himself.

23. To what extent are our own minds models for those of others? I take this question up in the next section.

24. I hold that one of the most important effects of genre is to signal points at which we are to understand the characters' motives and actions in ways other than by empathy. See my "The Metaphysics of Genre" (in preparation).

25. "Important ways" is a significant qualification; our response to fiction is not in all ways similar to the responses we do or would make to real life. See my "Paradox of Caring."

26. Roy Sorensen, "Self-Strengthening Empathy," *Philosophy and Phenomenological Research* (forthcoming). Sorensen has interesting things to say about why we are not wholly similar mentally.

27. Clear versions of this argument are hard to find in the critical literature, but it appears to stand behind certain kinds of skepticism about the value of art. Something like it seems to be implicit in some remarks toward the end of Peter Lamarque and Stein Haugom Olsen's *Truth, Fiction and Literature* (Oxford: Clarendon Press, 1994). Denying that art has a "learning effect," they claim that literary works are organized around

concepts like "freedom of the will" and "determinism" and that "[t]here is no similar order in the real world" (454–5).

28. Crispin Sartwell argues there is no difference. See his "Why Knowledge Is Merely True Belief," *Journal of Philosophy* 89 (1992): 167–80.

29. See, e.g., Alvin Goldman, *Epistemology and Cognition* (Cambridge, Mass.: Harvard University Press, 1986).

The ethical criticism of art

BERYS GAUT

This essay argues that the ethical criticism of art is a proper and legitimate aesthetic activity. More precisely, it defends a view I term *ethicism*. Ethicism is the thesis that the ethical assessment of attitudes manifested by works of art is a legitimate aspect of the aesthetic evaluation of those works, such that, if a work manifests ethically reprehensible attitudes, it is to that extent aesthetically defective, and if a work manifests ethically commendable attitudes, it is to that extent aesthetically meritorious.

This thesis needs elucidation. The ethicist principle is a pro tanto one: it holds that a work is aesthetically meritorious (or defective) *insofar as* it manifests ethically admirable (or reprehensible) attitudes. (The claim could also be put like this: manifesting ethically admirable attitudes *counts toward* the aesthetic merit of a work, and manifesting ethically reprehensible attitudes *counts against* its aesthetic merit.) The ethicist does not hold that manifesting ethically commendable attitudes is a necessary condition for a work to be aesthetically good: there can be good, even great, works of art that are ethically flawed. Examples include Wagner's Ring Cycle, which is marred by the anti-Semitism displayed in the portrayal of the *Nibelungen;* some of T. S. Eliot's poems, such as *Sweeney among the Nightingales,* which are similarly tainted by anti-Semitism; and Leni Riefenstahl's striking propaganda film, *The Triumph of the Will,* deeply flawed by its craven adulation of Hitler. Nor does the ethicist thesis hold that manifesting ethically good attitudes is a sufficient condition for a work to be aesthetically good: there are works such as

The ethical criticism of art

Harriet Beecher Stowe's *Uncle Tom's Cabin* which, though the ethical attitudes they display are admirable, are in many ways uninspired and disappointing. The ethicist can deny these necessity and sufficiency claims, because she holds that there are a plurality of aesthetic values, of which the ethical values of artworks are but a single kind.[1] So, for instance, a work of art may be judged to be aesthetically good *insofar as* it is beautiful, is formally unified and strongly expressive, but aesthetically bad *insofar as* it trivializes the issues with which it deals and manifests ethically reprehensible attitudes. We then need to make an *all-things-considered* judgment, balancing these aesthetic merits and demerits one against another to determine whether the work is, all things considered, good. And we should not suppose that there is any mechanically applicable weighing method that could determine the truth of such a judgment: overall judgments are plausibly ones that resist any form of codification in terms of mechanically applicable principles. These kinds of pro tanto and all-things-considered judgments are common in other evaluative domains, notably the moral domain.[2]

The notion of the aesthetic adopted here should be construed broadly. In the narrow sense of the term, aesthetic value properties are those that ground a certain kind of sensory or contemplative pleasure or displeasure. In this sense, beauty, elegance, gracefulness, and their contraries are aesthetic value properties. However, the sense adopted here is broader: I mean by "aesthetic value" the value of an object *qua* work of art, that is, its artistic value. This broader sense is required, since not all of the values of an object *qua* work of art are narrowly aesthetic. Besides a work's beauty, we may, for instance, aesthetically admire it for its cognitive insight (subject, as we shall see, to certain conditions), its articulated expression of joy, the fact that it is deeply moving, and so on. However, this broader sense of "aesthetic" does not mean that just any property of a work of art counts as aesthetic. Works of art have many other sorts of value properties that are not values of them *qua* works of art: they can have investment value, value as status symbols, and so forth.[3]

The notion of manifesting an attitude should be construed in terms of a work's displaying pro or con attitudes toward some state of affairs or things, which the work may do in many ways besides explicitly stating an opinion about them.[4] (Such attitudes can run the gamut from unmixed approval through neutrality to unmixed disapproval, and also include various complex and nuanced attitudes that display both approbatory and disapprobatory aspects, such as those

183

revealed in jealous or conflicted attitudes.) What is relevant for ethicism are the attitudes *really* possessed by a work, not those it merely claims to possess; so the attitudes manifested may be correctly attributable only by subtle and informed critical judgment. A novel may state that it condemns the sexual activities it describes, but from the subtly lubricious and prying manner in which it dwells on them, it may be correct to attribute to it an attitude of titillation, not of moralistic disgust. Just as we can distinguish between the attitudes people really have and those they merely claim to have by looking at their behavior, so we can distinguish between real and claimed attitudes of works by looking at the detailed manner in which events are presented.

Ethicism does not entail the causal thesis that good art ethically improves people.[5] Since the ethicist principle is a pro tanto one, it allows for the existence of great but ethically flawed works; and even if all aesthetically good works were ethically sound, it would not follow that they improve people, any more than it follows that earnest ethical advice improves people, for they may be unmoved by even the most heartfelt exhortation. Much of the ethical discussion about art, particularly concerning the supposedly pernicious effects of some popular films and music genres, has been concerned with the question of whether such art morally corrupts. This is a version of the causal thesis and should be kept distinct from ethicism. Further, ethicism has nothing to say about the issue of censorship, nor does it give any grounds of support to either the friends or foes of artistic censorship. All that follows from ethicism is that if a work manifests morally bad attitudes it is to that extent aesthetically flawed, flawed as a work of art. The fact that a work of art is aesthetically flawed is not grounds for its censorship: if it were, the art museums of the world would suffer serious depletion.

OBJECTIONS TO ETHICISM

1. Ethicism fails to distinguish sharply enough between ethical and aesthetic evaluation. There is an aesthetic attitude in terms of which we aesthetically evaluate works; this aesthetic attitude is distinct from the ethical attitude we may adopt toward works; and ethical assessment is never a concern of the aesthetic attitude. So the ethical criticism of works is irrelevant to their aesthetic value.

The existence of the aesthetic attitude has, of course, been much disputed.[6] But, even if we accept its existence, its adoption is compatible with ethicism. To see why, we need to specify in more detail what the aesthetic attitude is. There are two basic ways of doing this: the aesthetic attitude may be individuated by some feature intrinsic to it or by its formal objects.

Consider the case in which the attitude is individuated by its formal objects: these may be understood in narrow aesthetic fashion, as beauty and its subspecies, such as grace and elegance, or characterized more broadly by the criteria to which formalists appeal, such as Beardsley's unity, complexity, and intensity.[7] Since the presence of these properties arguably does not require, or suffice for, the presence of ethical properties, it may be held that ethical assessment is irrelevant to aesthetic evaluation.[8] Yet this objection is unconvincing, for the list of properties deployed is too narrow to embrace all those of aesthetic relevance. In the assessment of art, appeal is made to such properties as raw expressive power and deep cognitive insight as well as to beauty, elegance, and grace; and the relevance of these expressive and cognitive values explains how there can be great works, such as *Les Desmoiselles d'Avignon,* that are militantly ugly. So the narrow aesthetic view fails. In more sophisticated fashion, the formalist appeals to purely intrinsic properties of works as aesthetically relevant, an appeal motivated by a conception of the work of art as autonomous from its context. But that conception is flawed, for a work can be fully interpreted only by situating it within its generative context.[9] There is reason, then, to spurn the restricted diet of aesthetically relevant properties offered by the narrow aesthetic and formalist views, and as yet no reason to exclude ethical properties from a heartier menu.

The alternative is to individuate the aesthetic attitude by some feature intrinsic to it, and for the opponent of ethicism the most promising feature is the detachment or disengagement we purportedly display toward fictional events. Since it is logically impossible to intervene in such events, the will is detached, practical concerns are quiescent, an attitude of contemplation is adopted. Given the practical character of morality, it follows that ethical assessment plays no role in aesthetic attitude and therefore no role in aesthetic evaluation. But the step from the claim that the will is disengaged and therefore that ethical assessment has no role to play does not follow: there is similarly no possibility of altering historical events, and we are in this sense forced to have a detached or contemplative attitude toward them, but we still ethically assess historical characters and actions. If it is objected that we are ethically engaged in history because we hope to draw from it lessons for our current practice, the same may be said of the lessons we can draw from fiction, such as the psychological insights that Freud discovered there.

The point about ethics and the will deserves elaboration, for it will be relevant to the position defended later. On what might be termed the *purely practical* conception of ethics, the ethical assessment of a person's character is determined only by what he does and by the motives that determine his actions. Any feelings or thoughts that play no role in motivating actions are ethically irrelevant: thoughts, fantasies, and desires, however gruesome, inappropriate, or corrupt we would judge the actions they motivate to be, are not themselves ethically bad, unless they issue in actions that express these feelings and thoughts. So a person may be ethically good while having these feelings and thoughts, and his goodness may consist partly in his capacity to resist their influence on the will, for these feelings and thoughts may have arisen purely passively in him, and he is not to be held responsible for their occurrence.[10] This view, as has just been noted, speedily runs into problems in historical cases where the will cannot be engaged, yet where ethical assessment is still appropriate. But it can be shown to be flawed on other grounds too. Much of our ethical assessment is directed at what people feel, even though these feelings do not motivate their actions. Suppose that Joe is praised for some deserved achievement by his friends, but he later discovers that they are secretly deeply jealous and resentful of him. Their feelings have not motivated their actions, yet we would properly regard these people as less ethically good were we to discover this about them. They are flawed because of what they feel, not because of what they did or their motives for doing it. Also, that people feel deep sympathy for us, even though they are completely unable to help us in our distress, is something that we care about and that properly makes us think better of them. In fact, much of our vocabulary of ethical assessment is directed wholly or in part at the assessment of feelings: we criticize people for being crude, insensitive, callous, or uncaring; we praise them for being warm, friendly, and sensitive. So for the ethical assessment of character an *affective-practical* conception of assessment is correct, a conception which holds that not just actions and motives, but also feelings that do not motivate, are ethically significant. Virtue of character is "concerned with feelings and actions," as Aristotle correctly observes.[11] Such an affective-practical conception of ethical assessment allows the ethical assessment of the feelings that people have when they respond to fictions, even though they cannot act toward the fictional events described.

2. A more radical objection holds that ethical assessment has no place in the assessment of art. Works of art can at best manifest attitudes toward those fictional characters and situations they describe, and such attitudes are not ethically assessable, since they are directed toward merely imagined objects – such objects cannot be harmed or hurt in reality, for they do not exist. What is ethically assessable, in contrast, are attitudes directed toward real characters and situations, but works of art do not manifest attitudes toward such things, for they do not describe them. Hence, there is no place left for the ethical assessment of art.

Even at first blush, the objection is hyperbolic, since not all works of art are fictions: Riefenstahl's film is a documentary of the 1934 Nuremberg rally, and Hitler was not a fictional character. So, at best, the argument would apply only to a subclass of works of art. Second, attitudes directed toward only imagined states of affairs can in fact properly be ethically assessed. Consider a man whose sexual life consists entirely of rape fantasies, fantasies he has not about women he sees in real life, but about women he only imagines. Would we say that there is nothing to be said from an ethical point of view about the attitude he manifests in his imaginings about these fictional women? Clearly, what a person imagines and how he responds to those imaginings play an important part in the ethical assessment of his character. The mere fact that the women he imagines cannot be harmed does not bracket his inner life from ethical assessment, since what is at issue are the attitudes he manifests in his fantasy life. And nothing in our judgment about him requires us to assume that what is bad about his fantasies is that he may act on them – perhaps he is confined to prison for life. He stands ethically condemned for what and how he imagines, independently of how he acts or may act. (Here again, we return to the ethical importance of feelings, but see now that feelings toward merely imagined people can be ethically relevant too.) Further, the attitudes people (and works) manifest toward imagined scenarios have implications for their attitudes toward their real-life counterparts, for the attitudes are partly directed toward kinds, not just individuals.[12] When the rape fantasist imagines his fictional women, he is imagining them *as women,* that is, as beings of a kind that also has instances in the real world; and that he imagines them as women is, of course, essential to his imaginative project. Thus, by virtue of adopting such an attitude toward his imagined women, he implicitly adopts that attitude toward their real-life counterparts – and so reveals something of his attitude toward real-life women. Indeed, it is inevitable that, however apparently exotic the fictional world, the kinds shared between it and the real world will be vast, given the limits on the human imagination, the interests we have in fiction (which include exploring possibilities that reorder the actual world), and interpretive constraints, which involve drawing on background information about the real world in the interpretation of fictions. So the attitudes manifested toward fictional entities will have many implications for attitudes manifested toward real entities.

3. Ethical assessment is relevant to a work's aesthetic merit, but ethicism gives the connection the wrong valence: works can be good precisely *because* they violate our sense of moral rectitude. Often the most fascinating characters in works are the evil ones, such as Satan in *Paradise Lost.* And recall the passage in *King Lear* in which blind Gloucester asks Lear, "Dost thou know me?" and Lear replies, "I remember thine eyes well enough. Dost thou squiny at me? / No, do thy worst, blind Cupid, I'll not love." As Lawrence Hyman writes, "The dramatic effect requires our moral disapproval," but Shakespeare manages to "transfigure that moral shock into aesthetic pleasure."[13]

It is important to distinguish between the evil or insensitive characters represented by a work and the attitude the work displays toward those characters. Only the latter is relevant to the ethicist thesis. Satan is indeed fascinating because evil, but the work represents him as such, showing the seductive power of evil, and does not approve of his actions. Milton was not a Satanist. And while the power of Lear's bad joke does rest on its hearty heartlessness, it is part of the point of *Lear* that the flamboyant insensitivity displayed by Lear in his derangement is of a piece with the gross egoism that leads to disaster, an egoism overcome only by grief and loss, and transmuted into a finer moral wisdom. Lear's attitude toward Gloucester is represented by the play, but not shared by it. It is true that some works, such as de Sade's *Juliette,* not merely represent evil, but also manifest approval toward that evil. If this work has indeed any serious aesthetic merit, it can in part be traced to the literary skill with which it represents the attitude of finding sexual torture erotically attractive; yet the ethicist can consistently and plausibly maintain that the novel's own espousal of this attitude is an aesthetic defect in it.

It may be objected that the novel's approbatory attitude toward evil is a reason why it is aesthetically good: evil arouses our curiosity, for the evil person may do and experience things we can scarcely imagine, let alone understand; and the novel's ability to satisfy this curiosity, to show us what it is like to engage in such actions, is a prime source of its aesthetic merit. Yet from the fact that we are fascinated by the attitudes manifested, we cannot conclude that our interest in them is aesthetic: our fascination with Adolf Hitler or Jeffrey Dahmer is not an aesthetic one, and our interest in de Sade's work may similarly stem from a curiosity about psychopathic states of mind. Suppose, however, that our interest in *Juliette* is aesthetic, perhaps because of the way that interest is inflected by a concern with the work's stylistic and rhetorical system. This still does not undermine ethicism. For our interest here is in being able to imagine what it is like to have evil attitudes, and so in coming to understand them, and this is satisfied by the vivid *representation* of an evil attitude. But, again, representation of an attitude by a work does not require the work itself to share that attitude: works may manifest disapproval toward characters or narrators who are represented as evil. Moreover, if, as the objection holds, it is our curiosity that is aroused, we have a cognitive interest in not seeing evil approved of, for such approval implies that there is something good about an attitude we know to be bad.

SOME ARGUMENTS FOR ETHICISM

There are, of course, further objections and elaborations open to the opponent of ethicism, some of which will be touched on later, but enough has been said to give rational hope that they may be laid to rest. The question remains as to why ethicism should be endorsed. Part of the answer is to be sought in its congruence with our considered aesthetic judgments; we do decry works for their insensitivity, their moral crudity, their lack of integrity, their celebration of cruelty, their slimy salaciousness. But it is the mark of an interesting philosophical thesis that, while some find it obviously true, others find it obviously false; and ethicism is, fortunately and unfortunately, an interesting philosophical thesis. So it would be good to have an argument for its truth.

1. George Dickie has advanced a simple argument for the truth of ethicism. A work of art's moral vision is an (essential) part of that work; any statement about an (essential) part of a work of art is an

aesthetic statement about that work; so a statement about a work of art's moral vision is an aesthetic statement about the work.[14]

However, it is not true that any statement about an essential part of a work is an aesthetic statement about it. For instance, it is essential to a poem that it be composed of the particular words that comprise it. So it is essential to it that it have in it the particular letters that it has. So, if it is true of a particular poem that it has in it exactly as many letter *e*'s as it has letter *c*'s, then that is an essential feature of the poem. But that is not an *aesthetic* statement about the work, since it standardly plays no role in our appreciation of it.[15] Likewise, consider a statue carved in limestone. It is essential to its being the particular statue which it is that it be composed of the crushed shells of ancient sea creatures. But whereas the statue's texture and color are generally relevant to its aesthetic merits, the mere fact that it is composed of crushed shells is not. For, again, this fact standardly plays no role in our appreciation of it as a work of art. So a premise on which Dickie's argument rests is false.

2. Perhaps the most influential opponents of ethicism have been formalists.[16] However, David Pole not only has argued that ethicism is compatible with formalism, but has tried to derive ethicism from it. He holds that the immorality of a work is a formal defect in it, since it is a type of internal incoherence. For if a work of art presents a morally bad view, it will do so by distorting or glossing over something it presents. But then something is lacking within the work itself and so "some particular aspect [of the work] must jar with what – on the strength of the rest – we claim a right to demand." This jarring is an internal incoherence in the work and thus a defect that the formalist would acknowledge as such.[17]

If a work is morally corrupt, it follows that it distorts something and so jars with a truth about the world, but it does not follow that it has to jar with anything else in the work, for the work may be systematically immoral. *The Triumph of the Will,* for instance, is held together thematically by its offensive celebration of Nazism. So Pole's formalist derivation of ethicism fails.[18]

3. An approach glanced at by Hume and elaborated by Wayne Booth holds that literary assessment is akin to an act of befriending, for one assesses the implied author of a work as a suitable friend. A good friend may possess a variety of merits (being intelligent, good company, lively, etc.), and some of these are ethical: she is trustworthy, sensitive, kind, and so on. So assessing someone as a friend involves among other things assessing her ethical character, a char-

acter displayed in the case of the implied author in the literary work in which she is manifested.[19]

The approach has its merits, and captures the pro tanto structure of ethicism well, but it is ill-equipped to cope with some Hollywood films whose impersonality and industrial-style production may give the audience little sense of an implied author or authors, but whose ethical stance may elicit their aesthetic condemnation. And the approach also runs afoul of one of the objections considered earlier; for the implied author is a fictional construct, albeit one implicit in, rather than described by, the text. If fictional characters, such as Satan and Lear, can be interesting because of their moral failings, the corrupt fictional character of an author can similarly be interesting, and the aesthetic merit of her work be accordingly enhanced. Appeal to the characters of fictional beings will not ground ethicism.

4. More promising is an argument that may be extrapolated from views defended by Richard Eldridge and Martha Nussbaum. For Eldridge a person's moral self-understanding cannot completely be captured by general theories, but must be developed and sustained by an awareness of the relation of her story to the stories of others, an awareness that literature is peculiarly well placed to articulate and extend: "all we can do is to attempt to find ourselves in cases, in narratives of the development of persons."[20] For Nussbaum, too, morality is a matter of the appreciation of particular cases, and literature can refine our awareness of moral particularities in a way that eludes the flailing grasp of philosophy: "To show forth the force and truth of the Aristotelian claim that 'the decision rests with perception,' we need, then – either side by side with a philosophical 'outline' or inside it – texts which display to us the complexity, the indeterminacy, the sheer *difficulty* of moral choice."[21] This conception of literature as moral philosophy naturally suggests a cognitivist argument for ethicism: it is an aesthetic merit in a work that it gives insight into some state of affairs, and literature can yield insights into moral reality of a depth and precision that no other cultural form is well placed to match; so the moral insights delivered by literary works enhance their aesthetic worth.

There is much here that should be retained and accounted for in any successful defense of ethicism, and an attempt will be made to do so in what follows. Yet the argument rests on a radically particularist account of morality, which denies the existence of any general and informative moral principles. If that view be denied, as I believe it should,[22] the idea of literature as the culmination of moral philos-

191

ophy is rendered less compelling. And even if the claims of literature were rendered more modest, we would still require an explanation of why the insights literature can provide are aesthetically relevant. Works of art can be interesting and informative as social documents, but the fact that much can be learned from them about the attitudes and circumstances of their time does not ipso facto make them aesthetically better: one can learn much about Victorian agricultural politics from *Tess,* and on the subject of nineteenth-century whaling practices *Moby-Dick* is excruciatingly informative. Likewise, old photographs and films can have great value as documentary sources of their times, but these cognitive merits do not thereby improve these objects *qua* works of art. So the cognitivist approach must be supplemented in order to give an account of the conditions under which cognitive merits are aesthetically relevant.[23]

THE MERITED-RESPONSE ARGUMENT

Ethicism is a thesis about a work's manifestation of certain attitudes, but in what does this manifestation of attitudes consist? It is obvious that works prescribe the imagining of certain events: a horror film may prescribe imagining teenagers being assaulted by a monster; *Juliette* prescribes imagining that acts of sexual torture occur. Perhaps less obviously, works also prescribe certain responses to these fictional events: the loud, atonal music of the horror film prescribes us to react to the represented events with fear, *Juliette* invites the reader to find sexual torture erotically attractive, to be aroused by it, to be amused by the contortions described, to admire the intricacy of their implementation, and so forth.[24] The approbatory attitude that *Juliette* exhibits toward sexual torture, then, is manifested in the responses it prescribes its readers to have toward such torture. The attitudes of works are manifested in the responses they prescribe to their audiences.

It is important to construe this claim correctly to avoid an objection. Consider a novel that prescribes its readers to be amused at a character's undeserved suffering but that does so in order to show up the ease with which the reader can be seduced into callous responses. Then one response (amusement) is prescribed, but a very different attitude is manifested by the work (disapproval of the ease with which we can be morally seduced); hence, the manifestation of attitudes is wholly distinct from and independent of the prescription of responses. What this objection reveals is that prescriptions, like attitudes, come in a hierarchy, with higher-order prescriptions taking lower-order ones as their objects. Thus, my amusement at the character's suffering is prescribed, but there is a higher-order prescription that this amusement itself be regarded as callous and therefore as unmerited. So the complete set of prescriptions that a work makes must be examined in order to discover what attitudes it manifests: taking individual prescriptions out of context may mislead us about the work's attitudes. Here, as elsewhere, the application of the ethicist principle requires a grasp of interpretive subtleties and contextual factors. Talk of prescriptions from now on should be construed as involving the complete set of relevant prescriptions that a work makes toward fictional events.

The claim that works prescribe certain responses to the events described is widely applicable. *Jane Eyre,* for instance, prescribes the imagining of the course of a love affair between Jane and Rochester, and also prescribes us to admire Jane's fortitude, to want things to turn out well for her, to be moved by her plight, to be attracted to this relationship as an ideal of love, and so forth. Similar remarks apply to paintings, films, and other representational arts. Music without a text is also subject to ethical criticism if we can properly ascribe to the music a presented situation and a prescribed response to it. If Shostakovich's symphonies are a musical protest against the Stalinist regime, we can ethically assess them.

The notion of a response is to be understood broadly, covering a wide range of states directed at represented events and characters, including being pleased at something, feeling an emotion toward it, being amused about it, and desiring something with respect to it – wanting it to continue or stop, wanting to know what happens next. Such states are characteristically affective, some essentially so, such as pleasure and the emotions, while in the case of others, such as desires, there is no necessity that they be felt, although they generally are.

The responses are not simply imagined: we are prescribed by *Juliette* actually to find erotically attractive the fictional events, to be amused by them, to enjoy them, to admire this kind of activity. So the novel does not just present imagined events, it also presents a point of view on them, a perspective constituted in part by actual feelings, emotions, and desires that the reader is prescribed to have toward the merely imagined events. Given that the notion of a response covers such things as enjoyment and amusement, it is evident that some kinds of response are actual, not just imagined. Some philosophers have denied that we feel actual emotions toward fictional events, but there are, I believe, good reasons for holding this to be possible.[25]

Though a work may prescribe a response, it does not follow that it succeeds in making this response merited: horror fictions may be unfrightening, comedies unamusing, thrillers unthrilling. This is not just to say that fear, amusement, and thrills are not produced in the audience; for people may respond in a way that is inappropriate. Rather, the question is whether the prescribed response is merited, whether it is appropriate or inappropriate to respond in the way the work prescribes. If I am afraid of a harmless victim in a horror movie because of her passing resemblance to an old tormentor of mine, my fear is inappropriate. And my admiration for a character in a novel can be criticized for being based on a misunderstanding of what he did in the story. So prescribed responses are subject to evaluative criteria.

Some of these criteria are ethical ones. As noted earlier, responses outside the context of art are subject to ethical evaluation. I can criticize someone for taking pleasure in others' pain, for being amused by sadistic cruelty, for being angry at someone when she has done no wrong, for desiring the bad. The same is true when responses are directed at fictional events, for these responses are actual, not just imagined ones. If we actually enjoy or are amused by some exhibition of sadistic cruelty in a novel, that shows us in a bad light, reflects ill on our ethical character, and we can properly be criticized for responding in this fashion.

If a work prescribes a response that is unmerited, it has failed in an aim internal to it, and that is a defect. But not all defects in works of art are aesthetic ones. From the point of view of shipping them to art exhibitions, many of Tintoretto's paintings are very bad, since they are so large and fragile that they can be moved only at great risk. But that is not an aesthetic defect. Is the failure of a prescribed response to be merited an *aesthetic* defect (i.e., is it a defect in the work *qua* work of art)? That this is so is evidently true of many artistic genres: thrillers that do not merit the audience being thrilled, tragedies that do not merit fear and pity for their protagonists, comedies that are not amusing, melodramas that do not merit sadness and pity are all aesthetic failures in these respects. Works outside these genres, which similarly prescribe a range of responses, are likewise aesthetic failures if the responses are unmerited. And in general it is a bad work of art that leaves us bored and offers no enjoyment at all. We are also concerned not just with whether a response occurs, but with the quality of that response: humor may be crude, unimaginative, or flat, or may be revelatory, profound, or inspiring. And the aesthetic criticism of a work as being manipulative, sentimental, insensible, or crude is founded on a mismatch between the response the work prescribes the reader to feel and the response actually merited by the work's presentation of the fictional situation.

The aesthetic relevance of prescribed responses wins further support from noting that much of the value of art derives from its deployment of an affective mode of cognition – derives from the way works teach us, not by giving us merely intellectual knowledge, but by bringing that knowledge home to us. This teaching is not just about how the world is, but can reveal new conceptions of the world in the light of which we can experience our situation, can teach us new ideals, can impart new concepts and discriminatory skills – having read Dickens, we can recognize the Micawbers of the world. And the way knowledge is brought home to us is by making it vividly present, so disposing us to reorder our thoughts, feelings, and motivations in the light of it. We all know we will die, but it may take a great work of art to drive that point fully home, to make it vividly present. We may think of the universe as devoid of transcendent meaning, but it may take *Waiting for Godot* to make that thought concrete and real. We may believe in the value of love, but it may take *Jane Eyre* to render that ideal unforgettably alluring. On the cognitive-affective view of the value of art, whether prescribed responses are merited will be of aesthetic significance, since such responses constitute a cognitive-affective perspective on the events recounted. For such responses not merely are affective, but include a cognitive component, being directed toward some state of affairs or thing, and bringing it under evaluative concepts.[26] By prescribing us to be amused, to enjoy, to be aroused by scenes of sexual torture, *Juliette* aims to get us to approve of the imagined events, to think of them as in some way desirable, and so to endorse an evaluation about events of that kind.

These observations can be assembled into an argument for ethicism. A work's manifestation of an attitude is a matter of the work's prescribing certain responses toward the events described. If these responses are unmerited, because unethical, we have reason not to respond in the way prescribed. Our having reason not to respond in the way prescribed is a failure of the work. What responses the work prescribes is of aesthetic relevance. So the fact that we have reason not to respond in the way prescribed is an *aesthetic* failure of the work, that is to say, is an aesthetic defect. So a work's manifestation of ethically bad attitudes is an aesthetic defect in it. Mutatis mutandis, a parallel argument shows that a work's manifestation of ethically commendable attitudes is an aesthetic merit in it, since we have reason to adopt a prescribed response that is ethically commendable. So ethicism is true.

To illustrate: a comedy presents certain events as funny (prescribes a humorous response to them), but if this involves being amused at heartless cruelty, we have reason not to be amused. Hence, the work's humor is flawed, and that is an aesthetic defect in it. If a work prescribes our enjoyment (as almost all art does to some extent), but if we are supposed to enjoy, say, gratuitous suffering, then we can properly refuse to enjoy it, and hence the work fails aesthetically. If a work seeks to get us to pity some characters, but they are unworthy of pity because of their vicious actions, we have reason not to pity them, and hence the work is aesthetically flawed. Conversely, if the comedy's humor is revelatory, emancipating us from the narrow bonds of prejudice, getting us to see a situation in a different and better moral light and respond accordingly, we have reason to adopt the response, and the work succeeds aesthetically in this respect. If the enjoyment it offers derives from this kind of revelatory humor, we have reason to enjoy the work. And if a work prescribes pity toward characters who suffer unfairly and through no fault of their own, we have reason to pity them, and the work succeeds aesthetically in this way. Similar remarks apply to the range of other responses prescribed by works, such as admiring characters, being angry on their behalf, wanting things for them, and so forth.

The merited-response argument for ethicism captures what is plausible in the last two of the arguments surveyed earlier, but sidesteps the pitfalls into which they stumble. If a work prescribes certain attitudes, these may be sufficiently patterned to justify crediting an implied author to it, and this explains why the befriending argument looks plausible. But the merited-response argument has the advantage of avoiding the problems that stem from taking the implied author as foundational in an argument for ethicism. And the cognitive argument is not so much rejected as incorporated into the current argument, which makes use of a cognitive-affective view of art. Art can teach us about what is ethically correct, but the aesthetic relevance of this teaching is guaranteed only when the work displays it in the responses it prescribes to story events. While tacking on to a novel a claim that a certain type of committed love is an ideal will not do much for its aesthetic worth, getting us to *feel* the attraction of that ideal as embodied in a particular relationship is the central and animating excellence of several novels, including *Jane Eyre.*

OBJECTIONS TO THE ARGUMENT

1. The argument does not support ethicism. To say that a prescribed response is unmerited is to say that the work is emotionally unengaging; but then the work's failure is a result of the failure to engage, and not of its ethical corruption. Indeed, if, despite its ethical corruption, the work does emotionally engage, then its ethical badness is not an aesthetic defect.

The objection misconstrues the argument, even in respect of responses that are emotions. A work may engage an emotion even when it does not merit it (it may, for instance, manipulate us into feeling a sort of pity we know is merely sentimental), and only merited emotions are relevant to the argument. It is whether the emotion is merited that is important, and ethical merits are partly constitutive of whether the emotion is merited; hence, ethical values play a direct role in determining whether the work is aesthetically defective.

2. The argument is structurally unsound. Starting from a claim about ethical merit, ethicism ends up with a claim about aesthetic merit, so the argument commits a fallacy of equivocation in moving from an ethical reason to an aesthetic one, for there are no other resources available for making the transition.

There is no equivocation: the claim used to make the transition is that whether prescribed responses are merited is aesthetically relevant, and among the criteria that are relevant to determining whether they are merited are ethical ones. This is a substantive claim, and one that has been argued for by appeal to the language of art criticism and a supporting claim that art deploys an affective mode of cognition.

3. The aesthetic defects of a work cannot be reduced to a failure of prescribed responses: while some works clearly prescribe responses, other works need not, or may fail in respects in which no particular response is prescribed.

The point is correct, but the ethicist defense does not require that all aesthetic defects be failures of prescribed responses, for it is enough to establish its truth that some aesthetic defects are of this kind.

4. Works may prescribe responses that are not aesthetically relevant: a royal portrait may be designed to impart a sense of awe and respect toward the king depicted, and a religious work may aim at

enhancing the viewer's sense of religious reverence, but such responses are aesthetically irrelevant. So ethicism rests on a false premise.

This is not so. A painting is not just (or even) a beautiful object: it aims to convey complex thoughts and feelings about its subject, providing an individual perspective on the object represented. Thus it is that a painting not only can be a representation, but can also embody a way of thinking in an affectively charged way about its subject, and this perspective on its subject is an important object of our aesthetic interest in the work. So if a painting does not succeed in meriting the responses prescribed, it fails on a dimension of aesthetic excellence.

5. Finally, the argument rests on a claim that real responses, not merely imagined ones, can be had toward fictions. Yet that claim has in respect of emotional responses been powerfully contested: some philosophers have argued that certain emotions cannot be really directed at fictional entities.[27] Thus, ethicism rests on a contentious claim, and its truth is hostage to the fortunes of this thesis.

The merited-response argument has indeed been framed by appeal to real emotions directed at fictions, both because I hold that such emotions can be had toward fictions and because the argument proceeds smoothly with this claim. But it is not in fact essential to the argument to appeal to fiction-directed real emotions. (The thesis that fiction-directed real emotions are possible I shall refer to as *emotional realism,* as opposed to *emotional irrealism,* which denies the possibility of such emotions.) There is a class of responses toward fictions – responses of pleasure and displeasure – that both sides to the dispute can agree to be real. It is evident that one can actually enjoy or be displeased by fictional events: one can actually enjoy Jane Eyre's (fictional) happiness at the end of the novel. Scarcely more contentious is the thought that there are many other fiction-directed responses that are real: I don't have to check to see whether a story is fictional or not in order to know whether I am really amused by it or only imagining that I am so. I don't have to know whether described events really occurred to know whether I am disgusted by them.[28] The battle between realists and irrealists is over the reality of those specific kinds of responses that are emotions, and indeed chiefly over the reality of pity and fear directed at fictions.

Ethicism can be fully defended by appeal to those responses the reality of which is relatively uncontentious. For these include pleasure and displeasure, which are pervasive in our responses to fictions, and, as we noted, a person can be ethically criticized for what she takes pleasure or displeasure in. Someone who actually enjoys imagined suffering can properly be condemned for this response. Hence, pleasure and displeasure felt toward fictions are the only kinds of responses the reality of which one needs to appeal to in order to defend ethicism successfully.

Further, the appeal to actual responses was made in order to avoid a possible objection that the audience's responses are only imagined, and the audience is not ethically at fault if it only imagines a response, as opposed to actually possessing it. But the claim that imagined responses are not ethically assessable can be denied in its full generality. Certain imagined responses, particularly when they are compulsive, vivid, or ones that in various ways fully engage their imaginers, may ground ethical criticism, for they too may be deeply expressive of the imaginer's moral character (for instance, the rape fantasist discussed earlier may be ethically criticized, even if he only imagines being aroused by the imagined scenarios). Hence, emotional irrealists can support ethicism on the grounds that people can be ethically condemned for some of their merely imagined responses.[29] Further, as we noted earlier, works that manifest certain attitudes toward fictional entities implicitly manifest the same attitudes toward real entities of that kind. Reading this in terms of prescribed imagined responses, the irrealist can hold that works prescribing an imagined response toward fictional entities implicitly prescribe the counterpart real response to real entities of that kind. Since no one denies that real emotional responses can be directed at real entities, the irrealist can hold that artworks are aesthetically flawed by virtue of the moral reprehensibility of the implied emotions directed at real states of affairs.[30] Thus, it is not essential to the success of the merited-response argument that emotional realism be true: emotional irrealists can and should sign up to it as well.

So the merited-response argument stands. And the truth of ethicism shows that the aesthetic and the ethical are intertwined. While those who have supposed them to form a unity have overstated their closeness, the two evaluative domains have proved to be more tightly and surprisingly interconnected than many had thought possible.

Notes

I am grateful to Noël Carroll, Jerrold Levinson, Richard Moran, Alex Neill, Monique Roelofs, Kendall Walton, and Nick Zangwill for their many helpful comments on this essay, as well as to the participants in the 1994 American Society for Aesthetics national conference, at which an earlier version of this essay was delivered.

1. The view that the *only* aesthetic merits of works are ethical ones is known as *moralism* and is elegantly dispatched by R. W. Beardsmore, *Art and Morality* (London: Macmillan Press, 1971), chap. 2.

2. For a defense of this claim see my "Moral Pluralism," *Philosophical Papers* 22, (1993): 17–40, and my "Rag Bags, Disputes and Moral Pluralism," *Utilitas* (forthcoming).

3. For my account of what a work of art is, see my "'Art' as a Cluster Concept," *Theories of Art,* ed. Noël Carroll (Madison: University of Wisconsin Press, forthcoming). It may be objected to this broader sense of "aesthetic" that it does not encompass the aesthetic properties of nature. Since we are here concerned only with artworks, this restriction would not matter for present purposes; but also note that the notion naturally extends to include aesthetic properties of nature, since nature may share some of the value properties that objects have *qua* artworks. These include narrow aesthetic properties and also various formal and metaphorically ascribed properties. (For a discussion of the latter and their significance, see my "Metaphor and the Understanding of Art," *Proceedings of the Aristotelian Society* 97 [1996–7]: 223–41.)

4. Evidently, talk of works manifesting attitudes is quite in order – we can, for instance, properly talk of *Small World* manifesting an attitude of wry amusement toward academic conferences. Talk of works manifesting attitudes is, I would argue, equivalent to talk of artists manifesting attitudes in works, though the sense of the terms needs careful specification, and the artist here is not to be understood as a mere fictional construct. (See Guy Sircello, "Expressive Properties of Art," in *Philosophy Looks at the Arts,* ed. Joseph Margolis, 3d ed. [Philadelphia: Temple University Press, 1987], for a suggestive discussion of the relation between what artists do and the properties their works possess.) However, given the fact that we can properly talk of works manifesting attitudes, investigation of this equivalence need not be pursued here.

5. Those who evince sympathy with this distinct causal claim include Kant, Matthew Arnold, Anthony Savile, and Anne Sheppard. Kant claims that the harmonious accord between cognitive faculties that beauty produces in the man of good taste "at the same time promotes the sensibility of the mind for moral feeling." *Critique of Aesthetic Judgement,* trans. J. C. Meredith (Oxford: Oxford University Press, 1952), 39. See also Matthew Arnold, *Culture and Anarchy: an Essay in Political and Social Criticism,* 3d ed. (London: Smith, Elder, 1882), passim; Anthony Savile, *The Test of Time* (Oxford: Oxford University Press, 1982), chap. 5, sect. II; and Anne Sheppard, *Aesthetics* (Oxford: Oxford University Press, 1987), 151.

6. For the locus classicus of skepticism about the aesthetic attitude, see George Dickie, "The Myth of the Aesthetic Attitude," in *Philosophy*

Looks at the Arts, ed. Margolis. As noted later, Dickie also uses an attack on the aesthetic attitude to argue for a variant of ethicism.

7. Monroe Beardsley, *Aesthetics,* 2d ed. (Indianapolis: Hackett, 1981), 462ff.

8. However, as will be seen later, some formalists, including David Pole, would deny this claim, and argue for the validity of ethical criticism.

9. See my "Interpreting the Arts: The Patchwork Theory," *Journal of Aesthetics and Art Criticism* 51 (1993): 597–609. For an extended critique of autonomism in reference to its implications for the ethical assessment of art, see Noël Carroll, "Moderate Moralism," *British Journal of Aesthetics* 36 (1996): 223–38.

10. This conception is Kantian in spirit, though Kant's own view differs from it in salient ways. His view is in one way narrower: it is only duty (not feelings) that can motivate actions that have genuine moral worth (or, on one reading of his position, feelings can operate only as primary motives of morally good action, while the secondary motive must be duty; see Marcia W. Baron, *Kantian Ethics Almost Without Apology* [Ithaca, N.Y.: Cornell University Press, 1996], chap. 4). In addition, Kant holds that actions are not directly assessable; only their maxims are.

11. Aristotle, *Nicomachean Ethics* 2.6 1106b16, trans. Terence Irwin (Indianapolis: Hackett, 1985).

12. Interpretive skill is needed, of course, to establish what the relevant properties of fictional characters are toward which attitudes are manifested. This can be a subtle matter; for instance, in some jokes a character being Irish is merely a conventional way of indicating stupidity and need not imply any derogatory attitudes toward Irish people. For a discussion of humor that is closely related to the issues discussed in this essay, see my "Just Joking: The Ethics and Aesthetics of Humor." *Philosophy and Literature* (forthcoming).

13. Lawrence Hyman, "Morality and Literature: The Necessary Conflict," *British Journal of Aesthetics* 24 (1984): 149–55, at 154–5.

14. George Dickie, "The Myth of the Aesthetic Attitude," in *Philosophy Looks at the Arts,* ed. Margolis, 113. In his *Evaluating Art* (Philadelphia: Temple University Press, 1988), chap. 7, Dickie also endorses the cognitivist derivation of ethicism that I discuss later. I place 'essential' in parentheses, since Dickie makes the argument without explicitly using it, but appeals to it when giving the example of a novel; his argument is strengthened by appeal to the notion.

15. I do not mean to deny, of course, that in the case of certain poems this fact might play a role in the appreciation of the work. For instance, if a poet wished to demonstrate his skill by writing a poem containing exactly the same number of every letter of the alphabet, yet the resulting poem did not have this feature, this would reflect badly on his artistry. So in some unusual cases facts about the number of different letters in a poem might be aesthetically relevant. But Dickie's argument requires it to be *always* true that such facts are aesthetically relevant.

16. E.g., Monroe Beardsley, *Aesthetics,* 2d ed. (Indianapolis: Hackett, 1981). Though he attacks only moralism directly (564–7), it is clear from his remarks on page 457 that moral criteria play no part in the objective reasons that, he believes, exhaustively specify aesthetic evaluation.

17. David Pole, "Morality and the Assessment of Literature," in his *Aesthetics, Form and Emotion* (London: Duckworth, 1983), 49–50.

18. A parallel criticism is made by Dickie, "The Myth of the Aesthetic Attitude," 113.

19. Hume remarks, "We choose our favourite author as we do our friend" in his "Of the Standard of Taste," in *Critical Theory Since Plato* ed. Hazard Adams (San Diego, Calif.: Harcourt Brace Jovanovich, 1971), 321. See also Wayne Booth, *The Company We Keep: An Ethics of Fiction* (Berkeley: University of California Press, 1988), esp. chaps. 7 and 8.

20. Richard Eldridge, *On Moral Personhood: Philosophy, Literature, Criticism and Self-Knowledge* (Chicago: University of Chicago Press, 1989), 20.

21. Martha Nussbaum, "Flawed Crystals: James's *The Golden Bowl* and Literature as Moral Philosophy," *New Literary History* 15 (1983): 43.

22. See my "Moral Pluralism."

23. Richard W. Miller, "Truth in Beauty," *American Philosophical Quarterly* 16 (1979): 317–25, argues that truth is sometimes aesthetically relevant, since the "aesthetic goals of some works include the combination, in appropriate ways, of the true depiction of certain aspects of reality with other, exclusively and uncontroversially aesthetic virtues" (319). If there are ethical truths, this would yield a cognitivist defense of the relevance in certain conditions of the depiction of ethical truths to aesthetic worth. Miller's piece is important, since it seeks explicitly to meet the relevance problem, and his strategy shares some features with that advanced in the present essay though it differs in an important respect in appealing directly to truth rather than to merited responses. But given his stress on the fact that it is not the truth of ideas per se that is aesthetically relevant, but their cognitive manner of expression, his approach appears to yield the result that if immoral views (such as Baudelaire's sexism) are well expressed in his poems, then their immorality does not constitute an aesthetic defect in the poems (322). Thus, the position yielded by Miller's argument is incompatible with ethicism and, given the argument for ethicism advanced later, is to be rejected as it stands.

24. The notion of prescribing imagined feelings is to be found in Kendall Walton, *Mimesis as Make-Believe: On the Foundations of the Representational Arts* (Cambridge, Mass.: Harvard University Press, 1990), chap. 7.2. The claim that actual feelings can be prescribed is defended by Richard Moran in "The Expression of Feeling in Imagination," *Philosophical Review* 103 (1994): 75–106. I am indebted at several points in this section to Moran's discussion.

25. For defenses of the view that real emotions can be felt toward events known to be merely imagined, see Noël Carroll, *The Philosophy of Hor-*

ror or *Paradoxes of the Heart* (New York: Routledge, 1990), 60–88, and Patricia Greenspan, *Emotions and Reasons: An Inquiry into Emotional Justification* (New York: Routledge, 1988), esp. part I.

26. For cognitive-evaluative views of responses, see Greenspan, *Emotions and Reasons;* Robert C. Roberts, "What an Emotion Is: A Sketch," *Philosophical Review* 97 (1988): 183–209; and Elijah Millgram, "Pleasure in Practical Reasoning," *Monist* 76 (1993): 394–415.

27. See, e.g., Walton, *Mimesis as Make-Believe,* 241–55; and Gregory Currie *The Nature of Fiction* (Cambridge University Press, 1990), chap. 5.

28. Compare Carroll, *The Philosophy of Horror.*

29. A point I owe to Kendall Walton. See his "Morals in Fiction and Fictional Morality," *Proceedings of the Aristotelian Society,* suppl. vol. 68 (1994): 27–50, for an irrealist discussion of the ethical criticism of art.

30. I owe this point to Jerrold Levinson.

8

How bad can good art be?

KAREN HANSON

Worries about the immorality of art can arise from a number of apparently quite different considerations. One line of thought, as old as Plato and as current as Catherine MacKinnon, emphasizes the continuity of art and life and contends that some artistic productions may corrupt the minds, hearts, and behavior of those who experience them.

Another concern, less historically pervasive perhaps but still potent, is grounded on an assumption that art is removed, or removes us, from life and thus from the strictures and obligations that properly bind us. This anxiety may stand as a vexed tribute to the cultural power of the doctrine of art for art's sake. It may be that Oscar Wilde's claim that "[a]ll art is quite useless"[1] is granted, but the claim is treated as an anguished accusation and not a proud proclamation. Or one may believe, with Walter Pater, that "art comes to you proposing frankly to give nothing but the highest quality to your moments as they pass, and simply for those moments' sake,"[2] and yet want to turn from such a proposal, as from the seductive allure of the lotus land, because one remembers that one has duties, that there are tasks to attend to in the passing moments of the responsible life. The separation of art and life is also delineated in accounts of "psychical distance" and of "the aesthetic attitude" and "disinterestedness," and here again apprehension may arise that absorption in art can be defined in specific contrast to moral responsiveness.

I shall take up first this second line of concern, the worries about discontinuities between art and life. Critically examining a number of versions of this uneasiness about art, I shall conclude that there is, from this direction, little ground for strong complaint. Exploring this territory will lead, however, to a surprising point of contiguity with the first worry, the apprehension about the continuity between art and life. Returning, then, to the first, the historically recurrent complaint, and finding it both empirically and conceptually complex, I shall use it as a point of entry for a more general discussion of the role of ethical considerations in judgments of art. Defended in that discussion will be a particular idea of the invocation of moral considerations in aesthetic contexts, an idea that leaves some – but not unlimited – room for us to judge aesthetically excellent a work whose moral quality we firmly condemn.

First, though, we must canvass the idea that art can be condemned because of its separation from the moral life. An interesting version of this concern is voiced by Arthur Danto, who thinks

there would be cases in which it would be wrong or inhuman to take an aesthetic attitude, to put at a psychical distance certain realities – to see a riot, for instance, in which police are clubbing demonstators, as a kind of ballet, or to see the bombs exploding like mystical chrysanthemums from the plane they have been dropped from. The question instead must arise as to what one should *do*. For parallel reasons, . . . there are things it would be almost immoral to represent in art, precisely because they are then put at a distance which is exactly wrong from a moral perspective. Tom Stoppard once said that if you see an injustice taking place outside your window, the least useful thing you can do is to write a play about it. I would go further, suggesting that there is something wrong in writing plays about that sort of injustice in which we have an obligation to intervene, since it puts the audience at just the sort of distance the concept of psychic distance means to describe: something like this has been offered as a criticism of the photographs of Diane Arbus.[3]

Danto's disquieting rumination suggests ethical perils on all sides: the art itself may be immoral, because it puts the audience at a distance; the artist may be judged morally wrong, for producing an object that has this effect; the audience may be judged wrong or inhuman, for taking an aesthetic attitude or remaining still, at a distance, when there is an obligation to intervene. How serious are these dangers?

Before we gauge the perils, before we afix blame or condemnation, we need to think more about the conditions of this assessment. The grounds for censure seem always roughly the same: some circumstances or events require action, and art in those circumstances or about those events not only does not count *as,* but in fact *blocks,* appropriate action. How does it do this? The example of art that might have the Medusa-like power to turn those who look upon it to stone – namely, the photographs of Diane Arbus – seems to me not a help but a puzzle. Arbus's freakish or socially marginalized subjects do not, in any straightforward way, suggest injustice in need of our active intervention. If we had been there with Arbus as she shot photographs, had been there in the living presence of, say, a dwarf or a transvestite, what would morality have demanded that we *do?* If there is no obvious answer to this, if no action is obviously required in the presence of her subjects, then how can Arbus's photographs be blamed for blocking the requirements of morality or sapping our will to act?

Perhaps, in this example, the moral objection is subtler. Is it that Arbus's photographs put us in a position to stare, to look without consequences at sights from which, in practical life, we might turn away in discomfort? Perseus was able to see and slay the freakish Medusa because he avoided a direct, unmediated glance. He used Athena's shield to catch Medusa's reflection, and it was only the reflection that he kept in view. That might be a metaphor for the looking and seeing we can achieve through photographs, but it so far carries no hint of moral fault. I can imagine – I have seen – photographs that would elicit misgivings about the morality of looking, about personal privacy, exploitation, and unjustifiable intrusion. But if, with Arbus's work, we are made to stare frankly at those who, in life, we would ignore or spy upon with furtive glances, then it is not clear that our real-life responses have much positive moral weight. And we do not, after all, come close to killing or even wounding the dignity of Arbus's subjects. We do not, in looking at their photographs, override their wishes or participate in an evident abridgment of their sense of privacy.

We might also remember, about the medium in general and not just about Arbus's use of it, that a photograph offers the viewer a sight of the *past,* so the idea of active intervention in the very particular event or circumstances photographed is, strictly speaking, vain. It may be, of course, that that is a nicety of airy metaphysics that weighs very little in grave matters of morality. A photograph shows you a Sudanese child starving, and you are moved to *do* something. By the time you reach Sudan to help, perhaps even by the time you write a check to a relief agency, perhaps even when you first see the photograph, that child may have already died; but the famine goes on and a practical response is surely not in vain. But, then, if photographs – and plays (think of *A Doll's House*) and novels (think of *Bleak House* or *The Jungle*) and so on – can in fact thus serve as spurs to action, are we flatly rebutting the claims made by Danto and Stoppard, or obtusely missing their point?

If we focus on Danto's assertion that "there is something wrong in writing plays about that sort of injustice in which we have an obligation to intervene," we may see traces of a Rousseauian objection to theater, to its capacity to pervert and dissipate true sentiment and its role in obscuring the genuine needs of our fellow human beings.[4] If the spectacle in the theater provokes us to tears, but then, refreshed and self-satisfied, we step outside and are blind to the sight of our freezing coachmen – or the freezing homeless – isn't there room for moral complaint? It may not be clear, however, just where – against what or whom – the complaint should be lodged. If we do not see the connection between the pitiful events portrayed on stage and the dreadful circumstances on the street, why blame the play or playwright and not ourselves? The idea is farfetched that a play might exhaust our capacity for sympathy and purge us of any inclination to behave responsibly in the face of real opportunities for doing so; but if there were such plays, isn't it we who should still be faulted for indulging in them, in preference to other works, as we might be faulted for choosing to dull our reactions to the misfortunes of others by indulging in drink or drugs? It is, in any case, hard to see that – why or how – plays about *injustice* would *necessarily* have this deeply enervating effect.

It may well be that it is simply psychical distance itself, or some instances of it, that Danto wants to condemn, and plays and playwrights are viewed with moral disapproval insofar as they present occasions for the realization of blameworthy distance. Moral suspicion of psychical distance could certainly be grounded on the fact that the latter notion is routinely defined by differentiating it from practical attitudes and moral concerns. Thus Bullough speaks of "the *negative,* inhibitory aspect" of distance, "the cutting-out of the practical sides of things and of our practical attitude to them,"[5] so that distance can supply "one of the special criteria of aesthetic values as distinct from practical (utilitarian), scientific, or social (ethical) values."[6] And, of course, though Kant does not speak of "psychical distance," he may be understood to lay the foundation for the notion with his account of the judgment of taste as "devoid of all interest" and his conceptual location of the beautiful in contradistinction to the agreeable and the good.[7]

Now the very idea of a disinterested aesthetic attitude has been subjected to a great deal of critical scrutiny, and many philosophers question the coherence of the traditional accounts of psychical distance. (Indeed, and somewhat puzzlingly, Danto himself notes that art "has often had useful roles to play as . . . didactic, edificational, . . . or whatever, and the theory [of psychical distance and the aesthetic attitude] thus presupposes a degree of detachment available only in special periods of art history." "For this reason," he says, he "applaud[s] the polemic of George Dickie, who contests what he speaks of as 'the myth of psychic distance.'")[8] If psychical distance is a mythological construction, Danto's moral worry may collapse. It is worth remarking, however, that even if some plausible notion of psychical distance can be preserved, it is not immediately clear that such distancing ever in itself constitutes a moral mistake. Something that might be described as distance – a space for thought and choice – seems fundamental to the realization of a developed moral life. A salient feature of the human condition is that our responses to the world are not always reflexive reactions to immediate impingements. (Compare, for sharp contrast, the life of the clam or the slug.)[9] *Deliberate* action – with options held out enough to be weighed – may not be all there is to the good human life, and objectivity – understood to involve a distinction between knower and known, between a thinker and an object of thought – may be an overrated or misunderstood epistemological ideal. Still, if "the question [is to] arise as to what one should *do*," it seems one must *already* be at *some* sort of distance from what "must" be addressed.

Nonetheless, the examples used to suggest the moral questionableness of psychical distance seem somehow to carry argumentative force. Do they persuade by implying, perhaps illicitly and certainly without proof, that an aesthetic attitude or a distanced perception erases a prior, or precludes a subsequent or, say, alternating, practical or moral concern? Would we condemn a psychologist studying the development of toddlers' problem-solving strategies because, at a moment when a subject child exhibits unhappy frustration, the psychologist maintains a cognitive attitude, seeking not to offer immediate comfort to the child but to record and make sense of the child's behavior? If an individual shows nothing but a cognitive interest in others, we might, of course, be dismayed and disapproving, as appalled as we would be at one who sees a bloody riot only as a kind of ballet. But the scientific observer may also be a warm and responsive parent, may indeed, even at the same time as she is engaged in scientific observation, be emotionally attuned to register and react to the moment when a subject child's unhappiness should

208

be soothed and not merely noted. Similarly, one who attends to the perceptible form and sensuous surface of an event may also be capable of seeing the event's moral import and taking the implications for conduct. If by a definition of "psychical distance" aesthetic and moral attitudes cannot be *simultaneous,* why may they not be realized by an individual at what *practically* amounts to the same time?

If it is argued that split seconds can make a difference or, more plausibly, that something like the *order* or the *predominant* category of an individual's attitudes is signally important to our estimation of his or her moral character, this must be granted. After all, an adult whose first reaction to a crying child is always curiosity about what facts might now be revealed about the immature psyche, and who only subsequently remembers to offer some comfort, has a different – we might say "colder" – character than one who comforts first and reflects later. And so, with Danto, we might judge "wrong or inhuman" a person whose first or typical reaction to violence is to aestheticize it, even if this individual manages also to behave appropriately in the face of violent events. But this does not show that putting certain realities at a psychical distance is inherently wrong or inhuman, any more than the example of the cold psychologist shows that trying to understand people is *inherently* at odds with caring for them. Danto himself elsewhere recounts "Monet's anguished discovery that, sitting by the body of his late wife Camille, his model, love, support, angel, he had, instead of grieving, been studying the purple on her eyelids. He wondered what manner of monster he had become."[10] Monet's horrified self-discovery, if it showed him to be a monster, showed him to be a monster of the sort Pascal calls "human." In the combination of his reaction and his reaction to his reaction, Monet must be seen as neither angel nor beast but a fragile thinking reed – loving, creative, and perceptive, a complex man.

It might finally be said, now as a flat counterassertion, that Danto's claim "that there is something wrong in writing plays about that sort of injustice in which we have an obligation to intervene" just seems decidedly implausible. If, as Danto admits, art *can* be didactic and edifying, why prohibit the theater from, or condemn it for, addressing large social issues and serious moral and political problems? Stoppard's weaker line – "that if you see an injustice taking place outside your window, the least useful thing you can do is write a play about it" – is more tenable, but its reach as moral criticism is unclear. It echoes Wilde's "All art is quite useless," but while that is a defense against charges of immorality, Stoppard's comment is clearly deprecatory. Should it be taken as a summary of empirical evidence, a generalization about the marginality of theater's edifying powers or the fragility of art's connection to social action?

But if we are thus engaged in utilitarian calculations, then doesn't it matter keenly to know what *kind* of injustice is "taking place outside our window"? Is someone being assaulted by a gang of muggers, or is a deadly epidemic being ignored by the medical establishment because most of its victims are politically powerless or socially "other"? Don't we need to know, too, about our particular abilities and our other available options for action? If we see someone being mugged, then, depending on our strength and circumstances, it may be useful to intervene directly, and certainly we should call the police. (And might we not then also, when the immediate crisis is over, usefully incorporate something of this episode in our new play?)[11]

But suppose we are concerned about the epidemic. Should we demonstrate in the streets, write letters to our political representatives and to the NIH, go back to school to learn to do medical research, establish or contribute to a new charity? Both the nature and the extent of our obligations are, in this sort of case, much more difficult to discern. One of the obstacles to seeing the best course is that individual action, no matter how wisely chosen, is likely to be only slightly ameliorative, given the nature and the scale of the problem. This in fact is the case with most of the problems we might typically call "injustices" – economic inequities, violations of human rights, practices of racism, sexism, political domination, and so on. Now if these sorts of injustices cannot be solved by any individual's actions and may not be solved in any of our lifetimes, then, while we certainly have no excuse for doing nothing about these problems, we may have good reason not to belittle any serious attempts to address them. The cynic might note that the difference between "the least useful" and the most useful course of action is essentially negligible, given the enormity of these problems, and there is some truth to this. But the more optimistic assessment is that writing a play may be as good a way as any to take constructive action.

Writing a play about the neglect of the AIDS epidemic may be as good a way as any other to address the problem – the problem of this *injustice.* We can leave aside for now, as only strengthening this defense of art, that the play may offer or sustain moral values – for example, compassion, individual comfort – other than those directly related to promoting social justice. Writing a play may be as useful a mode of action as any other, provided, of course, that one has some writing talent and some opportunity to have the play produced and seen, provided one isn't already employed as, say, an AIDS researcher, or the head of the NIH, or the president of the United States, or. . . . Remembering that both our native endowments and our acquired roles, our untapped personal talents and our undischarged social debts are among the conditions that determine the reasonableness or defensibility of a given course of action, we must assume that for each of us, at each stage of our lives, there will be better and worse bets about what course of action is likely to be most useful. If I am a middle-aged scientist with a good track record in medical research but no previous literary experience or calling, it is probably true that devoting myself to writing a play about AIDS is likely to be among the least productive things I might do (about AIDS).[12] We should thus at least qualify, relativize, the flat generality of Stoppard's claim. Remembering, though, that action is *never* accompanied by a guarantee of its felicitousness, we may also want to challenge more directly the assurance of Stoppard's assertion, but now with a worry about the uncertainties of moral luck.

Bernard Williams memorably sketches the problem of moral luck by drawing out the considerations relevant to the personal justification of an *artist,* an exemplary or schematized Gauguin. When Gauguin leaves his family destitute in order to pursue in Tahiti the development of his art, there can be nothing, at the time of his departure, that can justify his action: "Justification, if there is to be one, will be essentially retrospective."[13] Success as an artist, the creation of world historically valuable art, is the only thing that can redeem his decision to depart, to abandon his domestic responsibilities, but success cannot be guaranteed – or even confidently predicted on reasonably adequate grounds – at the time of his departure. If the justification of important life projects – such as writing a play – sometimes depends on moral luck, on the projects' *happening* to turn out well, then we cannot say, as we commit ourselves to them, that these projects are definitely worthwhile or, more crucially, that they may rightfully take precedence over our standing obligations or over other tasks we might as reasonably undertake.

Philosophers who accept the idea that morality and rational justification are subject to the vagaries of luck have various reactions to this disturbing thought. Either the nature or the scope of morality, or both, may seem deeply unsettled. Without proceeding further into this contested conceptual territory, we can simply note that if there is a problem of moral luck, it affects not just art and the artist, but every human enterprise. It is not just Gauguin, after all, but also, say, the medical researcher, at the lab all day and into the night, who may, for example, neglect real family needs in order to pursue work. He or she might not need to discover a vaccine for AIDS in order to justify this one-track devotion, but something more than unimaginative dead ends and plodding bench work had better be discernible if a grim life judgment is to be escaped. If that is the bad news about moral luck, however, the good news is that the present decision to write a play cannot, at this moment, be definitively and conclusively . condemned.

Thus, Stoppard's particular judgment cannot be sustained. It may have been, in any case, only lightly offered. But another, more obdurate concern about the utility of art may still be pressed. If art is understood to be discontinuous with life, if it is thought that either the production or the enjoyment of art removes an individual from the practical and moral sphere of human existence, then, since the practical world is always brimming with injustice, indulgence in art must entail the gross neglect of some vital obligations. Given the apparent omnipresence of undeserved pain and dreadful suffering in the world we inhabit, there are *always* already some very basic claims upon our time and energy – so many, in fact, that we cannot possibly justify in terms of utility turning away from those problems and toward the development of art.

The austerity of this moral outlook will, of course, dry up not only art, but also science and all liberal learning, and its account of our moral obligations will render all but the Mother Teresas among us exhausted failures. That some forms of utilitarianism seem to have these sorts of implications for moral assessment is now generally seen as a problem for those *theories,* not as a revelation that should come to guide our lives. It is worth remarking, however, that this complaint about art, grounded as it is on considerations of utility, often gains cultural currency through an edgy political alliance with an opposing view.

If art can be condemned because, trafficking with it, we are moved to ignore the basic evil and suffering all around us, art can also, with adequate practical if not deep theoretical consistency, be condemned because, trafficking with at least some of it, we are corrupted, made more likely to contribute to the sum total of evil and suffering in the world. Blaming art for a purported *discontinuity* with life thus joins blaming art for purported *continuities* with mistaken lives, and the moral space from which one might praise or even just leave art alone seems precipitously eroded. We have not, however, so far found much real reason to worry about a depraved discontinuity between art and life. Is the moral quicksand in fact on the other side, in the *connection* between art and life?

We should step carefully here, if only to mark off one serviceable path for exploration rather than another. To investigate the idea that art may corrupt, we need, of course, not only a standard of morality or, at any rate, some defensible moral judgments, but also some detailed empirical evidence. It may be no more difficult to gather and interpret properly evidence about art's effects than it is to obtain useful evidence about a host of other matters, but it is certainly not obvious that philosophy, or even what philosophy may call "common sense," has this evidence to hand.

It must be admitted that current U.S. law has a different, a less cautious or more generous view of the disclosures here of common sense. Writing for the majority in *Paris Adult Theatre I v. Slaton,* and citing Justice Cardozo's assertion that "all laws in Western civilization are 'guided by a robust common sense,'" former Chief Justice Warren Burger dismisses the import of the argument that no scientific data conclusively demonstrate "that exposure to obscene materials adversely affects men and women or their society":

If we accept the unprovable assumption that a complete education requires the reading of certain books, and the well nigh universal belief that good books, plays, and art lift the spirit, improve the mind, enrich the human personality and develop character, can we then say that a state legislature may not act on the corollary assumption that commerce in obscene books, or public exhibitions focused on obscene conduct, have a tendency to exert a corrupting and debasing impact leading to antisocial behavior?[14]

Leaving aside the crucial issue of this case, the controversy about state censorship, we can focus just on Burger's string of suggestions about the relations between art and morality and on his sense of the logical connections between those basic propositions. There seem to be no clear rules of deduction guiding an inference to the "corollary" that grounds the legislative action here in dispute, but, after all, Burger also acknowledges that all these contentions may simply be assumptions. Is there in fact widespread, common, acceptance of these claims? Surely at least the first of these propositions – "that a complete education requires the reading of certain books" – is openly *debated.* That we do not have here a settled social assumption is shown by the intensity of current discussion about the content and aims of liberal education and by the attacks on, and even the defenses of, the viability of "the canon." (Given the reality that school time, and indeed life, is limited, and apart from an admirable commitment to the idea that no education is ever truly complete, even the most conservative of the proponents of a traditional canon are likely to offer not a fixed list of "certain books," but at least some range, usually open-ended, of prized options.) Still, acceptance – or rejection – of the first assumption may be quite irrelevant to one's sense of the plausibility of the other propositions. Perhaps these other two ideas – that good books (plays, etc.) uplift and enhance the character of the reader and that bad books (plays, etc.) debase the reader's character – are widely held. They are certainly not real corollaries of one another, but Burger may be right that, in many minds, they are convictions somehow bound together. Is Burger also right that nearly everyone would immediately admit that good books develop good character?

Too many people are acutely aware of the emblematic, but historically real and genuinely problematic figure of the cultivated Nazi officer, so that univeral assent to this simple account of the relations between art and life will probably not be forthcoming.[15] Moreover, polling ourselves about the plausibility of these substantive, general claims – that good art has good effects and bad art corrupts – may not be the only, or the best, way of investigating something that, in these matters, is often called common sense. We might notice instead that, whether we hold or reject what Burger calls "the well nigh universal belief" about art's effects, we seem to have accepted the referential clarity of the phrase "good books, plays, and art." What do we have in mind here when we think of "good art"?

What particularly needs sorting out, in the context of these issues, is the extent to which – willfully or not, appropriately or not – we intertwine or even fuse moral and aesthetic judgment. Burger, for example, must not *define* "good art" as art that will "lift the spirit, improve the mind, enrich the human personality, and develop character," or he would not feel obliged to give a hypothetical form to his consideration of what he takes to be common assumptions. Plato is sometimes thought to draw no distinction between aesthetic and ethical/political criticism of poetry, music, and drama, but his accounts of our common judgments of the poetry he would banish show that he recognizes, even as he hopes to counter, appraisals of art that are not drawn from ethical thought. (See, e.g., *Republic* 10, 605d [trans. Shorey]: "We praise as an excellent poet the one who most strongly affects us," [the one who makes us] "feel pleasure, abandon ourselves and accompany the representation with sympathy and eagerness.") Tolstoy, too, is often understood as a moralist about aesthetic merit, and he does argue that art's value is ultimately determined by the religious perception of each era and society, with the best art now being Christian art, uniting humanity. Even Tolstoy, however, wants to make a clear distinction between judgments of "the quality of art as art" and a definition of "good and bad art with reference to its subject matter."[16] It is only the latter that is grounded on the moral goal of human brotherhood. The quality of art as art is measured by its infectiousness – the individuality, clarity, and sincerity of the feelings it transmits – "apart from whether the feelings it transmits are good or bad."[17]

On the other hand, Wilde – with his famous assertion that "[t]here is no such thing as a moral or an immoral book. Books are well written or badly written. That is all" – presumably stands antipodean to Tolstoy, and yet Wilde too notes that "[t]he moral and immoral life of man forms part of the subject matter of the artist."[18] If it is generally agreed that morality may be a part of the subject matter of art, part of its content, we must still consider disagreements concerning moral judgments about that content. Is moral criticism of art a thing apart from aesthetic criticism, with moral concerns trumping aesthetic ones, or not reaching their rarefied heights, or coequal but simply different? Or should we expect a merging of moral and aesthetic values in our judgments about art? Or does art possess immunity from ethical criticism, existing on an altogether different plane?

The idea that art is somehow beyond the reach of moral criticism may seem immediately implausible. Since art is, or is a product of, human activity, and since human action is among the natural subjects, is perhaps the central object, of moral evaluation, a theory that exempts art from moral evaluation may seem an untenable deus ex machina. Faith in this doctrine can be made more reasonable by taking care to limit its scope. It can be acknowledged that art, art making, and the experience of art may be considered from a variety of perspectives, placed in a variety of categories of activity or social practice. Art is, for example, economic activity. Material resources are used to make, exhibit, buy, and enjoy it, and the economic ramifications of a given piece or the conditions for a whole practice of art may be morally criticized. Art may be employed, say, to educate the young or to enhance a community's sense of cohesion, to break down or to build up common prejudices, and so on; and when we focus on these sorts of functions, on how well or how poorly they are performed, on whether they should be performed at all, our concerns may be primarily moral. When art is considered *as art,* however, and not in terms of any of its functions, why should it not be understood to ascend to a dimension that is its alone?

A parallel for this line of thought, a confirmatory model, may perhaps be drawn from a popular view of science. Scientific truths may be supposed unsusceptible to ethical criticism, though it is readily admitted that their pursuit and application are appropriately evaluated from the moral point of view. Again, to sketch some parallel examples, the economic resources devoted to some scientific inquiry may be questioned, or we may praise or condemn the uses to which a discovery is put, but the discovery itself, the truth revealed through inquiry, cannot be placed on a moral grid.

Philosophers have, of course, disputed the accuracy of this picture of value-free science,[19] but even if we set aside those fundamental controversies, we should notice two ways in which this comparison between art and science – far from enhancing the plausibility of the idea of art's immunity to moral judgment – tends instead to diminish the prospects for that idea. The first problem is that, in both science and art, the distinction between pursuit or practice, on the one hand, and finished achievement or accomplishment, on the other, is not always sharp or easily discerned. This may be only a minor problem, if a problem at all, for science, with its working commitment to epistemological fallibilism, its open and productive embrace of the possibility that today's best scientific theory may one day have to be scrapped or revised, may not yet be the final truth. An equivalent fallibilism in the realm of art would, however, vitiate utterly the aesthete's prohibition of moral criticism of artistic productions. For then, whenever this theorist declared a book, play, painting, or whatever off limits to moral evaluation, the question would inevitably arise, and with real force, "But is that book [play, painting, or whatever] *art?*" If we cannot be sure that something *is* art, if the possibility always exists that what we are evaluating is instead only a wasteful attempt at art, or a shameless shamming of art, or retrograde political propaganda disguised as art, then we cannot be sure that moral evaluation *is* out of line.

Waiting behind and related to this difficulty is the second problem with the scientific model's usefulness as an ally in art's attempt to exempt itself from moral evaluation. When – or if – scientific truth is granted an exemption from morality's scope, it is *because* this truth is conceived to be responsive only to brute reality, to be utterly independent of human desires, needs, and efforts.[20] Scientific truths may be uncovered because of human efforts, out of human needs and desires, but, on this picture, we pursue and discover, we cannot *make,* the truth. We do, of course, make art. It is wholly a product of our desires, needs, efforts, skill, intelligence, and so on. If there is such a thing as free will, then art, perhaps more than anything else, is made freely and willfully. Why should it not be a candidate for moral judgment?

If, after all, we are judged for making bombs or making peace, why can we not be judged for making a painting? If we are judged for telling lies and for telling the truth, why can we not be judged for telling stories, writing novels? If it is now granted that *we,* and our choice of activities, may be subject to moral scrutiny, but it is still insisted that art, the product of our activity, is beyond morality, the distinction seems desperate. It is, we must note, the nature of peace and the properties and consequences of bombs that help make our efforts to construct one or the other so appropriately subject to moral evaluation. Furthermore, the lies we tell, not just we in telling them, may be judged from the moral point of view: this lie, because of its superficial content and its function as a routine social gesture, is not so bad; that one, because of its cruelty and its significance, is despicable. In the end, though, as at first glance, it is the obvious fact that people make art, that art making is a human activity, that makes it inappropriate to try to isolate the realm of art from all prospect of moral evaluation.[21]

Accepting the idea that the *content* of art may be subject to moral evaluation, we may still disagree about the force and operation of such evaluation and, in particular, about its import for aesthetic judgment. There are at least two leading possibilities: art may be subject to moral assessment, but ethical judgments always remain distinct from aesthetic ones; or moral considerations are sometimes properly invoked in aesthetic criticism.

Defending the first view, and arguing that the values of ethics and aesthetics (and all other "value areas") are "different and independent," William Gass admits:

In life, values do not sit in separate tents like harem wives; they mix and mingle. . . . A dinner party, for example, will affect the diners' waists, delight or dismay their palates, put a piece of change in the grocer's pocket, bring a gleam to the vintner's eye. . . . And if I, Rabbi Ben Ezra, find myself seated next to Hermann Goering, it may quite put me off the quail – quail which the

Reichminister shot by machine gun from a plane. We should all be able to understand that. It would be a serious misunderstanding, however, if I imagined that the quail was badly cooked on account of who shot it, or to believe that the field marshal's presence had soured the wine, although it may have ruined the taste in my mouth. . . . [T]he meal will be well prepared or not quite independently of the guests' delightful or obnoxious presence, and it would be simple-minded to imagine that because these values were realized in such close proximity they therefore should be judged on other than their own terms – the terms, perhaps, of their pushier neighbors.[22]

Granting the idea that a dinner party can be analyzed from a variety of perspectives – in terms of the calories the guests consume, or in terms of the monetary cost of the food and wine, and so on – the crucial question remains, even with this deliberately impudent example: Can we neatly separate aesthetic from moral judgment? If a dinner party were just the consumption of calories, Gass's claim might be easier to make. Then a "well-prepared" meal would just be one that makes those calories available for consumption, "quite independently of the . . . delightful or obnoxious presence" of the others sharing the trough. But a good dinner party requires conviviality, and conviviality may be a product of the *mix* of food, drink, and guests. A "well-prepared" meal is not just a matter of culinary expertise directed toward an abstract, idealized gustatory receptor. Beefsteak in bearnaise sauce prepared by Jacques Pépin doing his best is still not a meal well prepared for baby's dinner on her first birthday.

And what would Gass say if the field marshal brought to the cook not quail, but the body of a person he had shot? Would the moral circumstances of cooking and consumption still be utterly independent of this meal's aesthetic merit? Would this meal be well prepared if the thigh had been slow-roasted to an internal temperature of 165 degrees, or should it be 180? And is it only if the meat thermometer registers 200 that I may justifiably complain that this joint is "badly cooked"? Is it "simple-minded" of me to be unable to stomach, on any terms, the sight of this corpse on the table?[23]

Gass seems to assume that one who intelligently commands value judgments *can,* in the end, sort values into separate tents and that intercourse with one "value area" is unaffected by the presence of the other tents. But just as the women of the harem affect one another, apart from the presence of or unbeknownst to the male, before he sends them to their separate tents, our values may be more intimately interrelated than we admit, and our analytical separation of value areas may simply disclose the partiality of our perspective, our ignorance of the ways in which our "distinct" value "types" affect and depend upon one another.

In a memorable illustration of what he calls "a certain blindness in human beings," William James recounts his aesthetic horror when, journeying in the mountains of North Carolina, he saw valley after valley cleared of forest and scarred by primitive squatter farms. Upon hearing a mountaineer speak of these coves' "cultivation," however, James suddenly felt he had been missing "the whole inward significance of the situation." The clearings meant home, safety, and security for the mountaineers and their families: "[What] to me was a mere ugly picture on the retina . . . was to them a symbol redolent with moral memories and sang a very paean of duty, struggle, and success."[24] The values here realized evidently vary according to one's material relation to the clearings, but it is not merely that the mountaineer saw a positive economic value in the raw homestead, while James, from his comfortable academic position, had overlooked this aspect of the situation. It is rather that the very sight of the cove – the sight James initially saw as "ugly," "unmitigated squalor," oppressive "dreariness" – was *seen* by the mountaineer as suffused with spiritual warmth and the glow of fulfilled aspirations. Gass wants the aesthetic value of the sight to be judged "on its own terms," but it is the character of those terms, *not* just which term is "pushier," that is precisely what is often in dispute. Gass insists that the realization in close proximity of an array of values should not lead us to mistake one for another, but in fact the character of a term of evaluation – like our own character – may be deeply influenced by the neighborhood in which it was developed.

Gass contends that "[a]rtistic quality depends upon a work's internal, formal, organic character, upon its inner system of relations, upon its structure and its style, and not upon the morality it is presumed to recommend."[25] Among the problems with this blunt and sweeping declaration, however, is that it is not obvious that a work's "organic character" is inherently amoral or that the most salient inner system of relations will never have a moral cast. Nor is it clear that considerations of the morality of a work must take the form of a presumption about the work's "recommendations." Arnold Isenberg reminds us that even didactic literature – which, he says, either "features regular ethical terms, such as 'good', 'evil', 'right', 'wrong'," or is "cast in the imperative mood," or "assembles descriptive propositions in such a way as clearly to point to a moral conclusion"[26] – while it may seem the strongest case "of moral involvement among the fine arts,"[27] need not necessarily be understood as making recommendations. The content of, for example, a poem, what it says, may be moral (or moralistic), but whether the poem must – or even should – be taken to be hortatory is another matter.

It is not just that some apparently didactic stanzas may be, for example, part of a parody or satire, or that they may be dialogue in a play and thus the dramatic utterance, the expression, of a particular character in the drama, or that the lines may be quoted in another poem, only to be poetically disputed. The more fundamental point is that the moral content of a work of art does not always serve as a moral precept. If one does not see this, according to Isenberg,

it is because one does not understand what other roles may be played by moral ideas: one does not, for instance – though understanding very well how the side of a mountain can be an object of interest for one who is neither a geologist nor a surveyor – see how a "side" of a moral question can be an attractive thing, in itself and apart from its merits as a solution to that question.[28]

This way of putting what can serve as a rejoinder to Gass serves also, however, to lay the groundwork for Isenberg's own argument that didactic content can be put to a purely aesthetic use. The aesthetic assimilation of moral content occurs, according to Isenberg, when the moral understanding is called "into a kind of free play"; we "give ourselves over to the reception of moral ideas," "occupying a middle position between sensory enjoyment and moral deliberation."[29] But Isenberg's confidence that there *is* a middle position here may depend upon his situating deliberation too far toward the side of practical action – and indeed he suggests that, in aesthetic criticism, we stop "trying to evaluate moral ideas depthwise – that is, in terms of their connections with action and eventual result."[30] But in fact moral deliberation may often stop well short of fixing a course of conduct, and it can be called out by considerably less than a currently pressing practical problem. It is true that deliberation will weigh what might be called the "merits" of a given "side" of a moral question. But then how could something called "moral understanding," even if engaged in "free play," find a moral side "attractive" *apart* from its merits?

When Lionel Trilling argues for the aesthetic relevance – not assimilation or reductive resolution – of *ideas,* and intellectual cogency, in literature, he notes that

we can take pleasure in literature where we do not agree, responding to the power or grace of a mind without admitting the rightness of its intention or conclusion – we can take pleasure from an intellect's *cogency,* without making a final judgment on the correctness or adaptabilty of what it says.[31]

There seems no reason why ideas, in literature or in any other art that might supply them, may not be moral as well as nonmoral, but to respond to their cogency we must *see* their cogency, understand how they fit together (their "inner system of relations," according to Gass), and the relative force of the case this work makes for them. If we then can take pleasure in, or judge aesthetically excellent, a work whose moral quality we might judge evil, we may indeed be responding to "the power and grace" exhibited on behalf of that "side" of the moral question. It would be a mistake, however, to think of this response as "purely aesthetic." Power and grace are intellectual and moral virtues, as much as they are aesthetic qualities, and it may require clear thought and some moral deliberation to grasp their presence.

It is perhaps worth mentioning, in this context, that when Hume sets out his famous attack on immoral art – his denunciation of the "deformity" of vicious art, and his claim that to "confound the sentiments of morality and alter the natural boundaries of vice and virtue" is, in art, "an eternal blemish" – the factors he specifically mentions as art's deforming malefactors are "bigotry and superstition."[32] Hume may not have been careful enough, in his appraisal of art, to recognize that "vicious manners" could be "described without being marked with the proper characters of blame and disapprobation"[33] and yet still not be recommended. And he should have seen that even if an artwork were to recommend viciousness, the boundaries of vice and virtue would not then necessarily be conflated.

Nonetheless, in identifying bigotry and superstition as the spoilers of art, he effects a point of contact with those of us who are attracted to the case for the moral evaluation of art, but who grant the excellence of some art whose morality we deplore. For bigotry and superstition, as Hume understands them, are exactly the opposite of cogent thought and genuine deliberation. Thus, art marked by bigotry and superstition is art deprived, to that extent, of power and grace. This is not to deny that bigotry and superstition can be powerfully conveyed and inculcated by means of art. It is to insist that bigotry in art, patently weak thought, and intellectual confusion count as artistic, as aesthetic, flaws. The work is, as art, worse for their presence, and we should find unredeemed displeasure in the surfacing of these defects.

If it is objected that this suggestion aestheticizes morality, and we are brought curiously full circle to earlier worries about aesthetic distance and inaction, then we must note, first, that moral ideas, whatever their source, are felt as well as thought and, second, that the moral content of art, if such there be, is subject to deliberation as well as delectation. In our lives – and in and through the art that is a part of our lives – we can remain alive to the force of ideals we do not now share and to the pull of alternative evaluative schemes. We in fact cannot, in our conduct, honor all the moral ideals that may, in abstract thought and even in the lives of others, seem worthy, admirable, or in some way attractive. This is not because – or not alone because – of pervasive weakness of the will. The more fundamental problem is the practical incompatibility of, the friction between, a wide variety of recognized, or tempting, ideals. One may try to combine a commitment to, say, humility and nobility, but the sharp edges of each virtue are likely to be substantially smoothed if they are subject to a common incarnation. Or one may, out of deliberation or temperament, utterly reject some durable calls to moral responsiveness. One may, for example, conclude, and for good reason, that duty structures the moral life and that unprincipled compassion is a mistake. An artwork that makes a plea for the value of compassion may then seem troublesome. Alternatively one may, upon equally defensible reflection, see sympathy and fellow-feeling, not rules and laws, as the core from which the highest morality is built. An artwork that is a brief for duty and nobility may then seem worrisome.

But, as Emerson claims, "In every work of genius we recognize our own rejected thoughts: they come back to us with a certain alienated majesty. Great works of art have no more affecting lesson for us than this."[34] Art's capacity to keep alive certain moral perspectives, even if these views diverge radically from our present moral outlook, can help us remain alert to life's possibilities and our own potentialities. This is a benefit that is neither merely aesthetic, nor solely moral; it is both at once.

Notes

1. Oscar Wilde, Preface to *The Picture of Dorian Gray,* in *The Portable Oscar Wilde,* ed. R. Aldington (New York: Viking Press, 1946), 139.
2. Walter Pater, *The Renaissance* (New York: Modern Library, 1873), 199.
3. Arthur Danto, *The Transfiguration of the Commonplace* (Cambridge, Mass.: Harvard University Press, 1981), 22.

4. It would be exegetically crude to attribute this objection, in just this form, to Rousseau himself. But Rousseau certainly worries about the corrupting possibilities of theater and about tragedy's capacity to excite "a barren compassion indulging itself in a few tears, but never productive of any act of humanity" (*An Epistle from J. J. Rousseau to Mr. D'Alembert,* in *Miscellaneous Works of J. J. Rousseau,* vol. 3 [New York: Burt Franklin, 1972], 34).

5. Edward Bullough, "'Psychical Distance' as a Factor in Art and as an Aesthetic Principle," *British Journal of Psychology* 5 (1912): 89.

6. Ibid., 118.

7. Immanuel Kant, *Critique of Pure Judgment,* trans. J. H. Bernard, First Part, First Book, First Moment (New York: Hafner, 1968), 37–45.

8. Danto, *Transfiguration,* 23.

9. See the American pragmatists, especially G. H. Mead and John Dewey, on this point. Mead, in *Mind, Self, and Society* and *The Philosophy of the Act,* argues that conscious control and intelligent behavior depend upon a capacity for delayed reactions; and he and Dewey – the latter in, e.g., *Human Nature and Conduct* and *Experience and Nature* – characterize deliberation, including moral deliberation, as imaginative rehearsal, the playing out in thought of habits and tendencies to act that are temporarily blocked from external manifestations in conduct.

   Consider as well Emerson and Nietzsche on distance. Their different but related treatments of this idea are differently ambivalent and equivocal. Emerson and Nietzsche seem to agree, however, on the epistemological importance of the idea, and they suggest that a kind of distance is not merely a valuable human achievement but also a necessity for the realization of art. (For a comparison of Nietzsche and Emerson on the notion of distance, see K. Hanson, "Approaching Distance," *International Studies in Philosophy* 24, no. 2 [1992]: 33–40.)

   This notion that ideas of distance have surfaced in accounts of practical reason and successful epistemology – consider also the power imputed to "theoretical distance" – is not an assertion that, in these various occurrences, the meaning of "distance" is always the same. Indeed, part of what is in question here *is* the meaning, the import, of the idea of aesthetic or psychical distance. But if the latter is characterized essentially in negative terms, as the inhibition of the practical, then it certainly baffles an immediate moral condemnation of psychical distance that coherent accounts of moral deliberation seem to secure a space for this inhibition.

10. Danto, *Transfiguration,* 143.

11. I do not wish, with this question's utilitarian spin, to deflect attention from a different, and I think deeper, moral problem that hovers at the edge of this discussion. What constraints, if any, govern the use, in art, of events and experiences drawn directly from life? Morally salient questions about sincerity, authenticity, fidelity, and personal loyalty may well arise when there is narrative incorporation, within an artwork,

of one's own or others' particular experiences. Issues of privacy are also pertinent, and it must be remembered that even autobiography involves the appropriation, the use, of (at least one version of some portion of the lives of) others – friends, enemies, relatives, strangers.

12. For this schematic example to have force, the stipulations must of course be taken seriously, as must its probabilistic formulation; otherwise, one may well think of Dr. Chekov.

13. Bernard Williams, *Moral Luck* (Cambridge University Press, 1981), 24.

14. U.S. Supreme Court 413 U.S. 49 (1973).

15. Jerrold Levinson offers an interesting discussion of this sort of case, the cultivated Nazi, in "Evaluating Music," *Revue Internationale de Philosophie* 198 (1996): 593–614. He suggests that such cases are so striking precisely because they *are* exceptional, because they "violate an empirically based norm of artistic taste comporting with some degree of moral awareness." My own view is that it is the extremity of the case that is exceptional. It is the literal monstrousness of artistic sensitivity coupled with participation in *genocide* that strikes us. We would not be at all surprised, I think, by the case of a person with exquisite taste in music, someone who exhibits a sensitive ear and discerning appreciation, who nonetheless is, say, callous and self-centered, insensitive to friends and associates.

16. Leo Tolstoy, *What Is Art?* trans. A. Maude (Indianapolis: Library of Liberal Arts, 1960), 142.

17. Ibid.

18. Wilde, Preface to *Dorian Gray*, 138.

19. The issue goes back at least as far as William James, who argues for a conceptual connection between truth and human interests and values. More contemporary attention to a range of related questions about the content of science can be seen in, e.g., Thomas Kuhn's *The Structure of Scientific Revolutions* (Chicago: University of Chicago Press, 1962), 2d ed. 1970; Israel Scheffler's *Science and Subjectivity* (Indianapolis: Bobbs-Merrill, 1967) and "Vision and Revolution: A Postscript on Kuhn," *Philosophy of Science* 39 (1972): 366–74, reprinted in Scheffler's *Inquiries* (Indianapolis: Hackett, 1986); Evelyn Fox Keller's "Feminism and Science," in *Sex and Scientific Inquiry,* ed. S. Harding and J. O'Bar (Chicago: University of Chicago Press), 233–46; E. McMullin (ed.), *The Social Dimensions of Science* (Notre Dame, Ind.: University of Notre Dame Press, 1992); and many of the essays in *The Philosophy of Science,* ed. R. Boyd, P. Gasper, and J. D. Trout (Cambridge, Mass.: MIT Press, 1991).

20. It should be underscored that this point is intimately related to the one in the preceding paragraph. The embrace of fallibilism can work in science to reinforce the idea of objectivity because, if it is nonsubjective reality that ultimately controls or coerces scientific results, then the terms in which one might criticize proffered achievements – claims that proffered claims do not accord with reality – are relatively clear, clearly agreed upon, and clearly not moral. But comparable constraints on prof-

fered art are not clearly available. Thus, it will not do to pretend to embrace a comparable fallibilism in the realm of art, suggesting that we cannot be sure, for any candidate art, whether it really *is* art, but insisting, still, that true or genuine art may yet be immune from moral criticism. It is precisely because there is no practical agreement on the ultimate constraints of art that an adversion here to the idea of the "true" or the "genuine" is quite empty – radically undeveloped conceptually and, partly because of that, of no use in furthering a possible parallel between moral immunity in science and in art. (John Brown's useful commentary, at the University of Maryland conference for which this essay was originally prepared, prompted this elaboration.)

21. Indeed, the linkage between something's being the product of human activity and something's being an appropriate subject for moral concern is so tight that it may supply an inappropriate bit of support for Danto's thoughts about psychical distance. It is perhaps no accident that Bullough's original illustration of the phenomenon of psychical distance, the example he uses to establish the meaning of the term, is the sea fog abstracted in experience from "its danger and practical unpleasantness." The natural world, apart from human beings, is not a natural locus for moral concern and assessment, so when Bullough asks us to imagine putting aside practical considerations about the sea fog in order to achieve the thrill of psychical distance, morality does not impede our compliance by standing before us with stern practical demands. A move to relish the sensuous surface of the situation may proceed without serious obstacles. Danto's politically charged riot (with "police clubbing demonstrators") and bombs dropping from airplanes are, however, situations already fraught with moral agency and essentially defined by sociopolitical responsibilities. Abstracting in these situations from considerations of morality may indeed, then, be "wrong or inhuman," but not (just) because we have an obligation to intervene; the problem is rather that the human responsibility *for* these situations, the human agency that stands *behind* them, demands, appropriately calls out for, moral *assessment*. This is not to say that the issues at stake could not be recast in a less prejudicial form. We could consider whether it would be wrong or inhuman to put at a psychical distance a natural catastrophe now threatening or claiming human lives: an earthquake is beginning to rumble through our town, or the sea fog leads to the collision of two ships . . .

22. William Gass, "Goodness Knows Nothing of Beauty: On the Distance between Morality and Art," in *Reflecting on Art,* ed. John Fisher (Mountain View, Calif.: Mayfield, 1993), 110, 112.

23. In his conference commentary on this essay, John Brown suggested that this response to Gass turns on a conflation of the "well-planned party" and the "well-prepared dish." Brown noted that *dishes* are typically judged not by moral criteria but by culinary ones, the standards of a cuisine being assumed to be morally acceptable.

That is probably a correct account of our typical practice, but it begs the question I take the extremity of the example to highlight. We do not "assume" the acceptability of a cannibalistic cuisine, and if we were in the untypical position of being served cooked human flesh, then moral, not culinary, criteria would surely come to the fore. The more general lesson of the extreme example is that our assumptions about moral acceptability, or irrelevance, may sometimes be unsettled and our typical practices of judgment open to confoundment. Gass suggests that it is simple-minded not to judge things on "their own terms." But the very question at issue may be "What *are* the relevant terms of judgment?"

A focus on the cooked quail can lull us into the belief that we can always sustain a distinction between value areas, always make a distinction between a bad thing done and a thing badly done. For many of us, though of course not for all, the cooking of quail does not seem a bad thing, and the dish is simply well or badly prepared. But the idea of a thing "badly done" depends for its sense upon assumed standards, tacit expectations, a relatively clear notion of what the "thing" is that has been botched. The creative and innovative character of art, however, suggests there may be trouble, in this sphere, with the idea of assumed standards and tacit expectations.

24. William James, "On a Certain Blindness in Human Beings," in *Talks to Teachers* (New York: Norton, 1958), 152.
25. Gass, "Goodness," 115.
26. Arnold Isenberg, *Aesthetics and the Theory of Criticism* (Chicago: University of Chicago Press, 1973), 270.
27. Ibid., 269.
28. Ibid., 272.
29. Ibid., 274.
30. Ibid., 280.
31. Lionel Trilling, *The Liberal Imagination* (New York: Viking Press, 1950), 291.
32. David Hume, *The Standard of Taste,* in *Essays and Treatises on Several Subjects* (London: 1758), 146.
33. Ibid., 145.
34. Ralph Waldo Emerson, "Self-Reliance," in *The Works of Emerson* (New York: Tudor, n.d.), 1: 31.

9

Beauty and evil: the case of Leni Riefenstahl's *Triumph of the Will*

MARY DEVEREAUX

I

Leni Riefenstahl's documentary of the 1934 Nuremberg rally of the National Socialist German Workers' Party, *Triumph of the Will,* is perhaps the most controversial film ever made. At once masterful and morally repugnant, this deeply troubling film epitomizes a general problem that arises with art. It is both beautiful and evil. I shall argue that it is this conjunction of beauty and evil that explains why the film is so disturbing. My aim in this essay is to explore the relationship of beauty and evil in *Triumph of the Will* and to use this examination of a particular case as a way of investigating the more general problem of beauty and evil in art. Having looked at this case in detail, I want to draw some broader conclusions about the inadequacy of the usual solution to the problem of beauty and evil in art and to suggest the direction we should move in to develop an account of aesthetic value rich enough to handle cases as difficult as *Triumph of the Will.*

My main aim is philosophical, but I shall have to turn to more concrete matters before taking up the philosophical issues. I will briefly describe the historical background of the film and the circumstances in which it was produced (Section II). I will also provide some sense of *Triumph of the Will* itself, that is, of its artistic strategy and how it contributes to the film's overall effect (Section III). I will then be in a position to turn to the problem of beauty and evil in the film and to the more general problem of beauty and evil in art that is my central concern (Sections IV–VI).

II

The 1934 Nuremberg party rally was one of several mammoth political rallies sponsored by the Nazi Party between 1923 and 1939. It lasted seven days, involved tens of thousands of participants, and was estimated to have drawn as many as 500,000 spectators.[1]

The film of these events was made at Hitler's personal request and with his support. Hitler himself gave the film its title, *Triumph des Willens*. He also went to Nuremberg to help with the preproduction planning, carefully orchestrating the spectacle that would involve thousands of troops, marching bands, and ordinary citizens.

Like the rally, the film's production was a large, well-organized event. Riefenstahl's crew consisted of 172 persons: 36 cameramen and assistants, 9 aerial photographers, 17 newsreel men, 17 lighting technicians, and so on.[2] The crew, uniformed as SA (Sturmabteilung der NSDAP) men so that they would not be noticeable in the crowd,[3] used thirty cameras and worked nonstop for a week. Riefenstahl held daily directorial meetings at which each member of the camera crew received instructions for the next day. Scenes were rehearsed beforehand, and the front ranks of the Labor Service men were trained to speak in unison.[4]

Concerned that the long parades, endless speeches, and days of nearly identical events would bore her audience, Riefenstahl rejected the static format and voice-over commentary of the conventional newsreel. Instead, she adopted and expanded methods of mobile photography developed by Abel Gance and others for the (fictional) feature film. Wherever possible she had rails and tracks laid throughout the rally site, including a circular track built around the speakers' podium[5] and a lift installed on a 140-foot flagpole. The crew was even instructed to practice roller skating.[6] These devices enabled Riefenstahl to infuse shots of her frequently stationary subjects with action and motion.

Distilled from sixty-one hours of footage, in a process of editing that Riefenstahl worked twelve to eighteen hours a day for five months to complete, the final version of the film ran just over two hours. Its intensely dynamic visual material was set to a score of Wagnerian music, German folk songs, military marches, and party anthems (including the official party anthem, "Das Horst Wessel Lied") intercut with the sound of cheering crowds and party speeches. The result, in both style and effect, was a radical departure

from the standard newsreel. An innovation in documentary film-making, *Triumph of the Will* was also, as is generally recognized, a major contribution to the history of film.

The film premiered at the Ufa Palast in Berlin in March 1935 before an audience of foreign diplomats, army generals, and top party officials, including Hitler.[7] None of the Nazi officials, not even Hitler, had seen the film in advance[8] – an extremely unusual circumstance at the time, since no film could be screened in private or public until it was passed by the censorship board.[9] Some party members thought the film "too artistic," though whether the objection was to artistic technique itself or to the film's suitability for political use isn't clear. Others, especially members of the army, were angry at Riefenstahl's omission of most of the military exercises (the footage had been shot in bad weather). Hitler, however, was delighted with the film.[10] Although it is difficult to know exactly how widely *Triumph of the Will* was shown or how it was received,[11] it apparently enjoyed some popular success, despite the German public's preference for entertainment films.

In any case, artistically, *Triumph of the Will* immediately established itself, winning recognition not only in Germany (where it was awarded the 1935 National Film Prize), but also abroad, where it won the Gold Medal at the Venice Film Festival. Two years later, it won the Grand Prix at the 1937 Paris Film Festival, where, to their credit, French workers protested Riefenstahl's appearance when she came in person to accept her award.

III

In turning to the film itself, there are three things to note: its structure, its vision, and its narrative strategy. Each of these features contributes to the film's notable effect.

Structurally, *Triumph of the Will* has twelve sections or scenes, each focused on a particular party rally event: Hitler's arrival in Nuremberg, the Hitler Youth rally, the folk parade, Hitler's address to the SA, and so on. The film *appears* to present these events as they unfold. In fact, Riefenstahl ignores chronological order almost entirely, working instead to create a rhythmic structure for the film.[12] Her aim, she states, was "to bring certain elements into the foreground and put others into the background," to create a dramatic succession of highlights and retreats, peaks and valleys.[13] This musical structure was created largely in the editing room, where, working without a script, Riefenstahl used a variety of means – alternating scenes of day and night, moving from solemnity to exuberance, and generally altering the pace of the film from sequence to sequence and within the individual scenes themselves – to give the film a determinate rhythmic structure.

This rhythmic structure is manifest in sequences such as the film's third section, "The City Awakening." The portrait of early-morning Nuremberg begins slowly and lyrically as the camera travels high above the quiet, mist-covered rooftops of the old city. Church bells toll and the film dissolves to a lively shot of morning activity in the tented city used to house rally participants. Here, drums beat and bugles announce the start of day for residents, who emerge jauntily from their tents to wash, shave, and eat breakfast. The tempo and pace of this montage of daily activity increase, climaxing in brightly lit shots of healthy, bare-chested youths, working and singing old German folk songs as they polish shoes, haul wood for the camp stoves, and prepare for the more serious activities of the rally itself.

By building these scenes to a crescendo of dramatic intensity, Riefenstahl means to hold the spectator's attention and generate some of the same enthusiasm and excitement felt by rally participants. These same techniques are used throughout the film, in scenes of Hitler's speeches, troop reviews, and the like. Even the most prosaic subjects, such as the repetitive passages of military marching, are made visually interesting and dramatic by these techniques. Not surprisingly, these tightly organized rhythmic sequences are quite effective.

Much has been written on the formal features of Riefenstahl's art.[14] What has not been generally appreciated is that the film's artistic achievement is not merely structural or formal. Equally important is Riefenstahl's masterful command of traditional narrative means: theme and characterization, the use of symbolism, and the handling of point of view. It is the use of these devices to tell a *story* – the story of the New Germany – that, combined with the structural techniques already surveyed, creates the vision of Hitler and National Socialism that makes *Triumph of the Will* so powerful.

That vision is one in which the military values of loyalty and courage, unity, discipline, and obedience are wedded to a heroic conception of life and elements of German *völkisch* mythology. In Riefenstahl's hands, an annual political rally is transformed into a larger historical and symbolic event. *Triumph of the Will* presents the Nazi world as a kind of Valhalla, "a place apart, surrounded by clouds and mist, peopled by heroes and ruled from above by the gods."[15] Seen from the perspective of the film, Hitler is the hero of a grand narrative. He is both leader and savior, a new Siegfried come to restore a defeated Germany to its ancient splendor.

In establishing this heroic vision, Riefenstahl works with several striking motifs: the swastika, the German eagle, flags, Albert Speer's towering architecture, torches and burning pyres, moon and clouds, the roar of the crowds, Hitler's voice. Her strategy is to use these aural and visual motifs to establish three key ideas, encapsulated in the National Socialist slogan *Ein Volk. Ein Führer. Ein Reich* (One People. One Leader. One Empire). These three ideas, introduced by Riefenstahl in slightly different order, are the *Führerprinzip,* leader principle or cult of the leader (the *Führer*), the unity of the people or national community (the *Volk*), and the strength and power of the German nation (the *Reich*). Each has a central role both in the film's vision of Hitler and in its story of the New Germany.[16]

The first and most important idea, the *Führerprinzip,* has obvious roots in messianic Christianity.[17] The idea of a great historical figure or great man who has the will and power to actualize the true will of the German people was frequently dramatized in Nazi cinema. But *Triumph of the Will* is the only Nazi film that directly identifies this mystical leader with Hitler himself. From its very first frames, Riefenstahl's film presents Hitler as the leader long sought by the German people and as "the bearer of the people's will."[18] He is a god-like, mystical figure who descends – literally – from the clouds, his plane flying in over the mist-enshrouded towers and spires of medieval Nuremberg. These shots of the advancing plane are intercut with striking aerial footage of Nuremberg – a city representative of the old Germany and of the glorious Teutonic past, its castle a bulwark against foreign intruders. The shadow of the approaching plane falls over the columns and columns of marching troops who fill the streets below. All this takes place as themes from Wagner's *Die Meistersinger* slowly give way to the Nazi Party anthem, much as the old Germany slowly gives way to the new. The climax of this scene comes several minutes into the film when the plane lands, its door opens, and Hitler appears to a roar of approval from the waiting crowds. By such means, Riefenstahl makes Hitler's arrival at the rally – as well as his every subsequent appearance – resonate with deep historical and national significance for the German people.[19]

In the early sequences of the film, Riefenstahl stresses not only Hitler's messianic leadership, but his humanity. This is a leader who moves among the people, who shakes hands and smiles. Shots of Hitler are intercut with shots not only of enormous crowds but of individuals, especially children, laughing and smiling. Even small details, like Hitler stopping his motorcade to accept flowers from a mother and child along the road, are designed to support the film's vision of Hitler as the much-beloved father of the German people.

The second key idea of *Triumph of the Will* is the unity of the support for Hitler among the German people (*ein Volk*). Within the universe of the film, *everyone* supports Hitler. The crowds that fill scene after scene are staggering in number, their enthusiasm unending. Nowhere do we see anyone – a postman, a traffic cop, or a pedestrian – engaged in ordinary business. Day after day, the narrow Nuremberg streets are filled to overflowing with old and young. People hang from the windows; they throng the stadium. All yearn to catch a glimpse of the *Führer.*

The beauty and sheer exuberance of these scenes celebrate these pro-Nazi sentiments. Indeed, several scenes appear to have been explicitly constructed to demonstrate that Hitler's support knows no class or regional barriers. For example, in the fifth sequence of the film, the presentation of the Labor Services, 52,000 corpsmen appear in review before Hitler at an enormous outdoor rally. Riefenstahl begins with the usual documentary-like shots of the men as they stand in formation, shouldering their shovels like guns and reciting patriotic slogans. But then she does something unusual. She constructs a montage of individual faces calling out the names of their *Heimat,* or regional homeland. "Where do you come from, comrade?" asks their leader. "From Friesland." "And you, comrade?" "From Bavaria." "And you?" "From Kaiserstuhl." "And you?" "From Pomerania . . . from Königsberg, Silesia, the Baltic, the Black Forest, Dresden, Danube, from the Rhine, and from the Saar. . . ."

This carefully crafted passage makes the idea of a national community visually (and aurally) concrete. Hitler's supporters, the film shows us, are a unity – one people – despite their differences; it is Hitler – one leader – who brings them together. The stirring music, the marshaling of flags, and the great German eagle towering over the stadium underscore the importance of the contribution of even the most ordinary laborers to the New Germany – planting forests, building roads "from village to village, from town to town." In the words of the workers themselves: "*Ein Volk. Ein Führer. Ein Reich – Deutschland.*" The effect is one of order and national purpose, a national purpose made manifest in the final shot of the sequence: the Labor Services men marching toward the camera, their image superimposed over Hitler's raised fist.[20]

The third and final idea central to *Triumph of the Will,* one *Reich,* is most prominent in the film's final sequences. Here Riefenstahl's strategy is the visual display of power (*Macht*).[21] Her aim is to show the enormous military forces that stand behind the *Führer* and the solidity of their support.[22] In demonstrating power, the ritual of the mass meeting itself had a central role: the waving swastikas, the uniforms, the legions of marching, chanting followers, the torches against the night sky – all contributed to the spectacle designed to display Hitler's personal and political power.[23]

Triumph of the Will does more than present a set of ideas; it weaves them into a story, makes them part of a grand narrative. The 1934 party Congress had two titles: the Party Day of Unity and the Party

Day of Power. Riefenstahl works with the themes of both unity and power, manipulating artistic form not only to create enthusiasm for Hitler and the National Socialists but to evoke fear. As noted, the opening of the film focuses on cheerful scenes emphasizing the spontaneous loyalty of ordinary people. Party and military forces are little in evidence. In contrast, the two final sequences – the military parade with which the Nazis leave Nuremberg and the somewhat anticlimactic final congress – center on Hitler, high-ranking party officials, and regiment after regiment of tightly disciplined troops. There are no smiles or laughing children, no young boys, no women with flowers. These are men – ready to go to war.

235

Running nearly twenty minutes, the final parade sequence is the longest of the film. Riefenstahl presents a seemingly inexhaustible stream of massed forces. We see the straight-legged, stiff-kneed marching troops from every angle, constantly moving, in a dazzling display of dynamic editing. Riefenstahl cuts back and forth between shots of the men in uniform, party officials, and Hitler. In contrast to the opening scenes, Hitler stands alone, apart from the people: watching, saluting, receiving ovations. The mood is somber. The power of the Nazis is presented as daunting and unquestionable.

To summarize, then, Riefenstahl weaves the narrative and thematic elements of her film around the central National Socialist slogan *Ein Führer. Ein Volk. Ein Reich* as tightly as she weaves the visual elements of eagle and swastika. As she tells it, the tale of Hitler – stalwart and alone, heroic – is the tale of the German people. His will is their will. His power their future. It is all this and more that makes *Triumph of the Will* the powerful film it is.

IV

Clearly, *Triumph of the Will* is a troubling film. My claim is that it is so because of its conjunction of beauty and evil, because it presents as beautiful a vision of Hitler and the New Germany that is morally repugnant. But might not there be a simpler, more straightforward explanation of the film's disturbing nature? Can't it be wholly explained by the fact that the film is a documentary?

As a *documentary* film, *Triumph of the Will* is disquieting because the events it portrays are themselves disquieting. As a documentary *film, Triumph of the Will* conveys the sheer immediacy of these events. We view Hitler's speeches, the flag ceremonies, the spotlighted evening assemblies as if they were happening *now*. And our knowledge that what we are seeing stands in a causal chain of events that led to the Second World War and the Holocaust makes this immediacy chilling. It is as if we were watching the buds of these horrors unfold before our eyes.

But Riefenstahl's film does more than document historical events. And it is more than an ordinary documentary. *Triumph of the Will* is also troubling because it is a work of Nazi propaganda. The word 'propaganda' originated in the celebrated papal society for "propagating the faith" established in 1622. In modern contexts, the term has taken on more specifically political connotations. In claiming that *Triumph of the Will* is a work of propaganda, I mean that it is designed to propagate the Nazi faith – and mobilize the German people. *Triumph of the Will* thus unites the older religious connotations of 'propaganda' with the modern political connotations, presenting National Socialism as a political religion. Its images, ideas, and narrative all aim at establishing the tenets of that religion: Hitler is a messianic leader, Germany is one *Volk,* and the Third Reich will endure for a thousand years.

It may come as some surprise, then, to learn that the film's status as propaganda is controversial. Amazingly, Riefenstahl and her supporters deny that *Triumph of the Will* is a work of propaganda. And because there is a controversy – in fact, a rather heated one – we need to pause briefly to take up this issue. Riefenstahl and her supporters contend that her concerns in *Triumph of the Will* – as in all her films – were aesthetic, not political: that it was the cult of beauty, not the cult of the *Führer,* that Riefenstahl worshiped. The claim is that stylistic devices like the cloud motif in the film's opening sequence, the rhythmic montage of faces in the Labor Services sequence, and so on were *just* that: stylistic devices meant to avoid newsreel reportage, enrich the film artistically, and nothing more.[24]

Certainly Riefenstahl *was* preoccupied with beauty in *Triumph of the Will.* Her films of the 1936 Berlin Olympics, her photographs of the Nuba, indeed the whole of her artistic corpus, make clear that visual beauty was one of her central artistic preoccupations. But the claim that a concern for beauty and stylistic innovation is the only thing going on in *Triumph of the Will* is undermined by the film itself. As we have seen, the film is aimed not simply at stylistic innovation and formally beautiful images, but at using these means to create a particular vision of Hitler and National Socialism.

The pure-aestheticism defense is also belied by the historical record. Riefenstahl was, as she willingly admits, a great admirer of Hitler. Attending a political rally for the first time in her life in February 1932, she was "paralyzed," "fascinated," "deeply affected" by the appearance of Hitler and the crowd's "bondage to this man."[25] Even at the end of the war, by which point she, like many Nazi sympathizers, claims to have harbored doubts about Hitler's plans for Germany, Riefenstahl, by her own admission, "wept all night" at the news of his suicide.[26] To this day, Riefenstahl has never distanced herself from the political content of *Triumph of the Will* or any of the other films she made for Hitler.[27] Nor, despite years of ostracism and public controversy, has she shown – or even feigned – remorse for her artistic and personal association with many members of the Nazi Party.

It might be added that Riefenstahl agreed to film the 1934 Nuremberg rally only on condition that she be given complete artistic control over the project, a condition to which Hitler apparently agreed. She demanded, and got, final cut. Thus, we can assume that the film Riefenstahl made – the film organized around the ideas of *Ein Führer. Ein Volk. Ein Reich* that presents Hitler as savior to the German people, and that describes the Nazi future as full of promise – is the film she chose to make.

The film's history also supports its status as propaganda. Goebbels, who as minister for People's Enlightenment and Propaganda, was largely responsible for the creation of the *Führer* myth, thought the film a great achievement, unprecedented in its representation of Hitler as father of the German people and leader of the New Germany. In recommending that *Triumph of the Will* be awarded the National Film Prize, Goebbels proclaimed:

The film marks a very great achievement. . . . It is a magnificent cinematic vision of the Führer, *seen here for the first time with a power that has not been revealed before.* The film has successfully avoided the danger of being merely a politically slanted film. It has translated the powerful rhythm of this great epoch into something outstandingly artistic; it is an epic, forging the tempo of marching formations, steel-like in its conviction and fired by a passionate artistry.[28]

Indeed, so successful was *Triumph of the Will* in articulating the *Führerprinzip* that, as one historian of German propaganda put it, "there was no need to make another film about Hitler. . . ."[29] *Triumph of the Will* was the definitive Nazi documentary about the *Führer.* Although a series of later films associated Hitler with other great men of Germany's past (e.g., Bismarck and Schiller), no other documentary about the *Führer* was, in fact, ever commissioned.

Riefenstahl also maintains that *Triumph of the Will* was what might be called "a pure documentary," that it merely records the reality of the loyalty and hope Hitler once inspired. In her words, the film "is purely historical. . . . It is *film-verité*. It reflects the truth that was then, in 1934, history. It is therefore a documentary. Not a propaganda film."[30]

This second line of defense is clearly at odds with the first: her claim that the film's concerns are purely aesthetic. She wants, on the one hand, to tout her considerable artistic accomplishments in giving life to the boring speeches and endless marching and, on the other hand, to maintain that she did little but record events as they unfolded, that her film is *cinema verité*. Can she really have it both ways? But let us bracket the issue of consistency and good faith and simply note that the claim of pure documentation, like the claim of pure aestheticism, is refuted by the film's structure. As we have seen, *Triumph of the Will* is a carefully crafted, artfully constructed film. Its principles of organization are governed not by the chronological sequence of the events depicted in the film, but by the demands of the film's narrative vision: the highly selective (and distorted) story about Hitler of which Riefenstahl is the author.

Of course, documentaries are never just transcriptions of events. Documentary filmmakers always edit and construct. They always take a point of view. But even allowing for this general point, it remains true that *Triumph of the Will* is an extreme case of a documentary film whose organization is governed by political aims.

The pure-documentary defense also conveniently overlooks certain crucial features of the relation between the film and its subject matter. One of the most remarkable facts about *Triumph of the Will* is that the reality it records is a reality it helped to create. This is what Siegfried Kracauer was getting at when he made his famous "faked reality" charge:

... from the real life of the people was built up a faked reality that was passed off as the genuine one; but this bastard reality, instead of being an end in itself, merely served as the set dressing for a film that was then to assume the character of an authentic documentary.[31]

Riefenstahl, in other words, helped to set up the spectacle her film was designed to document. As she herself acknowledged in a now-famous remark, "[T]he preparations for the Party Convention were made in concert with the preparations for the camera work."[32]

One can of course argue that, unlike the staged scenes of Nazi events made in Hollywood, this "faked event" was part of Nazi history: a real event, not just the set of a movie. But this real event did not just "unfold"; it was constructed in part *to be* the subject of her film. By "faked reality," Kracauer can be understood to mean something like what we would now call a "media event." Furthermore, in filming this event, Riefenstahl gave form to Hitler's vision of Germany's future. To cite her own words, she took "nothing but

239

speeches, marches, and mobs" and brought this material alive, creating a stirring film spectacle that could be replayed again and again. Riefenstahl used her considerable talent and her art to create an image that helped further and sustain the vision of National Socialism shared by Hitler, Goebbels, and Speer. Surely much of the infamy of the 1934 rally is due to Riefenstahl's film.

We can close this discussion of the controversy over the film's status as propaganda by noting that both lines of defense (the aesthetic and the documentary) are framed in terms of Riefenstahl's intentions. Each of these arguments is of the form: "*Triumph of the Will* is not a work of propaganda, because Leni Riefenstahl did not intend to make a work of propaganda." Did Leni Riefenstahl *intend* to make a work of propaganda? If the question is "Did she think to herself, 'I'm going to make a work of Nazi propaganda'?" the answer is probably no. But this is the wrong question. The right question is: "Did she think something to the effect that 'I'm going to show Hitler in a way that will mobilize the German people in his support'?" And the answer to this question, presumably, is yes. Had Hitler won the war, Riefenstahl wouldn't be defending herself by disavowing the intention to make a work of propaganda.

In any case, the debate about Leni Riefenstahl's intentions (what was going on "in her head") is largely beside the point.[33] For the question whether *Triumph of the Will* is a work of propaganda is a question about the *film,* not a question about (the historical person) Leni Riefenstahl. And as we have seen, the answer to this question is plainly yes.[34]

So *Triumph of the Will* is a work of Nazi propaganda. And that is clearly part of what makes the film so troubling. But Riefenstahl is not the first or last artist to make fascist art. Hundreds of propaganda films were made in German between 1933 and 1945. Many, like the feature film *Jud Süss,* had much wider popular success. And some, like the virulently anti-Semitic "documentary" *Der ewige Jude* (The Eternal Jew, 1940), had arguably as harmful an effect on German thought and behavior.

Triumph of the Will is distinguished from these and other Nazi propaganda films in two ways. First, it is extremely well made. (And the fact that it is an excellent work of propaganda is part of what makes it so disturbing.) But the film is more than first-class propaganda. It is also a work of art. A work of creative imagination, stylistically and formally innovative, its every detail contributes to its central vision and overall effect. The film is also very, very beautiful. *Triumph of the Will* can be properly called a work of art because it offers a beautiful, sensuous presentation – a vision – of the German people, leader, and empire in a recognized artistic genre (documentary) of a recognized artistic medium (film). It is the fact that *Triumph of the Will* is an excellent work of propaganda *and* a work of art that explains why Riefenstahl's film has more than historical interest and why it has a place in film and not just history classes.

V

As art, *Triumph of the Will* is problematic for reasons other than those associated with its excellence as a work of propaganda (e.g., its capacity to mobilize the German people in the 1930s), and it is as art that *Triumph of the Will* is most disturbing. What makes *Triumph of the Will* problematic and disturbing as art is its artistic vision: its vision of the German people, leader, and empire. Riefenstahl's film portrays National Socialism (something morally evil) as beautiful. To view the film in the way in which it was intended to be seen is to see and be moved by (what Riefenstahl presents as) the beauty of National Socialism.

If this is right, it raises a question about how we are to respond to this film. Its every detail is designed to advance a morally repugnant vision of Hitler, a vision that, as history was to prove, falsified the true character of Hitler and National Socialism. Enjoying *this film* – recognizing that we may be caught up, if only slightly, in its pomp and pageantry or be stirred by its beauty – is likely to make us ask, "What kind of person am I to enjoy or be moved by this film?"[35] Isn't there something wrong with responding in this way to a Nazi film?

This worry arises because *Triumph of the Will* presents National Socialism as attractive and, in so doing, aims to make us think of National Socialism as good. Hitler and what he stood for are commended. This is different from a case like Klaus Mann's novel about Nazism, *Mephisto,* where the evil described is clearly not presented as attractive or as meant to win our allegiance. Riefenstahl doesn't just ask us to imagine finding the *Führer* and his message appealing, but actually to find them so.[36]

The concern is not only that if I enjoy such a film, I may be led to act badly (e.g., to support neo-Nazi movements), but also that certain kinds of enjoyment, regardless of their effects, may themselves be problematic. Pleasure in this work of art (like pleasure in a work of art that celebrates sadism or pedophilia) might lead one to ask not just about what one may *become,* but about who one is *now.* The point is an Aristotelian one. If virtue consists (in part) in taking pleasure in the right things and not in the wrong things, then what is my character now such that I can take pleasure in these things?

Triumph of the Will also raises pressing questions about the attitude we should adopt toward the film as art. Should we praise it for its widely acclaimed aesthetic qualities despite its celebration of National Socialism? We recognize D. W. Griffith's *Birth of a Nation* as an important film despite its racism, and we admire the Pyramids despite the great human cost paid for their production. Should we similarly bracket questions of good and evil in looking at *Triumph of the Will?* Alternatively, should we insist that the moral implications of Riefenstahl's work undermine its aesthetic value? Or is this formulation of the problem too simple?

These questions merely highlight the long-standing general problem of beauty and evil: that aesthetic and moral considerations may pull in different directions. The problem emerges not only with *Triumph of the Will* and the other cases mentioned earlier but with, for example, the literary works of the Marquis de Sade and T. S. Eliot. The problem posed by the conflict between the demands of art and the demands of morality is familiar. What are we to make of it?

For much of the twentieth century, the standard solution to this conflict has been to recommend that we look at art from an "aesthetic distance." As originally described by Edward Bullough in 1912, an attitude of aesthetic distance allows us to set aside the practical concerns of everyday life, including questions of a work's origins, its moral effects, and so on, and concentrate exclusively on the work of art itself. By "the work itself" Bullough means, of course, the work's "formal" (i.e., its structural and stylistic) features. Bracketing all nonformal features frees us, at least temporarily, "to elaborate experience on a new basis,"[37] much as we do in appreciating the beauty of a fog at sea despite its danger.

The basic strategy here is simple: when approaching a work of art that raises moral issues, sever aesthetic evaluation from moral evaluation and evaluate the work in aesthetic (i.e., formal) terms alone. This is the formalist response to the problem of beauty and evil. Formalism treats the aesthetic and the moral as wholly independent domains. It allows us to say that, evaluated morally, *Triumph of the Will* is bad but, evaluated aesthetically, it is good.

In recent decades, formalism has become rather unfashionable, having been subjected to serious criticism by feminists, philosophers of art, and others. Formalism nevertheless plays a dominant role in discussions of *Triumph of the Will.* One explanation for this is that the formalist strategy may seem especially well suited to cases such as *Triumph of the Will.* Like Bullough's fog at sea, the Nazi content of Riefenstahl's film *is* threatening. And it is certainly true that without some measure of distance, we risk being too overcome with emotion or too caught up in what is morally objectionable to attend to what makes the work aesthetically good. Viewing the film from a disinterested (what Bullough calls an "objective") point of view gives us a way of setting aside the components that make it morally objectionable. This enables us to appreciate at least some of the features that make it aesthetically good. If the strategy works, there *is* no problem of beauty and evil. Indeed, one of the aims of formalism is to show that there is really no such problem – to show that it is illusory.

But in the case of *Triumph of the Will,* the formalist strategy fails. It won't work here, not because we're too obsessed by the moral issues to assume a properly distanced standpoint, or because when we assume a posture of aesthetic distance we forget about the historical realities associated with the film, or because adopting an attitude of aesthetic distance toward a film like *Triumph of the Will* is itself an immoral position (though some may wish to argue that it is).[38] Nor does adopting an attitude of aesthetic distance require that we literally forget about the historical realities. Aesthetic distance is, after all, only a shift in perspective, and a temporary one at that.

The reason the formalist strategy fails in the case of *Triumph of the Will* is that distancing ourselves from the morally objectionable elements of the film – its deification of Hitler, the story it tells about him, the party, and the German people, and so on – means distancing ourselves from the features that make it the work of art it is. If we distance ourselves from these features of the film, we will not be in a position to understand its artistic value – that is, why this lengthy film of political speeches and endless marching is correctly regarded as a cinematic masterpiece. We will also miss the beauty (horrifying though it is) of its vision of Hitler.

Like all religious and political works of art (e.g., Dante's *The Divine Comedy,* Orwell's *1984,* Wright's *Native Son*), *Triumph of the Will* has a message.[39] We can bracket that message – that is, the political elements and aims of the film – in favor of its strictly formal elements, just as we can read *The Inferno* while ignoring its Christianity. But in doing so we omit an essential dimension of the film, and an essential dimension of its beauty. To see *Triumph of the Will* for the work of art it is and to fully grasp its beauty, we need to pay attention to its content – to just those elements of the film that formalism directs us to set aside.

In emphasizing the importance of the film's content, I don't mean to underplay the significance of its formal elements. Unquestionably, a large part of what the film is, and of what makes it artistically valuable, consists in its striking images and beautiful patterns of movement. Moreover, the purely formal features of *Triumph of the Will,* considered in abstraction from their contribution to the film's message, are (as formalism teaches us) unproblematically beautiful.

But *Triumph of the Will* is a work of artistic mastery – perhaps, I dare say, of genius – not merely because of the film's purely formal features (the beauty of Riefenstahl's cinematography, her skillful editing techniques, etc.) but, perhaps most important, because of its artistic vision, its particular, utterly horrifying vision of Hitler and National Socialism. That vision is the essence of the film.

If taking an attitude of aesthetic distance means paying attention only to the formal aspects of the work (to the image and not to what it means), then aesthetic distance fails in the case of *Triumph of the Will* because it requires us to ignore the essence of the film.

Now, defenders of formalism can opt for a more complex understanding of aesthetic distance, one that does not require us to bracket an artwork's content. According to this view (call it "sophisticated formalism"), understanding a work of art consists in grasping and appreciating the relationship between its form and content, that is, the connection between the message and the means used to convey it. Artistic success consists in expressing a particular message in an effective way. Sophisticated formalism thus allows – indeed requires – us to pay attention to the particular content of the work. On this subtler view, we can't just ignore the content of art or its message. We must attend to the relation between a work's form and content, if we are to appreciate the work itself.

Sophisticated formalism introduces a new conception of the aesthetic. The simpler version of formalism defined the aesthetic narrowly, in terms of a work's formal elements, considered by themselves. The new, more complex conception tracks the *relation* between form and content. A work's aesthetic achievement consists in the skill with which it expresses its content. Understood in this way, the aesthetic value of *Triumph of the Will* involves not just its formal accomplishments, but also how these stylistic means are used to convey feelings of awe, admiration, and oneness with Hitler.

Note that sophisticated formalism doesn't require abandoning the distinction between aesthetic and moral evaluation. As with the simpler version, with sophisticated formalism, aesthetic evaluation belongs to one domain, moral evaluation to another. Sophisticated formalism tells us to judge not the message but its expression. In this respect, the approach we are meant to take toward the National Socialist elements of Riefenstahl's documentary is no different from the approach we are meant to take toward the Christianity of *The Divine Comedy* or *Paradise Lost.* Our finding the message conveyed by *Triumph of the Will* repulsive (or attractive) should not therefore affect our aesthetic judgment. Nor should it affect our aesthetic response to the film.

Indeed, according to sophisticated formalism, *Triumph of the Will* and works of art like it shouldn't (from an aesthetic point of view) cause any problem at all. We can distance ourselves from – that is, set aside – the moral dimension of the work's content while still *paying attention to* that content – that is, the way in which the film's content figures in its expressive task.

Is this broader, more inclusive understanding of aesthetic distance satisfactory? The answer, I think, is no. Even sophisticated formalism, with its richer concept of the aesthetic, makes it impossible to talk about the political meaning of *Triumph of the Will,* the truth or falsity of its picture of Hitler, whether it is good or evil, right or wrong – *while doing aesthetics.* These cognitive and moral matters are ones we are meant to distance ourselves from when engaged in the business of aesthetic evaluation. Sophisticated formalism doesn't ignore content, but it does *aestheticize* it. When we follow its recommendations, we adopt an aesthetic attitude toward the Christianity of *The Divine Comedy* and an aesthetic attitude toward the National Socialism of *Triumph of the Will.* Sophisticated formalism is, after all, a kind of formalism. It focuses on the (formal) relation between form and content. From its perspective, the content of the film (its vision) is relevant to evaluation only insofar as it is expressed well or badly. Thus, even on sophisticated varieties of formalism, essential elements of *Triumph of the Will* remain irrelevant to its aesthetic evaluation. Hence, here too, formalism fails to respond fully to the work of art that *Triumph of the Will* is.

Content is not always as important as it is in the case of *Triumph of the Will,* but here, as in the case of much political and religious art, the formalist response makes it difficult or impossible to explain why works like *Triumph of the Will* should be considered problematic in the first place.

At this point there are two ways to go. We can say that there is more to art than aesthetics or that there is more to aesthetics than beauty and form. The first option allows us to keep the historically important, eighteenth-century conception of the aesthetic intact. (It is in effect the conception of the aesthetic introduced by sophisticated formalism.) This conception has the advantage of keeping the boundaries of the aesthetic relatively narrow and clearly defined. And it keeps aesthetic evaluation relatively simple. Questions of political meaning, of truth and falsity, good and evil, right and wrong fall outside the category of the aesthetic. One implication of adopting this option is that, since there are works of art that raise these issues, the category of the artistic outstrips the category of the aesthetic.

The second option broadens the concept of the aesthetic beyond its traditional boundaries. It says that we are responding to a work of art "aesthetically" not only when we respond to its formal elements or to the relationship between its formal elements and its content, but also whenever we respond to a feature that makes a work the work of art it is. (These features may include substantive as well as formal features.) On this second option, the aesthetic is understood in such a way as to track the artistic, however broadly or narrowly that is to be understood.[40]

It is this second route that I recommend. Let me at least briefly say why. The first option remains wedded to a conception of the aesthetic that preserves the eighteenth-century preoccupation with beauty. This is a rich and important tradition, but it focuses – and keeps us focused – on a feature of art that is no longer so important to us. Indeed, one of the significant and widely noted facts about the development of modern art is that beauty is no longer central to art. The price of regarding this conception of the aesthetic as the only legitimate one is to marginalize aesthetics – isolating it from much of the philosophy of art – and, indeed, from much of our experience of art.

Opting for this broader conception of the aesthetic gives us a more inclusive category, one more adequate to what art is in all of its historical and cultural manifestations and to the full range of its values. It sets much of what we humanly care about back into the aesthetic arena and offers a much more complete view of the value of art.[41]

My claim, which employs this richer conception of the aesthetic, is, then, that in order to get things aesthetically right about *Triumph of the Will,* we have to engage with its vision. And this means that we have to engage with the moral issues it raises. This nonformalist notion of the aesthetic rides piggyback on a nonformalist conception of art. It doesn't require wholesale abandonment of the distinction between aesthetic and moral value. We can, for example, still distinguish between the formal beauty of *Triumph of the Will's* stylistic devices and its moral status as a work of National Socialist propaganda. Nor does it require denying that art and morality belong to different domains. But it does require recognizing that there are areas where these domains overlap and that certain works of art, especially works of religious and political art, fall within this overlapping area.

VI

In Section IV, we began by canvassing different explanations for the troubling nature of *Triumph of the Will:* that it is disturbing because of the horrible events it documents, because it is a work of propaganda, because it propagates a highly selective and distorted picture of Hitler and National Socialism. Each of these factors helps to explain why the film is troubling, but none of them gets at what is, I have argued, the most unsettling feature of the film: its conjunction of beauty and evil.

We then, in Section V, considered the standard solution for dealing with the problem of beauty and evil, namely, formalism, which holds that aesthetic evaluation can be severed from moral evaluation and that art *qua* art must be evaluated in formal terms alone. Each of the two versions of formalism we considered, simple and sophisticated, maintained that the problem posed by the juncture of beauty and evil in *Triumph of the Will* (and works like it) is illusory. The simple version attempted to dissolve the problem of the juncture of beauty and evil by focusing on the formal features of the film and relegating the film's content to a domain outside the boundaries of aesthetic evaluation. The sophisticated version attempted to dissolve the problem by focusing on the relation of form and content in the film. It, too, held consideration of the film's morally objectionable content (its vision) to fall outside the domain of aesthetic evaluation. But, as we have seen, formalism fails in the case of *Triumph of the Will* because in bracketing the very components that make the film morally objectionable (i.e., its content), it also brackets the film's essence as a work of art – its vision of National Socialism.

The failure of formalism shows that the problem of beauty and evil is real. Indeed, each of the candidate explanations for the threatening nature of the film can be recast as accepting and giving different interpretations to this problem. As a documentary, *Triumph of the Will* conjoins beautifully rendered footage and the celebration of horrible historical events; as propaganda, the film conjoins a masterfully constructed political narrative and a distorted picture of Hitler's character and aims; as formal expression, it conjoins masterful cinematography and morally repugnant content. But the most trenchant account of the relation of beauty and evil in *Triumph of the Will* focuses on the fact that the film renders something that is evil, namely National Socialism, beautiful and, in so doing, tempts us to find attractive what is morally repugnant.

The upshot of these reflections is that the question we considered before – How are we to respond to *Triumph of the Will?* – can't be evaded. As we have seen, there are really two questions here, one about us, one about how we are to evaluate the film as art.

First, the question about us. What does it mean about us if we find this film beautiful? Does it show that there is something wrong with our character? That we really approve of or endorse fascism or the doctrines of National Socialism? That we approve of the Final Solution? The answer to the question about us depends on what, in finding the film beautiful, we are responding *to.* As the simple version of formalism showed, some elements of the film are unproblematically beautiful: the film's fine camera work, its rhythmic editing, and so on. Responding to these elements of the film isn't the same as endorsing its National Socialism. One can respond to the formal elements of the film without supporting the work's message. Nor is there anything problematic about responding to the relation between form and content in the film. If we are responding not to the film's content *per se,* but only to how that content is *presented,* then, here too, we are not endorsing the film's message.

My analysis, however, shows that there is another feature of the film that is not so innocuous: its vision. In order to respond fully to the film as a work of art, we must respond to this vision. Indeed, my analysis implies that appreciating the film as a work of art requires responding to the beauty of this vision of National Socialism. But this means that the proper formulation of the question about us is, What kind of people are we if we find this vision beautiful? It is not immediately obvious that we *can* find this vision beautiful without endorsing fascism or the doctrines of National Socialism.

Here it is important to be very clear about what is meant by the film's vision. When I speak of the film's vision, I do not mean something that might be meant by the word 'vision', namely the abstract doctrines or ideals of National Socialism, but rather the film's deifying portrait of Hitler as the beloved father of a happy, smiling people and of a national community unified by its desire to labor for the New Germany.

Appreciating the beauty of this vision (seeing the possible appeal of the idea of a benevolent leader, of a unified community, of a sense of national purpose) is not the same thing as finding the doctrines or ideals of National Socialism appealing. I can consistently see this concrete vision as beautiful (or attractive) and reject the doctrines and ideals of the National Socialists, be utterly horrified by what they did, and so on.

There is a step between finding the film's concrete artistic vision beautiful and endorsing the doctrines and ideals of National Socialism. The step is a moral one, a step we need not (and, of course, should not) take. So it is possible to appreciate the beauty of the film's vision without compromising ourselves morally. But, it is important to note, one of the central aims of *Triumph of the Will* is to move its audience to take this step, to find the historical realities and doctrines of National Socialism appealing. Part of the evil of the film consists in the fact that it is designed to move us in this way – in the direction of evil.

That the film aims to move us to find National Socialism appealing is also one of the things that makes responding to it so problematic. The film *is* potentially corrupting. To appreciate the beauty of its vision – or to acknowledge our appreciation – is to open ourselves to a work that presents us with the temptations of fascism. One reason that the sense that there is something troubling about *Triumph of the Will* will not – and should not – go away is that there *is* something morally dangerous about the film.

I want now to turn to the second question: How should the fact that the film is evil figure in our evaluation of it as a work of art? Having gotten clearer about the real insidiousness of the film, we may be tempted to claim that it is of little or no artistic value. But this response won't do. *Triumph of the Will* clearly is of artistic value. As we have seen, it is an extremely powerful film, perhaps even a work of genius.

Should we then say that *Triumph of the Will* is a terrific work of art, despite its insidiousness? Here I think we should hesitate. For all its accomplishments, *Triumph of the Will* is flawed. It is flawed because its vision is flawed. Its vision is flawed because it misrepresents the character of Hitler and National Socialism and because it presents as beautiful and good things that are evil, namely Hitler and National Socialism. These flaws are relevant to the evaluation of *Triumph of the Will* as art because, as our examination makes clear, the film's vision of National Socialism is part of the work of art that it is. If that vision is flawed, then so is the work of art.

One explanation of our enduring reservations about the film is that many of us have certain intuitions about the relation of beauty and goodness. One place those intuitions get articulated is in Plato. Even those of us who are not Platonists are heirs to a Platonic tradition that identifies beauty and goodness, a tradition that conceives of the beautiful as consisting not only in giving pleasure to the senses but also in engaging and satisfying the mind and spirit. (For example, in the *Phaedrus,* beauty is thought to awaken the longing and passion for what is higher, for the Good.)[42] It is this ancient, strongly entrenched strand of thinking which, I suggest, accounts for the sense that there is something paradoxical about a work of art that so tightly weaves the beautiful and the morally evil. Indeed, one of the most shocking things about *Triumph of the Will* is that it so clearly demonstrates that beauty and goodness can come apart, not just in the relatively simple sense that moral and aesthetic evaluation may diverge, but in the more frightening sense that it is possible for art to render evil beautiful.[43]

If *Triumph of the Will* shows that the Platonic tradition is wrong to identify beauty and goodness, it also provides support for the idea that the *unity* of beauty and goodness is a standard by which art should be measured. If good art must not only please the senses, but also engage and satisfy us intellectually and emotionally, then we are, I suggest, justified in criticizing *Triumph of the Will* for rendering something evil beautiful.

We are justified in doing so not just as moralists but as critics of art. This is not to say that works of art should only show good people doing good things, or that they are meant to endorse only conventional conceptions of goodness. Nor is it meant to deny that a work of art – even one as morally flawed as *Triumph of the Will* – may nevertheless be of artistic value. But there is reason, I am claiming, to withhold the highest aesthetic praise from works of art that present as beautiful, attractive, and good what, on reflection, can be seen to be evil.[44]

One question remains. If Riefenstahl's film is flawed in the ways I have described, why watch it? Well, we obviously don't sit down to watch *Triumph of the Will* for fun. But it is an important film. It is worth watching because of its historical value as a chronicle of the rise of fascism in Germany and of events leading to the Second World War and as a case study in how propaganda works. It is also worth watching for its formal beauty and expressive power. In addition, we may watch *Triumph of the Will* for much the same reason some feminists examine works of pornography: so that in confronting these works we may learn something about a way of seeing the world we reject.

There are at least two further reasons for watching the film. The more obvious one is that part of preventing a recurrence of fascism involves understanding how fascism came to be thought attractive, how parties like the National Socialist German Worker's Party called upon and met certain underlying human wishes of many Germans in the 1930s (e.g., for a strong leader, for community, for a sense of national purpose). Deciding not to ban (or avoid) materials like *Triumph of the Will* means learning not to deny, but to live with, the historical reality of the Third Reich. The second, related reason is that confronting the film's vision of National Socialism may allow us to understand more fully ourselves as human beings. Imagining seeing the world as Riefenstahl represents it, however disturbing, may enable us to confront, and come a little closer to comprehending, both the real and potential tendencies that have come to define human evil.

The most important reason, though, for watching *Triumph of the Will* is that it provides the very conjunction of beauty and evil we find so unsettling. It allows us to see that beauty and evil can, and have been, conjoined. And it allows us to see that one of the disturbing things about art is that it can make evil appear beautiful and good. Thus, what we might think is a reason for *not* watching the film is, upon reflection, the very reason we should watch it.

A methodological coda. In the course of our examination of the problem of beauty and evil, we have spent a great deal of time focusing on the historical and artistic details of one particular case. It is worth considering why. We had to look at the historical specificities of the film because, as a documentary and as a work whose subject is a particular historical event, *Triumph of the Will* is a historically specific work. We had also to look at the artistic details of the film in order to see how *Triumph of the Will* poses issues that give rise to the more general philosophical problem of beauty and evil. This detailed historical and artistic examination was part of a larger strategy of looking at a particular case as a means of exploring the more general problem of beauty and evil in art. But why start with a particular case? Why not begin with the more general issue and work to the particular case? The reason, which I can state here in only an abbreviated way, is that the problem of beauty and evil in art is real, but it becomes real only insofar as it arises in particular cases. We go to the particular cases because that is where the issue comes to life. The historical and analytic work of this essay is not mere propaedeutic to the philosophical inquiry but is inextricably bound up with the philosophical inquiry itself. This is not a new approach, but one whose locus classicus is Plato's discussion of Homer in Books 2 and 3 of the *Republic*.

Notes

For comments on earlier drafts of this essay, I thank Ted Cohen, Michael Hardimon, Deborah Lefkowitz, Jerry Levinson, and Claudine Verheggen.

1. Estimates of the number of people who came to the Nuremberg rally vary. The city already had a population of 350,000. For a detailed discussion of the 1934 rally and its attendants, see Hamilton T. Burden's *The Nuremberg Party Rallies: 1923–1939* (New York: Praeger, 1967), esp. 79, 85–7, 90.
2. Renata Berg-Pan, *Leni Riefenstahl* (Boston: Twayne, 1980), 99.
3. Ibid.
4. Siegfried Kracauer, *From Caligari to Hitler: A Psychological History of the German Film* (New York: Noon Day Press, 1960), 301.
5. Leni Riefenstahl, *Leni Riefenstahl: A Memoir* (New York: Picador, 1987), 160.
6. Ibid., 159. Erik Barnouw offers one of the most interesting and detailed descriptions of the film coverage of the Nuremberg rally and the lengths to which Riefenstahl went to get it. See his *Documentary: A History of the Non-Fiction Film* (Oxford: Oxford University Press, 1983), 101–3.
7. David Welsh, *Propaganda and the German Cinema, 1933–1945* (Oxford: Clarendon Press, 1983), 149.
8. Riefenstahl, *A Memoir*, 165–6.
9. The Reich Cinema Law, which went into effect in February 1934, stipulated that all kinds of films, even film advertising and film stills, were to be submitted to the censorship board. Both private and public screenings were covered by this law, and each film print was required to carry an embossed stamp of the German eagle. That *Triumph of the Will* by-

passed this considerable legal machinery suggests that Hitler had complete faith in Riefenstahl's political "soundness." See Welsh, *Propaganda,* 17–22.

10. Berg-Pan, *Leni Riefenstahl,* 131.

11. Some reports indicate that the film ran in all the major German cities but only for a short time, others that it continued to be shown throughout the Nazi era. In the absence of historical evidence, it is also unclear to what extent the film was used for purposes of propaganda or with what effect. Again, historians and critics disagree. Some credit the film with winning many to Hitler's cause; others maintain that the film was little seen outside the largest cities and not widely used by the Nazis.

12. See David B. Hinton, *The Films of Leni Riefenstahl* (Metuchen, N.J.: Scarecrow Press, 1978), 36–7.

13. Andrew Sarris (ed.), *Interviews with Film Directors* (New York: Avon Books, 1967), 461.

14. See, e.g., Welsh, *Propaganda,* and Berg-Pan, *Leni Riefenstahl.*

15. Richard Meran Barsam, *Filmguide to "Triumph of the Will"* (Bloomington: Indiana University Press, 1975), 27–8.

16. Unlike most commentary on *Triumph of the Will,* which stresses the film's idolization of Hitler (e.g., Riefenstahl's use of low-angle shots and backlighting), the interpretation I offer here, to my knowledge, stands alone in stressing the use Riefenstahl makes of the three interlocking ideas of *Ein Führer, Ein Volk,* and *Ein Reich.*

17. It also has roots in the Nazi's distorted reading of Nietzsche. For this history of the concept of the *Führerprinzip,* I follow Welsh's illuminating discussion in *Propaganda,* 145–7.

18. For more on this notion of Hitler as "the bearer of the people's will," see ibid.

19. On the symbolic importance of Nuremberg for the Nazi rallies, see Burden, *Nuremberg Party Rallies,* 3–9.

20. The extent of the staging of this sequence has been much discussed. Certainly this closing shot could not have been filmed without considerable advance planning and cooperation from the troops, none of whom look at the camera.

21. The idea that power must not only be held but visibly displayed is something that Riefenstahl takes from Hitler and the Nazis. As Eugen Hamadovsky, who later became the Third Reich's national broadcasting director, wrote in 1933: "All the power one has, even more than one has, must be demonstrated. One hundred speeches, five hundred newspaper articles, radio talks, films, and plays are unable to produce the same effect as a procession of gigantic masses of people taking place with discipline and active participation" (cited in Welsh, *Propaganda,* 149).

22. The solidity of Hitler's support was important to emphasize in light of the Roehm purge. In what came to be known as the Night of the Long Knives (June 30,1934), Ernst Roehm and other SA leaders suspected of treachery against Hitler were roused from their beds and shot without hearings of any kind.

23. For a discussion of the importance of mass meetings in the projection of the *Führer* cult, see Welsh, *Propaganda*, 148.
24. See, e.g., Hinton, *The Films of Leni Riefenstahl*, 58.
25. Riefenstahl, *A Memoir*, 101.
26. Ibid., 304–5.
27. In addition to *Triumph of the Will*, Riefenstahl made an earlier documentary for Hitler, a short, hastily organized film on the 1933 Nuremberg rally. This film, *Victory of Faith*, introduced Riefenstahl to the documentary film form. Following *Triumph of the Will*, she made a third party rally film, *Day of Freedom*. This last film was made to appease the Wehrmacht generals she had angered by their underrepresentation in *Triumph of the Will*.
28. *Volkischer Beobachter*, May 1, 1935. Cited in Welsh, *Propaganda*, 158. Emphasis added.
29. Welsh, *Propaganda*, 159.
30. Riefenstahl quoted in Sarris (ed.), *Interview*, 460.
31. Kracauer, *From Caligari to Hitler*, 301.
32. This remark is widely cited. Its source is Riefenstahl's book on *Triumph of the Will*, *Hinter den Kulissen des Reichsparteitag Films* (Munich: Franz Eher, 1935).
33. For a good introduction to the standard debates over authorial intention, see Gary Iseminger's collection, *Intention and Interpretation* (Philadelphia: Temple University Press, 1992).
34. As it is, the film cannot be legally shown in Germany because it is a work of National Socialist propaganda.
35. Ted Cohen raises similar questions about laughing at jokes in bad taste. See his "Jokes," in *Pleasure, Preference and Value: Studies in Philosophical Aesthetics*, ed. Eva Schaper (Cambridge University Press, 1983), 120–36.
36. The distinction between a work that asks us to *imagine* a certain response (e.g., being amused, being attracted to) and one that asks us really *to be* amused, attracted, and so on is discussed by Berys Gaut in Chapter 7, this volume.
37. Edward Bullough, "'Psychical Distance' as a Factor in Art and as an Aesthetic Principle," *British Journal of Psychology* 5 (1912): 87–98, 108–17.
38. Some have argued that by adopting an attitude of aesthetic distance toward certain kinds of artistic representations we risk hardening ourselves to real human suffering. Being willing to run that risk for mere aesthetic pleasure may be thought morally insensitive and a kind of moral fault.
39. What it is for a work of art to have a message is, of course, a matter of great complexity. On the general question of what an artwork's saying something amounts to and how we determine what, among various possibilities, it says, see, e.g., Jerrold Levinson's "Messages in Art," *Australian Journal of Philosophy* 73, no. 2 (June 1995): 184–98. While not addressing these issues directly here, I am assuming that works of art

are capable of communicating attitudes and beliefs toward what they describe or otherwise present. What those attitudes and beliefs are is something a work itself manifests when read against the background of its cultural and historical context.

40. An example of this general approach can be found in Wayne Booth's *The Company We Keep: An Ethics of Fiction* (Berkeley: University of California Press, 1988).

41. I am not, of course, suggesting that we abandon the older conception of the aesthetic completely; as I have acknowledged, it is a useful, although not exhaustive, conception.

42. In the *Phaedrus,* Plato also argues that the sight of beauty may arouse an appetite or lust unconnected with deeper feeling (the appetite of "a four-footed beast" [250e]). But, he maintains, in people of reasonable nature and training, the sight of beauty arouses complicated feelings of awe, reverence, and fear, which in turn warm and nourish the soul, motivating it to pursue the good. My concern in this essay, however, is with the broad outlines of a tradition inherited from Plato and not with the considerable subtleties of the Platonic texts themselves.

43. Making this move – allowing that the attitudes a work endorses may compromise its artistic value – is likely to meet with the objection that adopting such a (nonformal) standard of evaluation compromises art's autonomy. The worry here is that a standard that evaluates art in ethical or political terms will expose it – perhaps unwittingly – to various forms of interference, e.g., the whims of political fashion or religious intolerance. This is a serious worry, but it rests on a misunderstanding. The suggestion that moral or political considerations may be relevant to the evaluation of art does not entail that such considerations be the only factors relevant to their evaluation, nor does it imply that these considerations must invariably take priority.

Most important, such an evaluative standard does not entail the abandonment of the idea of artistic autonomy. The principle of art's autonomy, properly understood, is the idea that works of art deserve a "protected space," a special normative standing. The idea that art deserves this protection is traditionally defended by appealing to a formalist theory of art, but it can also be defended on straightforward political grounds. The basic idea here is that works of art are a political good. They deserve protection because, as forms of expression, they often play an important social and political role: articulating existing ways of seeing and thinking or challenging and pushing beyond them.

Thus, the suggestion that *Triumph of the Will* is of less artistic value because of its celebration of National Socialism is a rejection of formalist standards of artistic evaluation; it is not a rejection of artistic autonomy. This analysis of the idea of artistic autonomy is based on my "Aesthetic Autonomy and Its Feminist Critics," forthcoming in *The Encyclopedia of Aesthetics,* ed. Michael Kelly (Oxford: Oxford University Press). For a more developed response to worries about censorship,

see my "Protected Space: Politics, Censorship and the Arts," in *Aesthetics: Past and Present*, ed. Lydia Goehr, *Journal of Aesthetics and Art Criticism*, 50th Anniversary Issue (Spring 1993): 207–15.
44. The view that the endorsement of ethically bad attitudes can be an aesthetic failure of a work is defended by Berys Gaut in his contribution to this volume.

The naked truth

ARTHUR C. DANTO

"Is it true the natives think the camera steals their souls?"
"Some of them. The sensible ones."
                    Pat Barker, *The Ghost Road*[1]

Not so long ago I was discussing aesthetics with the junior faculty of a northern university, when one of them said, as a kind of joke, that whenever she saw a job opening in aesthetics posted, she could not suppress the thought that the department wanted someone who could do nails. She clearly came from a language community in which the term serves as the generic business name of enterprises ministering to the cosmetic requirements of patrons who would, if they lived in the United States, instead have had recourse to what, evidently without thinking it the least odd, we designate as "beauty shops." And her amusement derived from the appropriation, in one language, of a term that has come to mean, in another language, primarily a branch of philosophy, concerned, as the dictionary tells us, with "a theory of the beautiful and of the fine arts." It is more than slightly ludicrous to think of cosmetology as applied philosophy, and the permanent wave as an exercise in practical aesthetics, as if one might assure graduate students in aesthetics that they might always find employment in a tight market by trimming hair – or for that matter "doing nails" – just as students of logic are assured that careers in computer programming are fallback options in case academic positions are not to be had. The ludicrousness of applying a discipline almost defined by the contrast between the aesthetic and the practical is given an edge of slight revulsion by the image of the philosopher with clippers and rouge pot.

257

The philosophical beautician – or practical aesthetician – would of necessity be engaged in the activity of flattering the appearances, which Plato had already decreed as repugnant in the *Gorgias,* where no deep differentiating line is allowed to be drawn between the art of the hairdresser and that of the Sophist. It is this perhaps that explains the mild shudder: what better characterization of the beauty shop could we find than Plato's way of putting the vaunted practice of the Sophist down as "making the worse as the better case?" The beautician does what she can to make silk purses out of the sows' ears who wish under false colors to win contests in the skirmishes of flirtation.

There is no dialogue titled *to' Aesthetikos – The Beautician –* but it would not be difficult to imagine a conversation – it might be a pendant to the *Ion –* in which Socrates, true to character, undertakes the dialectical brutalization of the somewhat effete hairdresser who takes on the defense of appearances. It would take very few ironic pages before Socrates would score the point that ringlets and pomades will not make anyone better but at most momentarily happy, and that we ought to turn from appearance to reality, from what we aspire to look like to what we should aspire to be, and instead of a life of ephemeral attractiveness we should seek one of abiding goodness and justice. After all, it was Socrates' mandate to establish that it was better to be than to appear just, even if, in the limiting case, the just man should appear maximally unjust and the unjust man appear the embodiment of justice, as in the case, Colin McGinn pointed out to me, of Dorian Gray. But Aesthetikos might profess puzzlement: he cannot see how our unhappiness with the appearances nature dealt us has anything much to do with goodness and with justice: there just is the human propensity to look askance at ugliness, even if beauty is only skin deep, and why should the just man badly endowed not enhance his hopes for happiness by rectifying his appearances in such a way as to deflect the propensity to suspect the ill-favored, gain the trust of others, and actually do the just things his appearances render difficult? Possibly we would be better off if we could be indifferent to our appearances, but, Aesthetikos continues, this is tantamount to saying that we would be better off if we were not human. To be human is to care about how we are seen, and that means that, as humans, we endeavor to see ourselves as others might see us, and seek, so far as possible, to assure that they will find us, if not attractive, at least not unattractive. Our preoccupations with aesthetics might be something of a distraction, but hardly equivalent to leading unjust lives! And

Aesthetikos, who happens to be a student of Gorgias himself, driven into cosmetic engineering because of the sparsity of paying jobs in Sophistry, presses his point. "Look at you, Socrates, with your belly hanging out and your dirty feet bare like that! If anyone *looks* indifferent to looks, it is you! Nobody would hire you if they wanted a lawyer! Nobody would hire you for anything, especially when you run about the marketplace saying to everyone in earshot that you don't know anything except how ignorant you are. You are an absolute master of appearances, and through the way you look get people to relate to you precisely as you wish. It would really be a fit punishment were the rulers to make you get a haircut, put on a pair of decent sandals, and lose a bit about the middle! You would probably prefer execution to changing your looks." The dialogue breaks off here, but it is very popular in the classroom, where there are predictably lively undergraduate discussions of the instructor's beard and blue jeans, or the ethnic jewelry and Andean pocketbook affected by the professor of multiculturalism, though shunned in the School of Accounting.

I shall memorialize Aesthetikos by designating as *aesthetikoi* those whose profession it is to enable individuals to achieve the looks that in their view represents them as they are, and letting the representationality of looks serve as a bridge between cosmetology and the mimetic arts in general. Needless to say, the look is capable of deceiving others, especially in causing them to believe its possessor younger and more attractive than reality underwrites, and it is the inducing of false beliefs that has doubtless made of *aesthetikoi* and their patrons targets of moralistic condemnation down the ages. It certainly establishes a philosophical fellowship between Ion and Aesthetikos, as it does between them and the legions of poets and imitators swept into the camp of enemies of the truth in the great dialogue that succeeds *to' Aesthetikos* in the order of Platonic composition: Book 10 of *The Republic*. It does not matter that aesthetic mimesis is of an ideal, usually, which the acquirer of the false look falls short of, sometimes far short of, on her own. Mere works of art, however we fault them on Platonic grounds, in general do less damage than looks achieved through the mediation of *aesthetikoi,* which trap the unwary, as we see, for sad example, in the cruel case of the second Mrs. Dombey's meretricious mother, Mrs. Skewton, whom Dickens refers to as "Cleopatra" when she is made up to face the world:

Mrs. Skewton's maid appeared, according to custom, to prepare her gradually for night. At night, she should have been a skeleton, with dart and hourglass, rather than a woman, this attendant, for her touch was as the touch of

Death. The painted object shrivelled underneath her hand; the form collapsed; the hair drooped off; the arched dark eyebrows changed to scanty tufts of grey; the pale lips shrunk; the skin became cadaverous and loose; an old, worn, yellow, nodding woman, with red eyes, alone remained in Cleopatra's place, huddled up, like a slovenly bundle, in a greasy flannel gown.[2]

But of course the deception can be vastly more serious than anything padding, coloration, and false curls can achieve. Plato tips his hand at the end of Book 10, when he has Er watch supposedly purged souls choose their next lives. He tells us of a man who chooses the life of a tyrant, obviously the life painted in glowing colors by the Sophists Socrates wrangled with throughout, those who, like Callicles and Thrasymachus, tell us that the best life is the one in which a person can do what he wants with impunity. The assumption is that each of us really wants power and sex, whatever the appearances – and what Socrates has wanted to argue is that this is itself the most dangerous appearance of all: it represents a morally ugly life as beautiful – and when the duped soul sees the reality he has chosen "he began to beat his breast and lament over his choice." The Sophists have, in their portrayals of life, as usual made the worst appear better, given the natural appetites of those they deceive. This, by the way, might give Plato an answer for Aesthetikos. He has given Socrates his unprepossessing look in order that the reality of the good, just life he exemplifies be the one his readers choose. The point is to *be* like Socrates, since no one would choose to *appear* like him. "And it shall be well with us both in this life," Socrates tells Glaucon, "and in the pilgrimage of a thousand years which we have been describing."

In one of her *Matisse Stories,* A. S. Byatt has her heroine, a middle-aged university lecturer, patronize a beauty shop because of a print of Matisse's *Pink Nude* she sees through the window. She would sincerely attribute her patronizing the establishment to the artistic taste of the patron when in fact it is the sexual voluptuousness of Matisse's nude that draws her in, but we learn this, as she does, only late in the story. The lecturer affects a certain plainness in her appearance, wearing her hair straight and somewhat severe. One day she comes in to have her hair done, for she is to be on TV, and in the midst of the washing she lapses into a memory of intense lovemaking with an Italian student, when she was young. On this occasion, the *aesthetikos* has turned her over to an assistant, who does not know her preferences, and when she emerges from her memory she sees herself in the mirror wearing rather an elaborate coiffure, an architecture of curls and whorls, the kind, indeed, appropriate to a women of her age and her attainment. She throws a fierce tantrum, smashing the tinted mirrors with jars of gel. When she calms down it is clear to us, and it becomes clear to her, that her straight hair was a memorial to vanished youth and to that moment in her past when she and her flesh were as one, as in the Matisse. It is no longer appropriate, much, as Aristotle observes, as the young man's scarlet cloak is unbecoming when worn by an elderly man. The lecturer is not endeavoring to deceive nor disguise, but the look she has, with the collaboration of the *aesthetikos,* made her own has had a double meaning she only now is able to see through. It is meaning rather than mimesis that must be appealed to in seeing what appearances are in the moral lives of humans. When the curled replaces the straight in the lecturer's appearance, there is no question that she is being truer to what she is; it would be like putting aside scarlet cloaks and acting one's age. But that is because she now identifies with the meaning carried by the curled as against the more private meaning carried by the straight.

This might offer Socrates the basis of a reply to Aesthetikos. He can defend his looks by saying there is no stigma in carrying a potbelly when one has passed the age in which it is suitable to wrestle naked in the palaestra, where the belly would reduce effectiveness and would in any case be less – aesthetic. So his present lumpy middle is a way of signaling acceptance of middle age: diet and exercise would doubtless make him slim, but this would be a kind of scarlet cloak – part of the paraphernalia of youth. Socrates would be right, were he to have recourse to such an argument, but he would have lost the match, for he has conceded meaning to appearances of a kind his older way of contrasting appearance with reality was too coarse to capture. We live in a world of appearances, he would have to concede, but they define what we are at any given moment, and the *aesthetikoi,* like artists, are laborers in the field of symbolic reality. When Socrates first sets out to design his republic, the whole form of life to be lived by its inhabitants, while it ministers to basic needs, does so in a way to transmit to potential conquerors that this is not a polity worth the conquest. It has none of the gold and plate that countries go to war for. Nothing we do as human beings is innocent of meaning, and a Platonic Form of human reality that left meanings out of reckoning would be radically inadequate. The radical tack of turning one's back on appearances is a formula for ineffectiveness. The right tack would be to engage with the Sophists, but to make the better appear the better. And what else, after all, do the Socratic dialogues try to do? There is a truth in appearances that ensures as deep an affinity between Aesthetikos and Socrates as the falsity in appearances gives Aesthetikos his standing in applied Sophistry.

Byatt's dowdy lecturer turns out to be transformed by her coiffure into a grudging attractiveness, as an evidently unwonted kiss from her husband that evening demonstrates. Nor is attractiveness altogether alien to her personal agenda of looks. It is just that the attractiveness she wants is only symbolically facilitated by the style she affects: it is the attractiveness of a lank, humid female in the coils of young fleshly love. *She,* before her enlightenment in the beauty salon, would have justified her dowdiness by appeal to "what is fitting" for a person of her station, dedicated in almost Platonic fashion to higher scholarship. It is a kind of uniform of the professor who would suppose that she had left behind what she continues to live for in her heart of hearts, smouldering beneath the clinkers of middle age. Indeed, her husband tells her she looks twenty years younger, and the wry irony is that in seeking to retain her youth by means of straight hair, she made herself into something of a crone. The enlightenment is an accident, benign or cruel only the subsequent narrative of her life, beyond the narrative boundaries of the short story, could reveal. Byatt leaves her at a fork in her life path, where competing coiffures point, like signposts, in conflicting directions. And the enlightenment raises the difficult question of whether the truth inadvertently released to her consciousness by the well-meaning *aesthetikos* was a good thing. Conscious or unconscious, the projection of our image of ourselves through a system of symbolic appearances is something the ethical rights and wrongs of which are infrequently discussed, though everyone has intuitions in the matter, and the intuitions in a certain way are universal. In the domain of human rights, the moral inviolability of the body, appealed to in connection with torture and rape, and in connection as well with cruel and unusual punishment, is widely conceded. But what of the symbolic body, the body presented symbolically under a system of signals that convey the meaning a person intends to have acknowledged by others? The kind of meaning mediated by the mirror in the *aesthetikos*'s salon where patron and artisan collaborate on the production of an image?

In addressing this question, I want to make the mirror central: it is to one's mirror image that one assents or dissents, depending upon whether one believes that it expresses the truth of what one is. When

Byatt's lecturer sees reflected back a woman in a stylish coiffure, she has no doubts of the optical truth of the mirror image, but only of its moral truth – its *truth to* what she believes herself to be. And in a way her rage is explained less by the fact that the image is *false to* the belief than that the belief itself is false. She is no longer a student, no longer a girl; she has, as the mirror shows, taken on attributes she has systematically denied through affected plainness. Mirrors, like cameras, always tell the truth, optically speaking, but they do not always tell the moral truth, as I am using that somewhat uncomfortable phrase. I have in mind the distinction, made much of by Virginia Woolf in the character of Jennie in *The Waves,* between composing one's face before the mirror, so that one sees, hopefully, what one intends to see, and catching a glimpse of oneself in a mirror – one's mouth sullen, one's posture slack, one's belly out – and, using the mirror as a monitor, adjusting one's features, throwing one's shoulders back, sucking one's stomach in. One arranges oneself to conform with the mirror image that commands one's assent. Of course, the discrepancy may in the end conduce to the acknowledgment of the glimpsed image: one has taken on weight, and taken on years, and allowed the history of sorrows to show in one's features. And at that point one might have recourse to the *aesthetikos,* to diet and hair dye, a tuck here and a tuck there, a regimen of exercise, so that the distance between the glimpsed and the rehearsed mirror image closes. Or one just accepts the glimpsed image, in which case the distance may close again, this time in the opposite direction: one stops resisting gravity, age, and letting one's features tell the bitter story of one's suffering. When this happens one has stopped caring. One is beyond the hope and fear that open space for applied aesthetic mediation.

Such a state is by no means contemptible. It can even be a basis for admiration. We all know one or two persons whose indifference to appearance is the objective correlative of their dedication to higher matters: the distinguished thinker with unkempt hair and cigar ashes on his stained vest, the visionary who so internalizes the urgency of her mission that she throws on whatever garment is at hand and makes obeisance to cosmetic imperatives by running her fingers through her hair. And probably that was Socrates' situation as well, so bent as he was on the pursuit of self-knowledge that we can imagine him throwing a scarlet cloak over his shoulders, not because he was an older gentleman feigning youth but because the scarlet cloak happened to be at hand. The admirability of indifference, on the

other hand, does not itself define a universal ideal, though certainly
if it were universal, there would be one modality of vulnerability to
which human beings would no longer be exposed, and one modality
of suffering. They – we – would no longer be vulnerable to a certain
form of ridicule, and no longer be subject to the pain of mockery. And
with this I approach the ethics of aesthetic degradation, where persons are degraded through their looks. The unkempt visionary and
the disheveled thinker are obvious targets of ridicule and objects of
mockery. But their unconcern, the absence of care, immunizes them
against the suffering ridicule and mockery are intended to inflict.
Doubtless this can ground an imperative of aesthetic asceticism, a
further way to indemnify ourselves against suffering, a corollary of
the kind of Hellenistic philosophy that sought such indemnification
in its various stratagems to stultify pain. But that is tantamount to
enjoining sainthood as the solution to moral problems. And it is a
variant on blaming the victim. It appears as if it is our own fault if we
are open to suffering of this order when surely there is a moral mis-
demeanor in inflicting it. Surely it entails a violation of respect for
the person, even if it is "one's own fault" that one is vulnerable to it.
Theft remains a moral transgression, even if we would be immune
to it were we to forgo worldly possessions. One cannot exonerate
thievery by enjoining Hellenistic wisdom against the transgressed.
Besides, there is something brave in keeping up appearances in difficult times. One of Sartre's characters insists on shaving in the
prison camp, as a way of showing that his spirit is not in captivity.
Winnie, in Beckett's *Happy Days,* applies lipstick amid the ruins.
Colette's Julie de Carneihan knows that as long as she wears seductive lingerie, all is not lost.

I have read that when Elizabeth the Great grew old, she could no
longer bear to look at her image in the mirror. So she left the daily
task of applying makeup to her ladies-in-waiting, who, in the cruelty
of their youth, placed a spot of red on the queen's nose, to make her
look foolish. One can imagine their stifled giggles as the queen,
believing herself cosmetically armored, set forth to the ceremonies
and duties of her day, made up like a clown. I take it that the queen
must have ordered all mirrors removed from the court, and that none
would dare to tell her that she had been betrayed. Cruelty is cruelty,
even if it was the queen's own fault that she left herself, through vanity, open to this practical joke. Had she known the truth, she would
have felt at once degraded and betrayed, where the betrayal consisted
in co-opting the vanity that would keep her from acquiring that

knowledge. The queen was hurt even though she in fact felt no pain: she was hurt through the subversion of her appearances, where she was made, on the scale of dignity, to look opposite to what she believed herself to look.

A case like the smutched queen helps us thus to see the moral inadequacy of Hellenistic theories, which tended to identify hurt with felt hurt and went on to argue that what you do not know – do not feel – does not hurt you. It is difficult to see how the queen's ignorance exonerates the ladies-in-waiting, whose action, because of its gratuitousness, has a quality of evil. It is a standard intuitive counterexample to Utilitarian moral theories that if they are right, it is morally acceptable to make a promise to someone one knows will die, all the while intending not to keep it, giving the promisee a pleasure she would not have had had the promise not been made, and none of the pain that knowledge that the promise was broken, was insincere, would cause, since death removes the possibility of that knowledge. Absence of knowledge cannot neutralize the moral quality of an action, though the knowledge would, in this case, constitute part of the action's wickedness, inasmuch as were the queen to discover what had been done, that would not merely add a truth to the body of truths in her possession: it would be a hurtful truth, and lodge, like an arrow, in the flesh of the queen's self-esteem. So in my view one has to build the pain into the indictment, even if the pain is never felt. And the controlling factor in the case would be the mirror image, even if mirrors had been systematically removed from the precincts of the court. The self-image with which the queen would have been presented, had she seen it, is hurtful to her even if she has not. It is hurtful because it makes her ridiculous, an object of derision and contempt, of mockery and hurtful, if suppressed, laughter. And all that for the mere entertainment of mischievous attendants!

I want to interject a word on the immateriality of death to the relevance of appearances as a source of moral concern. I am not thinking merely of the cosmetic interventions of the mortician, who seeks to leave an image of the departed in the minds of the mourners which is of a piece with the eulogy that paints the departed in becoming colors. For reasons far too deep for me to understand, it is a human reflex to want to establish an image of the departed, as if death is not final if the image itself lives on in the minds of those left behind. I am thinking, rather, of cases such as this: a wave of suicides among young women in a town in ancient Greece was ended abruptly when it was decreed that anyone who took her own life would be carried naked to the graveyard. Nakedness in young men was not merely accepted but flaunted, but a woman's nakedness was a source of intense humiliation. It would not be a factor in not wanting to be seen naked that one would not know one was because dead. It would be even more painful to contemplate because one would be helpless to cover oneself. A New York medical examiner under the Koch administration was discharged because he entertained his wife and a group of her friends by showing them the reputedly anomalous penis of a famous actor when the latter had been taken to the morgue. Athena robbed Achilles of a gloating pleasure by preserving the body of the dead Hector against decay. And in general how we are to be remembered after death is an incentive to behave a certain way while alive, even if we know that we will not know how others represent us. Part of what concerns us is that the representations should be true. And this brings us back to the idea of the controlling image. The exposed maidens want to be remembered as virtuous, and for them being seen naked is inconsistent with that. The displayed actor wants to be remembered for interpretations and perhaps his romantic looks, but having his penis smirked at by strangers is inconsistent with that. Hector would want to be remembered as a hero, not a mass of decaying flesh, and Athena performed the function of mortician, keeping his beauty intact until he could be buried. Burial is a way of letting decay take place out of sight, so that the image is uncontaminated by it.

My interest in the rights of individuals over the way they appear, and my appeal to the endorsed mirror image as that through which the subject identifies himself, as how he wishes to be seen and of course thought of, was aroused by a certain concern with photographic images. Two concerns, in fact. The first is that there is no immediate assurance that a photographic image coincides with a look, just because there are differences between the speed with which visual images register and the speed with which photographic images do, so that there may be no way in which we can see something the way the camera shows it. This establishes a difference between the glimpsed mirror image, when we take ourselves by surprise, and being taken by surprise by a photograph of ourselves looking different from the way we would have looked had we composed ourselves for the camera. The difference is that it is unclear that what the "candid camera" shot shows and what the inadvertently glimpsed mirror image shows are on the same level, both being visually true. They are not on the same level because we cannot see with the speed of the camera, and what the camera accordingly shows may not be the way we look, where "looks" are indexed to what is available to the unaided eye. The second concern is where the photographer asserts her authority to show the subject as she sees the subject, rather than the way the subject sees herself: where the photographer, as it were, asserts the rights of the artist over the rights of the subject. Both of these concerns may be violations of the right to control one's representations of oneself – the right, as it were, not to allow our appearances to be used without our consent – where consent consists, canonically, in endorsing an image as ours. This is not an absolute right, and it can be overridden. But I want to see how far the claim that it is a right can be taken. For if there is this right, then there are grounds for a certain moral criticism of images that violate the right.

Elizabeth's ladies-in-waiting transformed the queen into a sort of walking caricature of herself, but there is a clear difference between what they did and an act of iconoclasm, in which someone smears with red paint the nose of a statue of the queen or a painting. The desecration is intended to cause pain – it is a way of showing disrespect – but the evaluation of the action is qualified by considerations of political expression, which have to be balanced against the right of a subject to be portrayed a certain way. And iconoclasm has to be further distinguished from a caricature in which the queen is painted as having a red nose, where a further matter of artistic freedom complicates the issue. There are pictorial practices in which the relationship between an individual and her picture is considered to be one of identity, so that a desecration of an image is an attack on the individual whose image it is. Iconoclasm more or less presupposes this identity, but caricature does not: caricature makes a statement about its subject that may be injurious enough, since it asserts, by pictorial means, a proposition through exaggeration: the red nose can be taken as an assertion of alcoholism, or "bad blood," or mere disfiguring blotchiness: an assertion that the queen is a sot, a syphilitic, a hag. Being depicted in these ways is certainly painful enough when the assertions are true – but what if they are maliciously false?

In a show of student work from the school of the Art Institute of Chicago some years ago, someone exhibited a painting of Chicago's black mayor, Harold Washington, wearing nothing but frilly underwear. It was an exceedingly cruel painting, implying secret vices on the mayor's part or suggesting a metaphor for which there was no obvious interpretation that corresponded to any known fact of the mayor's character or behavior. It was *merely* cruel: the painter wanted to hurt the mayor through damaging innuendo, and to justify his so doing not with reference to any truth but with reference to artistic freedom. An artist could paint what he wanted – and he wanted to paint Mayor Washington in a brassiere and panties. Shortly after the opening, a group of black aldermen entered the gallery and simply removed the painting, causing as great an uproar in the press as the painting itself had caused. The argumentation was predictable. Everyone in the art community regretted that the painting had been done, but saw no alternative but to show it once it was done. The premise was that any obstacle to its display was censorship and a violation of the artist's freedom of expression, however painful the content of what was expressed. The artist's First Amendment rights were at stake. But what of the subject's right to control over his image? I believe Washington had died by then, but as I have argued, that does not affect the right.

My own sense is that the aldermen's solution was correct. The painting was, literally as well as metaphorically, false, and it violated Washington's right to correct representation. The painting in question was essentially pictorial libel, as much so as it would be libel if a newspaper columnist, merely arguing freedom of the press, were to print an article claiming that Harold Washington wore women's underwear. One reads these days that J. Edgar Hoover liked to flit about in black cocktail dresses and fishnet stockings – but there is evidently testimony to this effect by people who actually saw him so garbed. The artist did not claim knowledge, but merely the freedom to assert pictorially what he did assert. He did not, as it were, believe it true. He simply did it as an act of aggression. The discussion on freedom of expression has from its inception allowed exceptions, notoriously in the example of shouting "Fire" in a crowded theater. I take it that the example intends the case of so shouting when there is no fire: in the situation where there is fire, shouting might save lives. It would be valuable to have some further examples, this perhaps being one, given the realities of racial antagonism in Chicago at that point. The removal of the painting would not open room for anyone to take down any painting found distasteful. The aldermen did not find this painting merely distasteful. They took it down because it falsely represented the mayor and appeared to justify false beliefs about him, and so violated the mayor's right not be falsely represented. Freedom of artistic expression is as limited as shouting in theaters is. My view would be that rights have to be balanced out.

Merely, for example, because someone finds the representation of nudity offensive does not override a gallery's right to exhibit an artist's nude paintings. Injured sensibilities do not constitute a right to remove the agency of injury. There is no slippery slope at the top of which is the action of the aldermen with, farther down, the cancellation of the exhibition of Robert Mapplethorpe's photographs. There is no abstract right to remove offensive images, any more than there is an abstract right to exhibit them. We have to proceed case by case.

For the most part, the sorts of cases I am interested in discussing do not arise with photographs, though the technology of computer simulation certainly would raise them: a simulated photograph of Mayor Washington in feminine underwear closes certain of the gaps between painting and photography. The kinds of cases I am thinking about do not raise the specter so much of libel – they do not connect with legal matters at all. But they do involve moral judgments and hence a form of criticism on moral grounds that leaves artistic freedom untouched. There is a question of artistic autonomy somewhat parallel to the legal questions of artistic freedom. And in the case of photography there is probably an evenly matched contest between the right of an artist over his images and the right of the subject over his appearances. I will bring this out by considering two ways in which this conflict might arise, only one of which raises interesting philosophical questions.

I want to contrast two photographs of the transvestite Candy Darling – aka James Slattery – a superstar, or at least a star, in various Andy Warhol films, who formed part of the flamboyant chorus of misfits that surrounded Warhol in the 1960s. Born in Massapequa on Long Island – the son of a policeman – Candy Darling achieved a triumph in Warhol's 1968 film *Flesh,* in which she and another transvestite, Jackie Curtis, read bits of gossip to one another from movie magazines as Joe D'Allessando, his back to the viewer, is apparently receiving oral sex. Of the transvestites in Warhol's stable, Candy Darling had perhaps the deepest vocation to be a female movie star: as a youth, he wanted to be Lana Turner, then, somewhat later, Kim Novak. He dyed his long hair blonde, had a willowy figure, and displayed, as if by upbringing, the most ladylike demeanor. Candy Darling – who had by then a devoted following – died of cancer in 1974, and I shall respect her memory by using the feminine pronoun. The photographs are respectively by Richard Avedon and by Peter Hujar. Avedon's picture, *Andy Warhol and Members of the Factory* – a rather large polyptych of 1968 – shows a number of figures, all of them male, naked. All but one of the women, several other men, and Warhol himself are fully clothed. Candy Darling is grouped with the naked males, and she stands, in makeup and garter belt, and with her long hair, looking like Venus in Botticelli's famous panel, but with a penis. It is an aggressive picture, like so many of Avedon's, and particularly so in the case of Candy Darling, whom it is clear the artist means to "uncover" or "expose": as if, had he left her clothed, the viewer would not know she was a man. Instead, she looks like something of a sexual freak. Candy Darling clearly had a fragile personality, and for someone who lived the fantasies of movie magazines and Hollywood allure, it would have been too much to ask her to resist the opportunity to be photographed by someone whose name signified fashion, beauty, and glamour. So for the sake of that opportunity, Candy Darling betrayed her true identity. When I speak of Avedon as aggressive, I mean that he did not simply disregard Candy Darling's values, he forced her to surrender them. I find it an exceedingly cruel image, but given that the subject was co-opted, there is no serious parallel between it and the painting of Harold Washington *en travestie.*

I contrast Avedon's image with a photograph by Peter Hujar, *Candy Darling on her Deathbed* (1974). It is an extremely moving picture of Candy Darling, in a black nightgown and mascara, dressed as it were for the occasion, with bouquets of flowers by her bedside and a single rose beside her on the sheet. She has arranged herself in the Hollywood pose required by a glamorous expiration and is clearly playing a role, that of *la dame aux camelias,* dying a beautiful death. Hujar has photographed her the way she would have wanted to be shown, and he has added something of his own: the black closes in on the beautiful lady as she leaves the world like a poem ending. Hujar lived in the closed world of transvestites, the world so marvelously recorded by Nan Goldin (who was also part of it), and accepted their values without question. I regard this as his masterpiece, and one of the truly great photographs of the century. What I admire is the profound respect he displayed for Candy Darling's project, and the way he presented this death portrait as an authentication and a gift. Hujar had deferred to the image Candy Darling would identify as her and submerged his artistic will to that of the subject. Avedon violates the subject's will to his own ends. He has whited out the background, which is a signature manner, displaying the truth of Candy Darling without qualification. Hujar has used the shadows to

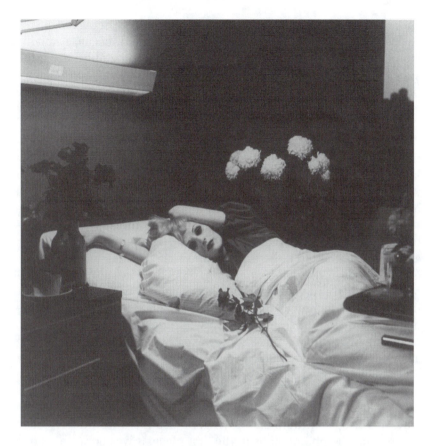

lend drama and pathos to fit the role and the fact of a dying beauty. There is nothing of libel in Avedon's image – he shows us what is, after all, the truth. But it remains a morally bruising artistic action whose harshness is not mitigated by the so-called autonomy of the artist.

My second example also turns on the claims of artistic autonomy, and may again be illustrated by the work of Richard Avedon. But it turns on a certain feature to which the high-speed camera gives rise in the sense that it produces images that do not correspond to the way subjects look, mainly because looks are indexed to certain limits on the visual of which nobody was especially aware until the invention of high-speed photography, where the camera shows things we are unable to see. But it is what we *are* able to see under normal conditions that defines a look. This can be brought home by considering a whimsical charge by the Russian émigré painter, Alexander Melamid, that the cave paintings recently discovered in the Ardeche were fakes. They were, Melamid argued, because nobody knew how to paint animals in motion before photography, the influence of which on whoever did the painting makes it impossible for them to have been executed before the invention of photography. The allusion, of course, is to the celebrated images of moving horses by Eadweard Muybridge of 1877.

It is well known that the unaided eye cannot answer certain questions regarding the locomotion of animals – for example, whether a horse in flying gallop ever has all four legs off the ground at once. It was in order to settle this (and decide a bet) that Muybridge set up a bank of fourteen cameras whose shutters were triggered by a horse running in front of them, tripping attached threads. These photographs were published in 1878 under the title *The Horse in Motion,* and it is doubtless to these that Melamid refers. They and the subsequent images in *Animal Locomotion,* published in 1887, made Muybridge famous, and when he projected them by means of his zoopraxinoscope – a technical forerunner of the modern motion picture mechanism – the illusion of motion was quite thrilling. No one who has seen Muybridge's images, however, which are stills showing arrested motion, would have the slightest temptation to see any resemblance between them and the running beasts of the Ardeche caves.

The reason is easy to state. We really don't see animals move the way Muybridge shows them moving, or else there would have been no need for the photographs in the first place: it was because no one knew the disposition of horses' feet when they run that Muybridge hit upon his awkward but authoritative experiments. Muybridge's published images had an impact on artists like Eakins and the Futurists, and especially on Degas, who sometimes shows a horse moving stiff-legged across the turf, exactly the way it can be seen in Muybridge's photographs, but never in life. Far more visually satisfying are the schematisms artists evolved down the centuries for representing animals in motion the way we *feel* they move. And what is striking about the Ardeche animals is the presence of such schematisms twenty centuries ago. Muybridge was, of course, positivistically contemptuous of the use of schematisms. His photographs showed how differently the horse uses its legs in the amble, the canter, and the gallop: it was, he told audiences, "absurd" to depict a galloping horse with all four feet off the ground. But a famous painting, which he made merry with – Frith's *Derby Day* of 1858 – shows no fewer than ten horses in this visually convincing but locomotively false posture. The animals at Ardeche dash headlong through space, vastly more like Frith's – or Gericault's or Leonardo's – than the reality Muybridge's photography disclosed. And the philosophically interesting point is that we do not really know what a horse in flying gallop looks like, since it does not look like Muybridge's unquestionably true images and unaided perception cannot support any existing description. That is why schematisms are indispensable. The schematism in a certain sense corresponds to the canonical image of the subject – the image of who the subject thinks he is.

Muybridge reproduced his images sequentially, like panels in a comic strip, so that we get, with qualification, some sense of a total movement, whether of an animal or a human. The qualification is that the point of view on the moving subject is distributed across the several cameras, so that it is as if we get concatenated glimpses by distinct observers, which are never fused into a single coherent movement. This was regarded as a blemish on Muybridge's achievement by Thomas Eakins, who invented a form of the modern motion picture camera by attaching a rotating disk with two apertures to a camera, thus referring the successive images to a single point of view. When a device was contrived for projecting them at a certain speed, so that the individual images fused into a single motion, one could no longer answer questions about the relative position of the feet in flying gallop: that could be answered only by stopping the film and examining what we now refer to as a still. But the still does not correspond to anything the unaided eye is able to take in: we do not see, as it were, in time-stop fashion. The motion picture camera (including Muybridge's prototype) is accordingly an optical device for arresting motion if we arrest the motion of the film and study the frame. It shows us things that are not part of the normal visual world, like the microscope does. When the microscope was invented, there were those who seriously raised the question whether God meant for us to see things as it enabled us to see them. In 1877, that kind of question was no longer asked, though a somewhat similar one was, namely whether God intended us to see one another naked. Indeed, that got to be a very vexed question in Philadelphia, where Muybridge was invited by Eakins, at that time the director of the Pennsylvania Academy, to lecture. But this takes me ahead of my story. The point is that Muybridge had, as it were, invented the still without having quite invented moving pictures. Up to that point there was a relatively simple correspondence between ordinary perception and the photograph: the photograph shows the world as we perceive it visually. The still, by contrast, shows the world as we are not able to perceive it visually. It shows us the world from the perspective of stopped time – the *fermata,* to use the title of Nicholson Baker's novel about a man able to stop time and explore the nakedness of women without their knowledge. The still is a kind of invasion into a world in which our eyes have no natural entry point.

In consequence of this contribution of Muybridge's, photographs became divided into two main classes, stills – which imply a reference to motion – and what one might, having in mind Fox Talbot's phrase "Nature's pencil," call "natural drawings." Talbot, after all, invented photography because of his own limitations as a draftsman: the camera was to do by means of light what he did by means of pencil – only, of course, more accurately and better. I am not recommending that we change our vocabulary to fit a distinction language has chosen to disregard. I make the distinction to draw attention to photographs that take normal perception as canonical, and photographs that disregard normal perception in showing us things the eye cannot see. Since the same kinds of cameras are used in making both kinds of photographs, with mechanisms for altering exposure by means of lens openings and shutter speeds, it gets to be a matter of the attitude of the photographer. Avedon makes stills, Hujar makes "natural drawings." And this in effect is the result of how they treat their subjects. Hujar posed his subjects as if he were a painter. They were not supposed to move. They *held* the pose, in the interest of an image that was a matter of negotiation between artist and subject. The controlling factor was what the subject wanted to look like, which the artist helped realize. Candy Darling was typical of the society of misfits and sexual fantasists from which Hujar drew his subjects (and his friends). They dressed for their portraits. Men wore women's clothing, or they posed in such a way as to proclaim their sexuality. And Hujar was unwavering in taking them at their own assessment, which is what gives his photographs their power and their truth. For what it is worth, my sense is that gay photographers are naturally drawn to "natural drawings," largely because of the fact that they are so singularly sensitive, through their sexual orientation, to appearances: the gay photographer and the *aesthetikos* probably share a sexual preference. Avedon has no interest in the sitter's wishes. He is after something the sitter may be unable to identify with at all. *Tant pis.* The sitter is a means to the attainment of an image that Avedon will not hesitate to claim is the truth of the sitter, a revelation or discloser of who she is. But often, typically, the image is false.

Avedon's portraits are stills, then, even if not cut from a filmstrip. What makes them stills is that they are of moving objects. In a sense, the world, as Buddhists might say, is in unremitted motion: even a rock is different from instant to instant as sunlight and shadow induce their changes. Those are changes we do not see, any more than we see grass growing. They are too slow, the way a horse's movement is too fast for us to see the way its legs go. The changes I refer to in the case of portraits are the changes in the human face as it moves from expression to expression. One does not register these motions, which is why the artistic discipline of physiognomy never sought to deal with them: it dealt with fear, anger, joy, hope, and the like. Nadar collaborated with a physiognomist to capture the basic facial expressions, which Cindy Sherman astutely observed looked all alike – which means, probably, that there were schemata for these, as for horses in flying gallop, though the same expression would take on different readings in different contexts.[3] Edgar Wind, for example, demonstrates in *Hume and the Heroic Portrait* that the expression that means wild sexual abandon on the face of a maenad means intolerable grief on the face of a *Mater Dolorosa* at the base of the Cross.[4] The "smile" we are urged to show by the photographer is as close as most of us can come, if that far, in complying with a schema. Probably the photograph of a real smile is a natural drawing, since the smile assumed for purposes of being photographed is willed, where real smiles are not. The *still* of a smile is probably a record of a fleeting facial expression that merely looks like a smile.

Most of what the human face shows is not so much expressions as transitions between expressions, and with ASA 160 and shutter speeds of a sixtieth of a second we can capture stages in these changes that the eye never sees. Avedon gets his severe effects by overexposure – he sets his openings about two f-stops above what a light meter would recommend – and then underdevelops. (Mapplethorpe kept his camera at f16, whatever that means here). The result is that faces are defamiliarized, all the more so as the typical Avedon portrait strips away the sitter's entire context. They are not the faces we know, if we know the subject, and certainly not what the subject sees in the mirror. My feeling is that in making stills Avedon asserts his autonomy over the subject, all the more so when he displays the image as the subject– for example, *Isaiah Berlin, Philosopher* – when anyone who knows the subject knows that this cannot be he. It is, moreover, false to say that he sometimes looks like this. He never looks like that to the eye. He only does so to ASA 160, f22 at 30 – which, of course, does not see. Apologists often say, "In a hundred years, nobody will know what Berlin – or anybody Avedon photographed – looked like." But given the natural authority ascribed to the photograph, namely "Photographs never lie," this is how people a hundred years from now will believe someone looked. And that is to use artistic authority in the propagation of a falsehood.

A photograph for which we are unprepared will often show us things we would not know about ourselves, of course, and we have to admit its higher authority than our own self-deceived self-image. "I saw you in the paper," someone tells the narrator in a story by Michael Byers. "'I've gained a little weight since you knew me,' I said. My picture had been on the inside front page. I was on the stage, receiving a plaque from the principal and superintendent. My suit jacket had been open and my stomach loomed out in its striped shirt, my tie barely reaching to the third button. I had been shocked by the picture, unpleasantly, but strangely fascinated, too, as if I were seeing myself for the first time in years."[5] But it will often lie as well. Candid shots, taken in a certain glaring artificial light, do not necessarily show people as they in fact are. Their expressions are unnatural, their gestures as wooden as Muybridge's horses' legs. They look like terrible people. I find this in Gary Winogrand's images, which in my view are often unmeritedly punitive. Catching people unawares does not automatically assure us that we have achieved the truth. Cameras do not lie, but photographers do, making "the better case look worse."[6]

I cannot recall reading a discussion of nakedness in the canonical literature of philosophical ethics, a surprising omission in view of the fact that the first discovery made by Adam and Eve upon partaking of fruit from the Tree of Knowledge of Good and Evil was that they were naked and that nakedness was something of which to be ashamed. The phenomenology of perception at Genesis I is brilliant: when their "eyes were opened," the disobedient pair saw nothing they had not always seen, including one another's naked bodies. But for the first time they saw themselves *as* naked, and hence as in a condition that called for hiding. "Who taught you that?" God wants to know, for he realizes that this is not so much a new truth as a special perspective on old truths. They have, as the serpent promised, become "as gods, knowing good and evil." And it is surprising that philosophers have not paused long enough in their endless mooting of promise keeping and truth telling to ask wherein the wrongness of being naked lies. My own sense is that the contrast with their prior state would be the same, even had Eve and Adam, in finding that they were naked, suddenly felt proud of their bodies. So that instead of making aprons out of leaves and hiding from God, they might have twisted flowers in their pubes, like Connie Chatterly and her lover. Shame and pride alike contrast with the state of innocence from which they had fallen. God would have known that they had knowledge only the gods had a right to, either way. And in particular, insofar as it is wrong to be seen naked, it is wrong to be shown naked, however the person in question happens to feel about his body.

Obviously there is something wrong in showing a person in some state of which the person is ashamed. Patricia Morrisroe describes an episode in her biography of Robert Mapplethorpe in which, untypically, the artist took photographs of someone against the latter's will: a particularly fat man let himself in for some masochistic thrills at the hands of leather-clad sadists, who forced him to submit to having the seance documented. It is not clear that the man was ashamed of the episode – it was very likely the acting out of a fantasy – but he was clearly ashamed of having it shown, and Mapplethorpe was wrong to show him this way, even if one is tolerant about what consenting adults do to one another in the name of sex. On the other hand, there exists a horrifying photograph of three Jewish women, stripped bare by the Nazis, waiting, terror in their eyes, to be executed. One would tend to think the humiliation forced upon these pathetic women vastly worse than the witness borne by the act of photographing it, and thus that the photograph stands today not as a self-indictment but as an indictment of inflicted shame. An enlargement hangs in a museum in Israel, devoted to what the Jews were made to endure by the Nazis. However, there is an Orthodox objection to the image, not because the women are ashamed of their nakedness, but because they are naked – as though the whole point of showing it were morally unacceptable because nakedness is morally unacceptable. Showing nakedness is morally disallowed by the rabbinate, even if there are compelling moral reasons for showing it.

In 1877, a writer in Philadelphia argued that it might be granted that "practice in every department is necessary to the thorough artist" without this committing one to the proposition that "what must be painted in the life-school, may surely be shown to the public." No, the writer continues, "To paint well the human figure, models are necessary: but . . . we deny that to paint the human figure utterly naked *is* to paint it well. And to paint it in any condition of exposure that lowers our sense of the dignity of the human being should be forbidden by directors of the life-schools." And he concludes with the rhetorical "Has a Hanging Committee no right of refusal if the *technique* be correct?"[7] This was in an era when there were serious problems regarding nudity in the "life-school" itself, when male models were required to wear loincloths, and female models given the option of wearing masks. Eakins (who has left us some powerful drawings of masked female nudes) was forced to resign the directorship of the Pennsylvania Academy because he removed the loincloth in the presence of female students, and he created a scandal a decade later when he did the same thing at Drexel in a course he had been invited to give on anatomy. His defense was based on pedagogical necessity: to learn to paint the male figure "well," one has to be able to follow the musculature all the way through, which even the minimal garment renders impossible. But no such argument justifies exhibiting a painting of a human male without a garment: the painted nude must as a matter of course be anatomically correct, but it is not the purpose of the painting to teach anatomical correctness. And this was the Philadelphia editorialist's point. What artistic justification could there be for "lowering our sense of the dignity of the human being" that nudity evidently a priori does?

One might think that little could be less compatible with the dignity of the wearer than an apron of leaves of the sort to which Eve and Adam resorted to hide their nakedness. And one of the tasks of artists, compelled by convention to depict the male nude in the achievement of the kind of historical painting that secured preferment in the salons, was to find a way of concealing the penis without reducing the dignity of the figure represented by means of a ludicrous garment: the wide scabbard worn diagonally across the groin, a fortunate twig, an architectural fragment would be typical academic stratagems. But the question of why nudity as nudity reduces human dignity remains to be answered. One is dealing, after all, with generic nudity, presumably, so that the kinds of considerations I have been pursuing in the body of this text would have no particular application: there is no one whose will is violated by her being shown nude. The painting of, say, Themistocles nude, where the artist employed a nude model, is not a painting of that model, not even if the artist copied that model's features exactly. And the same considerations apply to photographs of naked models, which were "legitimized" by photographing the figure next to a classical column, so that one could title it (say) "The Dream of Alcibiades." That way, men with certain tastes could glut their eyes on luscious youths, and draw as a kind of moral loincloth over their prurience the always acceptable excuse that they were admirers of the Classical. And of course this worked with female models as well: piety and family values disguised the real object of depicting, in *Roman Charity,* a young matron offering her breast to her imprisoned father, to keep him from starving. Eakins was revolted by these subterfuges in viewing the Salon of 1868:

The pictures are of naked women, standing, sitting, lying down, flying, dancing, doing nothing, which they call Phrynes, Venuses, nymphs, hermaphrodites, houris, and Greek proper names. The French court has become very decent since Eugenie had figleafs put on all the figures in the Garden of the Tuileries. When a man paints a naked woman, he gives her less than poor nature did. I can conceive of few circumstances wherein I would have to paint a woman naked, but if I did, I would not mutilate her for double the money. She is the most beautiful thing there is – except a naked man. . . . I hate affectation.[8]

Eakins would have muttered something about nakedness being "natural," and hence a representation of someone naked would itself have to be natural. His marvelous painting of the nude model in *William Rush Carving His Allegorical Figure of the Schuylkill River* of 1877 solves the problem of showing nakedness without resorting to artifice. But not being artifactual is not equivalent to being natural in the intended sense: nakedness had not been natural in the whole long history from Paradise to Philadelphia, at least in the Judeo-Christian tradition. If anything is natural to human beings it is to wear clothes. And when Eakins depicts naked males in his painting *The Swimming Hole,* he is clothing his figures in a form of nudist philosophy. When nakedness was natural to Adam and Eve, they did not think of nakedness as natural, since clothing had not been invented.

Eakins's powerful painting of William Rush and his model really solved the problem of how to show nakedness when artists no longer had the taste to set naked figures in classical landscapes: what they did was to paint models as models, rather than as Phrynes, Venuses, and nymphs. Artist-and-model, or model alone, became standard motifs in Modernist art, and the nude (typically female) figure became part of the vocabulary of studio interior, like the still life – or studio exterior, like the landscape – which turned out to be so attractive in the free markets of art from the late nineteenth century until very recently, when the life of the artist began to undergo powerful changes. Nude, still life, and landscape, for example, formed almost the entire range of Cubist and Fauvist canvases. In effect, by showing the nude as model, artists made an end run around the distinction that the Philadelphia critic took as canonical – between the studio and the gallery. The viewing public was given the privilege of the insider's view of naked flesh, not placed in edifying mythological and historical surroundings, but as so many planes and tones and shapes. The beginner in the life class was advised not to be shocked, but to look on the body as if it were a still life, an arrangement of forms. This of course did not prevent the artist from painting still lifes as if they were bodies – painting apples as surrogate breasts, as Meyer Schapiro insists Cézanne did.[9] Cubism and Fauvism were far over the horizon in 1877, but it is difficult to believe the Philadelphia writer would have understood their way of showing nudity as – showing nudity. He presupposed a naturalistic representational style. As in photography. In modernist representation, the nakedness of figures is, as it were, covered by the *style*.

In painting the model as model, artists painted women working, where nakedness was the condition of labor. That was not, of course, "natural," in the nudist sense of the term. But neither was it an assault on the woman's dignity, unless modeling itself was, given that she understood that in posing she very likely would be shown. And indeed, other than as models, there was no "natural" circumstance under which people would encounter nakedness in the regular course of life – except in the intimacy of the bedroom. The disjunction of artist's studio or bedroom then meant that unless shown as a model – which turned out to be in its own way an edifying context, as much so as the sylvan glade, the classical landscape, the picnic of the gods – the depiction of nudity was ipso facto associated with sex. And it is this, as much as anything, that must underlie contemporary feminist animadversions against the depiction of naked women as objects of "the male gaze." It must be a residue of received ideas from 1877 that in the 1990s females avert their eyes from naked men. In any case, in 1992, the directress of the National Museum of American Art – part of the Smithsonian complex – ordered the removal from an exhibition titled "After Muybridge" of an early work by the Minimalist master Sol Lewitt that showed the figure of a naked woman receding in space as one moved from porthole to porthole in a kind of stylized peepbox. It was claimed that the photograph, which was about as sexual as any of Muybridge's galloping horses or leaping men, was degrading to women.

The church fathers, Saint Augustine especially, saw the moral root of the discovery by Adam and Eve of nakedness as really the discovery of desire and of the clotting of reason by passion. Augustine's inference was that in Paradise there was no passion, that Adam planted the seed of his kind as coolly and as dispassionately as he would plant seeds in the ground, by sowing. For the first time Adam and Eve saw each other with desire, and they were ashamed of that feeling and, derivatively, of the state that occasioned it. The solution was to regain rationality by whatever improvised garment lay ready to hand, leaves as it happened. But it was too late. Sexualized beings could no longer look on one another save as potential objects of passionate desire. And that means we no longer see one another as rational beings seeing rational beings. Genesis was wise enough to recognize that this cut across the gender gap: both Adam and Eve undertook to screen their nudity from each other, at least until the privacy of whatever served them as bedroom: they had no business running about the garden in the "cool of the day" when their maker took a proprietary stroll. Nakedness belonged to the night – hence not under the full illumination allowed by the skylight in Philadelphia's Memorial Hall at the time of the centennial exhibition of 1876.

The knowledge of good and evil meant, in the language of the Bible, opening the eyes, and that meant seeing one another sexually. That is our condition, for better or worse, and the Bible simply takes it as something to be explained. Acknowledging it is not the same thing as returning to a state of innocence, but it is better, in my view, than seeing it as inimical to our dignity, for if the human being is a sexual being, the dignity of human beings must be consistent with that. No doubt we exploit one another through our sexuality, but the moral path to dignity is to recognize that sexuality itself is not exploitative but possibly fulfilling, at least along one of the dimensions of what it means to be human. But then neither is it exploitative to depict human beings as sexual, though by that I have in mind something rather stronger than merely showing human beings as naked. As far as showing a subject naked, the morality of that is altogether a matter of how the subject feels about himself as seen that way. Pauline Bonaparte was proud of her body when she posed for Bernini, but the *Man in Grey Polyester Suit* was sufficiently ashamed of his opulent sexuality that he made Mapplethorpe agree to crop his head when he photographed his immense penis hanging out of his fly. Pride and shame, those postlapsarian feelings, define the morality of the situation once the objections to generic nakedness have been removed – if they have been removed.

Notes

1. Pat Barker, *The Ghost Road* (New York: Dutton, 1995), 86.
2. Charles Dickens, *Dombey and Son* (London: Penguin English Library, 1979), p. 472.
3. See Michael Kimmelman, "Portraitist in the Halls of Her Artistic Ancestors," *New York Times,* May 19, 1995.
4. Edgard Wind, "The Maenad under the Cross: Comment on an Observation by Reynolds," in *Hume and the Heroic Portrait: Studies in Eighteenth Century Imagery* (Oxford: Clarendon Press, 1986), 74–6.
5. Michael Byers, "Settled on the Cranberry Coast," *Prize Stories, 1995,* ed. William Abraham (New York: Doubleday, 1995), 166.
6. An instructive example is the recent work of photographer Philip-Lorca diCorcia. "DiCorcia, 43, hides several synchronized strobe lights on signs or buildings, places his camera on a tripod and steps aside. . . . This technique allows his subjects no warning that they're being photographed, which seems to rankle New Yorkers more than most. 'They think I'm violating their rights,' says diCorcia, a New Yorker himself. 'Maybe I am.'" *New York Times Sunday Magazine,* May 18, 1997, 69.
7. In David Sellin, *The First Pose* (New York: Norton, 1976), 58.
8. Ibid., 47.
9. Meyer Schapiro, "The Apples of Cézanne: An Essay on the Meaning of Still-Life," *Art News Annual* 34 (1968). Reprinted in *Modern Art: 19th and 20th Centuries* (New York: Braziller, 1978).

Aesthetic derogation: hate speech, pornography, and aesthetic contexts

LYNNE TIRRELL

I felt a mental censor – product of the fears which a Negro feels from living in America – standing over me, draped in white, warning me not to write. . . . "What will the white people think if I draw the picture of such a Negro boy? Will they not at once say: 'See, didn't we tell you all long the niggers are like that? Now, look, one of their own kind has come along and drawn the picture for us!'" . . . I knew that I could not write of Bigger convincingly if I did not depict him as he *was:* that is, resentful toward whites, sullen, angry, ignorant, emotionally unstable, depressed and unaccountably elated at times, and unable even, because of his own lack of inner organization which American oppression had fostered in him, to unite with the members of his own race. . . . There was another constricting thought that kept me from work. . . . I asked myself: "What will Negro doctors, lawyers, dentists, bankers, school teachers, social workers, and business men think of me if I draw such a picture of Bigger?" . . . But Bigger won over all these claims; . . . I felt with all my being that he was more important than what any person, white or black, would say or try to make of him, more important than any political analysis designed to explain or deny him, more important, even, than my own sense of fear, shame, and diffidence.

Richard Wright, "How 'Bigger' Was Born"[1]

Nathan McCall, author of *Makes Me Wanna Holler,* credits Wright's *Native Son* with inspiring his love of reading and in turn his love of learning. McCall found Bigger Thomas's story familiar and frightening; he read Wright while in prison, sentenced to twelve years for robbing a McDonald's. Enthralled by Wright's writing, and "surprised that somebody had written a book that so closely reflected my experiences and feelings," McCall began a personal journey from convict to journalist to social critic. Nathan McCall is an example of a reader who identified first with the protagonist, partly because the protagonist's life emulated his own, but who made his subsequent life imitate not the art but the artist. Nathan McCall learned more from the writing than from what was written: he became fascinated with "the power of words."[2]

This is an essay about the power of words. In particular, I am concerned with the power of derogatory terms in aesthetic contexts. I am also concerned with the power of aesthetic contexts to legitimate or to undermine their own contents. Derogatory terms have long played various roles and achieved diverse ends in works of art, appearing in works by artists as different as William Faulkner and Ice-T. Recent discussions of these terms have been narrowly focused in their argumentation and yet quite sweeping in their application. The arguments against the use of such terms and images have not focused on aesthetic contexts, but have instead addressed racist epithets, on the one hand, and sexist images in pornography, on the other. Most of this essay is devoted to explaining the position of Absolutists, who would impose legal sanctions on the use of such terms, and Reclaimers, who would not.[3] Focusing on basic aspects of an aesthetic object or work, I look at the interpretive relation between point of view and content, asking how the method of presentation makes a difference to the nature of what exactly is presented. What does aesthetic context do to change our interpretation of these terms, if anything? Does aesthetic context serve as giant quotation marks, as it were, which thereby wipe away the author's commitment to the terms and which undermine the harm they would otherwise do? Even the assumption that quotation has this power to limit speaker endorsement is suspect, as we shall see. If aesthetic contextualization can do what quotation often cannot, then derogations in art could work for the Reclaimer rather than the Absolutist. If not, the Absolutist's position gains ground.

The debate about the viability and value of these terms is a debate about public morality, couched in terms of law or in terms of government funding. A common core unites such apparently diverse public issues as the protests about the 1993 staging of *Showboat* in Toronto, the debates about circumscribing funding for the National Endowment for the Arts on the basis of the content of proposed works, the efforts of Critical Race Theorists to enact anti–hate speech legislation, and the efforts of some feminist groups, aided by Andrea Dworkin and Catherine MacKinnon, to enact legislation prohibiting the sale and distribution of pornographic materials or opening the door to lawsuits against purveyors for damages. All concern the power of expression – words and images – to create or to reinforce a social reality that is morally contested. At stake in these debates is the range of permissible expressive commitments within our culture. This discussion will, I hope, make clear what I mean by that claim, and will help to clarify the cognitive and moral force of these terms and the debate surrounding them.

Further complicating matters when these issues are raised in aesthetic contexts is the fact that our society operates with a confused and internally incoherent conception of the nature of art. On the one hand, we often think that art is extremely powerful, that it has an immense capacity to control our perceptions and beliefs, and that there is little corrective once this power is exercised. Proponents of this view often hold that art is a cultural staple that ought to serve the social, political, or moral needs of the people. This view harks back at least to Plato, and probably motivates most discussions that take seriously the power of images to shape our lives. This view gives art great metaphysical and epistemological powers, while paradoxically condemning it to use those powers to no good. The other view of art that runs through our everyday thinking about the subject as well as some of our theories is the view that art is not a cultural staple, something with which everyone is or should be familiar and for which everyone is responsible, but rather that it is an expendable, superfluous aspect of human life, to be sequestered in museums and out-of-the-way corners of our lives, encountered on Saturday or Sunday afternoons and at some expense. On this view, artists are not revered cultural leaders or dangerous charlatans, but are rather part of an eccentric fringe making luxuries that are dispensable and largely irrelevant to the rest of life. On this view, art is decoration and window dressing; it has no real metaphysical or epistemological significance. On this view, restricting what artists can say or do has only symbolic import. The artist is made an example of, and others in the society learn their own boundaries from this example. I will not attempt to sort through these competing conceptions of art here, but this essay should lend some support to those who are engaged in such a project. In closing, I will sketch a picture of art that may help in thinking about these issues.

THE ABSOLUTIST AND THE RECLAIMER: WORDS

It has become commonplace to treat the aesthetic as a subspecies of the linguistic, to treat artistic acts and creations as species of expression, and to treat declarative speech as the paradigmatic form of expression. While maintaining some skepticism about the ease of such analogies between speech and aesthetic expression, it is also important to respect their power. So let us begin with a look at two approaches to derogatory terms such as racist, sexist, and ethnic epithets. The Absolutist argues that certain derogatory terms and subordinating images should be erased from our available repertoires, or at least that those who use such terms or images should be held liable in civil or criminal court.[4] In contrast, the Reclaimer holds that such terms, as terms of subordination, have a history that must be remembered and argues that these terms can be reclaimed by those against whom they are used. Attempting a sort of linguistic aikido, some members of the groups against which these terms have been used have been trying, with various degrees of success, to reclaim the derogatory terms and turn them into terms of endearment, or at least terms of in-group reference that differ significantly in their semantic content (or inferential role) from the original terms used by the dominant group. The reclaimer wants to disarm the power of these terms and images by internal reorganization – by effecting semantic change – rather than by imposing external sanctions. Making terms taboo grants them a certain power, so the Reclaimer does not want to strengthen the taboos against these terms. In contrast, the Absolutist sees the Reclamation project as doomed by the entrenchment of these terms and by the power of discursive practice to resist change.

Social practices and harms

Current discussions of derogatory terms (usually labeled *hate speech*) tend to focus on cases in which one person hurls a racist epithet as if it were a weapon inflicting pain and injury on its target. Such second-person cases surely are important, and just as surely such linguistic behavior is morally inappropriate. Critical Race Theorists like Mari Matsuda argue that such individual actions have the power they do only in the context of a society that sanctions these acts and offers no recourse to their victims. Derogatory terms and subordinating images gain their power from their coherence with other social practices. Racist language, for example, matters primarily in a context that sanctions the disparate treatment of members of races counted less valuable. Without the cultural and material "backup" of discriminatory practices, such as social isolation, economic discrimination, harassment, and violence, such derogatory terms would not have the force they do.[5] We have the power, through our laws, to stop the linguistic behavior or at least to punish it; we have the responsibility, Matsuda and others argue, to stop the harm.

This epithet-hurling model is unfortunate, however, for it obscures the larger social dimension of these terms and makes it seem as if the real problem were individual cruelty or individual attempts to sub-ordinate. The epithet-hurling case is attractive as a focus because it seems like a performative – an utterance that gets something done – in this case performing the act of subordinating the target. What force it has will depend on other aspects of the speech act. Further, this focus makes it seem as if the racism were a matter of the term's being *used*, but the logician's distinction between use and mention does not really work here to erase the associated derogatory commitments of the term. I will say more about this later.

Racist discourse has social force in all sorts of contexts and in most sorts of speech act. Just as important are the casual third-person uses of these terms – very different sorts of speech acts – which reinforce the mode of discourse and with it the conceptual framework and its social ontology. An exclusive focus on cases in which one person says to another "You so-and-so!" will yield a very different account than one that also attends to speech acts of the form "You know Fred, the so-and-so." Such third-person uses ultimately may be more insidious and more powerful. If the Absolutist is right that these terms cannot be rehabilitated, then even in third-person uses the terms carry a derogation. The derogatory force of the term does not depend on the term's being used in an explicitly derogating speech act such as shouting an epithet in someone's face; if the Absolutist is right, then the term is derogatory in *all* contexts.

The Absolutist sees derogatory terms as inextricably tied to stereo-types, which are themselves notoriously resistant to correction. Voic-ing a key tenet of Absolutism, one team of social scientists claims that derogatory terms "come to symbolize *all* the negative stereotypic beliefs associated with the group," adding that this comprehensive-ness makes them "extremely potent communicative devices."[6] Just as important, the Absolutist believes in the potency of discourse:

Words have the power to make a concept seem like something that actually exists in the world. For example, there are negative beliefs about blacks in the United States, but *the term 'nigger' crystallizes these beliefs into a con-cept or prototype that has a sense of concrete reality* to those who use the term.[7]

Derogatory terms have the power to shape our social ontology because they are broadly prescriptive, giving people a proclaimed reality to live down to. Because that "reality" is constituted by rigid stereotypes, the person labeled by the term cannot simply shake off certain aspects of the stereotype: what doesn't fit remains and rubs. The Absolutist advocates eliminating the terms used in racial epithets in order to break the language–culture cycle that keeps oppressive categories intact.

Both the Absolutist and the Reclaimer seek to break the power of oppressive category terms, but they have different strategies for doing so. Most of what I say in this essay about these approaches focuses on discrete terms or expressions – individual words and images. Lest we not settle for too benign a notion of what Reclamation would take, consider William Faulkner's attempt to depict racism in the United States. James Baldwin has said that "in the work of Faulkner . . . one sees the beginnings – at least – of a more genuinely penetrating search" for the way racism is woven into the patterns of our lives.[8] In a study of Faulkner's major novels, James Snead portrays Faulkner as a novelist who is actively engaged in a reclamation project that goes way beyond the mere reclamation of a particular word here or there. Taking very seriously the Absolutist's concern about the way that language shapes ontology, Faulkner set about to reshape both. Snead writes:

The stylistic strangeness of Faulkner's novels is not purely post-Joycean experimentalism, as often suggested, nor even a residue of his infatuation with Romanticism and French symbolism. Instead Faulkner's narratives are accurate reconstructions and dismantlings of linguistic and social classifications, proving that some extraordinary human beings struggle, against overwhelming odds, to reverse a separation that rhetoric has tried to make into permanent reality.[9]

Again we see the ontological power of language taken seriously, so seriously that Faulkner must wrestle with the structure of his prose to convey the restructuring he sees or sometimes only hopes for.

More recently, director Hal Prince revised some of the racist language in the Toronto production of *Showboat,* which premiered there in October 1993, because it had been described by critics as a trivialization of slavery. In response to such charges of racism, Prince cut all but two utterances of the word 'nigger', and those were uttered by a villain. Prince has been described as "reluctant to make more substantial changes to the language, adding 'You don't clean it up for the sake of rewriting history.'"[10] Protesters find this appeal to historical veracity rather disingenuous, given that the show is a musical depicting "blacks of the late 1800s and early part of this century as easygoing people who, despite unspeakable cruelties, will spontaneously burst into song and dance."[11] Cutting the racist terms is a beginning, but the protesters are right that it is not enough to render the play benign. The subordinating discourse is but one factor, the subordinating images are another; together, they are a very potent, very volatile combination. Prince's willingness to clean up the language is a willingness to do half the job. Doing the rest of the job would literally deconstruct the play.

The inferential role theory of meaning

To understand the social problems reflected in and the linguistic problems created by derogatory terms, it is helpful to use an inferential role theory of meaning.[12] Such a view makes good sense of the social and political dimensions of the discourse while making clear their connection to its basic linguistic and cognitive structure. The inferential theory, like the views of the Absolutist and the Reclaimer, is holist; it emphasizes the place of the expression in relation to its context and it emphasizes the significance of the relation of that context to other contexts (similar and dissimilar). Accordingly, the meaning of a sentence is a matter of its place in a pattern of inferences, and the meaning of a word or expression is a matter of its various actual and possible sentential roles. These patterns of inference are governed by commitments, which are a matter of speakers' issuing licenses and undertaking responsibilities. Social, cultural, and linguistic contexts govern which commitments a speaker may make. Communities license certain kinds of basic linguistic commitments, such as "It is raining" or "If this is College Park, we must be in Maryland," for nearly all community members. Some licenses require specific training or social positioning; specialization of labor and discretely distributed authority tend to yield parallel restrictions on linguistic licenses. So, in the United States, only some members of society can effectively say "Thirty days or thirty dollars" or "Take two Prozac daily." Most linguistic licenses tend to be less explicit, but similarly effective. When the Absolutist says that certain words should be expunged from the language or that speakers should be held liable for uttering them, she is urging that we, as a community, take *explicit* control over certain inference licenses – that we unlicense certain inferences across the board.

Whenever one speaks, one simultaneously undertakes commitments (of one's own) and issues licenses to one's audience. There are three basic kinds of commitments: assertional, identificatory, and expressive. When Jane says, "Mary is the dyke who went to the meeting," Jane's *assertional commitment* issues an inference license to her audience. That license allows her audience to use the claim as a premise in arguments of their own while deferring justification for the claim back to Jane. It also requires Jane to justify the claim if it should be challenged.[13] Suppose Jane outed Mary by using this term. Then Jane would have to justify two parts of her claim: that Mary went to the meeting and that Mary is a lesbian. Jane's *identificatory commitment* requires her to identify which Mary and which meeting, if her audience asks. Jane's *expressive commitment* here is complex, but it includes a commitment to the viability and value of dyke-talk.

As these descriptions suggest, linguistic commitments, like other commitments, are defined largely by their associated responsibilities. Identificatory and assertional commitments each carry an associated *task responsibility.* Assertional commitments, for example, are defined by the inferences they license and their supporting justifications – again inferences. Since an expressive commitment is a commitment to the viability and value of a particular way of talking, its task responsibility requires showing that this way of talking really is viable and valuable.[14] Showing viability requires showing that the expression is part of an inferential network that makes sense; showing value takes showing that the expression serves the goals of the discourse.[15] What one takes the expressive commitment of words and images used in works of art to be will depend upon both what one takes the goal of artistic practice to be and what one takes to be the goal or function of the particular artwork in which the terms or images abide. If one thinks that art is a practice or set of practices for the exploration of human subjectivity or for the development of our expressive powers (or both), then one is not likely to restrict its contents in the way that Jesse Helms would have us do.

Ordinarily, an expressive commitment is supported by supporting enough of the assertional commitments of the expression to show that the way of talking in which the expression fits is indeed viable and valuable. To illustrate the assertional commitments of perhaps the most derogatory of derogatory terms commonly used in the United States, we may turn to Jerry Farber's 1970 book, *The Student as Nigger.*[16] To make the as-claim stick, Farber tried to show that the inferential role of the term fits the lives of students. Farber contrasts students with faculty, citing segregated dining facilities, segregated lavatory facilities, segregated sleeping facilities, and anti-miscegenation rules as partial evidence of his analogy. Each of these features represents one assertional commitment of the term. Spelling it out, we would get a series of conditionals: "If X is a nigger, then there is a set of Ys such that Xs and Ys cannot sleep in the same facility"; similarly for each feature. Farber provides a partial list of the elements in the inferential role of the term: the referent is a being defined in reference to others to whom she is considered subservient, from whom she must be kept separate, by whom she may be exploited, and so on.

Sketching out the inferential role of the term by way of its assertional commitments shows viability. Sometimes viability alone shows value, since there is at least some value in the term's power to communicate so effectively. Both the Absolutist and the Reclaimer agree that the viability of a derogatory term does not show *enough* value to overcome the devastating pragmatic force of the term. The Absolutist holds that the term's subordinating assertional commitments undermine the value of the term; she holds that there is only one inferential role for all tokens of the term and that this role is morally and politically unacceptable. The Reclaimer holds that there are enough variations on the inferential role of the term that we are not really talking about one term with one expressive commitment, but rather several related terms with common pasts and overlapping but nonidentical presents and branching futures.

What is at stake between the Absolutist and the Reclaimer is the *expressive commitment* of the term. An expressive commitment is a commitment to the viability and value of a particular way of talking; it is a commitment to the inferential role of an expression. They agree about what the expressive commitment has been and perhaps even agree about what it currently is. Where the two camps always part company is over the future of the term. The Absolutist denies the possibility of there ever being a positive (nonderogatory) use of the term, while the Reclaimer urges that the subcommunity against which the term has been used can effect meaning change through the careful manipulation of context.

Some implications and applications

The Absolutist argument begins with the empirical claim that derogatory terms cause harm to those they label, and adds the normative claim that these harms are unjust and unnecessary. Since the assertional commitments of the term largely represent stereotypically assigned traits and relations, and since stereotypes are notoriously rigid, prescriptive, and difficult or impossible to undermine, the Absolutist holds that the assertional commitments of the derogatory terms are nondetachable. Richard Delgado claims, for example, that "words such as 'nigger' and 'spick' are badges of degradation even when used between friends; these words have no other connotation."[17] To stop the harms caused by the terms we would have to detach at least some of the stereotyped assertional commitments, but since these are nondetachable, there is no rehabilitating the term. Without rehabilitation, any use of the term is racist, sexist, heterosexist, or whatever, and so promotes injustice. So the Absolutist holds that since we cannot drop the derogation from the term, we should drop the term.

It is worth noting that the derogatoriness of a term in its sentential context is not a function of whether the term is asserted. Embedding the term in the antecedent or consequent of a conditional does not take away the derogatoriness of the term. If my neighbor says, "If a nigger buys the house down the street I'll sell mine," she is as responsible for justifying the expressive commitment of the derogatory term (for justifying "nigger" talk) as if she had said, "A nigger just bought the house down the street so I'm selling mine." Fictional discourse has great flexibility concerning what is asserted within the context and by the author, and this makes thorny the question of the status of racist language within fictional contexts. The current example shows that assertion in nonfictional cases may cement the speaker's expressive commitment, but nonassertion does not waive it. So if we take fiction to be a huge nonassertion marker, that still does not necessarily get us off the moral hook.

Similarly, the logician's distinction between use and mention does not help. Imagine a white supremacist linguist saying, "'Nigger' is a great word, for it keeps us all aware of who belongs where in the social order." The derogatory term is *mentioned,* not *used,* but the sentential context supports the derogatoriness of the term and the mentioning does not seem to wipe it away. The claim is racist, and the mentioned term helps make it so. Although the term's status as mentioned raises the question of whether the speaker endorses it, the question is settled by the content of the rest of the sentence. Now consider a liberal saying, "Fred is wrong to call blacks 'niggers' because there are no niggers – only black citizens." The first instance of the derogatory term is mentioned, and the second is used. Although the term is *used,* the sentential context condemns its derogatory aspect and its ontological presupposition. The claim is not racist, and the *used* term does not by itself render the claim racist. Of course, we would justly complain about the infelicity of the second occurrence of the derogatory term, for the speaker could just as well have said "there aren't any" without gratuitous repetition of the term.

The Absolutist would commend Hal Prince for dropping the many utterances of 'nigger' from *Showboat,* but would renounce him for keeping the two that remain, no matter that they are uttered by villains. Extending this position beyond language and into images, the Absolutist would reject the depiction of the cheerful slave as if it were historical reality and would challenge the value of re-presenting that image even if it were historically accurate. To depict the subordination is to impose it again, at least symbolically, according to this view. It is to libel and demean the group so depicted.

The Reclaimer would not wholeheartedly defend the restaging of *Showboat.* The terms in the play are not reclaimed, and the community against which the terms have been used does not provide the context in which the terms are used. Although the Reclaimer argues that sometimes derogatory terms recognize an important history of degradation without endorsing its continuation, in this case the question of endorsement is not made clear. Further, the question must arise concerning the point of restaging the show. To whom is it playing? About whom is it speaking? The fact of the derogatory terms will not settle these questions, but looking at the patrons of the theaters, the class implications of ticket costs, and so on yields a clearer picture. The 1990s *Showboat* plays to largely white, largely affluent audiences, people who can afford the $60+ per ticket and who take pleasure in seeing depictions of happy slaves. In this context, Prince's appeal to history seems outlandish. The Reclaimer would not attack the musical simply because its derogatory terms are unreclaimed, but would join the Absolutist in arguing that it subordinates the target community.

The Reclaimer wants the target community to have jurisdiction over the expressive commitments of its own self-referring labels. The Reclaimer would roundly deny Delgado's claim that derogatory terms are always "badges of degradation even when used between friends." Some African-Americans use 'nigger' as a term of endearment, and some lesbians use 'dyke' as a term of pride. When so used, such reclamations may in fact change the meanings of these terms through subversive uses within the subcommunity. By giving the

293

subcommunity this power, the Reclaimer hopes to change the norms that settle the assertional commitments of the term, and thus hopes to change the very meaning of the term.

Reclamation depends upon the possibility of somehow severing the derogation from the term, although not upon the possibility of severing the history of derogation *via* the term.[18] Here the Reclaimer directly contradicts the Absolutist's nondetachability thesis; she argues that in such contexts, some specific assertional commitments are dropped, others are relocated within the inferential network, and some stay the same but have different justifications or consequences. Generally, the Reclaimer's argument depends upon the claim that the derogation is a pragmatic effect, not a semantic aspect of the term. If the derogation *were* a semantic aspect, then there could be no nonderogatory use of the term. But there *is* a nonderogatory use: since some African-Americans use 'nigger' as an in-group term of endearment, we can see that the derogation is not built into the semantics. The pragmatic effect is a matter of the relation between the speaker's in-group and the referent's in-group, at least. When African-Americans use the term among themselves, it is *possible* for the term not to carry derogation, and this shows that group membership can enable disaffiliation from the common derogation.[19] Further, it may be that when others besides African-Americans use the term, it is impossible for the term not to carry derogation. If so, then if one is not a member of the group targeted by the term, one's use cannot disaffiliate. So there are nonderogatory uses of the term, and pragmatic factors are the means by which the derogation is detached.

The spirit of this argument is commendable and it captures our common folklore about who is entitled to try to reclaim the term, but it is unfortunately marred by confusions about the relations between semantics and pragmatics, interpretive methods and interpretations themselves, and similar issues.[20] Both inquiries into meaning-change in general and inquiries into the power of aesthetic contexts to facilitate deviant interpretations should find significant that group membership is crucial to determining whether a particular occurrence of a term is reclaimed. The question "Who speaks?" must be asked and answered in order to know what has been said. The Absolutist says that such terms have only one purpose – the subjugation of the person to whom they are applied – and that makes the terms uniformly morally inappropriate. The Reclaimer says that the story is not so simple. Sometimes a term is used within the oppressed group as a form of *accommodation* to the difficulty of their situation; we see this in some of Faulkner's black characters, like Nancy in "That Evening Sun," who says again and again, "I ain't nothin' but a nigger, it ain't none of my fault."[21] Sometimes the term is used within the target group as a way of establishing class difference within the group. And then, in a completely opposite move, it is sometimes used as a term of endearment, as in "'My main nigger' becomes 'my best friend.'"[22] The Reclaimer points out how context-sensitive the term is – it matters who says it, to whom, when, where, and why. An Absolutist position overlooks all this subtlety, and in the process overlooks the power of the community to allow or disallow very specific sorts of licenses.

The Reclaimer points out that to know what the sign-design 'nigger' means, one must place it in a linguistic context. The sign-design has its meaning in relation to a language and a context. The Absolutist ignores the importance of the many differences between the term's coming out of the mouths of white people as they harass black children on their way to school in South Boston, its coming out of my white middle-class mouth in the context of academic discourse like this, its coming out of Lenny Bruce's mouth along with a lot of other derogatory terms for a lot of other groups, its coming out of Richard Pryor's mouth (which it doesn't anymore), and its coming out of Ice-T's gangsta-rappin' mouth. Each of these contexts exists within a set of linguistic and social practices that shape the inferential role and the pragmatic function of the term in that context.

The Reclaimer also notes that the rehabilitation of a term or expression is a community-wide achievement that takes time to occur. For the reclaimed term to prevail, there must be community-wide agreement about the bulk of the assertional commitments. The problem for the members of a community as it moves from a derogatory inferential role to a laudatory one is epistemic. As interpreters of each other, we want, and sometimes need, to know who is committed to the old term, with its oppressive entrenchment, and who is committed to new linguistic and social practices. Sometimes knowing is a matter of comfort or ease, and sometimes it is a matter of safety. *We need to know who speaks.* Since the unreclaimed term represents the common past of the two versions of the term, its inferential role serves as the default when there are no clear markers that the less common and more recent reclaimed term is appropriate. Since there is so much at stake for those who have been targets, in the absence of community-wide consensus and clear markers for community membership, the default interpretation will probably always be the unreclaimed term. Thus, the old bad word stays ever active.

Both Absolutists and Reclaimers tend to be holists, but they differ about how to break the particular language–culture cycle that both want broken. Absolutists think that with terms like these, the expressive commitment, ranging as it does over the whole mode of discourse, is so powerful that it cannot be dismantled piecemeal but must be jettisoned completely. Reclaimers, on the other hand, think that we can change the structure of the assertional commitments and so change the very nature of the expressive commitment. Perhaps the most important issue between them is whether the speaker who uses the derogatory term may, through creative use of context, control which elements of the term operate within the context and what interpretive role they play. If so, then the Absolutist is out of business.

Even if one doubts that the Reclamation project can succeed, it is clear that the Absolutist's holism is too strong. Undertaking an expressive commitment does not require adhering to every possible element in the inferential role of the term. In general, we often quite carefully limit our endorsement of the inferential roles with which we work. We can narrow the scope of the endorsement, but if we reject something very central to the inferential role, then there is a real question about whether we are undertaking the expressive commitment at all. Without its central assertional commitments, the viability and value of the discursive practice that supports the term become questionable. Exploiting the metaphor of viability, the Reclaimer urges that just as careful pruning enhances the health of real trees, so too with "inferential trees." One might think that aesthetic contexts, providing a protected space in which the question "Who speaks?" and the issue of interpretation are ever-present, would be helpful to the project of making expressive commitment explicit and would be helpful in creating a starter culture from which a new world can rise. Art may just be able to facilitate the deviant interpretations that the Reclaimer needs.

CONTENT AND POINT OF VIEW: IMAGE ABSOLUTISM

Art is a complex set of context-dependent practices. These contexts include historical, art historical, and linguistic aspects, as well as genre constraints. Each of these aspects involves complex sets of interpretive practices. The arts are also wondrously expressively innovative. Sometimes they push the limits of an established form of expression; sometimes they create new forms, new practices. In art, the expressive medium is always an issue, at least to the artist. Further, the arts are remarkable in their consistent and often explicit development of authorial point of view. Whatever the medium or genre, the question "Who speaks?" arises whenever a work is interpreted. "Who speaks?" may ask about the poet, the novelist, the director, the painter, the sculptor, the choreographer, and so on. This question is also raised in philosophical inquiries into language used in nonaesthetic contexts, but it is obscured in modes of discourse, like science, that presume the objectivity of participating voices. In the arts, the authorial voice is rarely presumed objective; instead, the arts are often seen as practices through which we are encouraged to explore our subjectivity.

The Absolutist generally emphasizes that derogatory terms and pornography embody an objectionable point of view, and then argues that their restriction is not justified solely on grounds of the content of the expression, but primarily because of the point of view expressed. That point of view is one that advocates or *endorses* the subordination of one group of people to another. Anti–hate speech activists have tended to emphasize the content, while suggesting that the content and the point of view actually cannot be separated (they treat them as "thick terms"). On the other hand, until very recently, antiporn activists have tended to emphasize point of view, as we shall see. In her latest book, Catherine MacKinnon runs these together in the case of pornography, arguing that an image depicting subordination *just is* a subordinating image. She says that "elevation and denigration are all accomplished through meaningful symbols and communicative acts in which saying it is doing it."[23] Her arguments have strong rhetorical force – they ring out with self-proclaimed political correctness. There is a general point to be made that the Absolutist's arguments and political agendas are not really true to the goals she espouses, but here I will settle for suggesting that when such a discussion turns to aesthetic contexts these arguments especially do not make sense. The distinction between content and point of view will rarely be firm, for it is through the subtle manipulation of content that the nuances of point of view are conveyed. Even if we grant that neither the content nor the point of view represented by hate speech and pornography has aesthetic value, that is no reason to hold that there is no distinction between content and point of view, either generally or in particular. This is also no reason to deny the distinction between content and context, or to dispute the distinction between what is said and what is done in the saying of it.

Keep in mind Foucault's point that the author was created so that some speakers could be praised and others could be blamed. The author function is a responsibility function. To be an author, to have a byline, is to be accountable for what one says. MacKinnon, echoing a long line of speech act theorists, is right that saying is a kind of doing, but the *content* of what we say does not necessarily determine *the nature of the correlated action.* Context has a big hand here. If Foucault is right, and I think he is, then ever since there have been authors, words have been recognized as deeds. An author's words are her deeds, or at least a subset of them. These words/deeds embody a certain perspective or point of view, which is more or less coherent, more or less novel, more or less socially acceptable. What deed the words constitute depends on their associated identificatory, assertional, and expressive commitments, and these must be taken in light of the broader social and linguistic practices of the author's community. What deed the words constitute, what the author is responsible for, depends almost entirely on the social and linguistic context in which they appear.

Context, content, and point of view have long played a role in feminist definitions of pornography. Helen Longino has suggested a very useful tripartite distinction between pornography and erotica, on the one hand, and moral (or political) realism, on the other. Longino defines pornography as

verbal or pictorial material which represents or describes sexual behavior that is degrading or abusive to one or more of the participants in such a way as to endorse the degradation.[24]

This definition takes it to be *crucial* that pornography involves power relations, with a victim and a victor, a dominator and a subordinate. Gloria Steinem says of pornography that

its message is violence, dominance, and conquest. It is sex being used to reinforce some inequality, or to create one, or to tell us that pain and humiliation (ours or someone else's) are really the same as pleasure.[25]

Erotica, on the other hand, may be sexually explicit but does not depict and endorse the degradation or abuse of anyone. Its message and purpose are not domination. Erotica tends to be characterized by loving and caring gestures between peers; erotica is nice. Erotic images may be power*ful* but they are not *about* power.

On this picture, developed and endorsed by many U.S. feminists since the 1970s, the distinction between pornography and erotica is a content-based distinction. Pornography contains acts of subordination and humiliation, erotica does not.[26] The distinction between pornography and moral or political realism is, on the other hand, what jurists would call a point-of-view-based distinction. Both moral realism and pornography contain depictions of degradation and abuse, but pornography *endorses* the abuse, whereas moral realism makes no such endorsement. A film like *The Accused* counts as moral realism and not porn because although it graphically depicts the abuse and degradation of a woman being gang-raped, it does not glorify the rapists. It does not portray rape as providing pleasure to the woman or as something she sought or deserved. Presenting the woman *as a person,* as a person who has been harmed and violated by what has been done to her, is already a radical step away from most pornographic images. The image of the rape scene is colored by a perspective, which is reinforced by the overall context of the film. Any film portrays a perspective, which may endorse or protest what it depicts; the less a film or image *seems* to have a perspective, the more likely it is that the perspective matches the dominant cultural ideology. The perspective of *The Accused* is noticeable largely because of its opposition to common sexist views of women's sexuality; the film clearly protests rape, and its re-presenting the rape serves that end. The difference between pornography and moral realism lies in its endorsement, in whether it advocates or protests what it represents. Such a distinction can be countenanced only within an account that respects distinctions between content and context, and between content and point of view.

This feminist taxonomy is not far from standard views of representation in art. In his classic *Languages of Art,* Nelson Goodman points out that "with a picture as with any other label, there are always two questions: what it represents (or describes) and what sort of representation (or description) it is."[27] In Goodman's terms, the "what it represents" of both pornography and moral realism would be "acts of sexual subordination," and the key question is "what kind of representation it is." We might join MacKinnon in calling pornography's kind "subordinating image," but part from her by still reserving a category of moral realism, for which the kind-of-representation-it-is might be described as "liberating image" or "educating image."

Consider the performances of Italian playwright and actress Franca Rame, whose radical presentations have reached many outside the safe confines of high culture. Margaret Spillane describes Rame in this way:

In her "Tutta Casa, Letto e Chiesa," for example, Rame presents a serious, hilarious, and sometimes devastating look into the minute-to-minute limitations, responsibilities, and exasperations of a working-class woman. Her character must maintain heroic stamina to deal with the endless incursions of boss, husband, men in the street, children, and appliances upon her life. Rame has also made theater out of a horrific event; the night she was abducted from the street by far-right-wing thugs and brutally gang-raped. She spares nothing of the humiliation, the sexual slurs, the cigarette burns to her thighs. Rame has forged her own agony into a passionate social declaration: Those unspeakable details of a woman's brutalization, which a censorious society would quickly close the lid upon and bury, Rame propels into the spotlight of the stage.[28]

If Longino is right, then we must ask *why* Rame propels these brutal facts into the spotlight. What point of view is represented here? Again, Goodman's now-standard terminology helps. Goodman distinguishes between a representation of a man (as when that gray spot in the photo is my brother), a man-picture (which may be of no one in particular but is a man-type image), and a representation of someone or something *as* a man (e.g., a sketch of my dog wearing a necktie and suit jacket, smoking a pipe). Content and point of view intermingle here. When Rame presents these brutal details, she presents them *as* brutal, *as* violations; in doing this, she presents the victim, herself, as a person, which is something that is not done in most pornography. Moral realism respects and represents the agency of the victim, even when it is thwarted agency, whereas pornography tends to lie about the agency of those subordinated, usually presenting them as thoroughly complicit in the crimes against them while overlooking the forces that generate such complicity as exists.

Recently, MacKinnon has been roundly criticized for arguing that pornography is not just a picture of a particular act that subordinates a particular woman, but that *pornography itself subordinates.* On her view, pornography is pernicious because it does more than just depict sexual subordination – it is itself a subordinating image. MacKinnon is an Absolutist about pornographic images in the same way that Critical Race Theorists are Absolutists about derogatory terms. MacKinnon calls an image *subordinating* in order to convey that there is no neutral use of the image or expression – every moment of its production and viewing promotes violence to women. It should be clear from what I have just said that one problem with MacKinnon's view is that all depictions of the sexual subordination of women are thereby pornography, because she does not make the distinction Longino makes between porn and realism. It sounds like an ad hominem to say that if MacKinnon is right, then her own books and law review articles are or contain pornography, since she often recounts rather sordid pornographic practices and their associated images in her own texts. This is worth mentioning not in the hope of silencing MacKinnon, as some have tried to do, but to make explicit one problem that the Absolutist has in virtue of ignoring Longino's distinctions and in obfuscating the distinction between point of view and content. If there can be no nonsubordinating uses of the images or expressions, then to discuss them is to endorse them or to be saddled with at least some of their filthy residue. MacKinnon's practice shows her practical, if not theoretical, adherence to the distinction between pornography and moral realism. (This consideration may ground an argument for the collapse of Absolutism into Reclamation.)

Pornography is worth discussing at so much length in considering the relation between ethics and aesthetics because pornographic images, while generally not art, are images that many diverse members of our society take to be worth fighting against; they are images that many say should be controlled or eradicated. Pornography raises the question of the power of images. It is obvious that pornographic images can be powerful. The question is, what is it in their power to do? An image is generally taken to have power if it somehow affects our behavior. When an advertisement makes you want whiter wash or gets you to buy one brand instead of another, the images in that ad are considered powerful. If the image makes you change your attitude toward someone or something, and so alters your behavior in that regard, the image has power. Pornographic images have been said to have such effective power – they are said to *cause* violence against women.

There are two strategies for defending the claim that pornography causes violence against women. The strongest arguments against this claim maintain that no one can establish a direct link between pornography and, say, rape. Such a direct one-to-one link would require documenting many particular cases of many individual men viewing pornography and then raping. The critic argues that such a link has not been established, saying that studies that have sought to show this have been methodologically flawed or inconclusive. Without such evidence, we cannot establish that the images have the presumed causal power, and this shows that pornography is not a sufficient condition for rape. So, they would like us to conclude, we need not fear or control these images. Without a direct link between particular viewings and particular crimes, the antiporn feminists don't seem to have a case.

Now if we cannot establish the power of images in this kind of case, in what case can we establish it? How could such a claim be shown? This question is relevant to all the visual arts – not just the lowest forms; high art offers no safe haven from the power of the image. Having forgotten about some of the more gruesome of Rubens's paintings until I was in the midst of an exhibit at Boston's Museum of Fine Arts with my three-and-a-half-year-old son, I found myself concerned about the effect of his seeing Rubens's brilliant and yet horrible *Medusa*. The image is gripping, and given its effect on me I had to wonder what its effect on my young son would be. What he said was "Wow! Look at all those snakes coming out of her head! Mommy, her eyes look kind of green – I don't think she is okay. . . . Why are all those snakes there like her hair? And how come her head is cut off? Is she awake? . . . She looks mad!" These are good questions, and their unsettling answers attest to the power of the image to disturb. *Of course* images have power to shape and reshape our thoughts, our attitudes, our deeds, but given the complexity of the human mind, the complexity of our many social, psychological, and intellectual situations, capacities, and practices, there really is little hope of finding a simple formula for what picture X has the power to do to viewer Y. What a word or image has the power to do depends both on its role in the interpreted object (or sentence) and on various features of the interpreting agent. With pornographic images, this possible multiple effect is amply illustrated by the remarkable galvanizing effect that Women Against Pornography's slide shows have had over the years. Those who see these slide shows do not usually respond with violence against women. The effects powerful images have on us depend a great deal on who we are when we see them and the context in which they are presented.

In an early work, Catherine MacKinnon emphasizes an indirect rather than a direct link between pornography and violence against women with her proclamation that "fantasy expresses ideology."[29] Holding that pornography is a practical tool of the ideology of sexism, the early MacKinnon argues that the images, taken in the context of the ideology of sexism, cause violence against women. Pornography is about power over women via their sexuality; it mystifies and eroticizes male dominance and female submission. Pornography promulgates images of women and men that fuel practices that are damaging to women.[30] MacKinnon's point is to establish this more indirect link between pornography and harm to women by appeal to pornography's role in supporting sexism as a force that oppresses women. She puts the images back into their broader context and then argues that, in that context, they operate as efficient causes of violence against women. In her more recent work, she builds the oppressive social structure right into the images. (The structure would be captured within whatever serves as assertional commitments in the case of images. Simply moving it from context to content begs many questions.)

Oppression is a matter of there being systematic barriers and penalties that keep one group subordinate to another; oppression is about power. It is about the power of the social system and how that system grants power to members of one group because they are members of that group and denies it to those who are not members of that group. In the United States in the late twentieth century it is fairly easy to document the systematically interrelated ways in which women are oppressed. This is not a conspiracy theory of sexism, for it neither claims nor requires any intentional establishment or explicitly intentional perpetuation of the system. The virtue of this way of thinking about oppression is that it captures the fact that when considered individually many of the forces of oppression may be trivial or innocuous, but they gain force through their connection with similar actions and practices.[31] This account of oppression was developed by Marilyn Frye, who uses the analogy of a birdcage to illustrate her point, saying that of course if one looks only at one bar of the cage one will ask incredulously why the bird doesn't just fly away. It takes seeing the interrelated barriers – all of the bars and how they are joined – to see the bird's real situation. To see oppression, one must move from a microscopic perspective to a macroscopic one. A particular behavior counts as oppressive only against the background of a set of social practices; similar behavior in other contexts may not be oppressive at all.

This appeal to oppression gives the Absolutist's position its punch. Those who are most harmed by hate speech and pornography are also those who are historically oppressed. On classic views of censorship, like Hobbes's, the censor's job is to enforce the standards of the majority, so it is the minority that is censored. The Absolutist seeks censorship that works the other way around. In explaining why "stopping pornographers and pornography is not censorship," Andrea Dworkin claims that

pornographers are more like the police in police states than they are like the writers in police states. They are the instruments of terror, not its victims. Intervening in a system of terror where it is vulnerable to public scrutiny to stop it is not censorship; it is the system of terror that stops speech and creates abuse and despair.[32]

At issue is who has power. Dworkin, MacKinnon, and others who would ban pornography, like other Absolutists, use the moral authority of the plight of the powerless to ground a grasping of expressive control. Since the contested social and linguistic practices have served the powerful at the expense of the powerless – in fact, have helped to create and maintain the two groups – they argue that we should not see the righting of this wrong as censorship but as a substantive corrective to injustice. Dworkin's *substantive* conception of censorship takes seriously the relative power of speakers' positions and could serve as a corrective to the injustices that slip by procedural approaches, but it fails to note that new practices would emerge from this corrective that would yield but a different set of procedural injustices. Neither Dworkin nor MacKinnon can explain how her envisioned system would protect artists like Franca Rame and the makers of films like *The Accused.* Absolutism, while generally springing from such lofty moral concerns as the liberation of the oppressed, has also been used to silence the oppressed and is today being used in less than lofty ways. Similarly, although Reclamation may get good press when we look at the way blacks have reclaimed 'nigger' and lesbians have reclaimed 'dyke', we should also keep in mind that the logic of Reclamation really doesn't change much when Italian-Americans reclaim 'guido' and 'guinea' as part of a white supremacist political agenda.[33]

For MacKinnon, the question of the power of images is, at bottom, the question of the legitimation of ways of life. Acknowledging that part of the power of art is its power to legitimate, we can see that this power increases exponentially when it is combined with the dominant social ideology. Robert Mapplethorpe's work, for example, is both condemned and praised for its very artistic images of gay male sadomasochistic sexuality that seem through their artistry to legitimate the acts depicted and the lifestyles associated with them.[34] That legitimization is what gets Jesse Helms so worked up. But what Helms fails to see is that Mapplethorpe's images just cannot have the naturalized force that heterosexist images have, as long as Mapplethorpe is presenting a minority view. To someone who accepts the dominant heterosexist ideology Helms seeks to protect, Mapplethorpe's images are unlegitimated and unnatural (because unnatural*ized*). What Helms fears is that Mapplethorpe's images, and others like them, will legitimate their contents, thereby moving them away from the margins.

I said earlier that Hal Prince's willingness to eliminate gratuitous utterances of the word 'nigger' in his production of *Showboat* is a willingness to do only half the job. He will clean up the subordinating discourse but not the subordinating images. The Absolutist and the Reclaimer would surely agree that the show's musical format is inappropriate to the subject matter, especially since it depicts enslaved and mistreated Africans in the United States as responding to the cruelties of slavery with happy faces and lilting songs. The Absolutist sees no value in maintaining such a play, and, as I suggested earlier, the Reclaimer sees a problem with the play's purpose and its relation to its own history and the period it depicts. The Reclaimer might see the potential for virtually the same content to be presented nonoppressively, with changes to the context that would provide an assertion of authorial or directorial point of view. If the play were staged as a play-within-a-play, with the internal play represented as a relic of our racist past, then a condemnation of that past might help mitigate the racist content. That is, the Reclaimer can accept some racist content if the point of view expressed is opposed to that content. One obvious way to preserve content while expressing a variant point of view is through the manipulation of context; in this case the framing play does that job.

This external-frame approach to the problem is ultimately unsatisfying. Although there are good reasons for maintaining the distinction between content and point of view, some of which I have rehearsed here, the distinction is not a firm one generally and it is especially infirm in aesthetic contexts. Think, for example, about Arthur Danto's theory of artworks, according to which interpretation *makes* an object *into* an artwork.[35] Of course, an interpretation is not the same as a point of view, but they are kin, linked by the practices that constitute them. On Danto's view, even what is an element of an artwork is settled by the interpretation that constitutes the object as art. Danto adds that "if interpretations are what constitute artworks, there are no works without them and works are misconstituted when the interpretation is wrong. . . . The interpretation is not something that arises outside the work: work and interpretation arise together in aesthetic consciousness."[36]

The interpretive aspect of the ontological status of artworks, in part shown by their history of innovation, may be why artworks and aesthetic contexts have enjoyed a certain level of privilege – a degree of freedom not always extended to other expressions and situations. Mary Devereaux calls this "protected space" for artists, and argues that art deserves protected space because it

has a high social value. It makes us think twice, think differently, relive the past, imagine the future. . . . In allowing art the independence to function in these ways, we seek to protect a political good.[37]

That political good is complex. All the features of the political good that Devereaux cites involve interpreting our lives and our situations, which we do as part of our project of self-development and political action. Art has the power to fuel our efforts at self-transformation and the transformation of the world. Such protection of aesthetic contexts would amount to refusing to abridge or restrict art on the basis of objectionable content or on the basis of objectionable point of view. That's because at least part of the point of art is to explore points of view, perspectives on content.

While few people are really willing to embrace Romanticism, at least not wholly and not publicly, this is the position that best motivates an absolute expressivist freedom. The Romantic argues that art makes new things – it opens new ontological possibilities – and it has the power to change existing things in significant ways. Refusing content-based abridgments allows us to explore all the aspects of our lives, even the ugly and the trivial, with the media we have developed. Refusing point-of-view abridgments safeguards our subjectivity, which is on some views the core of our identity. Protecting point of view protects us as we develop our subjectivity – as we become who we are. Developing a point of view is part and parcel of what it is to be a person, and we do it through the manipulation and interpretation of our words and deeds, and through the restructuring of the patterns of significance that govern our lives. Sometimes we try to appropriate a ready-made point of view – something another person has set out for us through her words and deeds. Even in this case, however, the act of appropriation involves undertaking a commitment to the basic structures of the interpretive patterns that constitute that point of view. That undertaking of the commitment makes the point of view one's own, whether one created it or not. The gift that those who develop new interpretive models and new points of view give to others is just this potential for eclecticism – for being able to appropriate, recombine, and put together an interpretive structure and a point of view without having to start from scratch.

Consider the unsettling image of Bigger Thomas. Wright felt censored by two opposite social forces denying the value of the image. Against the background of white culture, Wright felt that writing Bigger would be a reinforcement of whites' claims of supremacy. So he ought not do it on social justice grounds. Against the background of black middle-class culture, writing Bigger would be a denial of black middle-class achievement and a reinforcement of the claim of black inferiority. So, again, he ought not do it, this time on grounds of honesty and race solidarity. A different kind of honesty – an honesty to a different black experience – prevailed for Wright. Remember what Wright says about why he ultimately wrote about the politically dangerous Bigger Thomas:

> But Bigger won over all these claims; . . . I felt with all my being that he was more important than what any person, white or black, would say or try to make of him, more important than any political analysis designed to explain or deny him, more important even, than my own sense of fear, shame, and diffidence.[38]

How could this fictional character win out over all the very real needs of these very real people? Well, Bigger is really only partly fictional. Writing Bigger was an act of creation but it was also an act of re-presentation that could be called "faithful portrayal" in Goodman's sense. In describing faithful portrayal as the conveying of "a person known and distilled from a variety of experiences,"[39] Goodman acknowledges the possibility of the faithful portrayal of someone who does not actually exist; he allows for the possibility of *creative* faithful portrayal. That is just what Wright saw himself doing in writing Bigger Thomas. That is also why James Baldwin, like Nathan McCall, was grateful to Wright. Baldwin said, "Growing up in a certain kind of poverty is growing up in a certain kind of silence"; the basic elements of your life are unnamable because "no one corroborates it. Reality becomes unreal because no one experiences it but you." Wright's *Native Son* was a faithful portrayal of a way of life, a condition of life, that had been invisible to and invalidated by the world, especially the reading world, until he wrote. Writing Bigger Thomas was a brave and radical act, which Baldwin did not see as retarding the chances for black liberation despite the disdain of the black middle class and the joys of the white racists. Baldwin says:

"Life was made bearable by Richard Wright's testimony. When circumstances are made real by another's testimony, it becomes possible to envision change."[40]

If the Absolutist is right that there is no way for an artist to distance herself from the derogation carried by these terms and images, and yet if these terms and images are somehow necessary to convey the form of life and the artistic message she seeks to convey, as they are to Franca Rame, Richard Wright, James Baldwin, Grace Paley, William Faulkner, Alice Walker, and many, many others, then the radical artist is stuck with a double bind. She is stuck with the double bind of being forced by her sense of aesthetic honesty to portray the form of life faithfully (using the derogatory terms, portraying the derogation and degradation) while undermining her condemnatory point of view through her inclusion of these terms. She must choose between portraying faithfully and silencing herself.

If the Reclaimer is right, then the condemnatory point of view and the manipulation of context can undermine the derogatory expressive commitments of these terms and images. That these derogations have occurred would not be contested, but that the author/artist questions or condemns them would be on the record, and what their expressive and assertional structure and force are would be disclosed in a new light.

The power of our words and images to make things real by naming them is the heart of the issue. Wright's point about Bigger's importance is kin to William Gass's claim that works of art are socially important because "they insist more than most on their own reality; because of the absolute way in which they exist."[41] For Gass, a work of art has a lasting social value not because of its interpretations, but because of what it is: works of art are originals, like we are, and should be lived with and loved for their own sakes. Gass writes:

We live, most of us, amidst lies, deceits, and confusions. A work of art may not utter the truth, but it must be honest. It may champion a cause we deplore, but unlike Milton's Satan, it must in itself be noble; it must be *all there*. Works of art confront us the way few people dare to: completely, openly, at once. They construct, they comprise, our experience; they do not deny or destroy it; and they shame us, we fall so short of the quality of their Being.

Here we see Gass at his most unabashedly aestheticist. Gass may be right about the "utterness" of art (at least great art); what he is wrong about is us. We are more like art and art is more like us than Gass allows. We do live "amidst lies, deceits, and confusions," but it is also true that most people are much more transparent than they think. Like artworks, we are complex, but not inscrutable. Even if some works of art do have a higher quality of being than some or even many people, it does not follow that art by its very nature is superior in being to people by their nature. At bottom, works of art and people are very much alike: a few great, a few terrible, and most in between. As David Luban has pointed out, this analogy goes further: just as we may forgive but not forget or ignore the serious moral faults of people we love, we may also require a measure of forgiveness with respect to morally flawed works of art.

Stravinsky, speaking of Monostatos and the Moor, refers to "their absurdity *apart from their music.*" Their music is the virtue that we love, and while it cannot and must not lead us to excuse racism, the possibility remains of forgiveness. I suspect that our appreciation of a great deal more art depends on forgiveness than we might like to think.[42]

Luban suggests that we should condone nothing but forgive much. The Absolutist thinks there is no room for forgiveness when it comes to either intentional or inadvertent promulgation of racist, sexist, and other forms of hate. There is a substantive issue here: what is forgivable and what is not?

Words and images do have the power to make something *seem* real, and sometimes seeming is the first step toward *being.* The words and images alone do not carry or convey the danger to our lives; ignoring context is something we do at our own peril. Social practices, including our linguistic (inferential) practices, practices of aesthetic interpretation, practices of respect and disrespect toward others, are what make the terms and images subordinating. Change these practices and you change the power of the expressions. This power to create is why art deserves special expressivist freedoms. Why should art be so special? What makes it deserve such expressive freedoms, when other arenas of our lives are losing them more and more? Here we must face our conflicting conceptions of art's extreme power and its utter uselessness. Consider the fact that the most widespread and effective legal intervention in the United States during this century has been in our schools and our workplaces; these are arenas in which opportunities must be protected, because they have an impact on the individual's long- and short-term prospects for survival and success. Does art have such an impact? It would be a stretch to put art and education or art and employment on equal footing, even though it is no stretch to argue that a sound education includes solid arts programs or that the best forms of employment allow the worker

309

creative growth through her work. Considering consequences, it may in fact be art's initial ineffectiveness that makes it a great candidate for expressivist protection. It takes a confluence of factors for the interpretations artists create to actually catch on, to actually have an influence. Let artists create, and let a lot of art fall fallow, but protect the failures as well as the successes. Given the role of art in our culture, we need not constrain art the way we need to constrain employers and school systems. The artist is our model of a human creator and, in making new things, teaches us our own power. So in the end, I suggest that it is absolutely crucial to safeguard the power to create new things and, with them, new forms of interpretation. That is what art is and does for us.

The Absolutist does us a favor by challenging the expressive commitments of some of the terms in our collective repertoires, demanding that we defend them or eliminate them. The Absolutist's challenge spurs us to consider just what is at stake when we create new works, to make explicit our expressive commitments and think of ways to change them. Radical writers and artists do this all the time, without the help of the theory I have articulated. Against the Absolutist, I am suggesting that we listen to these voices and think about their images, so that we can see the power of their creative recasting of these terms and images. At issue is whether a politically just social ontology should be achieved by controlling the expressive process and product, or by other means. The analysis presented here suggests we look to other means. The Absolutist's challenge should help us see more clearly what is at stake in our forms of expression; she goads us into making the politics of discourse and the politics of imagery explicit. Such explicitation can help us to make our own decisions about what is acceptable and what is not, what is forgivable, and what is not. She makes it clear that we need to take responsibility for our expressive commitments. Let us thank her for that, while not acceding to her demand that we silence even those who try to overcome by other means.

Notes

This essay was first presented at the University of Maryland Philosophy Department's 1994 D. C. Williams conference entitled "Aesthetics and Ethics." My thanks to the audience on that occasion, and especially to David Luban for his insightful comments. My warmest thanks to Chico D. Colvard for his enthusiastic and reliable research assistance.

1. Richard Wright, "How 'Bigger' Was Born," in *Black Voices: An Anthology of Afro-American Literature,* ed. Abraham Chapman (New York: Penguin, 1968), 551–3.
2. Nathan McCall, *Makes Me Wanna Holler: A Young Black Man in America* (New York: Random House, 1994), 157, 158.
3. This account has been developed more fully in my "Derogatory Terms: Racism, Sexism, and the Inferential Role Theory of Meaning," in *Language and Liberation: Feminism, Philosophy and Language,* ed. Kelly Oliver and Christina Hendricks (Albany, N.Y.: SUNY Press, 1997).
4. This position is held by Critical Race Theorists like Delgado, Matsuda, Lawrence, and Crenshaw, in *Words That Wound,* ed. Richard Delgado et al. (Boulder, Colo.: Westview Press, 1993), and it is also held by antipornography activists like Catherine MacKinnon and Andrea Dworkin. See MacKinnon's *Only Words* (Cambridge, Mass.: Harvard University Press, 1993), *Feminism Unmodified: Discourses on Life and Law* (Cambridge, Mass.: Harvard University Press, 1987), and, with Andrea Dworkin, *Pornography and Civil Rights: A New Day for Women's Equality* (Minneapolis: Organizing Against Pornography, 1988), and Andrea Dworkin, *Pornography: Men Possessing Women* (Harmondsworth: Penguin, 1979, 1980, 1981).
5. Consider the difference between invoking the history of slavery by saying "She is the great granddaughter of a freed slave" versus saying "She's a nigger." Both invoke the history of slavery, but one carries a default endorsement of that history and the other does not. For more on the importance of social backup, see Lynne Tirrell, "Definition and Power," *Hypatia* 8, no. 4 (1993): 1–34.
6. Jeff Greenberg, S. L. Kirkland, and Tom Pyszczynski, "Derogatory Ethnic Labels," in *Discourse and Discrimination,* ed. Geneva Smitherman-Donaldson and Teun A. van Dijk (Detroit: Wayne State University Press, 1988), 77; emphasis added.
7. Ibid., 77.
8. James Baldwin, "Autobiographical Notes," in *Black Voices,* ed. Chapman, 320.
9. James Snead, *Figures of Division: William Faulkner's Major Novels* (London: Methuen, 1986), xiv.
10. Tom Fennel, "Navigating Troubled Waters," *MacLeans,* November 1993, 72.
11. Ibid.
12. This sort of view is played out on many different fields: it is seen in Hempel's discussion of the importance of nonblack nonravens for understanding confirmation, in Quine's holism, and in Saussure's structuralism, to name but a few variations. For more on holism, see Jerry Fodor and Ernest LePore, *Holism: A Shopper's Guide* (Oxford: Basil Blackwell, 1992). For a development of an inferential role theory of meaning, see Robert B. Brandom's "Asserting," *Nous* 4 (November 1983): 637–50. This account is clearest in the case of assertion, although

311

it can easily accommodate other sorts of speech acts. Portions of the next two sections are condensed from my "Derogatory Terms."

13. This language of undertaking the commitment is not meant to preclude the possibility that someone might categorically refuse to ever justify anything she asserts, might never actually be forthcoming with an identification, and so on. These commitments represent a reconstruction of our social practices, and as with all social practices there are normally a few free riders and general noncooperators. When someone generally shirks her linguistic responsibilities, we tend to treat her as an unreliable interlocutor.

14. This concept was first developed to account for the way that metaphorical interpretation involves not only what is said but also how it is said and how that method of presentation influences both the assertional and the identificatory commitments associated with the expression. When Romeo says, "But soft, what light through yonder windows breaks / It is the east, and Juliet is the sun," he undertakes a commitment to the viability and value of using sun-talk to talk about Juliet. See Lynne Tirrell, "Extending: The Structure of Metaphor," *Nous* 23 (March 1989): 17–34.

15. Sometimes that goal is seeking truth, sometimes it is seeking power, and often it is a combination of these. The Supreme Court has a history of deciding the value of modes of discourse and particular bits of speech almost exclusively in terms of their utility in promoting truth. I say "almost exclusively" because the tendency to decide on these grounds is very strong, but can be overridden by considerations of threats to the public peace.

16. Jerry Farber, "The Student as Nigger," in *The Student as Nigger* (New York: Pocket Books, 1969). All the quotes in this paragraph are from pages 90 and 91. Farber is not asserting that students are blacks, but rather that they are second-class citizens if citizens at all. I don't think this claim requires metaphorical interpretation, as the rest of the paragraph should illustrate. The claim is literally interpretable and literally supported (or not).

17. Richard Delgado, "Words That Wound: A Tort Action for Racial Insults, Epithets, and Name-Calling," in *Words That Wound,* 107; see also 94 and 109–110. Delgado uses 'connotation' here and elsewhere in his article colloquially rather than technically; I take him to mean something like "attitudes conveyed or associated with the expression." (In contrast, the logician's use of 'connotation' refers to the usual sort of dictionary meaning, while 'denotation' refers to the objects of reference for the term.) For more about this argument, see my "Derogatory Terms."

18. One argument for the possibility of reclaiming derogatory terms like 'nigger' and 'dyke' depends on *not* taking the terms to be what Blackburn, McDowell, Gibbard, Williams, and others call 'thick'. 'Thick' terms are terms or expressions that carry with them or convey an attitude, an approval or a disapproval, in which the description and the atti-

tude "form a compound or amalgam, rather than a mixture: the attitude and the description infuse each other, so that in the end, in the repertoire of the mature speaker, the two elements are no longer distinguishable" (Simon Blackburn, "Through Thick and Thin," forthcoming).

19. Not all uses of the term by African-Americans will effect the detachment.

20. For a more detailed account of the weaknesses of this argument, see my "Derogatory Terms."

21. William Faulkner, "That Evening Sun," in *Major American Short Stories,* ed. A. Walton Litz (New York: Oxford University Press, 1975), 576–90. Also in *These 13* (1931) and *The Collected Stories of William Faulkner.* This story provides an interesting case of both blacks and whites using 'nigger' clearly as a derogatory term but none seeming to mind the linguistic derogation. (It simply is not the case that any use of the term to one's face constitutes fighting words, in the legal sense.)

22. Johnetta Cole to Mary Catherine Bateson, in Bateson, *Composing a Life* (Harmondsworth: Penguin, 1989), 44.

23. MacKinnon, *Only Words,* 13. She lists all performatives: signs saying "Whites Only" or "Help Wanted – Male" or speech acts like "You're fired."

24. Helen E. Longino, "Pornography, Oppression and Freedom: A Closer Look," in *Take Back the Night: Women on Pornography,* ed. Laura Lederer (New York: Morrow, 1980), 40–54. Even though this definition leaves room for depictions of victims who are not women, it is important to note that in most pornography the actual victim depicted is a woman, and in many cases the victim is functionally a woman.

25. Gloria Steinem, "Erotica and Pornography: A Clear and Present Difference," in *Take Back the Night,* ed. Lederer, 37.

26. The obvious question is: what is an act of subordination and humiliation? There are many clear-cut cases, but critics tend to focus on the more difficult ones to urge us to think that the determination of content is itself the product of a point of view, and thus they urge us to abandon this distinction. The distinction may not be precise, and it may not be exclusive and exhaustive, but it serves an important heuristic purpose.

27. Nelson Goodman, *Languages of Art* (Indianapolis: Hackett, 1976), 31.

28. Margaret Spillane, "The Culture of Narcissism," *Nation,* December 10, 1990. Reprinted in *Culture Wars,* ed. Richard Bolton (New York: Free Press, 1992), 305–6.

29. MacKinnon, *Feminism Unmodified,* 149.

30. We may add that it damages men too, by perverting their sexuality in a way that makes whole healthy relationships impossible. Such damage pales beside the damage to women, but it is real nonetheless and helps explain why men should resist and undermine pornography as well.

31. Marilyn Frye, "Oppression" and other papers, in *The Politics of Reality* (Trumansberg, NY: Crossing Press, 1983).

32. Andrea Dworkin, "After the Male Flood: Censorship, Pornography, and Equality," in *Letters from a War Zone* (New York: Dutton, 1989), 264.

33. Maria Lugones pointed this out to me in conversation at the Midwest Society for Women in Philosophy, Minneapolis, 1994.

34. Obviously not all gay men are sadomasochistic, and one must worry that the talk of lifestyles here, even pluralized, involves stereotyping.

35. Danto says, for example, that "an object is an artwork at all only in relation to an interpretation." Arthur C. Danto, *The Philosophical Disenfranchisement of Art* (New York: Columbia University Press, 1986), 44.

36. Ibid., 45.

37. Mary Devereaux, "Protected Space: Politics, Censorship, and the Arts," *Journal of Aesthetics and Art Criticism* 51, No. 2 (1993): 214.

38. Richard Wright, *Black Voices,* ed. Chapman, 553.

39. Goodman, *Languages of Art,* 20.

40. Spillane, "Culture of Narcissism," 304.

41. William Gass, "The Artist and Society," in *Fiction and the Figures of Life* (Boston: Godine, 1958), 276–88.

42. David Luban, unpublished comments on an earlier draft of this essay.

Bibliography

This bibliography is weighted toward writings on ethical issues in art and aesthetics and on comparison of ethical and aesthetic judgments or values. Representation of writings in ethical theory per se is rather selective, focusing mainly on writings concerned with moral realism.

Ackerman, Diana. "Imaginary Gardens and Real Toads: On the Ethics of Basing Fiction on Actual People." *Midwest Studies in Philosophy* 16 (1991).

Altieri, Charles. *Canons and Consequences: Reflections on the Ethical Force of Imaginative Ideals.* Evanston, Ill.: Northwestern University Press, 1990.

Arrington, Robert. *Rationalism, Realism, and Relativism: Perspectives in Contemporary Moral Epistemology.* Ithaca, N.Y.: Cornell University Press, 1989.

Attali, Jacques. *Noise: The Political Economy of Music.* Minneapolis: University of Minnesota Press, 1985.

Barrett, Cyril. "The Morality of Artistic Production." *Journal of Aesthetics and Art Criticism* 41 (1982).

Beardsmore, R. W. *Art and Morality.* London: Macmillan Press, 1971.

"The Censorship of Works of Art." In *Philosophy and Fiction,* ed. Peter Lamarque. Aberdeen: Aberdeen University Press, 1983.

Bender, John. "Art as a Source of Knowledge." In *Contemporary Philosophy of Art,* ed. John Bender and H. G. Blocker. Englewood Cliffs, N.J.: Prentice-Hall, 1993.

Bloom, Allan. *The Closing of the American Mind.* New York: Simon & Schuster, 1987.

Bolling, Doug (ed.). *Philosophy and Literature.* New York: Haven Publications, 1987.

Bontekoe, Ron, and Jamie Crooks. "The Interrelationship of Moral and Aesthetic Excellence." *British Journal of Aesthetics* 32 (1992).

Booth, Wayne. *The Company We Keep: An Ethics of Fiction.* Berkeley: University of California Press, 1988.

Bibliography

Critical notice of Martha Nussbaum, *Love's Knowledge. Philosophy and Literature* 15 (1991).

"On Relocating Ethical Criticism." In *Explanation and Value in the Arts,* ed. Salim Kemal and Ivan Gaskell. Cambridge University Press, 1993.

Brink, David. *Moral Realism and the Foundations of Ethics.* Cambridge University Press, 1989.

Brodsky, Joseph. *On Grief and Reason.* New York: Farrar, Straus & Giroux, 1995.

Brooks, David. "Taste, Virtue and Class." In *Virtue and Taste,* ed. David Knowles and John Skorupski. Oxford: Basil Blackwell, 1993.

Budd, Malcolm. *Values of Art.* London: Penguin / Allen Lane, 1995.

Carroll, Noël. "The Image of Women in Film: A Defense of a Paradigm." *Journal of Aesthetics and Art Criticism* 48 (1990).

"On Jokes." *Midwest Studies in Philosophy* 16 (1991).

"Film, Rhetoric, and Ideology." In *Explanation and Value in the Arts,* ed. Salim Kemal and Ivan Gaskell. Cambridge University Press, 1993.

"Moderate Moralism." *British Journal of Aesthetics* 36 (1996).

A Philosophy of Mass Art. Oxford: Oxford University Press, forthcoming.

Cascardi, Anthony (ed.). *Literature and the Question of Philosophy.* Baltimore: Johns Hopkins University Press, 1987.

Cavell, Stanley. *Must We Mean What We Say?* Cambridge University Press, 1976.

The Claim of Reason: Wittgenstein, Skepticism, Morality, and Tragedy. Oxford: Oxford University Press, 1979.

Cohen, Ted. "Jokes." In *Pleasure, Preference and Value,* ed. Eva Schaper. Cambridge University Press, 1983.

"Sports and Art: Beginning Questions." In *Human Agency,* ed. Jonathan Dancy et al. Stanford, Calif.: Stanford University Press, 1988.

"High and Low Thinking About High and Low Art." *Journal of Aesthetics and Art Criticism* 51 (1993).

Collinson, Diane. "'Ethics and Aesthetics are One.'" *British Journal of Aesthetics* 25 (1985).

Copp, David, and Susan Wendell (eds.). *Pornography and Censorship.* Buffalo, NY: Prometheus Books, 1983.

Crowther, Paul. *The Kantian Sublime: From Morality to Art.* Oxford: Oxford University Press, 1989.

Currie, Gregory. "Interpretation and Objectivity." *Mind* 102 (1993).

"The Moral Psychology of Fiction." *Australasian Journal of Philosophy* 73 (1995).

Danto, Arthur. "Art and Disturbation." In *The Philosophical Disenfranchisement of Art.* New York: Columbia University Press, 1986.

"Censorship and Subsidy in the Arts." In *Beyond the Brillo Box.* New York: Farrar, Straus & Giroux, 1992.

"Beauty and Morality." In *Embodied Meanings.* New York: Farrar, Straus & Giroux, 1994.

Playing with the Edge: The Photographic Achievement of Robert Mapplethorpe. Berkeley: University of California Press, 1995.

Bibliography

"From Aesthetics to Art Criticism and Back." *Journal of Aesthetics and Art Criticism* 54 (1996).

Davies, Stephen (ed.). *Art and Its Messages.* University Park: Penn State Press, 1997.

Devereaux, M. "Oppressive Texts, Resisting Readers and the Gendered Spectator: The *New* Aesthetics." *Journal of Aesthetics and Art Criticism* 48 (1990).

"Can Art Save Us? A Meditation on Gadamer." *Philosophy and Literature* 15 (1991).

"Protected Space: Politics, Censorship, and the Arts." *Journal of Aesthetics and Art Criticism* 51 (1993).

Diamond, Cora. "Martha Nussbaum and the Need for Novels." *Philosophical Investigations* 16 (1993).

Diffey, T. J. "Morality and Literary Criticism." *Journal of Aesthetics and Art Criticism* 33 (1975).

Dubin, Steven. *Arresting Images: Art and Uncivil Actions.* New York: Routledge, 1992.

Dutton, Denis (ed.). *The Forger's Art.* Berkeley: University of California Press, 1983.

Dworkin, Ronald. "Objectivity and Truth: You'd Better Believe It." *Philosophy and Public Affairs* 25 (1996).

Dwyer, Susan. *The Problem of Pornography.* Belmont, Calif.: Wadsworth, 1995.

Eagleton, Terry. *The Ideology of the Aesthetic.* Oxford: Basil Blackwell, 1990.

Eaton, Marcia. *Aesthetics and the Good Life.* Madison, N.J.: Fairleigh Dickinson University Press, 1989.

"Integrating the Aesthetic and the Ethical." *Philosophical Studies* 67 (1992).

"Aesthetics: Mother of Ethics." *Journal of Aesthetics and Art Criticism* 56 (forthcoming).

Eldridge, Richard. *On Moral Personhood: Philosophy, Literature, Criticism, and Self-Understanding.* Chicago: University of Chicago Press, 1988.

"Narratives and Moral Evaluation." *Journal of Value Inquiry* 27 (1993).

"How Can Tragedy Matter for Us?" *Journal of Aesthetics and Art Criticism* 52 (1994).

Ellos, William. *Narrative Ethics.* Aldershot: Avebury, 1994.

Feagin, Susan. "The Pleasures of Tragedy." *American Philosophical Quarterly* 20 (1983).

Reading with Feeling: The Aesthetics of Appreciation. Ithaca, N.Y.: Cornell University Press, 1996.

Fenner, David (ed.). *Ethics and the Arts.* New York: Garland, 1996.

Fisher, John Andrew (ed.). *Reflecting on Art.* Mountain View, Calif.: Mayfield, 1993.

Gardner, John. *On Moral Fiction.* New York: Basic Books, 1978.

Gaskin, Richard. "Can Aesthetic Value Be Explained?" *British Journal of Aesthetics* 29 (1989).

Bibliography

Gass, William. *Fiction and the Figures of Life.* Boston: Godine, 1958.
  "Goodness Knows Nothing of Beauty: On the Distance Between Morality and Art." *Harper's* 274 (1987).

Glidden, David. "The Elusiveness of Moral Recognition and the Imaginary Place of Fiction." *Midwest Studies in Philosophy* 16 (1991).

Goehr, Lydia. "Political Music and the Politics of Music." *Journal of Aesthetics and Art Criticism* 52 (1994).

Goldblatt, David. "Do Works of Art Have Rights?" *Journal of Aesthetics and Art Criticism* 35 (1976).

Goldman, Alan. "Aesthetic Versus Moral Evaluation." *Philosophy and Phenomenological Research* 50 (1990).
  "Realism About Aesthetic Properties." *Journal of Aesthetics and Art Criticism* 51 (1993).
  Aesthetic Value. Boulder, Colo.: Westview Press, 1995.

Gracyk, Ted. "Pornography as Representation: Aesthetic Considerations." *Journal of Aesthetic Education* 21 (1987).

Graham, Gordon. "Aesthetic Cognitivism and the Literary Arts." *Journal of Aesthetic Education* 30 (1996).

Grice, Paul. *The Conception of Value.* Oxford: Oxford University Press, 1991.

Griffiths, A. Phillips (ed.). *Philosophy and Literature.* Cambridge University Press, 1984.

Guyer, Paul. *Kant and the Experience of Freedom: Essays on Aesthetics and Morality.* Cambridge University Press, 1993.

Haines, Victor Yelverton. "No Ethics, No Text." *Journal of Aesthetics and Art Criticism* 47 (1989).

Hampshire, Staurt. "Logic and Appreciation." In *Aesthetics and Language,* ed. W. Elton. Oxford: Basil Blackwell, 1954.

Harrison, Bernard. *Inconvenient Fictions: Literature and the Limits of Theory.* New Haven, Conn.: Yale University Press, 1991.

Hein, Hilde. "Aesthetic Rights: Vindication and Vilification." *Journal of Aesthetics and Art Criticism* 37 (1978).

Heinrich, Natalie. "Framing the Bullfight: Aesthetics vs. Ethics." *British Journal of Aesthetics* 33 (1993).

Hermeren, Goran. *Aspects of Aesthetics.* Lund: Gleerup, 1983.

Herzog, Patricia. "Music Criticism and Musical Meaning." *Journal of Aesthetics and Art Criticism* 53 (1995).
  "The Practical Wisdom of Beethoven's *Diabelli Variations.*" *Musical Quarterly* 79 (1995).

Higgins, Kathleen. *The Music of Our Lives.* Philadelphia: Temple University Press, 1991.

Hjort, Mette, and Sue Laver (eds.). *Emotion and the Arts.* Oxford: Oxford University Press, 1997.

Hughes, Robert. "Art, Morals, and Politics." *New York Review of Books,* April 23, 1992.

Hyman, Lawrence. "Moral Attitudes and the Literary Experience." *Journal of Aesthetics and Art Criticism* 38 (1979).

Bibliography

"Morality and Literature: The Necessary Conflict." *British Journal of Aesthetics* 24 (1984).

Isenberg, Arnold. *Aesthetics and the Theory of Criticism.* Chicago: University of Chicago Press, 1973.

Jacobson, Daniel. "Sir Philip Sidney's Dilemma: On the Ethical Function of Narrative Art." *Journal of Aesthetics and Art Criticism* 54 (1996).

"In Praise of Immoral Art." *Philosophical Topics* (forthcoming).

Janaway, Christopher. *Images of Excellence: Plato's Critique of the Arts.* Oxford: Clarendon Press, 1995.

Jenkins, J. "Aesthetic Education and Moral Refinement." *Journal of Aesthetic Education* 2 (1968).

John, Eileen. "Subtlety and Moral Vision in Fiction." *Philosophy and Literature* 19 (1995).

Kalin, Jesse. "Philosophy Needs Literature: John Barth and Moral Nihilism." *Philosophy and Literature* 1 (1977).

"Knowing Novels: Nussbaum on Fiction and Moral Theory." *Ethics* 103 (1992).

Kekes, John. "On There Being Some Limits to Morality." In *The Good Life and the Human Good,* ed. E. Paul, F. Miller, and J. Paul. Cambridge University Press, 1992.

Kieran, Matthew. "Art, Imagination, and the Cultivation of Morals." *Journal of Aesthetics and Art Criticism* 54 (1996).

Kulka, Tomas. *Kitsch and Art.* University Park, Pa.: Penn State Press, 1996.

Kundera, Milan. *Testaments Betrayed.* New York: HarperCollins, 1995.

Kupfer, Joseph. *Experience as Art: Aesthetics in Everyday Life.* Albany, N.Y.: SUNY Press, 1983.

Lamarque, Peter. "Truth and Art in Iris Murdoch's *The Black Prince*." *Philosophy and Literature* 2 (1978).

"Tragedy and Moral Value." *Australasian Journal of Philosophy* 73 (1995).

Lamarque, Peter, and Stein Haugom Olsen. *Truth, Fiction, and Literature.* Oxford: Oxford University Press, 1994.

Levinson, Jerrold. "Being Realistic About Aesthetic Properties." *Journal of Aesthetics and Art Criticism* 52 (1994).

"Messages in Art." In *The Pleasures of Aesthetics.* Ithaca, N.Y.: Cornell University Press, 1996.

"Evaluating Music." *Revue Internationale de Philosophie* 198 (1996).

"Erotic Art." In *Routledge Encyclopedia of Philosophy.* London: Routledge, forthcoming.

Lipman, Matthew. "Can Non-aesthetic Consequences Justify Aesthetic Values?" *Journal of Aesthetics and Art Criticism.* 34 (1975).

Livingston, Paisley. *Literature and Rationality: Ideas of Agency in Theory and Fiction.* Cambridge University Press, 1991.

Lloyd, Genevieve. "Iris Murdoch on the Ethical Significance of Truth." *Philosophy and Literature* 6 (1982).

Margolis, Joseph. "Moral Realism and the Meaning of Life." *Philosophical Forum* 22 (1990).

Bibliography

Markowitz, Sally. "Guilty Pleasures: Aesthetic Meta-Response and Fiction." *Journal of Aesthetics and Art Criticism* 50 (1992).

McDowell, John. "Aesthetic Value, Objectivity, and the Fabric of the World." In *Pleasure, Preference and Value,* ed. Eva Schaper. Cambridge University Press, 1983.

"Values and Secondary Qualities." In *Morality and Objectivity,* ed. Ted Honderich. London: Routledge & Kegan Paul, 1985.

McGinn, Colin. *Ethics, Evil, and Fiction.* Oxford: Oxford University Press, 1997.

McNaughton, David. *Moral Vision.* Oxford: Basil Blackwell, 1988.

Miller, Richard. "Truth in Beauty." *American Philosophical Quarterly* 16 (1979).

Moore, Ron. "The Aesthetic and the Moral." *Journal of Aesthetic Education* 29 (1995).

Moran, Richard. "The Expression of Feeling in Imagination." *Philosophical Review* 103 (1994).

Murdoch, Iris. *The Sovereignty of Good.* London: Routledge & Kegan Paul, 1970.

Nehamas, Alexander. *Nietzsche: Life as Literature.* Cambridge, Mass.: Harvard University Press, 1985.

"Plato and the Mass Media." *Monist* 71 (1988).

Neill, Alex, and Aaron Ridley (eds.). *Arguing About Art.* New York: McGraw-Hill, 1994.

Newton, A. Z. *Narrative Ethics.* Cambridge, Mass.: Harvard University Press, 1995.

Novitz, David. *Knowledge, Fiction and Imagination.* Philadelphia: Temple University Press, 1987.

The Boundaries of Art. Philadelphia: Temple University Press, 1992.

Nussbaum, Martha. *The Fragility of Goodness: Luck and Ethics in Greek Tragedy and Philosophy.* Cambridge University Press, 1986.

Love's Knowledge: Essays on Philosophy and Literature. Oxford: Oxford University Press, 1990.

Poetic Justice: The Literary Imagination and Public Life. Boston: Beacon Press, 1996.

Palmer, Frank. *Literature and Moral Understanding: A Philosophical Essay on Ethics, Aesthetics, Education, and Culture.* Oxford: Oxford University Press, 1992.

Parker, David. *Ethics, Theory, and the Novel.* Cambridge University Press, 1994.

Passmore, John. *Serious Art.* LaSalle, Ill.: Open Court, 1991.

Phillips, D. Z. *Through a Darkening Glass: Philosophy, Literature, and Cultural Change.* Oxford: Oxford University Press, 1982.

Platts, Mark. "Moral Reality and the End of Desire." In *Reference, Truth and Reality,* ed. Mark Platts. London: Routledge & Kegan Paul, 1980.

Pole, David. "Morality and the Assessment of Literature." In *Aesthetics, Form and Emotion.* London: Duckworth, 1983.

Bibliography

Quinn, Philip. "Hell in Amsterdam: Reflections on Camus's *The Fall*." *Midwest Studies in Philosophy 16* (1991).

Railton, Peter. "Facts and Values." *Philosophical Review* 95 (1986).

"Moral Realism." *Philosophical Topics* 14 (1986).

"Subject-ive and Objective." *Ratio* 8 (1995).

Ridley, Aaron. "Desire and the Experience of Fiction." *Philosophy and Literature* 14 (1992).

"Tragedy and the Tender-Hearted." *Philosophy and Literature* 17 (1993).

Robinson, Jenefer. "L' Education Sentimentale." *Australasian Journal of Philosophy* 73 (1995).

Robinson, Jenefer, and Stephanie Ross. "Women, Morality, and Fiction." In *Aesthetics in Feminist Perspective,* ed. H. Hein and C. Korsmeyer. Bloomington: Indiana University Press, 1993.

Rorty, Richard. *Contingency, Irony, and Solidarity.* Cambridge University Press, 1989.

Rosebury, Brian. *Art and Desire: A Study in the Aesthetics of Fiction.* London: Macmillan Press, 1988.

Sagoff, Mark. "On Restoring and Reproducing Art." *Journal of Philosophy* 75 (1978).

Sankowski, Edward. "Blame, Fictional Characters, and Morality." *Journal of Aesthetic Education* 22 (1988).

"Ethics, Art, and Museums." *Journal of Aesthetic Education* 26 (1992).

Sartwell, Crispin. *The Art of Living: Aesthetics of the Ordinary in World Spiritual Traditions.* Albany, N.Y.: SUNY Press, 1994.

Savile, Anthony. *The Test of Time.* Oxford: Oxford University Press, 1982.

"Architecture, Formalism and the Sense of Self." In *Virtue and Taste,* ed. David Knowles and John Skorupski. Oxford: Basil Blackwell, 1993.

Sayre-McCord, Geoffrey (ed.). *Essays in Moral Realism.* Ithaca, N.Y.: Cornell University Press, 1988.

Schier, Flint. "Tragedy and the Community of Sentiment." In *Philosophy and Fiction,* ed. Peter Lamarque. Aberdeen: Aberdeen University Press, 1983.

"The Claims of Tragedy: An Essay in Moral Psychology and Aesthetic Theory." *Philosophical Papers* 18 (1989).

"Van Gogh's Boots: The Claims of Representation." In *Virtue and Taste,* ed. David Knowles and John Skorupski. Oxford: Basil Blackwell, 1993.

Scruton, Roger. *The Aesthetic Understanding: Essays in the Philosophy of Art and Culture.* London: Methuen, 1983.

Seamon, Roger. "The Story of the Moral: The Function of Thematizing in Literary Criticism." *Journal of Aesthetics and Art Criticism* 47 (1989).

Serra, Richard. "Art and Censorship." *Critical Inquiry* 17 (1991).

Sharpe, R. A. "Moral Tales." *Philosophy* 67 (1992).

Sheppard, Anne. *Aesthetics.* Oxford: Oxford University Press, 1987.

Shusterman, Richard. "Aesthetic Education or Aesthetic Ideology: T. S. Eliot on Art's Moral Critique." *Philosophy and Literature* 13 (1989).

Pragmatist Aesthetics. Oxford: Basil Blackwell, 1992.

Bibliography

Silvers, Anita. "Aesthetic Akrasia: On Disliking Good Art." *Journal of Aesthetics and Art Criticism* 31 (1972).

"Aesthetics for Art's Sake." *Journal of Aesthetics and Art Criticism* 51 (1993).

Sinnott-Armstrong, Walter, and Mark Timmons (eds.). *Moral Knowledge? New Readings in Moral Epistemology.* Oxford: Oxford University Press, 1996.

Sircello, Guy. *Love and Beauty.* Princeton, N.J.: Princeton University Press, 1989.

Slote, Michael. "Admirable Immorality." In *Goods and Virtues.* Oxford: Oxford University Press, 1983.

Solomon, Robert. "On Kitsch and Sentimentality." *Journal of Aesthetics and Art Criticism* 49 (1991).

Sontag, Susan. "The Pornographic Imagination." In *A Susan Sontag Reader.* New York: Farrar, Straus & Giroux, 1982.

Sparshott, Francis. "Why Artworks Have No Right to Have Rights." *Journal of Aesthetics and Art Criticism* 42 (1983).

Stalker, Douglas, and Clark Glymour. "The Malignant Object: Thoughts on Public Sculpture." *Public Interest* 66 (1982).

Stecker, Robert. *Artworks: Definition, Meaning, Value.* University Park: Penn State Press, 1996.

Steiner, Wendy. *The Scandal of Pleasure: Art in an Age of Fundamentalism.* Chicago: University of Chicago Press, 1995.

Stern, J. P. "History in Robert Musil's *Törless.*" In *Teaching the Text,* ed. S. Kappeler and N. Bryson. London: Routledge & Kegan Paul, 1983.

Tanner, Michael. "Sentimentality." *Proceedings of the Aristotelian Society* suppl. 50 (1976–7).

Taylor, Charles. *Sources of the Self.* Cambridge, Mass.: Harvard University Press, 1989.

Tilghman, Ben. *Wittgenstein, Ethics, and Aesthetics.* Albany, N.Y.: SUNY Press, 1991.

Tirrell, Lynne. "Storytelling and Moral Agency." *Journal of Aesthetics and Art Criticism* 48 (1990).

Tormey, Alan. "Aesthetic Rights." *Journal of Aesthetics and Art Criticism* 32 (1973).

Van Camp, Julie. "The Colorization Controversy." *Journal of Value Inquiry* 29 (1995).

Van Peer, Willie. "Literature, Imagination, and Human Rights." *Philosophy and Literature* 19 (1995).

Walton, Kendall. "How Marvelous! Toward a Theory of Aesthetic Value." *Journal of Aesthetics and Art Criticism* 51 (1993).

"Morals in Fiction and Fictional Morality." *Proceedings of the Aristotelian Society* suppl. 68 (1994).

Wiggins, David. "Truth, Invention, and the Meaning of Life." In *Needs, Values, Truth.* Oxford: Basil Blackwell, 1987.

Bibliography

Williams, Bernard. "Moral Luck." *Proceedings of the Aristotelian Society* suppl. 50 (1976).

Ethics and the Limits of Philosophy. Cambridge, Mass.: Harvard University Press, 1985.

Wilson, Catherine. "Literature and Knowledge." *Philosophy* 58 (1983).

Wittgenstein, Ludwig. "Lecture on Ethics." *Philosophical Review* 74 (1965).

"Lectures on Aesthetics." In *Lectures and Conversations on Aesthetics, Psychology, and Religious Belief,* ed. Cyril Barrett. Berkeley: University of California Press, 1967.

Wolf, Susan. "Moral Saints." *Journal of Philosophy* 79 (1982).

Wollheim, Richard. "Flawed Crystals: James's 'The Golden Bowl' and the Plausibility of Literature as Moral Philosophy." *New Literary History* 15 (1983).

The Mind and Its Depths. Cambridge, Mass.: Harvard University Press, 1993.

Wreen, Michael. "Aesthetics." In *Encyclopedia of Ethics.* New York: Garland, 1993.

Young, James. "Destroying Works of Art." *Journal of Aesthetics and Art Criticism* 47 (1989).

Zemach, Eddy. "Thirteen Ways of Looking at the Ethics/Aesthetics Parallelism." *Journal of Aesthetics and Art Criticism* 29 (1971).

Zuidervaart, Lambert. "The Social Significance of Autonomous Art: Adorno and Burger." *Journal of Aesthetics and Art Criticism* 48 (1990).

Index of names and titles

Index